BRITISH MILITARY AIRFIELD ARCHITECTURE

As part of our ongoing market research, we are always pleased to receive comments about our books, suggestions for new titles, or requests for catalogues. Please write to: The Editorial Director, Patrick Stephens Limited, Sparkford, Nr Yeovil, Somerset BA22 7JJ.

BRITISH MILITARY AIRFIELD ARCHITECTURE

FROM AIRSHIPS TO THE JET AGE

Paul Francis

Patrick Stephens Limited

© Paul Francis 1996

All rights reserved. No part of this publication may be reproduced, stored in a retrieval system or transmitted, in any form or by any means, electronic, mechanical, photocopying, recording or otherwise, without prior permission in writing from Patrick Stephens Limited.

First published in 1996

British Cataloguing-in-Publication Data:
A catalogue record for this book is available from the British Library

ISBN 1 85260 462 X

Library of Congress catalog card no. 96-75818

Patrick Stephens Limited is an imprint of Haynes Publishing, Sparkford, Nr Yeovil, Somerset, BA22 7JJ

Designed & typeset by G&M, Raunds, Northamptonshire
Printed and bound in Great Britain by
J. H. Haynes & Co. Ltd

CONTENTS

Introduction and Acknowledgements 7
Glossary 8

PART 1: THE EVOLUTION OF AERODROMES 9

PART 2: TECHNICAL BUILDINGS 30
Guardhouse 30
Safety Section Buildings 32
Motor Transport 36
Engine Test House 40
Bomb Stores 40
Station Armoury 42
Station Headquarters 43
Operations Buildings 46
Photographic Block 52
Workshops 52
Stores 54
Second World War Dispersed Buildings 57
Airfield Defence 60

PART 3: BALLOON AND AIRSHIP BUILDINGS 65
Airship Stations 1909–19 65
Cardington between the Wars 73
Barrage Balloon Stations 75

PART 4: HANGARS 81
Aeroplane Sheds and Hangars 1913–19 81
Interwar Hangars 90
Transportable Hangars 100
Ministry of Aircraft Production Hangars 107
Miscellaneous Types 110

PART 5: CONTROL TOWERS 111
Military Air Traffic Control 111
Air Traffic Control Signals 114
The First Buildings 118

Permanent Buildings 1934–40   120
Second World War Temporary Buildings   124
Royal Naval Air Station Control Towers   131

PART 6: SYNTHETIC TRAINING   138
Aircrew Training   138
Link Trainer   139
Gunnery and Crew Procedure Centre   142
W/T Operational Instruction Centre   143
Synthetic Navigation Classroom   147
Hawarden Trainer   148
Modified Haskard Range   149
Modified Hunt Trainer   150
Panoramic Trainer   150
Turret Gunnery Training   150
Elementary Deflection Teacher   155
Edmonds Deflection Trainer   155
Fisher Front Gun Trainer   155
Torpedo Attack Trainer   155
Air Ministry Laboratory Bombing Teacher   161
Camera Obscura   166
Anti-aircraft Dome Trainers   166

PART 7: DOMESTIC BUILDINGS   172
Barracks   174
Sergeants' Mess and Quarters   179
Officers' Mess and Quarters   181
Airmen's Dining-room and Institute   183
Gas Decontamination Buildings   186
Station Sick Quarters   193
Water Supply   194
Electrical Services   194
Squash Racquets Court   198
Gymnasium   199
Grocery and Local Produce Store   202
Tailor's, Shoemaker's, and Barber's Shop   203

PART 8: HUTS   204
Timber Huts   206
Half-brick Huts   207
Plasterboard Huts   208
Corrugated Iron Huts   209
Asbestos Huts   211
Plywood and Asbestos Huts   214
Concrete Huts   215

Index   221

INTRODUCTION AND ACKNOWLEDGEMENTS

This book describes the development of military airfields in Britain from 1909 to 1949 and complements the *Action Stations* series and *Britain's Military Airfields 1939–45*, both published by PSL.

Readers will notice that the terminology used throughout this book changes according to the period in question. This is quite deliberate; the terminology has been taken from the original drawings and plans issued by the Royal Engineers, Air Ministry Works and Buildings, Royal Marine Engineers, and the Air Ministry Directorate General of Works. The terminology used depended on the type of station and the date of the original plan: for example, aerodrome becomes airfield; aeroplane shed changes to hangar; office for duty pilot (1920s) becomes watch office (1934–43) which then changes to control tower. The terminology used in this book reflects these changes.

Although many types of building are described in this book, it has not been possible to include every type. *British Military Airfield Architecture* is the result of many years research cataloguing airfield building plans held at various sites. These include the former Property Services Agency, the Fleet Air Arm Museum, Yeovilton, the RAF Museum, Hendon, and the Imperial War Museum, Duxford. Another important source of information was the Airfield Research Group, many of whose members provided valuable help with individual building surveys. I would especially like to thank the following members of the Airfield Research Group for their assistance: Barry Abraham, W. B. Baguley, D. Benfield, Ken Border, Maurice Cole, Denis Corley, Graham Crisp, Fred Cubberley, Len Cullen, Paul Doyle, Huby Fairhead, Aldon Ferguson, Mick Fisher, Cliff Gardner, Bill Haggan, John Hamlin, A. J. L. Hickox, Peter Homer, John Horne, Guy Jefferson, David Lee, Alan Lowe, Brian Martin, John Nicholls, Norman Parker, Ian Reid, Brian Robinson, D. J. Smith, Bill Taylor, Julian Temple and Roger Thomas.

My thanks also go to Arnold L. W. Allen, Dr Martin Cherry (English Heritage), Wing Commander Keith Currans, Major Haslop, Jeremy Lake (English Heritage) Leslie Pegg, Frank Phillipson, V. H. Spencer, Angus Wainwright (National Trust), and Dr Alister Ward (English Heritage) for their help in researching this book.

The following companies were very helpful in my researches: En-Tout-Cas Ltd, Ferranti International (Simulation and Training), and Maurice Hill Ltd.

I would also like to thank the many RAF and USAF service personnel stationed at bases now closed in the UK, who assisted me with access to material at former RAF stations, including RAF Bentwaters, RAF Bicester, RAF Swanton Morley, RAF Swinderby, RAF West Raynham, RAF Weathersfield and RAF Woodbridge. In addition, personnel on the following Army bases located on former RAF stations also gave me much help: Bassingbourn, Hullavington, Larkhill (Rollestone Camp), Netheravon and Upavon. Last but no means least, I would like to thank the service personnel at RNAS Lee-on-Solent for their assistance.

Paul Francis
Ware, Herts

GLOSSARY

AAP	Aircraft Acceptance Park	MB	medium bomber
AC	Army Co-op	Met	meteorological
ACR	airfield control room	MoS	Ministry of Supply
ADGB	Air Defence of Great Britain	MoW	Ministry of Works
ADT	attack, dummy, torpedo	MT	motor transport
AGS	Air Gunner School	MTB	motor torpedo boat
AID	Aeronautical Inspection Department	MU	Maintenance Unit
ALG	Advanced Landing Ground	NAAFI	Navy, Army, and Air Force Institutes ('institute')
ALT	attack, light, torpedo	NFE	night flying equipment
AML	Air Ministry Laboratory	OTU	Operational Training Unit
AOC	Air Officer Commanding	PBX	private branch exchange (telephone system)
AOS	Air Observer Schools	PRU	Photo-reconnaissance Unit
ARD	Aircraft Repair Depot	PSP	pierced steel plank
ARS	Aeroplane Repair Section	RAE	Royal Aircraft Establishment
ASU	Aircraft Storage Unit	RFC	Royal Flying Corps
ATC	air traffic control	RFTS	Reserve Flying Training School
B	bomber	RNAS	Royal Naval Air Service or Royal Naval Air Station
BABS	beam approach beacons		
BCF	British Concrete Federation	ROC	Royal Observer Corps
BTU	Balloon Training Unit	RSJ	rolled steel joist
C	Coastal	R/T	radio telephony
CFS	Central Flying School	RU	ready use
CH	Chain Home (radar)	S	seaplane
D/F	direction finding	SBA	Standard Beam Approach
DTN	Defence Teleprinter Network	SFGT	standard free gunnery trainer
EFTS	Elementary Flying Training School	SFTS	Service Flying Training School
ENSA	Entertainment National Service Association	SHQ	station headquarters
F	fighter	SLG	Satellite Landing Ground
FAA	Fleet Air Arm	SMT	square mesh track
FCO	flying control officer	SS	submarine scout
FTS	Flying Training School	SSQ	station sick quarters
GGS	gyro gun-sight	T	training
GOC	general officer commanding	TAT	torpedo attack trainer
GPO	General Post Office	TDS	Training Depot Station
HDS	home defence squadron	TGST	turret gun sighting trainer
HE	high explosive	WAAF	Women's Auxiliary Air Force
IFF	identification friend or foe	W/T	wireless telegraphy
ITW	Initial Training Wing		

PART 1

THE EVOLUTION OF AERODROMES

The commercial potential of flying was recognized long before the creation of the Air Battalion of the Royal Engineers on 1 April 1911. However, the Imperial Defence Committee was uncertain about which flying machine should be chosen for military service, the airship or the aeroplane. Eventually No. 1 Company operated balloons at Farnborough, while No. 2 operated box kite aeroplanes at Larkhill. Lord Haldane, the Secretary of State for War addressed the Imperial Defence Committee in November 1911 and proposed the creation of a British Aeronautical Service with a Naval Wing, a Military Wing and a Central Flying Training School. As a result, the Royal Flying Corps was formed in April 1912 with five squadrons, two more being created just before the outbreak of war. The Central Flying School was established at Upavon, and technical training was carried out at Coley Park, Reading and at Netheravon. From 1913 onwards, pupil pilots from Upavon graduated to the Military Wing at an average rate of 30 per quarter.

By the end of 1913, Winston Churchill, the First Sea Lord, announced the impending independent status of the Naval Wing under the significant title of the Royal Naval Air Service. At this time, the RFC claimed responsibility for the aerial defence of Great Britain but with the limited funds available most aeroplanes were earmarked by Lord Haldane for the British Expeditionary Force. Meanwhile

Aeroplane sheds dating from 1910 at Larkhill. (Photographed 1994)

First World War station offices at Upavon. (Photographed 1994)

the semi-permanent RNAS under Captain Murray Sueter planned the construction of seaplane stations along Britain's east coastline: Calshot, Dundee, Eastchurch (training), Felixstowe, Fort Grange, Isle of Grain, Great Yarmouth, Killingholme, and Skegness. Airship stations were later established at Kingsnorth and Wormwood Scrubs.

From June 1914, Squadrons 2, (based at Montrose), 5 (based at Fort Grange), and 6 (based at Farnborough), and a Kite Section of the RFC Military Wing joined 3 and 4 Squadrons at the Netheravon 'Concentration Camp' for important combined exercises. Squadrons 3 and 4 were housed inside wooden 1913-pattern side-opening aeroplane sheds, while the visiting squadrons were allocated Piggott, Hervieu and Royal Aircraft Factory tents. The Piggott marquee was large enough to house all the aeroplanes of 2 Squadron; the other tents contained one machine apiece. The exercises involved the sighting and reporting of the positions of 'enemy' columns which included Army lorries and small groups of men belonging to the RFC, as well as the sighting of two MT lorries travelling along a road, requiring an estimation of the distance between them. A balloon was used to simulate an airship with its engines disabled and pilots had to identify the position of the 'airship' as a form of contest between squadrons.

Eventually, four squadrons were at Netheravon in instant readiness for dispatch to Europe, but on the outbreak of war the squadrons went to Farnborough. Here they were made up to full strength with aeroplanes and transport before moving to the embarkation points. The transport equipment of each squadron included:

- a car for the Squadron Commander
- six light Crossley-type tenders for carrying riggers, men and boxes of equipment
- six heavy tenders for transporting spare parts and camp equipment
- three reserve equipment lorries for other spare parts
- three lorries for transporting a set of components for a hangar
- three flight repair lorries with tools and electric lighting plant
- one lorry containing heavy machine tools and stores for mechanical transport
- one baggage lorry
- one lorry for petrol and lubricants
- six motor cycles and six trailers

An important feature of the layout of Netheravon was the large number of MT garages required to accommodate all the necessary vehicles that each squadron needed to take to France.

When war was declared on the 4 August 1914, the RNAS became responsible for the air defence of the British Isles. The German submarine menace soon emphasized the need for rapid expansion in the production of non-rigid airships and the design and construction of parent airship stations as well as operational patrol airship stations. As a result of raids by Zeppelins and long-range

Former offices of the Motor Transport Depot at Netheravon dating from 1914. (Photographed 1994)

A corrugated iron hut dating from 1914 which belonged to the Motor Transport Depot at Netheravon. (Photographed 1994)

**Yatesbury Aerodrome Training Depot
Stations Nos 36 and 37, 1918**

C1W camp No. 1 west
C1E camp No. 1 east
C2 camp No. 2

Gotha bomber aircraft, the War Office established a Home Defence Scheme in 1916 with aircraft, anti-aircraft guns and searchlights. The RFC took over the air defence role from the RNAS, at first using obsolescent aircraft from France. Many new stations established on the eastern side of Britain were designated Home Defence stations. There were two types: small aerodromes became 6th Brigade Flight Stations (such as Buckminster, Catterick and Goldhangar), and the larger ones became known as 6th Brigade Squadron Stations (such as Biggin Hill, Detling, Hainault Farm and Sutton's Farm).

Training was decentralized in late 1915 to cope with the flood of local volunteers. New training aerodromes were established at Beaulieu, Castle Bromwich, Catterick, Northolt and Norwich. The need to replace pilots lost on the Western Front led to the formation of Reserve Squadrons which were redesignated in 1917 as Training Squadrons. Some stations for these squadrons were built on existing aerodromes but the bulk were new stations which, for the first, time were built to a standard layout. From June 1918, their aerodromes became known as Training Depot Stations. No. 3 Training Squadron was based at Lopcombe Corner, No. 6 at Boscombe Down, No. 12 at Netheravon, and Nos 36 and 37 were based at the twin aerodromes at Yatesbury.

Aircraft acceptance parks (AAPs) were established to receive new aeroplanes from the constructor's premises. The new machines could be delivered by air, road or rail. At the AAPs they were examined and equipped for operational purposes before delivery to units at home or overseas. AAPs were manned by a mixture of Service and civilian personnel. Two AAPs were Bracebridge Heath which received Clayton & Shuttleworth Handley-Page 0/400s, and Brockworth which received aircraft from the Gloucestershire Aviation Company. Minor aeroplane repairs and overhauls were carried out in the Aeroplane Repair Section (ARS) shed but extensive damage or a complete overhaul meant that the aeroplane had to be sent to an Aircraft Repair Depot (ARD). These were built close to existing main line railways and each was sited on a designated geographical basis: aeroplanes were repaired and reissued to units within the designated area. For

Aerodromes 1911–18

The choice of a particular site for use as an RFC aerodrome was quite often left to a group of officers assigned the task. They were told roughly where the aerodrome was required and their job was to find the most suitable spot. Biggin Hill and Sealand both came into being in this way. Quite often, when a suitable location was found the standard Training Depot Station layout was drawn on a large-scale Ordnance Survey map before a more detailed site investigation was carried out. However, when the site was thoroughly investigated it was sometimes discovered that it was not suitable after all. For example, poor drainage – something not necessarily obvious from the OS map – would make the proposed site unsuitable. In some cases, such as at Hooton Park, the layout of the standard arrangement of aeroplane sheds had to be adjusted to suit the site conditions.

RFC aerodrome buildings were normally laid out in four separate groups: the officers' mess and quarters; regimental buildings; technical buildings (including hangars); and the women's hostel. During the First World War, technical buildings on Home Defence and Training Depot Stations were built immediately behind rows of hangars. Technical buildings were defined as those in which aircraft maintenance was carried out, vehicles were housed, instructional work was conducted, or which served the day-to-day running of the station such as administration, supply of electric power and water.

Construction was mainly in temporary brick with brick piers at 10 ft centres, or concrete blocks with either timber or concrete wall-posts. Perhaps the most impressive feature of First World War buildings was the hand-built timber roof trusses, both the scissors type and the composite trusses of timber and vertical iron tension rods. Cladding was usually diagonal boarding with either felt or corrugated asbestos sheeting.

Huts were normally designed as standard buildings, the only variation being an occasional switch from brick to concrete construction. But at a few stations deemed important enough, such as Aldeburgh, Biggin Hill, Henlow and Kenley, specially designed accommodation was built from drawings prepared solely for these sites.

Technical Buildings
- aeroplane shed
- armoury
- blacksmith's shop
- camera obscura
- coal and wood store
- depot offices
- dope shop
- guard house
- instruction hut
- motor transport yard
- plane store
- powerhouse
- sail-maker's/carpenter's shop
- salvage shed
- squadron office
- technical store
- water tower
- workshop (metal)

Not every station had all the buildings listed here and not every building is listed; hangars (sheds) are dealt with elsewhere.

The central heating and boiler house built at No. 5 Eastern Aircraft Repair Depot, Henlow. (Photographed 1982)

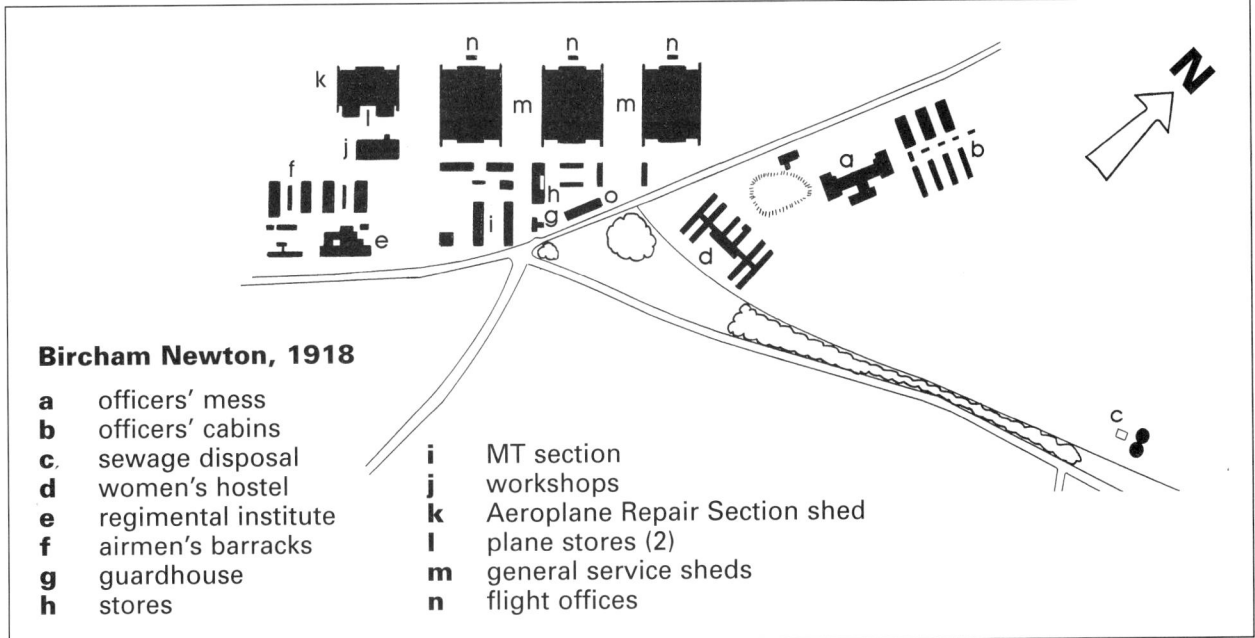

Bircham Newton, 1918

a officers' mess
b officers' cabins
c. sewage disposal
d women's hostel
e regimental institute
f airmen's barracks
g guardhouse
h stores
i MT section
j workshops
k Aeroplane Repair Section shed
l plane stores (2)
m general service sheds
n flight offices

example, Farnborough No. 1 covered the southern area, while Henlow No. 5 covered the eastern area.

The first Chief of the Air Staff, Air Chief Marshall Hugh Trenchard, devised a plan in January 1918 for combining American bomber crews with British crews to create an inter-Allied bombing force that would operate using Handley-Page 0/400 heavy bombers. Training for both American and British crews was to be carried out in Britain at Ford, Manston, Netheravon and Tangmere, and operational bases were to be established at five locations close to Nancy in France. The Handley-Page 0/400 had a 100 ft wing-span and consequently was given folding wings to enable it to fit into specially designed hangars at AAPs and training bases as well as the storage sheds on factory sites. The bigger Handley-Page V/1500 which Trenchard wanted for operations from bases in Norfolk would be not available until after the Armistice so this idea came to nothing.

A committee was formed in 1918 to look at measures for Home Defence. It was chaired by General Jan Christian Smuts who said: 'The day might not be far off when aerial operations may become the principal operations of war, to which the older forms of military operations may become secondary and subordinate.' This led to the belief that an air arm launching its own offensive could win a future war. Smuts went on to recommend the amalgamation of both the RFC and RNAS. This duly took place on 1 April 1918, creating the Royal Air Force. By the time the Armistice was signed on 11 November 1918, the RAF was the largest air service in the world with 22,647 aircraft and 188 squadrons. However, many of the squadrons returning from France were disbanded and many stations were closed down as the RAF reorganized itself for peacetime conditions. The Air Estimates published by Parliament in March 1919 consisted of £66.5 million with no fixed sum being allowed for reconstruction; most was earmarked for demolition.

After the war, Trenchard fought hard for the very existence of the new service, a fight that lasted 10 years. On 11 December 1919, he wrote a White Paper outlining

14 British Military Airfield Architecture

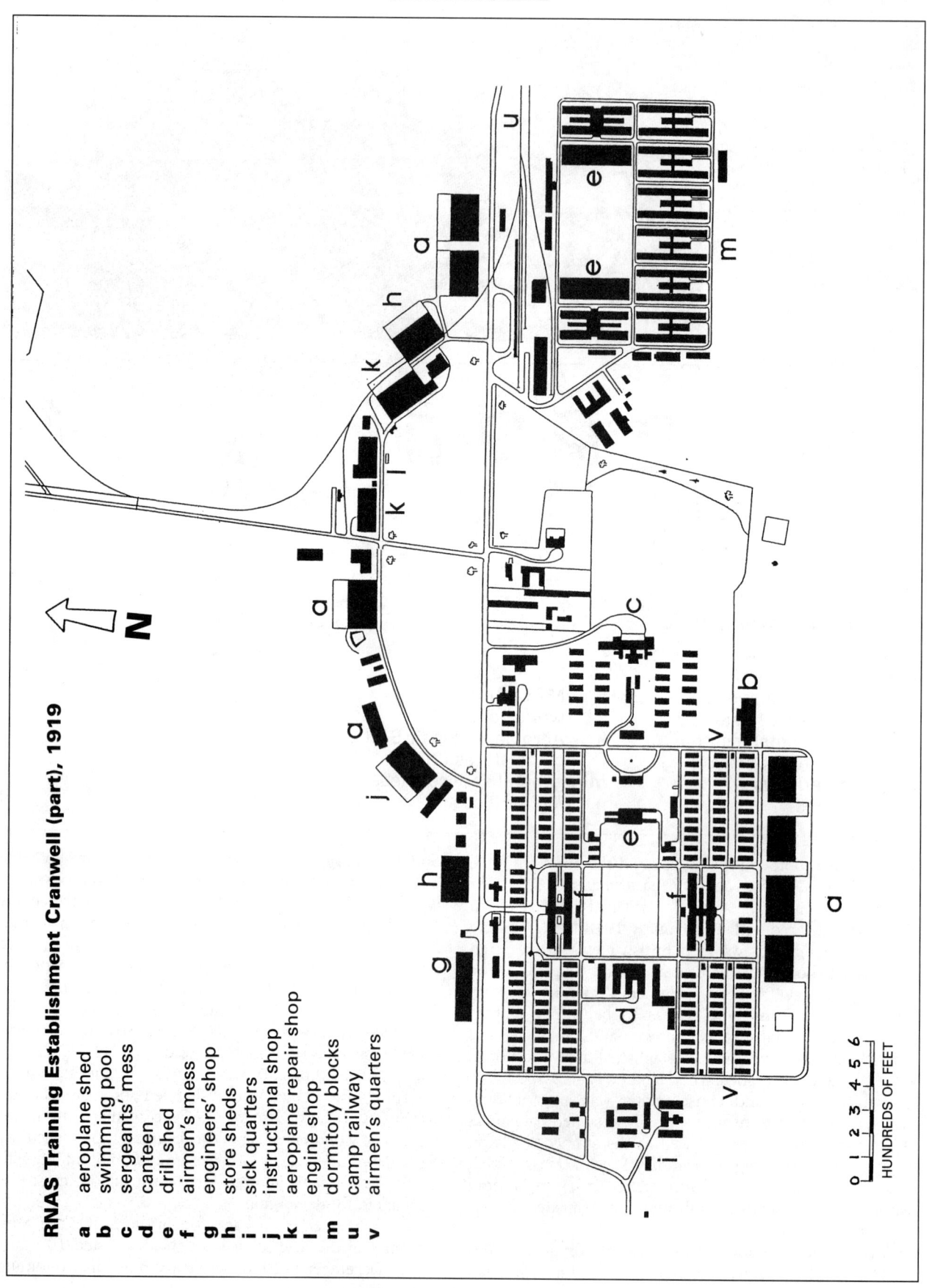

RNAS Training Establishment Cranwell (part), 1919

- **a** aeroplane shed
- **b** swimming pool
- **c** sergeants' mess
- **d** canteen
- **e** drill shed
- **f** airmen's mess
- **g** engineers' shop
- **h** store sheds
- **i** sick quarters
- **j** instructional shop
- **k** aeroplane repair shop
- **l** engine shop
- **m** dormitory blocks
- **u** camp railway
- **v** airmen's quarters

the form the new service should take: a proposed strength of 25 squadrons (19 overseas), aircrew and ground crew training to be centralized (achieved with the founding of No. 1 School of Technical Training at Halton in 1920), and a reorganization of the Air Ministry. That same year, the Prime Minister, Lloyd George, as a means of establishing financial control of the three services, reminded service chiefs that under the Treaty of Versailles Germany was banned from building aircraft and submarines. Thus, he did not anticipate a major war within the next 10 years; this was repeated by successive governments in 1925, 1926 and 1927 and became known as the 10 Year Rule. This goes some way to explain why there was so little defence expenditure during the 1920s.

In 1920 and 1922, the RAF successfully justified its existence during the intervention in British Somaliland; a single bomber squadron successfully attacked the forts and camps of the 'Mad Mullah'. Following the peace treaties of 1919, Britain had received mandates to police three areas of the Middle East: Palestine, Trans-Jordan and Iraq. In 1922, Iraq was in revolt and the RAF bombed the villages of the turbulent tribes, quelling the revolt far more cheaply than a ground force could have done. Here at last was an independent strategy for air power, showing that bombs could not only quell revolts but win wars as well. Taking full advantage of these successes Trenchard created the RAF Staff College at Andover and the RAF Cadet College at Cranwell.

By 1922, Great Britain only had 12 squadrons located at aerodromes in the UK, while France possessed the best-equipped air service in Europe. In August, Lloyd George's Coalition Government announced the terms of the first postwar expansion of the RAF, increasing the number of aircraft on strength to 500. This was to be achieved with funds provided by a more efficient Air Ministry. A committee, created in 1923 under Air Commodore J. M. Steel of the Air Ministry and Colonel W. B. Bartholomew of the War Office, produced a plan for defence based on the assumption that an attack on the British Isles would come south and south-west across the Channel – from France. By 1925, it was estimated that with the proposed expansion of their air service the French would be capable of dropping 325 tons of bombs per day against a mere 67

The 30 ft diameter acoustic bowl mirror built at Hythe in 1929 as seen in 1988.

tons per day which the RAF could drop. Britain's strategic aim therefore depended on building an air force large enough to counter an attack from France.

The plan involved a defensive belt curved round London. This would provide a small tactical advantage to the RAF by allowing it to fight in a prepared zone above its own bases; this was called the air fighting zone. This was sandwiched between inner and outer artillery zones. The belt was divided into sectors served by existing fighter stations with two squadrons based at each station south of London and one squadron at each station north of the capital. When it was later extended to the Bristol Channel, three squadrons were provided for the defence of the south coast. It was very important that early warning of an attack could be given to enable the fighters to reach sufficient altitude before the attacking enemy aircraft arrived. This was to be provided by both mobile and fixed sound locators under Major General C. F. Romer. A subcommittee of the Committee of Imperial Defence voted in 1923 for continued control of the naval air units by the RAF. The new government under Baldwin also

The 1930 acoustic wall at Denge, as seen from the seaward side. (Photographed 1988)

accepted the committee's recommendation for a Home Defence Air Force with 52 squadrons.

This expansion of the RAF planned for 1923–4 involved designing a completely new range of permanent buildings for the modernization of existing stations. It also necessitated buying back, but without compulsory powers and in the face of local opposition, many former First World War aerodromes that the Air Ministry had only recently sold back to the original landowners. Many had been abandoned, almost all had boundaries restricted in area, and many of the buildings were of timber construction. The Lords Commissioners of the Treasury of the new Labour Government allowed £3 million for eight new Home Defence squadrons and granted limited funds for the remodelling of (among others) Bicester (B), Biggin Hill (F), Bircham Newton (B), Catterick (F), Duxford (F), Filton (F), Gosport, Lee-on-Solent, Tangmere (F), and Upavon (CFS). In 1924, the new Cabinet approved Trenchard's Auxiliary Air Force project which at last brought the RAF in-line with the Army which had maintained a similar reserve with the Territorial Army units since 1909.

On 1 January 1925, a change came with the introduction of the Air Defence of Great Britain (ADGB) with which one Fighter Area and three Bomber Areas were grouped geographically. Bomber stations were mostly located in the western area, centred on Berkshire, Hampshire, Oxfordshire, and Wiltshire. Fighter stations were located mainly for the defence of London at aerodromes in Cambridgeshire, Essex, Kent, Middlesex, Surrey, and Sussex. By the end of October, the first four Auxiliary squadrons were formed: No. 600 (City of London), No. 601 (County of London), No. 602 (City of Glasgow), and No. 603 (City of Edinburgh). By the Spring of 1925, there were 54 squadrons, including 18 for the defence of Britain under ADGB. But in early 1926, the financial situation of the Air Force Expansion Scheme was so dire that the cost of running a squadron at home had to be reduced by reducing the number of aircraft per squadron from 18 to 12.

On 23 March 1932, the Cabinet decided that the 10 Year Rule should be abolished. In 1933, Hitler became Chancellor of Germany. For the first time since the end of the First World War, Germany posed a threat because of its re-emergence as a military power. At this time, the RAF was in a position of weakness with very few aircraft, most of which were obsolete. In 1932, a new aerodrome opened at Abingdon (MB) and in 1934 another opened at Beck Row (Mildenhall). In November 1935, the Prime Minister, Baldwin, authorized rearmament plans to expand the RAF with the introduction of the first of a series of Schemes that came into effect between 1934 and 1938. Five Schemes were passed by the Cabinet: A, C, F, L, and M. Another three, H, J, and K, were formulated but never went beyond the proposal stage although many new stations proposed under them did become part of the next Scheme to be passed by the Cabinet. This expansion led to a large-scale rebuilding programme, the RAF requiring numerous new stations of permanent construction.

Scheme A came into effect during 1934–5. On 19 July 1934, the Government announced its intention to increase the strength of the RAF by 41 squadrons and the Fleet Air Arm by eight squadrons. The locations of new fighter and bomber bases were determined by a plan recommended in 1935 by the Air Ministry Reorientation Committee under Air Marshal Sir Robert Brooke-Popham. For the first time since the First World War, this created a continuous system of fighter defence covering the whole country. Plans for new permanent stations requiring standard types of building designs were first started in 1934 for construction in 1935. These included Church Fenton (F), Cranfield (B), Feltwell (B), Harwell (B), Odiham (AC), Marham (B), Stradishall (B), Ternhill (SFTS), Thorney Island (C), and Waddington (B). Alterations and additions were carried out to replace unsatisfactory accommodation at Catterick (F), Cranwell (T), Halton (T), Hornchurch (F), Leuchars (F), North Weald (F), Sealand (S), Tangmere (F), Turnhouse (F), Upper Heyford (B), and Wittering (F). The first of the new Armament Training Camps was started at Warmwell in timber hutting.

Reserve Flying Training Schools (RFTS) were set up in 1935 to relieve SFTS of preliminary flying training. The Air Ministry awarded contracts to civilian companies already experienced in flying training to

AERODROMES 1922–33

In some cases, stations were split by having the living quarters separated from the airfield and technical area by a public highway. Although this was unsatisfactory in the eyes of the RAF Building Committee, it had to be accepted on the grounds of limited funds. There were now three distinct groups of buildings: technical buildings; communal buildings and barracks; and married quarters.

New designs replaced existing buildings and new types of building appeared: the operations room; the parachute store; and the watch office. Furthermore, individual workshops such as blacksmith's, carpenter's and metal shops were now located in a single building.

Redesigned Technical Buildings
- aeroplane shed
- armoury
- duty pilot's block (watch office)
- engine test house
- guard house
- main stores
- main workshop
- motor transport yard
- operations room
- powerhouse
- station headquarters
- water-tower

The Evolution of Aerodromes 17

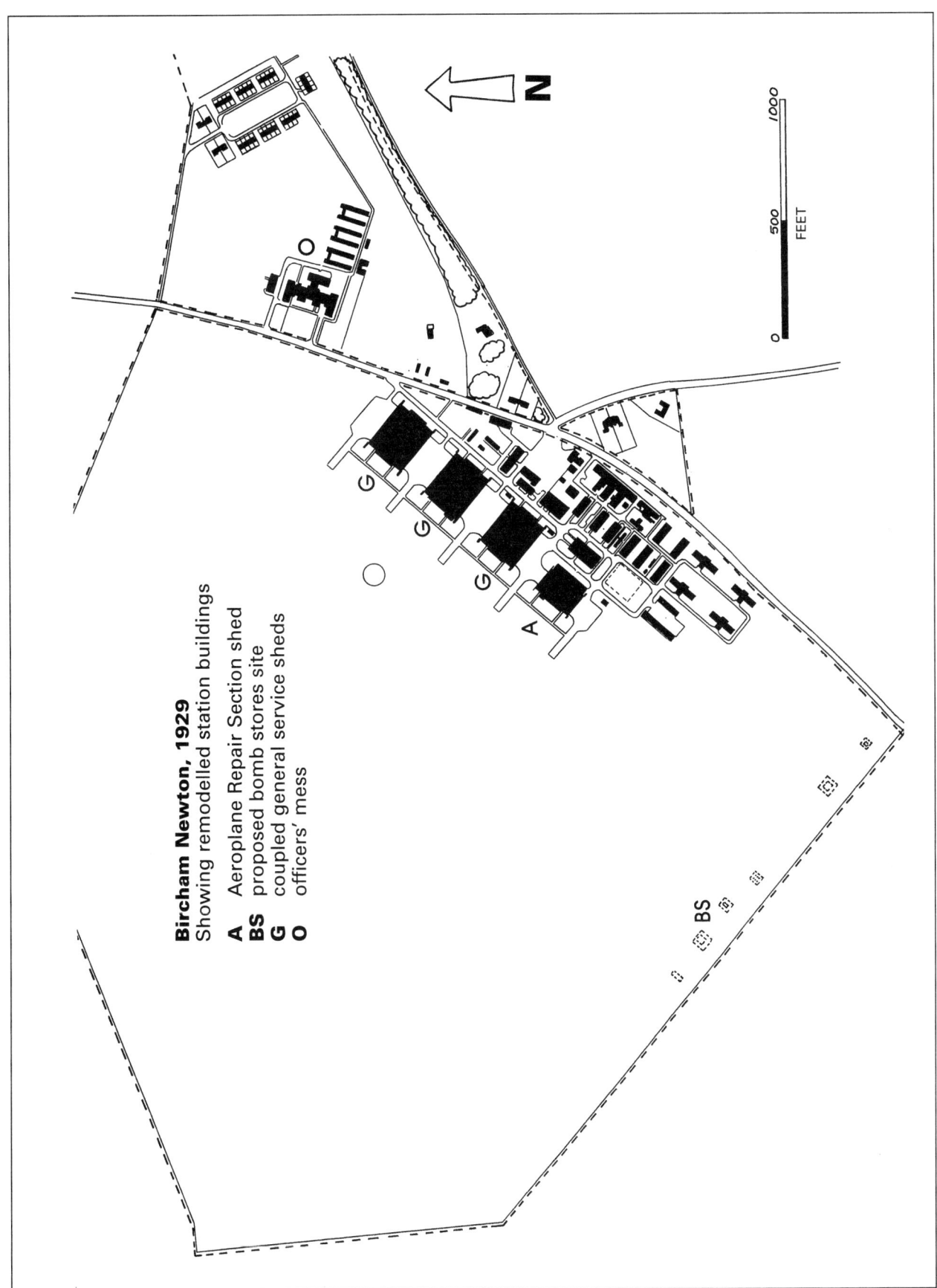

undertake this task. For example, at Sywell Brooklands Aviation undertook flying training, while at Woodley it was undertaken by Philips and Powis, and at Yatesbury by the Bristol Aeroplane Company.

Scheme C was announced in Parliament on 22 May 1935 to provide a Metropolitan Air Force of 123 squadrons with 1,500 aircraft. These figures had been calculated using reliable information which showed that Germany would have as many front-line aircraft as France by 1937 and enough with which to go to war in 1939. Therefore, the expansion programme had to be completed by 1937, but even this did not make any allowance for aircraft reserves. The programme was superseded by Scheme F before C was completed, however. Scheme F was announced in February 1936 and allowed for 124 squadrons with 1,750 front-line aircraft. For the first time, provision was made for aircraft to be held in reserve with the introduction of the first Aircraft Storage Units, each with a designed capacity of 400 aircraft. The construction of Aircraft Storage Units began at existing Service Flying Training Schools: Aston Down, Hullavington, Kemble, and Shawbury. This was the only Scheme to run its full term and was completed before the outbreak of war. The requirement for new aircraft under Scheme F was too large for existing aircraft companies to cope. So in March 1936 the Secretary of State for Air, Lord Swinton, announced the building of state-owned shadow factories. These would be managed by aircraft or motor car manufacturers and produce either aircraft or aero-engines designed by other companies: the shadow factories would manufacture the aircraft reserve.

The administration of the expanded RAF was now becoming too complex. As a result, the Air Council disbanded the ADGB and a reorganization took place to form the first four specialized commands: Bomber Command (HQ Uxbridge), Fighter Command (HQ Stanmore), Coastal Command (HQ Lee-on-Solent), and Training Command (HQ Ternhill). New permanent stations were started in 1936 at Debden (F), Dishforth (B), Driffield (B), Finningley (B), Hemswell (B), Hullavington (SFTS), Leconfield (F), Scampton (B), Shawbury (SFTS), Upwood (B), and Wyton (B). New Armament Training Camps and Air Observer Schools were commenced in timber hutting, requiring special designs of instructional, technical and domestic buildings for 500 personnel, at Acklington, Evanton, Penrhos, and West Freugh.

Aerodromes in the Expansion Period 1934–9

From the beginning of the expansion period in 1934 came the first real opportunity for the Works Directorate to design and construct a comprehensive range of specialist permanent buildings of character and uniformity. Plans were prepared around standard type designs so that buildings of the same design were erected at many stations, modified only in keeping with local conditions in respect of facing materials. At Hullavington, for example, stone facing work conformed with the traditions of the Cotswolds. The architectural style of simple well-proportioned Georgian architecture was adopted, with hand-made facing bricks and roofing tiles which were selected for colour, texture and pointing to be appropriate to the district. Due to shortages of bricklayers and the requirements for protection against bomb blast, later expansion period buildings were of concrete construction instead of brick.

The elevational treatment of all architectural designs was subject to review and approval by the Royal Fine Arts Commission. The Society for the Preservation of Rural England advised on the positioning of buildings in relation to the countryside.

Expansion period airfields were of 'compact' layout without being bisected by a public road. There were four distinct groups of buildings, three groups (the technical buildings, the communal buildings and barracks, and the married quarters) were located close to each other, but the fourth, the bomb store, now completely redesigned, was located well away from the main camp. The powerhouse became a stand-by set house as a commercial electricity supply was available and it was now only necessary to have a back-up supply in case of a failure of the main circuit. A central-heating station was provided because most buildings were connected to the district heating scheme.

Technical Buildings
- aircraft shed
- armoury
- bomb stores
- bulk fuel store
- central-heating station
- engine test house
- fire tender shelter and NFE store
- guardroom
- high-level water-tower
- main stores
- main workshops
- 25 yd machine-gun range
- motor transport yard
- operations block
- parachute store
- petrol tanker sheds
- stand-by set house
- station headquarters
- watch office
- works services yard

In addition, hangar annexes were designed to accommodate squadron offices, rest rooms, changing and locker rooms, map and briefing rooms, armouries, wireless and instrument workshops, dope and aircraft equipment stores.

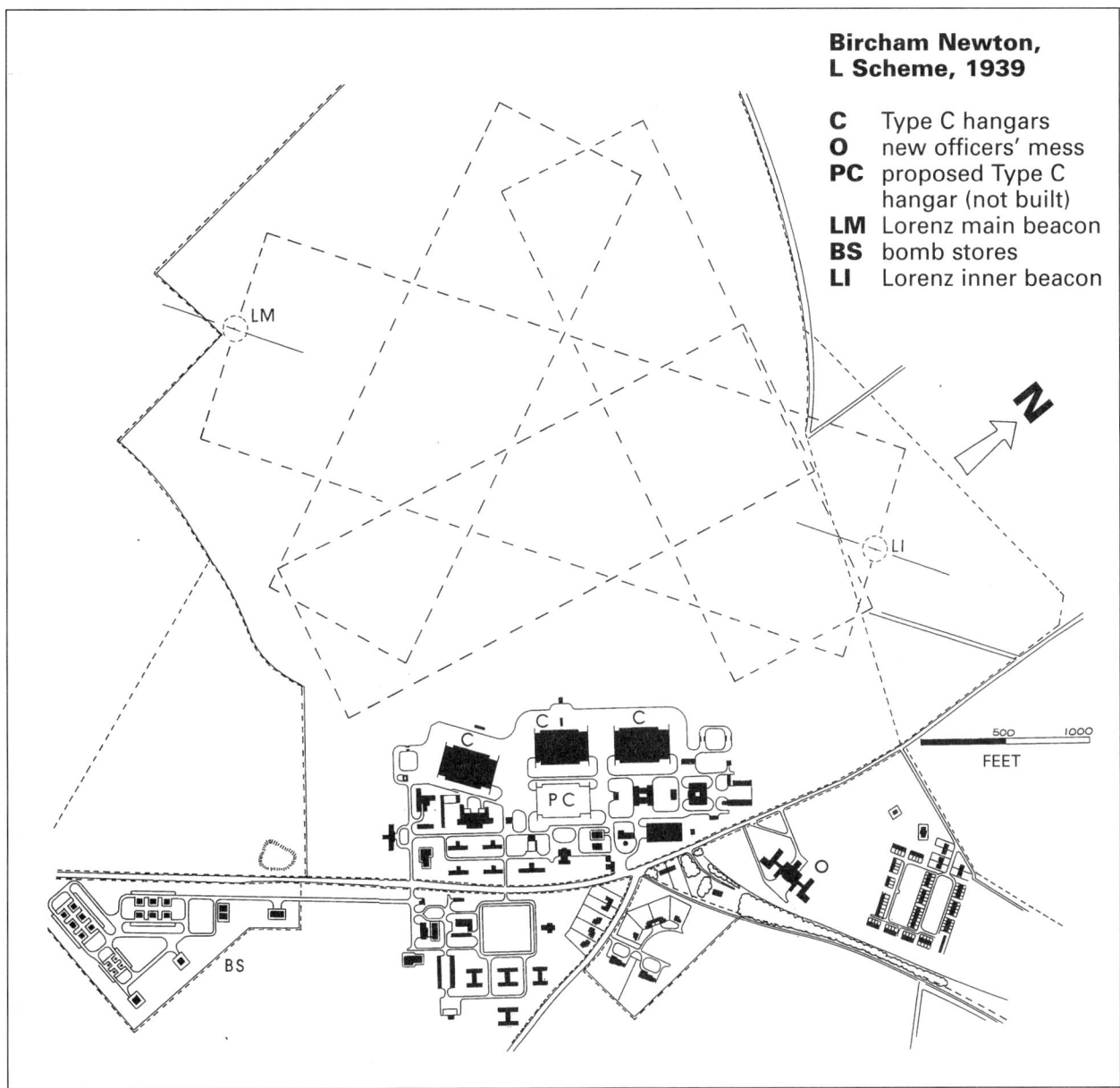

Reconstruction took place at existing stations, including Castle Bromwich, Catfoss (ATS), Digby (F), Duxford (F), and Hawkinge (F).

In 1937, the RAF relinquished control of the Fleet Air Arm to the Navy. That same year, the building of new permanent stations started at Bassingbourn (B), Benson (PRU), Brize Norton (SFTS and ASU), Cottesmore (B), Honington (B), Linton-on-Ouse (B), Little Rissington (SFTS and ASU), South Cerney (SFTS), Wattisham (B), Watton (B), and West Raynham (B). At Cosford, a combined Aircraft Storage Unit and new training establishment in both permanent and temporary timber constructions for 1,000 personnel was commenced. This included the design of large instructional workshops, lecture blocks and special domestic buildings. Additional accommodation for stations of increased size or a change in function was built at Bicester, Bircham Newton, Boscombe Down, Felixstowe, Mount Batten, North Coates, Sutton Bridge, Upavon, Upper Heyford, and Usworth.

The first of the Universal Equipment Depots for the storage of complete ranges of consumable items were designed and built at Carlisle and Hartlebury at locations chosen on a geographical basis. Each site was close to an existing main line railway line; marshalling sidings were provided for each one, capable of holding 100 trucks. Each depot was divided into a headquarters site and six subsites, all being well dispersed round the countryside. The subsites each contained up to five storage sheds of three different types: a fully protected type with walls and roofs of concrete capable of standing up to small incendiary bombs; a semi-protected type; and an unprotected type. The planning of accommodation for Barrage Balloon Depots took place and work started on the first four sites for the squadrons that were to be used for the protection of London. New Volunteer Reserve Training Centres were established at existing civil airports.

In October 1937, several high-ranking German officers, including Generals Milch, Udet (the Director of the Technical Department of the German Air Ministry), and Stumpff, were given a guided tour of selected RAF airfields, Hullavington among them, and shadow factories.

Scheme L was announced on 27 April 1938 but the Munich Crisis intervened and it was replaced by Scheme M on 7 November. New Type Design Scheme L stations were planned for Colerne (ASU), Coltishall (F), Horsham St Faith (F), and Kirton-in-Lindsey (F). The requirements of Scheme L also called for large increases in accommodation of both technical and domestic buildings at all existing stations to meet the demands of increased numbers of personnel. The first of the new permanent RAF hospitals was planned and started at Ely. Timber hutting was purchased in vast quantities to supplement the buildings on existing stations and three new Armament Training Camps and Air Observer Schools were commenced in timber at Jurby, Pembrey, and Stormy Down. A new station for general reconnaissance aircraft with semi-permanent Type C hangars and hutted technical and domestic buildings was started at Wick. Similar accommodation was provided with a mixture of permanent buildings for an Aircraft Storage Unit at Kinloss and Lossiemouth. The construction of new Barrage Balloon Depots was also started in 1938 for the protection of many towns and cities including Birmingham, Bristol, Cardiff, Derby, Glasgow, Hull, Liverpool, Manchester, Newcastle, Plymouth, Sheffield, Southampton, and Warrington.

During 1939, the construction of new permanent stations planned under the L and M Schemes were started at Aldergrove (ASU), Binbrook (B), Bramcote (OTU), Chivenor (SOAN), Coningsby (B), Dumfries (ASU), Leeming (B), Lindholme (B), Lichfield (ASU), Middle Wallop (F), Middleton St George (B), Newton (B), North Luffenham (B), Oakington (B), Ouston (F), St Eval (C), Swanton Morley (F), Swinderby (B), Syerston (B),

AERODROMES IN THE SECOND WORLD WAR

In the early stages of the war, in anticipation of concentrated bombing, a policy of dispersed layout was adopted for all new stations. Vital buildings such as the high-level water tank, the operations block, the stand-by set house, and station offices were built away from the technical area. The number of sites for such buildings varied from station to station but the main ones were the bomb stores, the RAF communal site, the WAAF communal site, the administration/ operations block, the instructional site, the living sites (of which there were usually several), the technical site, the sewage farm, and the sick quarters.

Permanent buildings designed in the expansion period were neither economical in materials used nor speed of construction, and the anticipation of war led to a rapid redesign. Drawings now had to be prepared for temporary buildings as well. At the outbreak of war there were a number of stations in various stages of construction and many of these had to be completed with modifications in the interests of immediate economy. Many thousands of drawings of standard type design buildings were prepared along with layouts, working drawings, structural engineering drawings, and drawings showing water, sewage, heating and ventilation (H & V), and mechanical and electrical (M & E) systems, and schedules of fittings. Many temporary buildings were designed to keep pace with the development of aircraft and weapons: aircraft became more sophisticated requiring dedicated buildings for the repair, servicing and storing of aircraft systems and weapons. Furthermore, station personnel had to be informed about events happening on the station. Aircrew had to be briefed about missions.

Construction was in cement-rendered temporary brick for most technical buildings (with half-brick thick walls). Some important buildings such as the watch office were built with walls 9 inches thick. The use of timber for roof trusses was common in the early part of the war until the timber shortage; steel trusses then became standard. Also, some designs called for timber floors but the shortage meant that reinforced concrete was used instead.

Technical Buildings
- squadron armoury
- station armoury
- bomb-sight store and repair facility
- crew briefing room
- maintenance block
- instrument repair shop
- radar workshop
- speech broadcasting room
- substation
- transformer enclosure

In addition to those listed, with the standard use of T2 hangars it was necessary to provide annexes for these hangars in the form of adjacent huts. Although there were many specialist functions involved, they were all accommodated in similar designs of standard buildings, only varying in length (number of bays) and internal arrangement. T2 Annexes included:

- minor workshops
- battery-charging rooms
- squadron and flight offices
- instrument rooms
- maintenance blocks housing squadron armouries
- aircraft equipment stores

Topcliffe (B), Waterbeach (B), West Malling (F), and Wick (C). Five small anti-aircraft co-operation units were built in hutting on new sites at Aberporth, Cleave, Kidsdale, Manobier, and Morfa Towyn. Stations for the reception, kitting out and accommodation of 4,000 recruits were planned and commenced at Bridgenorth, Padgate, Saughall Massie, and Wilmslow.

When war was declared in September 1939, the first-line strength of the Metropolitan Air Force did not exceed 1,500 aircraft (excluding reserves) which was not even sufficient to meet the requirements of Scheme F. Immediately on the outbreak of war, austerity measures were applied to those stations still not completed and to new Scheme M stations, involving a change from Type C to Type J hangars. These included Coningsby, Burtonwood, Middleton St George, North Luffenham, Kinloss, Lossiemouth, Lichfield, Oakington, Swanton Morley, Swinderby, Syerston, and Waterbeach. Parent stations designed before the outbreak of the Second World War continued to be built on the compact layout but those started at the beginning of war had a dispersed camp layout. All were equipped with a single Type J hangar and two or four Type T2 hangars. These included Chelveston (B), Chipping Warden (BOTU), Elsham Wolds (B), Goxhill (F), Holme on Spalding Moor (B), Honeybourne (BOTU), Molesworth (B), Moreton in Marsh (BOTU), Pershore (BOTU), Pocklington (B), Polebrook (B), Snaith (B), and Wellesbourne Mountford (BOTU).

AERODROME DEVELOPMENT 1920–45

Before construction operations could begin, the Air Ministry Airfield Board had to select a suitable site. This was done with the assistance of a lands officer. Preference was given to a large field with a convex contour – to allow natural drainage – rather than to a completely flat field which drained slowly since this would require an extensive drainage system. The soil had to be of high density and solidity, with a minimum water absorbency. Other considerations were access, amenities and obstructions both within the aerodrome boundaries and on the approaches.

Having chosen a site, the first operation was to clear the area of hedges, fill in ditches, clear timber, demolish existing structures, and remove root crops. With this work completed, any depressions and hillocks were obvious to see. Using scrapers drawn by Caterpillar tractors, the hillocks were levelled and the material used to fill in any depressions. Contouring of the site was obviously important: a convex contour allowed surface water to drain away towards the airfield boundaries. The flying ground was consolidated by repeated actions of rollers and tampers of various sizes and weights, after which the area was lightly ploughed with wide-span ploughs to a depth of 6 inches.

After careful analysis of the soil and of the conditions created by exposure, altitude and rainfall, the species of grass to be sown was chosen. The most suitable species were hard fescue, fine-leafed sheep's fescue, smooth-stalked meadow-grass, rough-stalked meadow-grass, crested dog's-tail, creeping bent, wavy mountain hair-grass, and wild white clover. One or more of these was selected, and the seeds were sown at a rate of 100 lb per statute acre. When the young grass was 4 inches tall, it was cut with sharp mowers drawn by tractors. It is now rather amusing to note that the standard Air Ministry test for determining whether the surface of the new aerodrome was suitable for general use, consisted of driving a car at 20 mph across the aerodrome; if this caused no undue discomfort to the passengers, the aerodrome passed the test.

Specialist aerodrome construction firms evolved during the 1920s and 1930s, such as En-Tout-Cas (Catfoss, Lee-on-Solent, Sealand and Sutton Bridge) and James Hunter (Barton, Gatwick, Great West Aerodrome, Portsmouth and Radlett). They all tended to develop similar methods of aerodrome construction. Most early aerodromes entailed few engineering problems and were therefore inexpensive to construct, but as the requirement for new sites increased during the Expansion Period, less suitable sites had to be chosen. Because of the extra preparation required by such sites, costs became progressively higher.

Construction of airfields during the RAF Expansion Period commenced in 1935, most of the preliminary site investigations and designs having been carried out in 1934. The work was carried out under contract to the Air Ministry by public works contractors using civilian labour from the building and civil engineering trade. The Directorate General of Works – under Ernest Holloway who was knighted in 1945 – a technical branch of the Air Ministry, was responsible for the design, execution and maintenance of all RAF civil engineering works and buildings. The Directorate's personnel were drawn from the civil engineering professions: architects, municipal engineers, and quantity surveyors, as well as mechanical and electrical engineers.

Sites selected by the Airfield Board were investigated by the Directorate General of Works with regard to the preparation of the aerodrome surface and the siting of buildings. To save time in finding new sites, a number of derelict former First World War stations such as Hemswell, Scampton, Waddington and Wyton were investigated. Quite a few were then redeveloped and became Expansion Period stations.

The best aerodrome shape was considered to be a rectangle or square, giving full-length runs from every direction. In early 1938, the Aerodrome Improvement Board was set up as a result of requirements of the Lorenz blind approach system. The board investigated every aerodrome and prepared stripping plans. Up to 1939, an area of land developed as an airfield usually contained an imaginary 1,100 yd diameter circle known as the bombing circle. This provided a safe area for practice bombing. Specified rectangular strips were set across the circle in appropriate directions for landing and taking off. The early practice was four strips, the main one of 1,300 yd by 400 yd with subsidiaries of 1,000 yd by 200 yd.

Aircraft weights and take-off and landing speeds, even

22　*British Military Airfield Architecture*

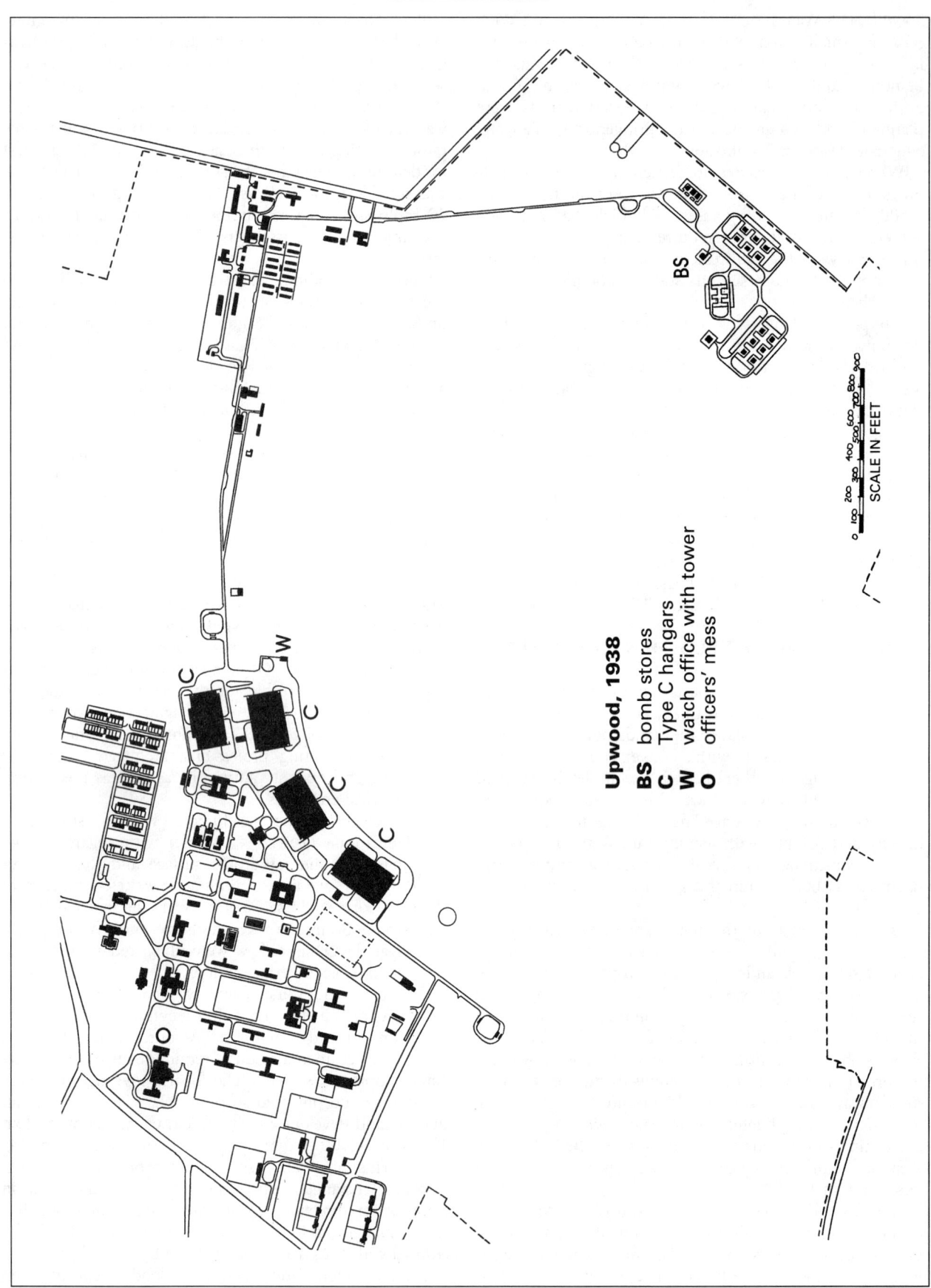

before 1939, were reaching a state where a normal grass surface was inadequate to withstand the wear of repeated traffic and became unreliable under wet weather conditions. So in 1938, two particularly 'wet' aerodromes, Odiham and Gosport, were developed with hard runway surfaces. At Odiham, two 700 yd runways were laid; at Gosport 350 yd and 400 yd long tracks were laid. By the autumn of 1938, paved runways were recognized as essential. At eight fighter stations, the construction of two runways of 800 yd by 50 yd were commenced: Biggin Hill, Church Fenton, Debden, Hendon, Kenley, Northolt, Tangmere and Turnhouse.

By December 1940, bomber airfields were being designed with three strips, each a minimum of 1,100 yd, and set as near to 60° to each other as possible. The main strip was 400 yd wide while the two subsidiary strips were 200 yd wide. Runways along the centre of two strips were 50 yd wide and 1,100 yd long, the main runway having a length of 1,400 yd. From 1942, the standard operational airfield became known as Class A. The main runway, usually sited in a north-east to south-west line, was increased to 2,000 yd by 50 yd, while the subsidiaries were increased to 1,400 yd with 100 yd cleared areas at both ends to allow for overshoots. Perimeter tracks were built to a standard 50 ft width, connecting the ends of the runways. Construction of all new airfields between 1942 and 1945 conformed to this specification, and existing operational airfields were brought up to this standard. It was not essential to fully meet Class A requirements ie 2,000 + 1,400 + 1,400, but if any runway was less than the ideal, it was recommended that another would exceed the ideal.

Between 1944 and 1945, several airfields were developed beyond the Class A standard. Airfields for heavy bombers were planned with three runways: the main runway 3,000 yd by 100 yd with subsidiaries of 2,000 yd by 100 yd. Lakenheath, Marham and Sculthorpe were three such airfields. Paved emergency runways built at Carnaby, Manston and Woodbridge were each 3,000 yd by 250 yd.

The continued use of grass surfaces at some Service Flying Training Schools sometimes resulted in the failure of aircraft undercarriage retracting gear due to mud building up on moving parts. Another problem was stones being flicked up causing serious damage to propellers. It was therefore decided in 1941 to construct concrete runways and perimeter tracks at permanent SFTS stations and to use metal tracking at temporary SFTS stations. Two types of metal tracking were commonly used: Army Track and Sommerfeld Track. Army Track was a pre-war temporary road surface consisting of wire woven into a diamond chain-link mesh, supplied in rolls 10 feet wide and 37 ft 6 in long. This was laid at Cranage, Kidlington and Southrop. Sommerfeld Track consisted of woven wire chain-link mesh with metal rods threaded transversely through it at 8-inch intervals. The ends of the metal rods were looped so that when the tracking was laid flat on a grass surface metal bars could be inserted through the loops to join it up into a continuous surface. Sommerfeld Track was laid initially at Bramcote, Chipping Norton, Henlow, South Cerney and Windrush.

Twenty-four Advanced Landing Grounds were constructed in southern England prior to the D-Day invasion. It was one of the most important pre-invasion tasks given to the Airfield Construction Service. The RAF's 2nd Tactical Air Force operated from these airfields during the Normandy campaign until airfields were established in France, softening up the enemy's defences immediately behind the invasion beaches on D-Day itself, and flying ground support sorties. Each airfield had two metal track runways (1,600 yd by 50 yd) made with Sommerfeld Track, Square Mesh Track (SMT), or Pierced Steel Plank (PSP), with 2.5 miles of perimeter track with an additional MT track running parallel with the perimeter track. Accommodation was kept to a minimum using existing farm buildings, but up to four blister hangars were often provided. Airfields that used Sommerfeld Track include Appledram, Funtington, Horne and Swingfield.

Square Mesh Track consisted of parallel rows of steel wire welded at right angles to more parallel rows of wire. It was available in 7 ft 3 in wide strips in rolls 77 ft long. Lengths of SMT were overlapped and held together by clips. Airfields using SMT included Christchurch (ALG) and Sherburn in Elmet. Pierced Steel Plank was an American track 1 ft 4 in wide and 12 ft long, made from pressed mild steel sheet. To increase stiffness, two longitudinal ribs were formed in the sheet, and three parallel rows of 4-inch holes were punched out to reduce its weight. Besides being used to make runways, PSP was used to triple the width of the ends of concrete runways at stations used by airborne forces to assist with the marshalling of tug/glider combinations. Brize Norton, Down Ampney, Fairford and Harwell all had PSP areas at the ends of runways. Examples of Advanced Landing Grounds that used PSP include Headcorn, High Halden, Kingsnorth, and Woodchurch. Another type of tracking was bar and rod track. This was a panel type of tracking consisting of parallel mild steel bars welded to another mild steel bar at each end to form a panel 3 feet wide and 12 ft long. Stiffness was provided by traverse rods welded to the bars to form a square pattern. Airfields with this tracking included Brackla, Elgin, and Stormy Down.

Immediately before the beginning of the Second World War it was realized that provision would have to be made for aircraft dispersal around the aerodrome boundary so that concentrations of aircraft in hangars could be avoided. Soon after the start of the Second World War there was an immediate requirement for quick and easy access to the runways; the temporary tracks laid at operational aerodromes in peacetime were no longer adequate. With the development of hard surface runways connected by perimeter tracks, 150 ft diameter 'frying pan' hard standings were now built, approached by an access track and sited irregularly around the airfield boundary. By 1942, with the huge increase in aircraft numbers, this system had become unworkable; the access tracks were clogged with aircraft. Therefore, the 'spectacle' type of hard standing, sited immediately off the perimeter track, was introduced. These became the standard dispersal and marshalling areas on bomber stations.

24 British Military Airfield Architecture

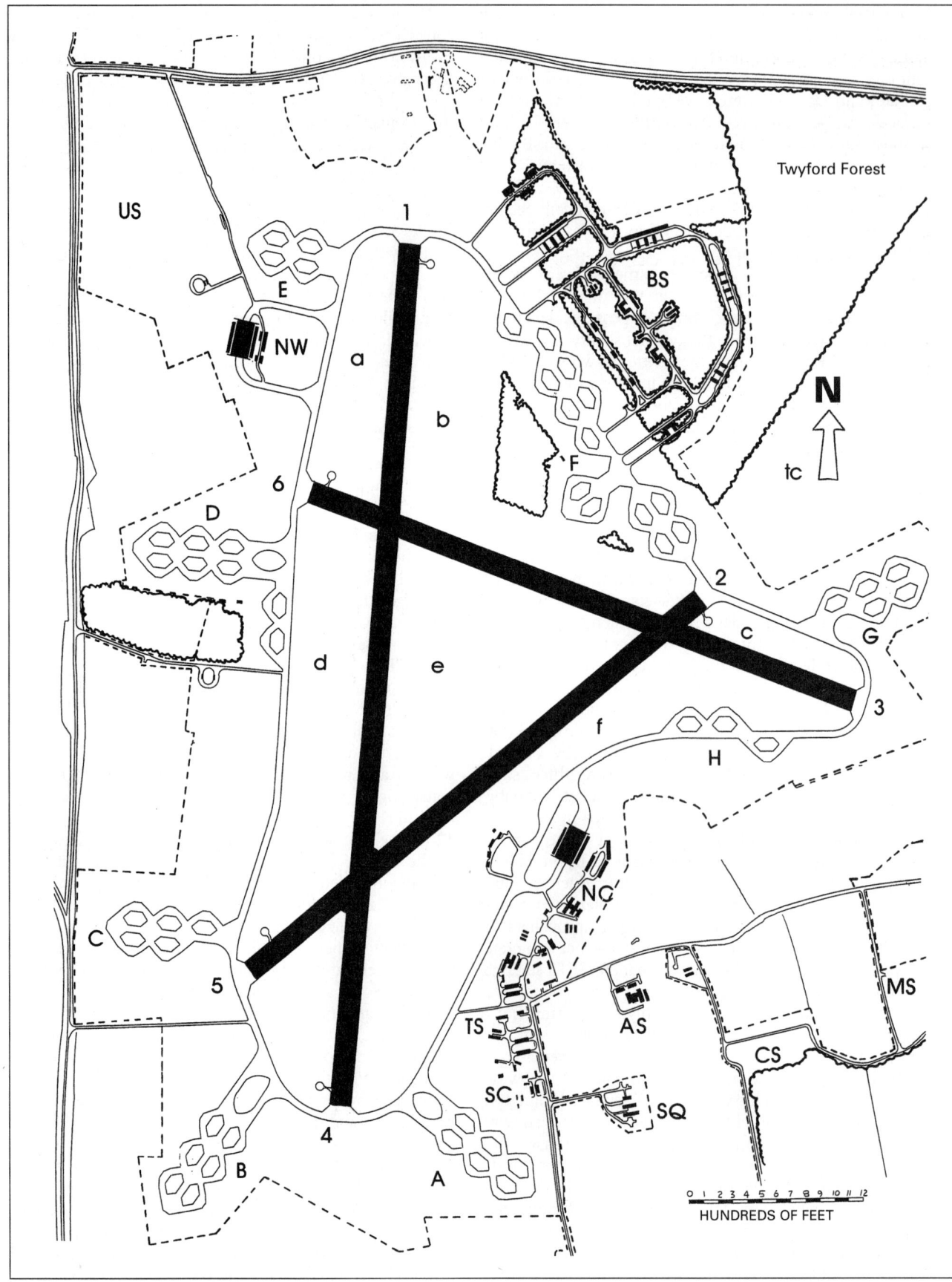

North Witham 1945 Class A Aerodrome

a	17 acres
b	51 acres
c	6.5 acres
d	36 acres
e	43.5 acres
f	50.5 acres
g	12.5 acres
r	requisitioned properties, demolished
tc	tree clearance
A	group A hard standings
B	group B hard standings
C	group C hard standings
D	group D hard standings
E	group E hard standings
F	group F hard standings
G	group G hard standings
H	group H hard standings
AS	administration site – 2.75 acres
BS	bomb stores site – 46 acres
CS	communal site – 6 acres
MS	mess site No. 1 – 7 acres
NC	north camp
NW	north-west camp – 5.5 acres
US	USAAF temporary tented camp – 45 acres
SQ	sick quarters site – 2.5 acres
TS	technical site – 18.5 acres

runway 1
total length – 2,000 yd by 50 yd wide
100,000 sq yd

runway 2
total length – 1,400 yd by 50 yd wide
70,000 sq yd

runway 3
total length – 1,400 yd by 50 yd wide
70,000 sq yd

taxi track total length – 5,521 yd

There were two main types of fighter dispersal pens in use during the Second World War, both with earthwork traverses, intended for the protection of two aircraft: Type B and Type E. The former, FCW 4513 (7151/41) pen differed from the Type E in that its outer arms were cranked whereas the arms of the E were straight. Cranking offered better protection to the aircraft but as space was limited with this arrangement it was necessary to have two different sizes of pen. One had a maximum width of 54 ft for an aircraft the size of a Hurricane and the other at 76 ft was large enough to accommodate a Blenheim. It was the normal practice to provide six Type B fighter pens per squadron of 12 aircraft while satellite airfields were provided with just six pens. Other stations had two separate groups of six pens.

The floor of the pen, either concrete or tarmac, was of two thicknesses, the greater thickness being in the centre underneath the undercarriage to take the weight of the aircraft. An arch-shaped precast concrete shelter 15 ft by 7 ft to accommodate 25 men was located at the apex of the bays within the traverses with access from each bay and a single emergency exit. The earthwork traverses had brick end walls, a brick or concrete dwarf retaining wall, and were built to extend 25 ft out from the aircraft to give maximum protection. Six Type B pens were built at each of the following: Bottisham, Culmhead, Matlask, and Stapleford Tawney. Twelve were built at each of the following: Coltishall, Fairlop, and Merston. Type E pens could be found at Biggin Hill, Hornchurch, Kenley, and North Weald.

Prior to the outbreak of the Second World War, the Air Ministry had to rely upon the Defence Act of 1842 for compulsory acquisition of land. Under this Act, the procedure for obtaining possession was largely done by consent. But with the introduction of Defence Regulations made under the Emergency Powers (Defence) Act, 1939, the difficulties of obtaining possession by consent were removed. It was now possible to take immediate possession of land and buildings. The ever increasing demand for new airfields in the early part of the war required several hundred sites to be inspected field by field, involving thousands of acres and the scheduling of the names of owners and occupiers for compensation. There was also an urgent need to safeguard the country's food production; arrangements had to be made with the agricultural authorities before a purchase could be made.

The process of purchase and development can be seen at Chipping Norton. The airfield was first developed from 68 acres of land originally purchased by the Air Ministry in 1937 from East Downs Farm. A further 88 acres were acquired before 1939 and the airfield was used in this form as a Relief Landing Ground. When Sommerfeld Track runways were laid and two Bellman hangars built, it was necessary to purchase another 35 acres east of the original boundary owned by the Dean Buildings Estate and 25 acres to the south owned by St Johns College. This area of land was worth about £500. Walls and fences were removed and a public road destroyed. Technical buildings were located on the west boundary on land owned by

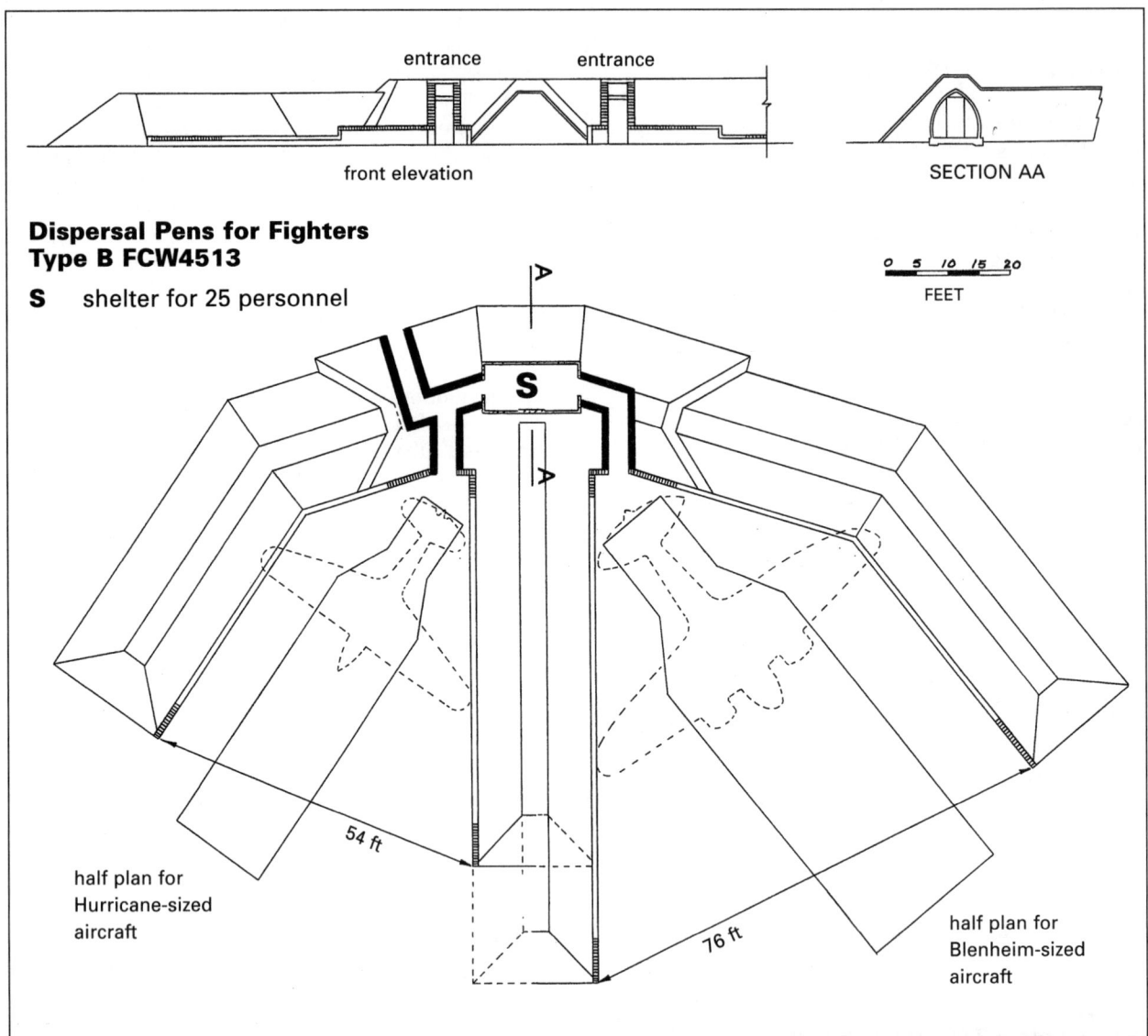

Chadlington Downs Farm. Finally, another 18 acres further east towards Dean Buildings were purchased for the erection of blister hangars.

Sometimes the normal Air Ministry procedure with notices of land requisition could not be followed as the situation was so urgent, as with Llandwrog and Llanbedr in North Wales. These were required as forward airfields for operations against enemy raiders in the Irish Sea. In late June 1940, Claude A. Brown, managing director of En-Tout-Cas was summoned to the Works and Bricks Section of the Air Ministry in London. Here a senior official handed him two Ordnance Survey maps covering the north and west coasts of Wales. The official explained that two aerodromes with hard-surfaced runways were required to be constructed and work was to start in two days.

Mr Brown immediately went to North Wales with the company architect, Cecil Jones. They inspected the sites, noting in particular the adjacent mountains as these would have an important bearing on the design of the airfield with regard to the angle of approach to the runways. The following day, the machinery and labour force began to arrive at the two sites, much to the astonishment of the local people, and the farmers and landowners in particular. There was an outcry when tractors began tearing down trees and hedges. The workmen were challenged on several occasions. One particular landowner came up in a warlike mood and asked them to explain what right the company had to invade his property as no one had consulted him or even asked permission to enter. The reply was that they were not permitted to tell him anything except to warn him that they had taken over his land and that within the next 24 hours they would have hundreds of men and fleets of large earth-moving scrapers at work. He was then given a London telephone number to ring. One hour later he came back with a beaming smile on his face. 'Go ahead Mr Brown, do what you like and if I can help in any way I shall be glad to.'

The company purchased locally hundreds of thousands

The Evolution of Aerodromes 27

There are two groups of six Type B fighter pens for two squadrons

Culmhead, 1944

A administration site
BR bombing range
SD sewage disposal
TS technical site

28 *British Military Airfield Architecture*

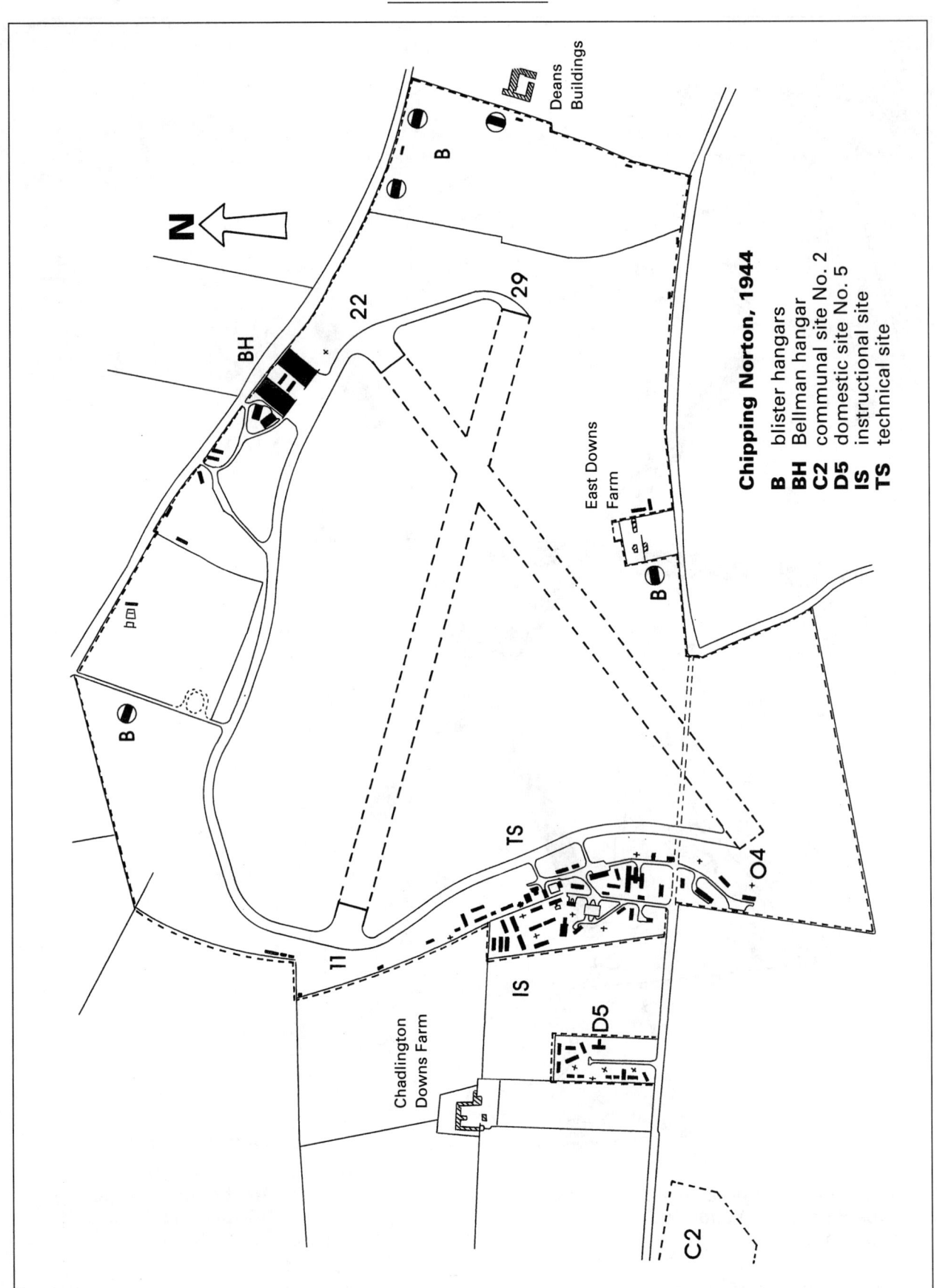

of tons of quarry waste. The Air Ministry provided 70 tipper lorries. The drivers were paid according to the number of loads they brought each day, and in consequence travelled at the highest possible speeds. Owing to the very heavy volume of high speed traffic over narrow and twisting roads it was necessary to have special traffic control points at all the bad corners. The police appointed a number of special constables for this task.

The company built runways of stabilized stone at the two sites, and were paid in the usual manner of a 'cost plus' contract with 5 per cent allowed for profit on cost, the total bill coming to £470,000. After the work had been completed, the company received the formal contract documents covering all the work and airfield site plans. The figures included the sum that had already been paid to the company, incorporated as their tender for the work. This somewhat irregular means of conducting business was nevertheless a practical way of dealing with a most unusual situation. Llandwrog opened in January 1941 and Llanbedr on 5 June 1941.

PART 2

TECHNICAL BUILDINGS

GUARDHOUSE

The guardhouse was the first, and last, building on any RAF station; visitors reported here on arrival for verification that they had the correct authority to enter the camp, and signed out here when they left. Airmen stationed on the camp reported to the guardhouse where their leave passes were checked before they were allowed to leave the station. The guardhouse was the working office of an orderly officer who operated the building in an efficient workmanlike manner to create a good impression. Other duties of the orderly officer included the issuing of keys, basic investigations of crime, controlling station transport on leaving the station, providing an escort when required, dealing with lost and found property, and the dress and discipline of airmen on the station.

An important function of the guardhouse was the holding of prisoners pending their appearance before the section officer or CO which depended on the seriousness of their 'crimes'. Prisoners were confined to the general detention room although a lone prisoner would be confined to the service detention room. In either cell, windows were usually top lighting or lantern lights. Electric lighting was of the guarded type. There were no doors on the WC or showers, and only a plank bed with a pillow board were provided. Defaulters (perpetrators of minor crimes) had to report periodically throughout the day to the guardhouse but still carried on with their everyday jobs, reporting for inspection in full 'marching order' morning and evening, and at lunch-time in normal dress. There were 2 hours of cleaning at 18:00 hrs.

The drawing for the RFC Training Depot guardhouse was also shared by a number of instructional huts used for elementary training. The guardhouse was 41 ft long and 15 ft 9 in wide and consisted of just two rooms each 20 ft wide comprising a detention room and a guardroom. At the rear was a small enclosed yard with walls 7 feet high finished with barbed wire and housing a WC block. The roof had a simple timber-framed coupled truss with purlins projecting away from the building to form a veranda, all clad with asbestos sheeting.

The original guardhouse on the accommodation site at Calshot built to drawing number 1357/18 was 50 ft long and 24 ft wide, and contained six 10 ft by 8 ft detention cells. Other rooms included a cabin, a master-at-arms office, a guardroom and WCs. It was constructed with a steel framework and a 4-inch concrete block infill supporting steel trusses.

An expansion period guardhouse was lozenge shaped in plan view, with rooms arranged round a central exercise yard. It was built of brick with a flat concrete (protected) roof that extended away from the main building to form a veranda at the front. The left-hand entrance led to the

A First World War guardhouse with fire party accommodation at Marske. (Photographed 1990)

Technical Buildings 31

A First World War guardhouse constructed with a timber frame and concrete blocks at Orfordness. (Photographed 1994)

The guardhouse with accommodation for the fire party built to 166/23 at Filton. (Photographed 1993)

Built to 494/38–497/38, this guardhouse at Swanton Morley also had accommodation for the fire party. (Photographed 1993)

guardroom and general detention room. A corridor gave access to the exercise yard which was completely enclosed by the building, as well as to WCs, the service detention room and a calorifier room.

Immediately at the front, in rooms set back from the main block, was an NCOs' office and small-arms ammunition store. The right-hand door (moving round the building in an anti-clockwise direction) led to an office for civilian wardens and a corridor connected a bathroom and fire party barrack room.

Outside on the right-hand side was a fire tender house, a paint and repair shop, and at the rear was the prophylactic treatment room.

12404/41 Type A guardhouse of the Second World War was a Nissen hut 84 ft 7 in long with a 24 ft span. An entrance almost in the centre of the long side of the building gave access to a T-shaped corridor with WC, store and warden's office. A right turn led to the fire party barrack room, while a left turn led to the guardroom and two detention rooms. Outside, against the left-hand end wall was the prophylactic room, while against the opposite end wall was a small-arms ammunition store and fire extinguisher store.

12404/41 Type B consisted of two 16 ft span Nissen huts built end to end and separated by a temporary brick entrance corridor, with a WC block at the rear. The left-hand hut functioned as the guardhouse with a single detention room. The other hut housed an NCOs' office, small-arms ammunition store and fire extinguisher store.

A Type A or Type B picket post was located at the entrance to all dispersed domestic sites. Both versions were Nissen huts 18 ft long with a 16 ft span, the only difference between them being that Type A contained a prophylactic store.

drawing no. 290/17   1357/18   494/38–497/38
examples   Calshot   Hemswell,
                                        Swinderby

drawing no. 12404/41
examples   Chilbolton

SAFETY SECTION BUILDINGS

Parachute Stores

From 1927 when parachutes became standard equipment, all aircrew had to be measured for and issued with their own parachutes which had to be periodically inspected to ensure that they were fit for service. This was carried out on a monthly basis by safety-equipment workers under the supervision of a senior NCO. Each parachute pack was issued with a small card on which was noted the date of the last inspection. Details such as to whom it was issued and when were all recorded on log cards, and RAF Form 1125 was signed to confirm that the parachute was fit for use.

One of the main problems with parachutes was that of condensation and to prevent shrinkage they had to be dried. The object was to evaporate 6 lb of moisture per parachute every 24 hours. A dry atmosphere with constant ventilation and a temperature of between 55°F and 65°F was required. The building had to be free of dust and built with a lobby so that the outer door could be closed before the inner one was opened. The main room had to have sufficient height to permit parachutes to be suspended by their apices for airing and drying without any part of the silk canopy touching the floor. In this position, rigging lines were placed on smooth-top tables. The lighting of packing tables was also very important to allow each parachute to be thoroughly inspected.

The parachute store was a specially designed building which met the requirements for parachute drying, inspection, packing, and storage. The solving of the problem of how to quickly dry parachutes can clearly be seen in the development of this building.

The first purpose-built parachute store was to 2355/25. This was a red-brick structure with four small-paned windows on the north-facing wall. The pitched roof was clad with slates with a dormer roof light on both sides.

Similar to 2355/25 was 3633/35, except that it was constructed of timber instead of brick and was a sectional Type B hut. This was 51 ft long and 20 ft wide with a maximum internal height of 16 ft. Walls were prefabricated units of posts and studwork in 5 ft wide bays with 1-inch timber boarding on the outside and plasterboard on the inside. The roof was made up of timber king-post trusses with principal rafters, tie-beam and compression struts. The ridge was exposed above a flat dormer which had three sets of timber opening lights on both sides. Entrance was through a porch with two sets of double doors. A fuel store serving a single anthracite stove was positioned in a small annexe built against the south facing wall at the front of the building.

A protected design 6351/37 was built at Middleton St George. It had permanent brick cavity walls, supporting a roof of reinforced-concrete slabs built in two heights. Separating the two were lantern lights for additional natural lighting to that provided by those in the north-facing wall. Similar to 6351/37 was 175/36, except that it was built entirely of reinforced concrete.

Parachute store 2355/25 at Filton. (Photographed 1993)

Parachute Store, 10825/42

A storage racks
B parachute
C tray
D packing table
E pulleys

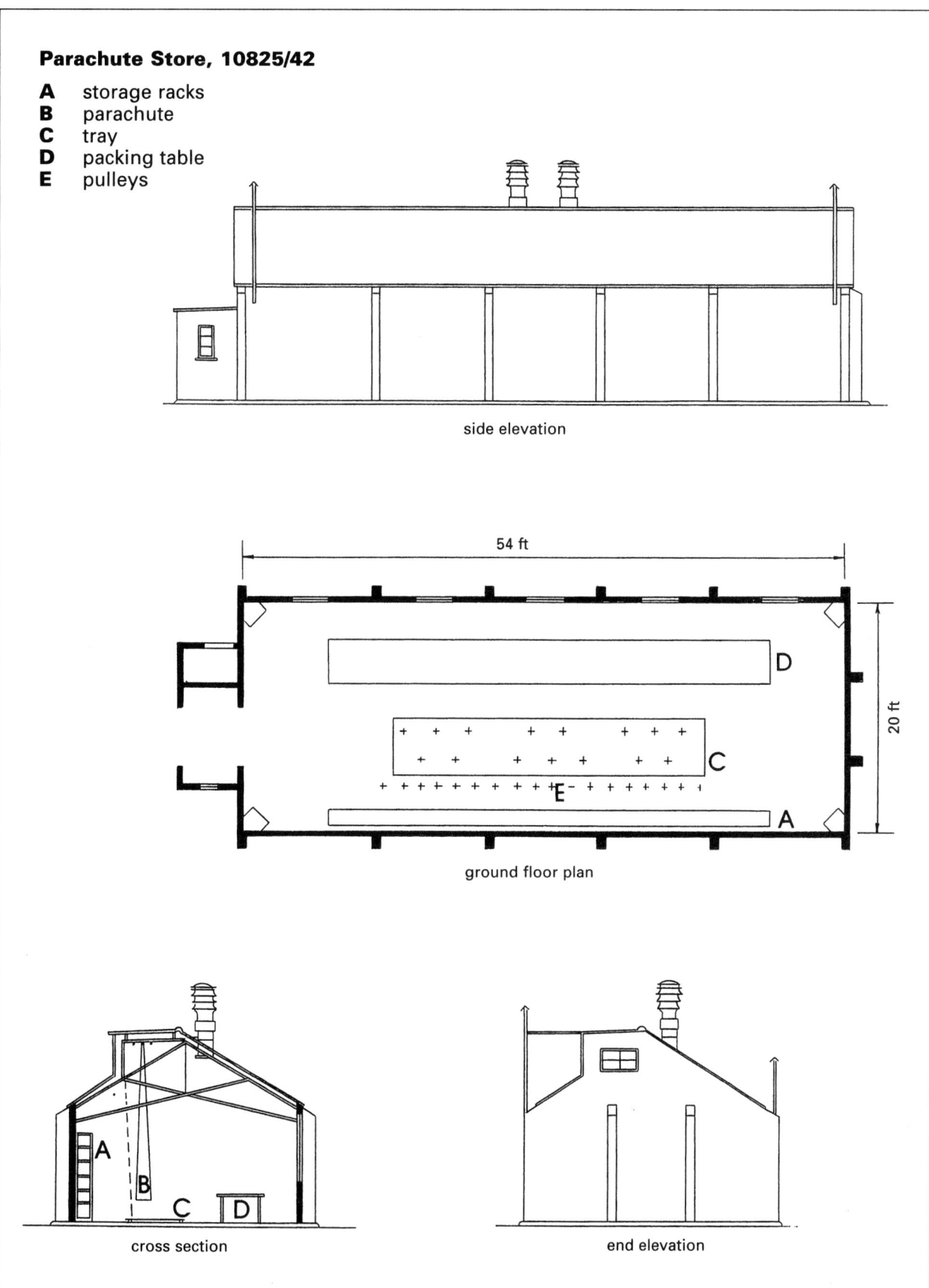

Parachute store 11137/41 at Chivenor. (Photographed 1991)

Parachute stores designed and built during the Second World War were constructed of 4.5-inch walls with brick piers making up to five 10 ft bays (17865/39 and 11137/41) or three 10 ft and two 12 ft bays (10825/42). All walls were cement-rendered both inside and out although Debach and Booker are exceptions. The north-facing wall had a single row of windows, one in each bay, while the opposite wall had none because the parachutes were stored against it. Early buildings had a symmetrical two-stage pitched roof with vertical side-panels between the stages. The lower roof and vertical sides were clad with corrugated asbestos sheets supported on steel trusses, while the upper roof had bituminous felt attached to boarding and supported on timber rafters. Although this form of cladding was recommended on the drawing, it could also be entirely in corrugated asbestos sheeting, with the ceiling lined with plasterboard leaving the steel trusses exposed.

Parachutes were suspended from the highest part of the ceiling to dry and were winched up and down with the aid of a pulley system. When dry, they were lowered to a tray on the floor which helped prevent them from getting dirty. From here they were placed on the packing table, repacked, then stored on the racks. Drawings of the earlier buildings show that the pulleys were located on the ceiling near the centre of the room. But at Debach a modification was carried out to include a separate drying room by building a wall between the two brick piers of the last bay. This small room with its own stove had the advantage of keeping drying time to a minimum.

The superseding design 10825/42 consisted of a single room for all three functions side by side. Condensation was reduced by two adjustable Universal Asbestos Aerolete ventilators mounted on the roof. These allowed clean dry air to enter the room and circulate, the amount being controlled by a pulley and cord. These can be seen on the former parachute store at Shepherds Grove. They had unusual asymmetrically shaped roofs, the roof pitch on either side of the upper section being of unequal lengths so that in cross-section the upper section was off centre. This was designed to cut down on the cross-sectional area of the roof space as a means of conserving heat, thus reducing drying time.

Parachute store 10825/42 at Chivenor. (Photographed 1991)

drawing no.	2355/25	3633/35	175/36
examples	Evanton, Hendon, Upavon	St Athan, Jurby, Staverton	Debden, Driffield Bassingbourn

drawing no.	6351/37	17865/39	11137/41
examples	Middleton St George	Lichfield, Marston Moor	Shobdon, Raydon, Sawbridgeworth

drawing no.	10825/42
examples	Gamston, Oulton, Winthorpe

Drying Towers

Drawing 9290/42 was for an existing brick hut, Nissen hut, or parachute store to be modified by the addition of a tall drying tower extension. Drawing 9294/42 was for a new building similar to the usual brick hut but built with a drying tower on an end wall.

The drying tower 11595/42 had a steel frame with a sloping roof clad with Universal Asbestos Super Six corrugated sheets. Three Aerolete ventilators and two steel flues lined the roof, and two Romesse stoves were located in a small single-storey extension either side of the hut (9294/42). A bosun's chair allowed access to the top of the tower for maintenance, and a winching system was provided for the parachutes. The tower measured internally 10 ft 6 in long by 29 ft wide with a clear height of 34 ft. Parachute stores at Membury (17865/39) and Shepherds Grove (10825/42) were both modified to have drying towers although they are quite different in construction.

Today, very few buildings survive and some have been put to industrial use, such as offices at Calveley or a metal machine shop at Shepherds Grove where the drying tower was subdivided into small rooms some years ago but is now not used. The tower at Membury has now unfortunately been demolished. This was a superb unaltered example of 11595/42.

Parachute store 10825/42 with drying tower at Shepherds Grove. (Photographed 1981)

drawing no.	9290/42	9294/42	11595/42
examples		Aldermaston	

Dinghies

An inflatable dinghy was stored on the aircraft in a compartment covered by a panel sealed with fabric. This would be ejected in an emergency, the dinghy being inflated by a cylinder of compressed gas.

The servicing and inspection of dinghies for signs of cracking or leaks was also carried out by the safety section. Dinghies were returned on a three-monthly inspection roster. Each had a log card showing the aircraft number and date of inspection. The installation of emergency packs and dinghies carried out by safety equipment assistants was recorded on the aircraft RAF Form 700.

There were two main building types found on the main technical site, either temporary brick 2901/43 or Nissen hutting 2900/43. These were used for the repair, packing and storage of dinghies.

Dinghy shed 2901/43 at Ingham. (Photographed 1982)

drawing no. 2900/43 2901/43
examples Blyton, Bodney,
Boreham, Lisset,
Langham Sculthorpe

Motor Transport

An important part of an active RAF station was the motor transport section, responsible for the garaging, repair and maintenance of all station vehicles. The MT section was based at the MT yard which essentially consisted of two rows of MT vehicle sheds facing each other, separated by a large concrete manoeuvring area.

Drivers had to have a current Licence Schedule G Certificate which gave exemption from the Licensing Provisions of Finance Act 1920 and the Roads Act 1920. The recording of journeys was made on different forms depending on the nature of the journey; internal movements were all logged together on RAF Form 658, except vehicles used for the conveyance of bombs, pyrotechnics or explosives. On leaving an RAF station or unit, all RAF drivers had to have the correct journey authorization form and had to produce it at the guardhouse.

Vehicle Sheds

Aircraft acceptance parks had two vehicle sheds of equal length, both with nine open bays, 100 ft long by 31 ft wide, which were built facing each other but separated by a concrete yard. One bay with a motor pit was used for vehicle repair. The other bays each had two concrete tracks, with gravel infill, for lorries to stand on. Construction was of rendered temporary brick with piers at 11 ft centres. Alternatively, it was timber-framed with precast concrete walls. In both cases, the piers or frame supported composite timber trusses allowing a 12 ft high door opening, the trusses being clad with corrugated asbestos sheeting.

Training Depot Stations also had two vehicle sheds, one having 13 bays with a total length of 144 ft, while the other was only eight bays long. They faced each other and were separated by a concrete yard. The last three bays of one shed were repair bays, two being provided with motor pits. At the opposite end, a single bay had a small office in one corner with the remaining area and the next bay reserved for motor cycles. The opposite shed just had 13 open bays. Construction of both was the same as the AAP shed but with skylights over the repair bays. Probably the best preserved First World War motor transport shed is

MT garage 289/17 at Orfordness seen before restoration by the National Trust. (Photographed 1992)

MT shed 1929/26 at North Weald. (Photographed 1982)

Technical Buildings 37

The MT at Burnaston used this Type B sectional timber hut. (Photographed 1984)

Sectional timber hutting used by the MT section at Jurby. (Photographed 1983)

that at Orfordness, where the National Trust has recently refurbished the building to a very high standard.

A total redesign took place in the 1920s when the vehicle sheds took the form of two steel-framed sheds, one longer than the other. Often the smaller one was later extended by two more bays of lower height. Built with red brick infill walls and diamond-shaped asbestos roofing slates, the sheds faced each other, separated by a yard. The number of bays varied from station to station but seven or nine was common. One was always a repair bay with another for motor cycles and store. A small attached office annexe with a drivers' rest room and WCs was attached to one end wall.

The second shed normally had 11 open-plan bays. Originally, both sheds had timber doors but these were later replaced with chain-operated roller-type steel shutters.

Although 660/36 was built entirely of concrete it was similar to the brick version, 2782/34, and had a pitched roof. It consisted of two flat-roofed vehicle sheds of unequal lengths facing each other with an MT yard between. One shed was built in three parts. The first part comprised office accommodation with compressor house, store, oil and paint store, and rest room. The centre section comprised a four-bay vehicle shed, each 12 ft (average) by 30 ft, with one repair bay having a revolving Tecalemit 7-ton lift (the doors of the bay opened to form a large workshop area when required). Another bay used for brake testing. Extra natural lighting was achieved through lantern lights above the glazed tangent folding doors. The third section consisted of four or more smaller bays 10 ft by 20 ft, built without lantern lights. The doors were roller-type steel shutters giving a clear opening of 10 ft 6 in.

The MT yard was 80 ft wide and the length of the longest shed. At the opposite end to the entrance was a 30 ft square washing platform. The opposite shed normally consisted of six open bays of 12 ft centres and 30 ft deep; doors were steel roller-shutters giving a clear height of 12 ft 6 in.

MT vehicle shed 6879/37 was a detached permanent brick and concrete shed, with either single or multiple bay bays. It was designed to accommodate heavy articulated trailers of 44 ft by 7 ft 6 in. It was similar to the petrol tanker shed 2773/34 with the difference that the bay was 10 ft 6 in by 51 ft.

MT vehicle shed 778/38 was similar to 660/36 but with the two revisions. Firstly, the walls were permanent brick

38 *British Military Airfield Architecture*

MT Vehicle Shed, Concrete Construction, 660/36

MT Vehicle Shed, Brick Construction, Protected Roof Design, 778/38

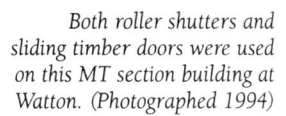

Both roller shutters and sliding timber doors were used on this MT section building at Watton. (Photographed 1994)

A 3-bay petrol tanker shed at Watton with roller shutters removed. (Photographed 1980)

cavity walls, supporting reinforced-concrete roof slabs (protected roof) and beams similar to those of 660/36. Secondly, all openings in the main shed had glazed timber sliding and folding doors, all 13 ft 8 in tall.

The largest MT sheds of the Second World War had 16 bays. Each shed was 200 ft by 28 ft. To create a 32-bay shed, a pair of these faced each other separated by a paved yard. One had an MT office built on to a side elevation. They were built with rendered temporary brick walls. Steel roof trusses carried corrugated asbestos sheeting.

By far the most common wartime MT shed design was 12775/41. This could be built with two (rare) to nine bays; the most common was a single four-bay shed. Construction was of rendered temporary brick walls with piers at 13 ft centres with timber purlins; no trusses were required as each bay was separated from the next by a brick wall. All openings had lockable doors which opened out to concrete hurters.

The MT office could be a detached Nissen hut 24 ft by 30 ft, or an attached temporary brick building with a 28 ft span. Room arrangement included airmen's rest room, office, store, WAAF rest room, oil paint store and Wcs.

On expansion period aerodromes, the petrol tanker sheds were located away from the MT section and built near aircraft hangars, nearer to where the vehicles would be needed – out on the airfield. Typically, the sheds were to 2733/34, four bays wide, 30 ft long and 13 ft high, and of permanent brick construction with reinforced-concrete roofs. Doors were steel roller-shutters operated by chains.

drawing no.	289/17	391/17	1929/26
examples	Duxford, Orfordness	Bracebridge Heath	Bicester, Biggin Hill, Upper Heyford
drawing no.	2733/34	2782/34	660/36
examples	(3 bays) Bicester, Harwell; (4 bays) Cranfield, Marham	Little Rissington, Marham	Bramcote, Debden, Bassingbourn
drawing no.	6879/37	778/38	7216/41
examples	Cosford, High Ercall (2 bays), Middleton St George	Bircham Newton, Swanton Morley	Bovingdon
drawing no.	12775/41		
examples	Gamston, Metfield, Long Newton (2 bays)		

MT Petrol

MT petrol was originally dispensed by hand-operated pumps which were only capable of discharging about 3 gallons per minute. By 1937, with the installation of electrical metering columns, petrol could be pumped at 15 gallons per minute from underground fuel tanks each containing 5,000 gallons. On airfields constructed during the Second World War, MT vehicles were filled up from an electrically metered column pump located immediately above a buried 2,000-gallon tank encased in concrete. This installation was located close to the MT yard.

Aviation Fuel

First World War semi-underground circular-type petrol tanks were of three different capacities: 2,000 gallons with a diameter of 9 ft 3 in; 4,000 gallons with a diameter of 13 ft; 6,000 gallons with a diameter of 15 ft 9 in. They were built with walls 5 ft high of hard stock bricks reinforced with steel rods and internally rendered with 'Super Cement' on a reinforced concrete base with a reinforced concrete roof.

In 1935, the RAF's mobile tanker system of refuelling aircraft became the standard practice. Expansion period aerodromes had petrol storage installations capable of holding enough petrol for a six-week period, protected in underground blastproof and splinterproof tanks. On an operational station, between one and three fuel farms were built, each remote from the others. The capacity of a single fuel tank, 9 feet in diameter and 30 ft long, was 12,000 gallons. Six of these were buried inside a concrete-walled cavity. They were connected up to pumps located inside an underground pump house. Aircraft petrol tankers would park on special perfectly flat hard standings where two petrol standposts could dispense petrol to the tankers. A similar hard standing was used by an off-loading petrol tanker.

An aircraft 24,000 gallon petrol installation consisted of two buried petrol tanks of 12,000 gallon capacity separated from each other by 100 ft with a centrally disposed pump house supplied by pipes at ground level. Further pipes from each tank terminated at a five-point manifold positioned next to a concrete hard standing used for a tanker to off-load and fill up the tank. A similar hard standing located in front of the pump house was for the aircraft fuel tanker.

Petrol tanker filling point on the fuel farm at Bicester. (Photographed 1994)

drawing no.   2132/18   1423/37   1612/39

Engine Test House

This was a single-storey brick building for the testing of aero-engines, built on home defence squadron stations and at Flying Training Schools. It normally had two or more bays (one bay per squadron) with simple timber collar-beam roof trusses clad with asbestos slates. Inside the test cell was a brick pier supporting a runway with block and tackle used for lifting the engines on to the test bench. The rear of the cell was open with torpedo netting fixed between piers. The test bench itself was also caged in with torpedo netting for containment in the event of an engine failure. On the front elevation were two large top-hung sliding doors enabling the engine trolley to enter.

Although there was an expansion period design, it seems only to have been built on the early stations. This was possibly a result of a change in policy. Engine test runs prior to flight were instead carried out on the aircraft.

drawing no.   702/26
examples   Bicester, Hendon, Hornchurch, Sealand, Tangmere

Bomb Stores

Bomb stores on First World War aerodromes were in the form of 40 ft by 14 ft 6 in semi-sunk buildings with 8 ft high walls of reinforced concrete, the lower 6 ft being below the natural ground level with the upper 2 ft hidden by an earth bank. The roof was the only part of the building exposed above ground and consisted of standard timber trusses with purlins clad with asbestos sheeting and a central steel exhaust vent.

Technical Buildings 41

Engine test house 702/26 at Bicester. (Photographed 1993)

The method of storing munitions was to load the bombs on to a wooden sledge mounted on runners; this was then carefully pushed to the entrance and down the slope to the floor of the store where the bombs were taken out and stored. The process of unloading the store simply involved pulling the loaded sledge back up the runners by means of a rope.

Between 1934 and 1945, the station armourers were located at the bomb stores and it was their task to select and fuze the correct bombs, then load them on to trolleys. These were then hauled by tractors, driven by the MT staff, round the perimeter track to the various dispersals so that the squadron armourers could winch them on to the aircraft.

Airfield bomb dumps were designed to store the following items: high explosive bombs, incendiary bombs, fuzed bombs, tail units, small bomb containers, bomb components (eg detonators, delay pistols), and small-arms ammunition. The bomb dump was always located well away from the main technical area.

There were three distinct phases to the development of the aerodrome bomb store: expansion period; early wartime; and late wartime. Stations in the expansion period utilized a classical symmetrical layout comprising two sets of six detached brick-and-concrete HE store buildings (3054/36) arranged back-to-back in two rows of three. Between each store and around the edge of the complex were traversed blast-walls. Each store was fitted with a high-level gantry, complete with block and tackle to lift bombs in and out of the building, and three sets of double steel doors. Other buildings were twin or triple-compartment incendiary and pyrotechnic stores, up to three fuzing-point buildings (two for heavy bombs and one for small bombs). These were arched sheds of curved RSJ and corrugated iron construction, covered with earth and turf. There was also a facility for the temporary storage of fuzed and ready-use weapons, consisting normally of four open compartments all fitted with lifting gantries.

Early wartime stations adopted a much simpler idea

HE bomb store (3054/36) with six compartments, arranged back-to-back in pairs, at Wick. (Photographed 1993)

Blast wall traverses of the HE bomb store, and gantries for lifting bombs at Wick. (Photographed 1993)

Barbed-wire fencing surrounding the bombs stores area at Wick. (Photographed 1991)

(5416/40). New stations built in the first two years of the war had detached 30 ft square open stores protected by traverses, each capable of storing up to 24 tons of HE Bombs. These were stored round the edge of the construction so that cranes and loading vehicles could enter.

Later stations, all of them temporary bomber airfields, had a completely redesigned airfield bomb store from late 1941. The aim was to increase handling efficiency. Design 3164/42 consisted of up to four open compartments arranged side by side, each protected by traverses and with an access road for lorries at one end and another for bomb trolleys at the other. The compartments were built with a slight slope so that the 'upper' lorry road could be used to fill the dump, gravity being used to position the bombs. The 'lower' trolley road was used to empty it by means of a simple lifting device. A further improvement was the provision of drive-through 36 ft length Nissen hut fuzing points, located between the bomb dump and the airfield. Incendiary bombs were stored in a number of ways. One method known as Type C 1932/43 was an open storage area with a U-shaped traverse wall; another was Type B on the same drawing which consisted of two temporary brick buildings built side by side, separated by a traverse wall or Nissen.

drawing no.	(WW1)	3054/36	5416/40
examples	Mousehold Heath	Bicester, Finningley	Polebrook, Lichfield

drawing no.	3164/42	1932/43

STATION ARMOURY

A typical station armoury, as built at Upper Heyford, served three squadrons. Originally, half of this building (1052/24) was two storeys high with a timber queen-post hipped roof, the other part a single storey with a flat roof. The flat roof annexe was the armoury; the upstairs in the two-storey part functioned as lecture room, library and office.

During the expansion period, a two-storey extension was built at right angles to the existing building in matching bricks with roof line and windows in keeping with the original. The new ground floor contained lecture room, gas respirator workshop and armament instruction classroom. Upstairs was the photographic laboratory with rooms devoted to chemical mixing, developing, film fixing, instruction, printing, and a workshop.

The front half of the bomber station building (7616/37) was two storeys high to include a large photographic section at first-floor level. Assessment of photographs taken during bombing missions was a very important part of operational analysis. Rooms included a photographic laboratory with separate developing and printing rooms, a workshop and lecture rooms. Also on the first floor was the projection floor of the AML bombing teacher. The ground-floor arrangement was similar to the fighter version, only smaller, as the photographic laboratory was on the floor above. The building therefore terminated after the three squadron armouries.

The fighter station building (1639/38) was similar to the bomber version but was only a single storey, built of brick with a flat reinforced-concrete roof. It was designed so that it could easily be converted to a bomber station armoury. This could be achieved by building an extension above the centre section of the roof in which could be housed a large photographic laboratory and the upper floor of an AML bombing teacher.

The fighter version had offices and a lecture room at the front with a hallway and passage leading round an enclosed area (which would be used for the ground floor of the bombing teacher should one be built) to a central workshop. On the left were three armouries (one for each squadron) and on the right was the station armoury, oil and paint store, and belt-filling room. The rear contained a small photographic laboratory. The roof of this room had a circular trapdoor so if the station changed function it could easily be adapted to house the lens of a camera obscura. There were also a camera-gun room, station small-arms store, and two more belt-filling rooms.

drawing no.	1052/24	7616/37	1639/38
examples	Bicester, Upper Heyford	Bassingbourn, Watton	Swanton Morley (converted to bomber version)

STATION HEADQUARTERS

Squadron offices on First World War Home Defence aerodromes were used as the station headquarters and were built close to the main entrance of the camp. The building (469/17) at Biggin Hill was 15 ft wide and 72 ft long, divided into three general offices, offices for clerks, officers and the squadron commander. In contrast, the standard RFC squadron office 370/17 was 15 ft wide and only 45 ft long, divided into three offices with one for the squadron commander.

Both buildings were built of temporary brick rendered

The station armoury for fighter stations of the three-squadron type 1639/38 at Swanton Morley which was modified to the bomber type. (Photographed 1993)

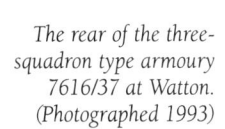

The rear of the three-squadron type armoury 7616/37 at Watton. (Photographed 1993)

Protected roof design of station headquarters 1235/31. (Photographed 1989)

with reinforced cement, having internal piers at 10 ft centres supporting a simple timber truss. Roof cladding was corrugated asbestos sheeting.

In the 1930s, a protected roof design was the most common bomber station SHQ, with attached operations room, originally built without a second-floor meteorological office. At some stations, a meteorological office extension was built above the connecting annexe between the SHQ and operations block.

The structure consisted of a central two-storey office block with a single-storey annexe on either side. Behind the main block was a two-storey annexe with a corridor, staircase and WCs, the corridor being connected with the operations room. The main entrance in the centre of the main block led into a hall and a T-shaped corridor connecting with all rooms on the ground floor. One annexe wing contained stores and accounts where payments were made through sliding windows to airmen queuing outside under a veranda. The opposite annexe was office accommodation for the engineer officer, clerks, and the commanding officer.

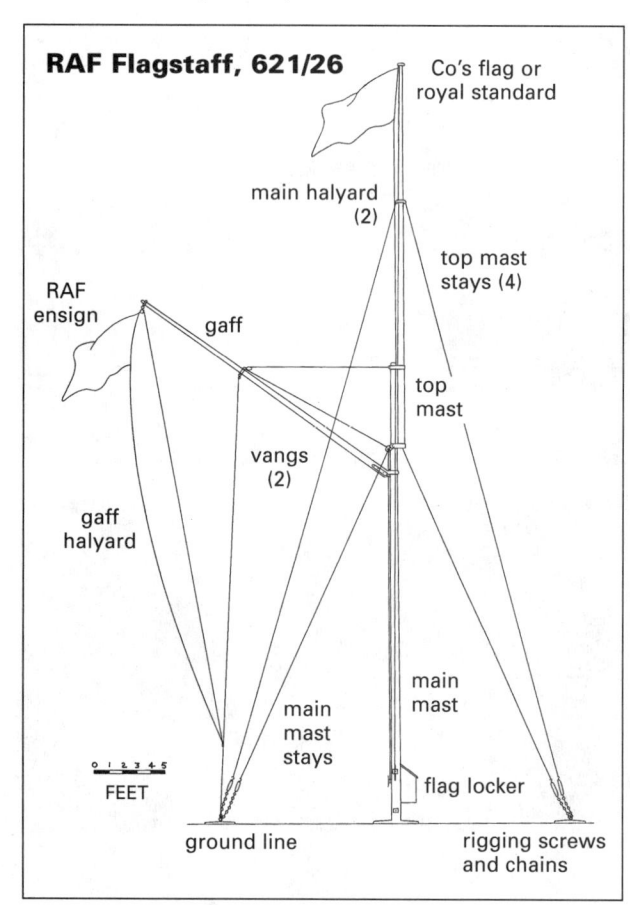

The ground floor of the main block featured offices for the sergeant major, accounts officer and assistants, waiting-rooms, and orderly rooms. Down the corridor, past the WCs and staircase, was the operations room at the rear of the main block. There were three main rooms at first-floor level of the main block, two lecture rooms and a library.

At those stations requiring a meteorological section 8550/37, such as Bassingbourn, this was simply added as a second-floor extension above the WC block annexe. The new accommodation consisted of general office, bedroom, store, and teleprinter room. The layout of this block was operations room, wireless and telephone rooms, offices for the commanding officer, meteorological section, traffic and signal officer, and battery room for emergency 110-volt lighting.

Construction of the office administration block was of permanent brick cavity wall with reinforced-concrete floor and roof. The operations block was built with thicker-section brick walls supporting a thick-section reinforced-concrete subroof with a thin-section upper roof, the void between being filled with a layer of sand and gravel to a thickness of 4 ft 6 in. Further protection against bomb blast came from a thick-section hollow traverse wall surrounding the block, the cavity being filled with gravel.

The temporary offices 12400/41 of the Second World War consisted of two 24 ft span Nissen huts built side by side and originally joined by a T-shaped temporary brick entrance lobby and corridor connecting the operations block 15586/40. It was later used as SHQ in conjunction with other operation block designs such as 228/43.

One Nissen hut was 72 ft 6 in long and had

Station Headquarters (offices) and W/T Lecture Room, 1329/27, Gosport

front elevation (west)

end elevation (south)

The station headquarters at Hullavington. (Photographed 1995)

The rear of the station headquarters at Swinderby, showing the operations block. (Photographed 1992)

accommodation for stores clerks and accounts clerks (these rooms had safes), an orderly room, and offices for the assistant accounts officer, chief accounts officer, warrant officer, and defence officer. The other Nissen hut was 60 ft 5 in long with offices for the engineer, engineer clerks, an orderly room for WAAF officers, and offices for station administration, the adjutant, and commanding officer.

drawing no.	370/17	469/17	1329/27
examples		Biggin Hill	
drawing no.	1723/36–	8550/37	12400/41
examples	1725/36	Bassingbourn	Bodney, East Kirkby, Gosfield

OPERATIONS BUILDINGS

The standard operations room for stations under the Air Defence of Great Britain Scheme was a brick-built bungalow-like building to 1161/24. It accommodated up to three squadrons. At bomber stations a similar building (1211/24) was used, built immediately behind the station headquarters and connected to it by a corridor. At fighter stations it was often a detached building which required a basement to house a heating chamber. This was omitted at most bomber stations as the operations room was heated from a heating chamber in the SHQ.

Fighter stations under ADGB were thought to be liable to attack in the event of war. Therefore, the operations rooms were protected by 6 ft high earthworks. The bomber version built at bases in Berkshire, Oxfordshire and Wiltshire were thought to be fairly safe from attack and therefore did not require a protective earth bank. The building was 97 ft 9 in long and 27 ft 9 in wide, built with solid walls 13.5 inches wide and faced with red facing bricks. King-post timber trusses with hipped gable ends and large-size purlins supported by vertical struts carried rafters supporting rough boarding and slates.

A protected central entrance through the earth bank gave access to a corridor connecting a store and workshop on the far left, while the operations room was at the opposite end. The PBX, battery room, wireless and signals office were all in the centre of the building.

In contrast to the 1920s design, the protected roof version to 5000/37 was very well protected against the effects of incendiaries and bomb blast from near misses. Surrounding the whole building was a 9 ft high reinforced-concrete traverse wall with an angled earth bank having a maximum thickness of 17 ft. The building

Fighter operations block 5000/37 at Swanton Morley. (Photographed 1993)

Technical Buildings 47

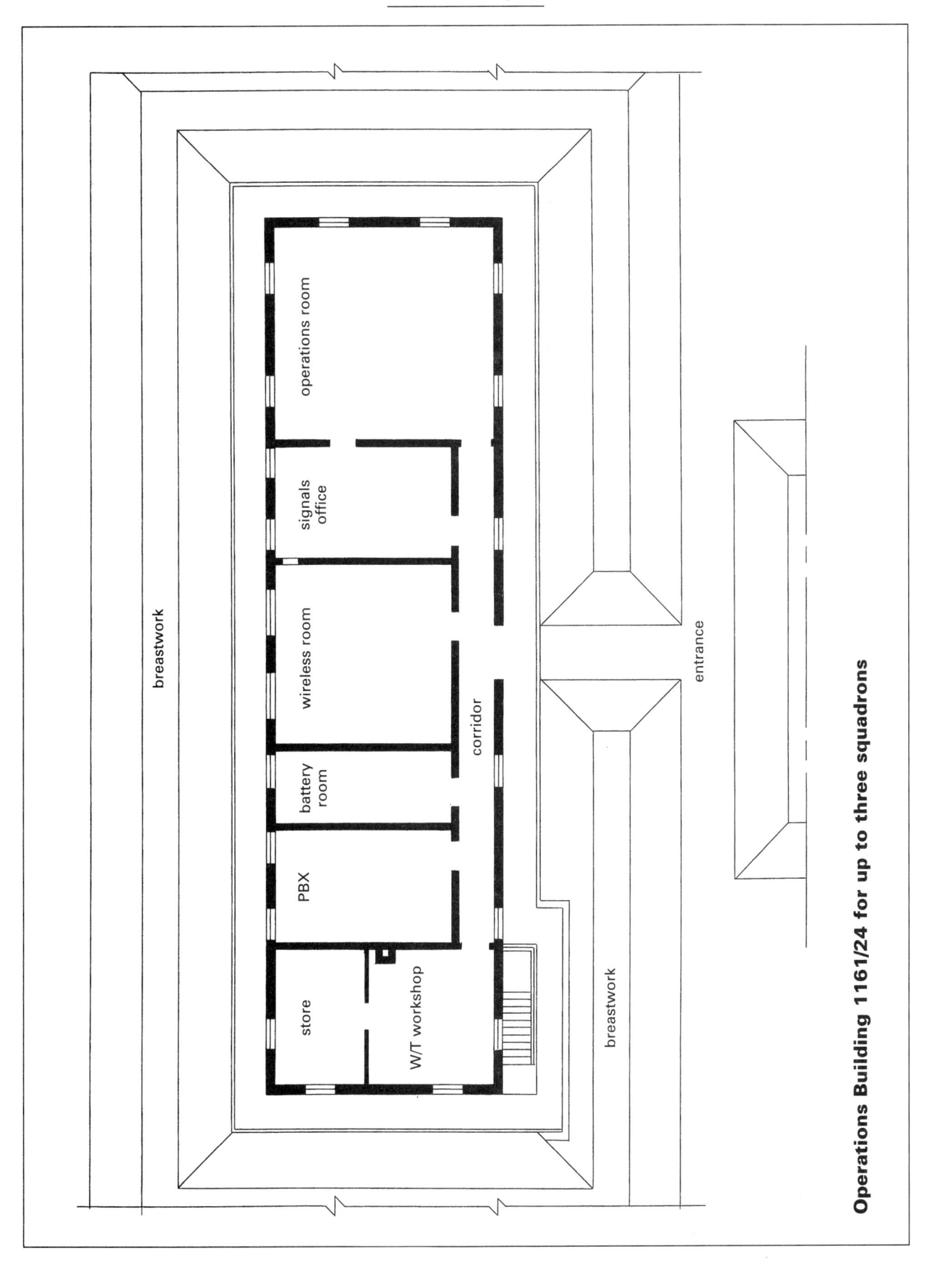

Operations Building 1161/24 for up to three squadrons

was further protected with a thick-section concrete subroof slab supported by 20 large-section RSJs. Above the subroof was a thin-section concrete upper roof, the void (4 ft 6 in) being filled with a 2 ft 6 in layer of sand and shingle with another layer of shingle on top. An airlock was provided at the two entrance points so that the internal air pressure could be raised above that outside to ensure protection in the event of a gas attack.

The block included battery room, four R/T chambers, meteorological office, operations room, plotting room, ventilating plant room, receiving room, searchlight room, teleprinter room, traffic office, workshop, and receiving room.

drawing no.	1161/24	1211/24	5000/37
examples	Duxford, Filton, Hawkinge, North Weald, Upavon		Debden, North Weald, Ouston, Swanton Morley, Wittering

FIGHTER COMMAND OPERATIONS

In 1938, the decision was made to erect a chain of 18 Chain Home (CH) stations between the Isle of Wight and St Abb's Head, the first operational masts (apart from research masts at Orfordness) being erected at Bawdsey and handed over to the RAF in May 1937. These were followed by masts at Dover and Canewdon. By the start of the Battle of Britain, there were 21 Chain Home stations and 30 Chain Home Low stations.

The Radar Reporting System came into being to provide sufficient warning of enemy aircraft approaching the UK coast to allow appropriate action to be taken, and to allow the tracking of all friendly aircraft and surface craft. Some reporting stations were linked to sector operations rooms for emergencies such as the breakdown of a filter room. With the limited performance of single radar stations it became necessary to operate stations of the same type to duplicate cover in azimuth and to operate stations of different type to provide cover in elevation.

The Royal Observer Corps was a civil organization consisting of part-time and full-time members, administered by Air Ministry (S5) through Headquarters ROC. Observer posts, deployed all over the UK, reported information concerning the tracking of all aircraft seen or heard flying to their parent ROC centre. At the ROC centre, reported information was filtered and identified. Selected tracks were indicated with distinguishing counters and plotted on a table map. Information such as raid number, whether the aircraft were seen or heard, their position, direction of flight, number and estimated height were reported to group filter rooms.

During the Battle of Britain, Fighter Command was organized into four fighter groups, each with its own operations and filter rooms. It consisted of Nos 10, 11, 12, and 13 Groups. Each Group was subdivided geographically into sectors, each sector including a main fighter station, with a sector operations room, and one or more satellite airfields.

The AOC-in-C Fighter Command was responsible for the air defence of Great Britain and delegated detailed responsibility to the AOC of his fighter groups. The AOC of each fighter group directed the operation of his fighters both in defensive and offensive operations through the group operations room. The group controller had several responsibilities: ordering the disposition of squadrons on the ground and their states of preparedness; estimating the scale and probable objectives of enemy air attack; ordering fighter aircraft off the ground in sufficient strength and in time to meet the enemy; control of aircraft while airborne; co-ordinating and supervising the control action of sectors within the group.

The group operations room was the centre of a network of operational communications with in-coming information from a wide area being received from ROC and radar reporting systems. A link was maintained by telephone and teleprinter with Fighter Command filter rooms, ROC centres, balloon depots, sector operations rooms within the group and numerous other authorities. Information regarding airborne aircraft was displayed with counters on a large table map watched over by the group controller and his staff. This included track number and direction, height, number of aircraft and speed. This amount of information created a problem during heavy raids in the early part of the Battle of Britain. It took up so much room that an alternative method for displaying it had to be found. In September 1940, a vertical slotted board known as a Totalizator was introduced to record ancillary information such as height, number of aircraft and speed.

The fighter squadrons were the final link in the chain and were controlled directly by the sector operations room. Sectors covered the area from Dorset up to Edinburgh and Glasgow, each sector being identified by a letter from A to Y. The commander of each sector was responsible to the AOC of his group for the control of fighters in accordance with filtered information received from Bentley Priory. This was achieved through the sector operations room. On receipt of an order number from group, the controller ordered a selected squadron to scramble, through a direct telephone link to the fighter dispersal points on the sector airfield or its satellite stations. Fighters in sufficient numbers had to be correctly positioned and at the correct height to intercept enemy aircraft. Once contact had been made, the fighter leader assumed tactical control of the battle in the air and the controller listened in. When combat was broken off, the controller resumed command to guide the aircraft back to their home airfield or to the nearest when this was necessary.

The information displayed in sector operation rooms was similar to that displayed in group operation rooms except that the table covered a smaller geographical area. The fighter plotting table was displayed with counter type indicators which showed the position of fighters under control of the sector controller and the enemy aircraft.

On the wall opposite the controller's position hung the 5-minute colour change clock. The current colour was displayed by the minute hand and corresponded to a

The operations building 1161/24 at Upavon. (Photographed 1994)

similar system displayed on the main table with details of identification, track number and direction. This ensured that information more than 10 minutes old was eliminated.

Filter Room

The filter room concept was developed by Squadron Leader Hart at Bawdsey. The building design was formed within No. 10 Department of the RAE at Farnborough under Squadron Leader Rose. The first to be built was at Bawdsey but parts were later removed and taken to Bentley Priory in October 1938. The first filter training school opened in March 1940 at Bawdsey.

The filter room collated, sorted and filtered all incoming reports before the information was used operationally. This was intended to eliminate duplication and to display identified tracks on the group operations room plotting table. The results were broadcast to all operational users within the designated area of responsibility of a fighter group such as sector operations rooms and Royal Observer Corps centres. The filter room was originally part of the group operations room but later became a protected building in its own right known as a filter block, built using the cut-and-cover technique in two levels. The roof consisted of a 1 ft thick reinforced-concrete subroof and a thinner upper roof with a 4 ft 6 in void filled with sand and gravel, the complete area then being covered with earth.

drawing no. 4820/41, 4821/41
examples Whittingham Lane

Operations Block

This building for a parent Fighter Operational Training Unit was a temporary building. It was unusual in that it consisted of a standard Laing hut (60 ft by 18 ft 6 in) on top of a brick ground-floor structure to form a two-storey building. The ground floor consisted of the operations room containing a 10 ft square map table and a raised dais from which the controller could oversee the table. Also provided was a D/F plotting room, four R/T rooms, a controller's office and WCs. The first floor contained the upper part of the D/F and operations rooms, the plant room, VHF room, and a large spare room at the rear.

drawing no. 289/42, 5819/42
example Rednal

BOMBER COMMAND OPERATIONS

Bomber Command, with its headquarters at High Wycombe, was also divided geographically into groups, each with a headquarters normally located in the grounds of a stately home. Each group was divided into a number of parent stations with one or more satellite aerodromes.

In the operations room at High Wycombe, the planning of the actual bombing operations took place under the direction of the Commander-in-Chief; the type of target was chosen by the War Cabinet. A choice of target was made after consultation with Air Ministry meteorological officers, after the final weather forecast was known. A primary and a secondary target were chosen; the later was only attacked if the weather over the primary target was unfavourable. The selected targets were of a similar type requiring the same types of bombs and weight of petrol. The written order passed on to the headquarters of each group for a bombing operation, called The Daily Allotment of Targets Form, was then filled in with the appropriate code formula for the targets to be attacked, the number of available aircraft in each group to take part in the operation, and the proportion of incendiary and high explosive bombs to be carried.

The order from Bomber Command Headquarters arrived at the group operations room via teleprinter. The decision about how many squadrons and from which stations was then taken. The final planning – the course to be flown, the aiming points and plotting the targets on the target maps – was carried out in the station operations room. Details of aircraft serial numbers, code letters, and an Order of Battle listing crew and aircraft would be produced and displayed for the benefit of the crews. The final link in the chain was to brief the crew some hours before the raid. In the briefing room, details of what to expect from enemy defences was discussed, photographs

Operations block 15586/40 built at Halesworth. (Photographed 1982)

of the target area were shown, and the signals officer informed the wireless operators which radio frequencies were to be used and the homing and distress procedures. After the briefing, each navigator decided on the best course to the target within the parameters set by the operations officer.

Operations Blocks 1941–3

At those stations with the new 1941 standard design watch office (13726/41) for bomber satellite stations, the operations room and crew briefing room were built on a dispersed administration site to drawings 13023/41 and 13742/41 respectively. This design was similar to the ops room and briefing room which were built as part of the combined watch office and operations room complex to 7344/41 and 7345/41.

The building was divided into three sections: an operations room built with 13.5-inch solid walls supporting a flat roof of concrete slabs; a teleprinter room; and PBX. A crew briefing room was provided in a seven-bay 24 ft span Nissen hut, joined to the operations block by a temporary brick main entrance lobby, corridor, kitchen and WC.

The large 4891/42 complex of buildings was on the dispersed administration site. The main block was a large building containing an operations room 36 ft by 29 ft. This room had a minimum height of 14 ft, while the remaining area containing the battery-room, cipher office, meteorology room, PBX, traffic office, and teleprinters was only 9 ft high. Entrance to the block was through airlocks

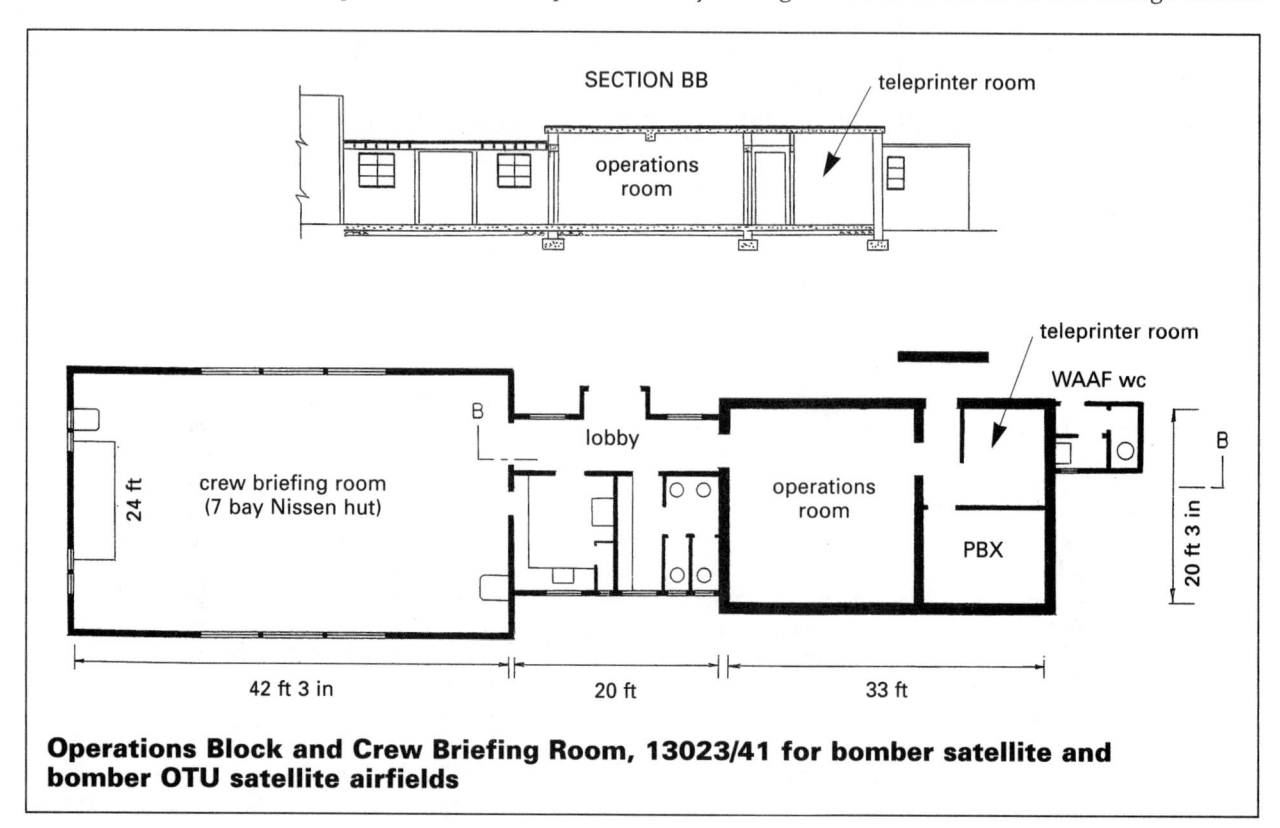

Operations Block and Crew Briefing Room, 13023/41 for bomber satellite and bomber OTU satellite airfields

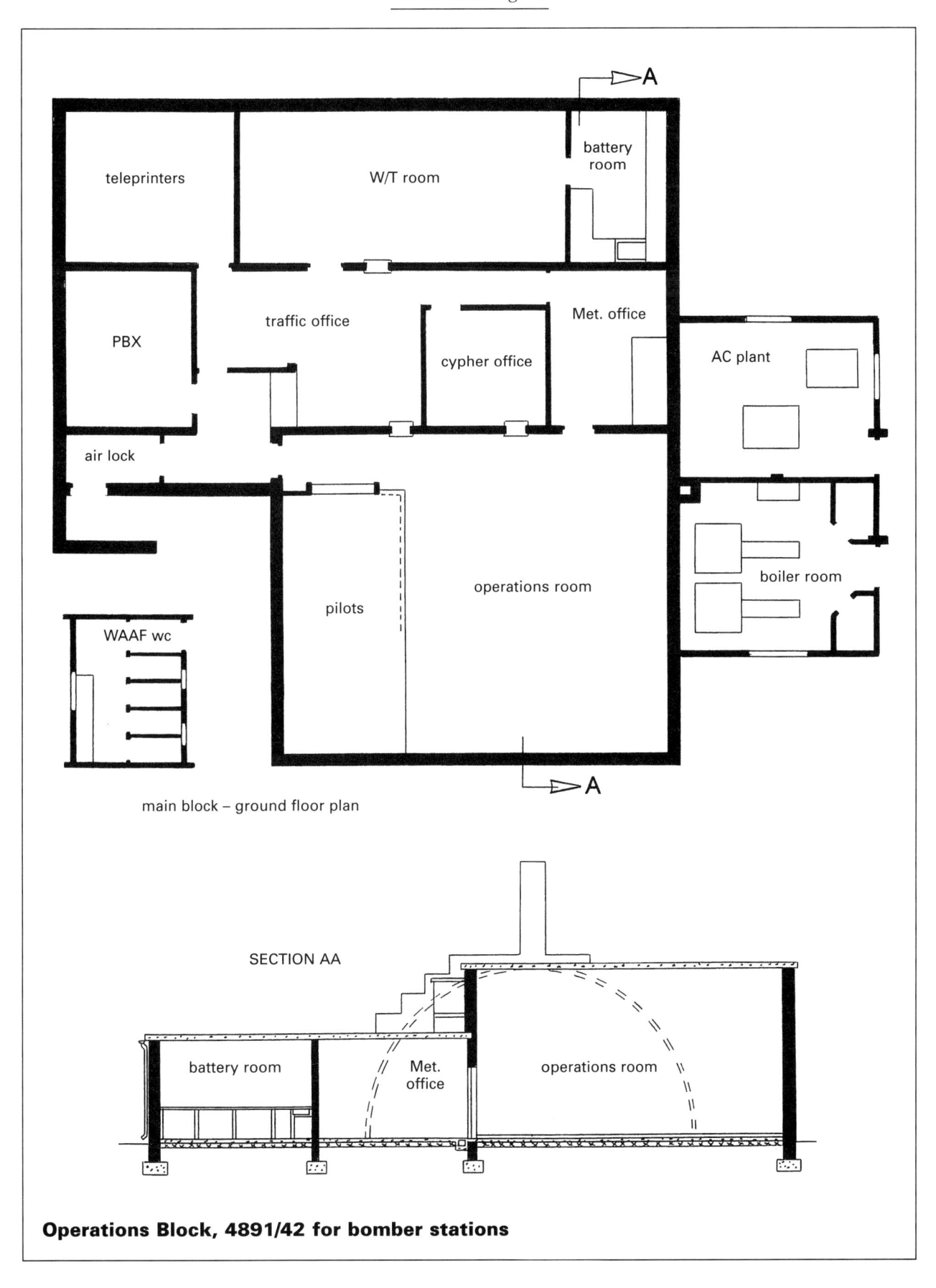

Technical Buildings 51

main block – ground floor plan

SECTION AA

Operations Block, 4891/42 for bomber stations

Operations block 228/43 at Seething. The AC plant and boiler-room are front left. The airlock is on the right. It once joined the interrogation room but this has been demolished. (Alan Mountford)

protected by brick traversed walls. A feature of its design was the use of a three-bay 30 ft span Nissen hut housing the plant equipment and boiler-room built against an end wall. A stepped wall connecting the two roof levels of the operations room formed one wall of a water tank house which fed a tap in the battery room below.

Other buildings included two detached 11-bay 30 ft span Nissen huts. One functioned as a crew briefing room and was open plan; the other was subdivided into an interrogation room, signals office, and various other offices for the intelligence officer, anti-aircraft operations officer, rest room and kitchen. WCs were provided in the form of detached blocks for WAAFs and semi-detached blocks for officers and other ranks.

The 228/43 design of January 1943 was similar to 4891/42 but with the following differences. The plant and boiler-room was housed in a temporary brick annexe. The interrogation room complex was connected to the main block by an airlock and corridor. The crew briefing room and interrogation block could be constructed in temporary brick or Nissen hutting.

drawing no.	13023/41, 13742/41	4891/42	228/43
examples	Burn, Metfield, Nuneaton, Turweston, Woolfox Lodge	Ludford Magna, Melton Mowbray, Metheringham, North Witham, Lasham, Snitterfield	Grove, Husbands Bosworth, Little Snoring, Metfield

PHOTOGRAPHIC BLOCK

In the First World War, a temporary brick hut was used. It was 62 ft by 15 ft 9 in with a simple collar-beam truss clad with asbestos sheeting. There were rooms for developing photographic plates, two printing rooms, a store, and an office.

On airfields built during the Second World War, the photographic section was housed on the main technical site in a temporary brick building or two 24 ft span Nissen huts. These were joined together by a temporary brick corridor and arranged at right angles to each other (T-shaped in plan). The largest hut (66 ft 5 in) functioned as the photographic laboratory, while the other hut (36 ft 3 in) was an open-plan projection and lecture hall. The laboratory had a central corridor with rooms on both sides for washing, drying, printing, developing, chemical mixing, a darkroom, a paper and film store, an office, another store, and a workshop.

drawing no.	290/17	12401/41
examples		Ashbourne, Framlingham, Silverstone

WORKSHOPS

The engine repair shop (288/17) of the First World War was 110 ft by 30 ft and built in temporary brick or with a timber frame and concrete blocks; both types had composite timber trusses. Natural lighting was aided by windows and four skylights. The main part was used as an engine repair shop with a 30 ft length divided into two; half for a coppersmith and welder, half for a blacksmith.

A Home Defence Squadron workshop of the 1920s was intended to serve three squadrons. It was a U-shaped brick-built building with a steel-framed roof supporting slates. One wing contained an engine-fitting shop and machine shop; the other wing contained a carpenter's woodworking and plane shop. The rear half was used as a carpenter's machine shop. Acetylene and blacksmith's shops with a boiler-room were located in a yard between the two main wings.

The first designs of the expansion period were 2048/34, 2049/34 and 4923/35. Each was intended to serve three squadrons. The designs replaced 1788/25 and 2315/25. Each was similar in internal arrangement but the 1934 brick designs had steel-framed pitched roofs with hipped trusses at the gable ends above two main wings with a flat-roofed machine shop located between the two. The 1935 design was built entirely of reinforced concrete including a flat roof above all sections. The internal arrangements were similar. One wing contained an airframe repair shop, the other was an engine repair shop and small engine

Technical Buildings 53

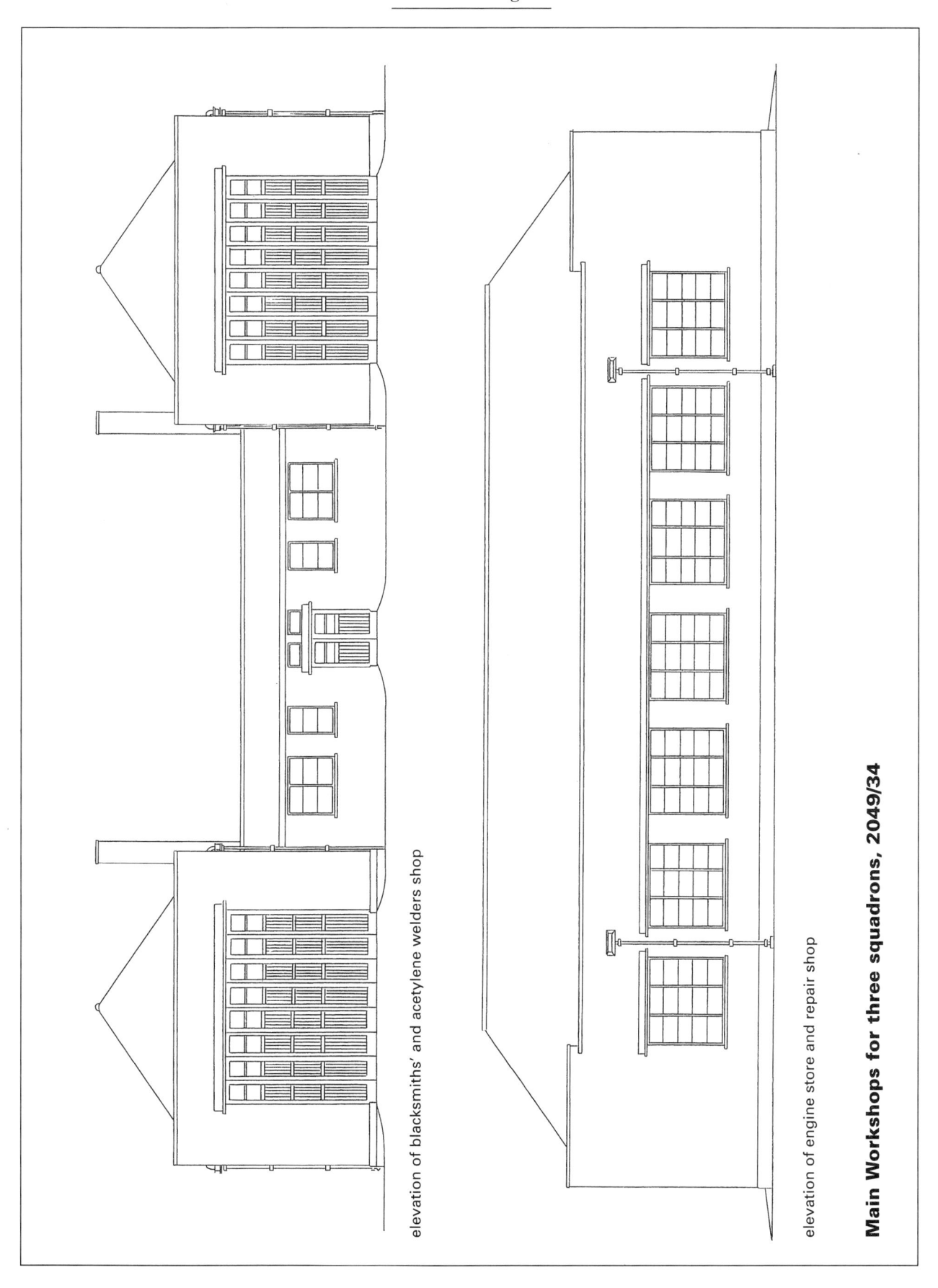

elevation of blacksmiths' and acetylene welders shop

elevation of engine store and repair shop

Main Workshops for three squadrons, 2049/34

These main stores to 814/30 served two squadrons at North Weald. (Photographed 1982)

The main stores built to 4287/35 at Watton. (Photographed 1994)

store. Separating the two were a number of smaller workshops for acetylene welders, blacksmiths, a machine shop, a fabric-workers' shop, and stores and office.

The 12774/41 version of the Second World War main workshop consisted of two 30 ft span Nissen huts, one 16 bays long, the other 12 bays long, built side by side with a 16 ft span Nissen hut between them, all three connected by a corridor. Room layout was similar to the permanent designs where one wing was used for airframe repairs and carpenter's shop, the other being used for engine repair, storage, and a combined acetylene welders and blacksmith's shop. The smaller Nissen hut contained a machine shop, fabric workers' shop, store, and office.

Another version, built to drawing 5851/42, used two 18-bay 30 ft span Nissen huts built adjacent to each other. The final version, built on some American bases, used two 95 ft long, 35 ft span Romney huts built adjacent to each other to drawing 2423/43.

drawing no.	288/17	1788/25, 2315/25	2048/34, 2049/34
examples		Hornchurch, Upper Heyford	Cranfield, Harwell, High Ercall, Ternhill

drawing no.	4923/35	12774/41	5851/42
examples	Bramcote, Cottesmore, Debden, Driffield		Bottisham, Framlingham, Rougham, Silverstone

drawing no. 2423/43
examples East Moor, Wombleton

STORES

Main Stores

The main stores was a facility for the storage of both non-technical items such as clothing and technical equipment such as small serviceable aircraft components – all necessary for an operational station. All in-coming material from RAF Equipment Depots was unloaded at the rear of the building into a receiving bay where it was sorted, logged and stored ready to be issued.

The first expansion period designs were based round an E-shaped building. The basic room arrangement of the two drawings was similar, the only real difference being the nature of construction. The earlier brick design had a steel-framed roof with hipped trusses at the gable ends, while the 1935 design was built entirely of reinforced concrete.

front elevation

side elevation (technical stores)

Main Stores for three squadrons, brick construction, protected Roof Design, 7064/37

A protected fabric store used as a lubricant store at North Weald. (Photographed 1982)

The left-hand outer wing functioned as a general technical store for aero-engine and MT spares, while the right-hand wing contained the non-technical stores. This included barrack furniture and clothing. There was a reception area containing a fitting space and local produce stores. In the centre of the front elevation was the main feature of all main stores: the tall fabric store with large timber folding doors. Designs dating from 1937 offering better protection against incendiary bombs, such as 7064/37, had steel-framed trestles both sides of the fabric store for supporting additional steel-framed and clad doors.

Both sides of the fabric store were rubber and bedding stores, and behind these were offices. The rear of the building contained a receiving area and packing case store, the floor level of the receiving bay being raised to the level of a vehicle unloading platform. Ramps were provided inside for ease of manoeuvring packing cases and boxes to the various storerooms. The walls of the receiving bay were steel-framed wire-mesh screens with steel doors.

A main stores complex of the Second World War consisted of two 16-bay 30 ft span Nissen huts built adjacent to each other and connected by a corridor which also connected a six-bay 24 ft span Nissen hut located at the front elevation and a six-bay 16 ft span Nissen hut at the rear. A detached fabric store was located nearby, built with 9-inch thick brick walls; it was 45 ft by 18 ft.

The internal arrangement was similar to that of permanent buildings with two wings used as technical and non-technical stores, while the 24 ft span hut was the reception area, and the small Nissen hut contained the offices.

Interestingly, 35 ft span Iris hutting was used as the two main stores buildings to drawing number 4889/42 at Little Snoring, Metheringham, North Pickenham, and Snitterfield.

drawing no.	2056/34	4287/35	7064/37
examples	Cranfield, Feltwell, Harwell, Marham	Debden, Driffield, Finningley, Upwood	Middleton St George

drawing no.	12773/41
examples	Ashbourne, Hixon, Framlingham, Toome

Fabric store 12773/41 at Framlingham. (Photographed 1982)

Lubricant Store

The main part of this 1920s building was built with its floor 3 ft above ground with a covered unloading platform. Vehicles parked next to the platform and unloaded barrels of oil which were simply rolled through double sliding doors and stored in a room 25 ft wide and 42 ft 9 in long. The second part of the building was a liquid container store, 16 ft long, its floor at ground level.

Built with 9-inch red-brick walls with piers at 10 ft 8 in centres supporting steel trusses carrying roof lights and ridge-mounted ventilators. Roof cladding was asbestos slates.

drawing no.	329/26
example	Bicester

Pyrotechnic Store

Ready-use pyrotechnic stores were usually found in pairs. It is quite common for them to have different drawing numbers, for example, 2847/38 and 5488/42. The stores were built of rendered brick with felt-covered flat concrete roofs. Inside were two compartments with up to five shelves and two air vents.

drawing no.	2847/38	5488/42
examples	Melbourne	Melbourne

Lubricant store 329/26 at Filton. (Photographed 1993)

The main stores 840/30 at Hendon. (Photographed 1992)

Ready use pyrotechnic store at Ingham. (Photographed 1983)

Towed Target Store

Built on parent fighter and bomber OTU stations, this was a 24 ft span Nissen hut 72 ft 6 in long. It was open plan with a small office in one corner.

drawing no.   12782/41
examples   Marsworth,
                Peplow
                Silverstone

SECOND WORLD WAR DISPERSED BUILDINGS

New airfields were constructed using drawings of the latest standard Type designs and often made use of sequential sets of drawings so that, for example, stations built in 1942 had groups of small buildings with drawing numbers beginning with 124 and 127. The 124 series covered a number of different small huts, many of which

The night flying equipment store 17831/40 at East Fortune.

shared a common drawing, for example 12408/41, 12410/41, and 12411/41.

Drawing 12408/41 was for a group of two small Nissen huts for the storage of gas detection and decontamination equipment. Both had 16 ft spans and were 36 ft 3 in long; one was used as an equipment store for wheel barrows, warning signs, oil and lamps, bleach, spades and ash bins, while the other functioned as an undressing room. Drawing 12410/41 was for a fire tender house and shelter. Both buildings were 24 ft span Nissen huts and were similar in appearance. The fire tender house was built near the guardhouse. It had a flat concrete floor and a bench at the rear. The fire tender shelter was built close to the watch office and had two concrete runways separated by ashes.

Drawing 12411/41 was used for several buildings including a gas chamber, a gas chamber and practice bomb store, a night flying equipment store, and a floodlight trailer and tractor shed.

An example of the gas chamber had 10 ft spans and 18 ft long with walls 7 ft high, and contained a small lachrymatory generator store, airlock and gas chamber itself. The gas chamber and practice bomb store was, for example, 18 ft by 40 ft with walls 7 ft high. This was simply a bomb shelter with one end used as a gas chamber. The chamber at Mendlesham was built like this. A night flying equipment (NFE) store was a three-bay garage, each bay with double doors, built close to the watch office. It accommodated a goose flare trolley, a glim lamp trolley and an illuminated landing tee. Each bay measured 10 ft by 18 ft; walls were 10 ft 6 in high, built of 4.5-inch rendered brick with steel trusses and corrugated asbestos sheeting.

The floodlight trailer and tractor shed was a garage containing a single floodlight trailer and tractor in a building 18 ft by 35 ft with walls 13 ft 6 in high, arranged open plan with large double doors at both ends. Construction was similar to the NFE store.

drawing no.	12408/41	12410/41	12411/41
examples	Thorpe Abbotts	Tempsford, Tilstock	Mendlesham, Little Staughton, Little Walden, Matching Green

Maintenance Buildings and Workshops

On airfields constructed during the Second World War, hangars were built without attached annexes, a number of detached huts being provided instead. They were positioned so that they were immediately available to the aircraft they served, dispersed round the airfield. If the hangars were located on the main technical site, they were part of the main site. Typically, a dispersed T2 hangar on a bomber station could have a couple of maintenance unit huts and a squadron armoury, but the station armoury was located only on the main technical site. Many buildings belonging to this category came under the 127 series of drawings: 12777/41, 12778/41, 12781/41 and 12782/41.

Several types of maintenance building were built from 24 ft span Nissen hutting using drawing 12777/41, including a maintenance and armoury unit with oil-bowser garage, a maintenance and armoury workshop, and maintenance unit staff blocks.

The maintenance and armoury unit with oil-bowser garage was 126 ft 10 in long and consisted of a tractor oil-bowser garage and the following stores facilities: camera, oil and dope, small bomb container, gun-cleaning room, armament officer's office, and turret repair and armament workshop. The maintenance and armoury workshop was 90 ft 7 in long with a similar internal arrangement but without tractor oil-bowser garage.

The maintenance unit was 126 ft 10 in long with battery-charging room, W/T store, office and workshop, instrument section office, auto-control shop and instrument repair, and two flight equipment stores. The maintenance unit staff blocks were 42 ft 3 in long, subdivided into engineer's clerks office, electrical engineering officer's office, NCO rest room, and airmen's rest room.

Maintenance blocks on parent bomber OTU stations were 24 ft span Nissen huts built to 12784/41. Block A was a hut 120 ft 10 in long. There were rooms for battery and accumulator charging, an oil paint and dope store, and offices for the engineering officer and his clerk. The main part of the building was the aeroplane equipment store. Block B was the same size as A but with different rooms, including a tractor and oil-bowser garage, W/T workshop, store and office, airmen's rest room, NCOs' rest room, kitchen, and lock-up equipment store.

Block C was the same length as A and B but arranged with the following rooms: auto-control shop and instrument repair, instrument section office, camera store, armament officer office, room for cleaning machine-guns, small bomb container store, and turret repair and armament workshop. Maintenance Wing offices were in a hut 72 ft 6 in long and subdivided into offices for the commanding officer, the adjutant, the technical adjutant, the warrant officer (discipline), the engineering warrant officer, the maintenance officer, and a library for publications and records.

The flight workshop to drawing 13732/41 for towed targets was 60 ft 5 in long with a battery-charging room, oil paint store, office and towed target/general engineering workshop. The gunnery flight workshops (Types A and B) to the same drawing were similar except Type B did not have a battery-charging room; other rooms included an oil, paint and dope store, one for cleaning and stripping machine-guns, and armament inspection room. Type A was 60 ft 5 in long while Type B was 48 ft 4 in.

The maintenance unit huts were manned by tradesmen attached to the flight whose job was the daily inspection of aircraft. These included electricians who would check all aircraft warning lamps, microswitches and electrical controls such as bomb release equipment; engine fitters who carried out daily and routine maintenance of aircraft engines, and in particular spark plugs, starter motors and magnetos; and riggers looked after the aircraft structure and certain equipment inside it such as air brakes, windscreen de-icing kit, flying controls and hydraulics. The instrument section was responsible for maintaining the autopilot, bomb-sight, gun-sight, instrument flying panel, magnetic compass and oxygen system. Another important function was the checking of each aircraft compass for deviation by carrying out a compass swing. Sometimes (on pre-war stations) a special circle of concrete was set aside for this purpose where the aircraft could be towed in a circle so that it could be lined up with the various points of the compass. The aircraft compass readings were checked against a hand-held calibrated standard instrument and an estimation was made of any deviation which was recorded on a Compass Corrector Card (RAF Form 316).

A flight sergeant, who had an office in the maintenance unit staff block, would be responsible for the aircraft Form 700 and would obtain the necessary signatures from all trades to confirm the serviceability of the aircraft.

drawing no.	12777/41	12784/41	13732/41
examples	Andrewsfield, Blyton, Melbourne		

Station Armoury

It was the job of the station armourers in the bomb dump to select the correct type of bombs, load them on to the bomb trolleys and fuze them prior to delivery to the squadron armourers waiting at the aircraft dispersal. When the loaded bomb trolleys arrived at dispersal, a team of squadron armourers would winch the bombs and their carriers into the aircraft, the exact position of each load being worked out to balance the aircraft.

Another group of station armourers filled ammunition belts in the station armoury using special machines. They operated a colour-code system to arrive at the correct mix of ammunition. A loaded belt could include tracer (red), armour-piercing (green), incendiaries (blue) and ball (purple). Gun harmonization was another important task carried out by armourers. This involved adjustment of the guns to give the correct cone of fire. The object was to have all four guns from a turret producing an intersecting cone of fire at 400 yd. This was tested with a large board with coloured circles at the four corners and an aiming mark between them. This was placed at the correct distance from the turret. With a periscope fitted in the barrel, the cross-hairs were lined up with the appropriate circle. When this had been carried out on all four guns the gun-sight was aligned with the aiming mark and fixed in this position.

The station armoury built to 12778/41, was a 24 ft by 66 ft 5 in Nissen Hut. It was divided into storerooms for unbelted ammunition, belted ammunition, and oil, next to which was a filling room with hoppers connected to the ammunition stores, and a belt-filling machine. Other rooms included one for armament inspection, an office, and the station armoury where revolvers and rifles were kept.

The temporary brick station armoury 9105/41 was originally similar in layout to 12778/41 but some examples were extended to drawing 2428/43 to include a larger filling room with more belt-filling machines and lining-up equipment. The 30 ft extension was added to an end wall creating a building 90 ft long. Where this happened, a complete reorganization of the internal arrangement took place.

Found mainly on bomber OTU stations, the armoury blocks to 12781/41 were 24 ft span Nissen huts of two different types: armoury block A which was 96 ft 8 in long, divided into gun maintenance room, containers and bomb-gear room, and turret-filling gear and magazine maintenance workshop; and armoury block B which was 72 ft 6 in long, containing storerooms for paint and oil, ammunition belt, and the magazine. There was also a filling room which contained three belt-filling machines, an office, and an armament inspection room and station armoury.

drawing no.	9105/41	12778/41	12781/41
examples		Boreham, Horham, Ridgewell	

drawing no.	2428/43

Squadron and Flight Offices

These were 24 ft span Nissen huts to drawing 13732/41. The internal layout of flight office blocks, both the gunnery and the towed target types, were essentially similar. The towed target block had an extra two bays making it 72 ft 6 in long, while the gunnery office was only 66 ft 5 in long. Office accommodation was for flight commander, flight sergeants, pilots' rest room (officers) and pilots' rest room (NCOs), a storeroom, and a locker room. The extra two bays were to accommodate additional lockers.

On bomber stations and bomber OTU satellite airfields, 24 ft span Nissen huts were built to 14532/41. The flight office was 54 ft 4 in long and had a central corridor with offices for three flight clerks, three flight officers, and had three flight storerooms. Squadron offices again had a central corridor but with two storerooms, and seven offices for the administration officer, commanding officer, two clerks, station adjutant, defence officer, and a warrant officer.

drawing no.   13732/411   14532/41
example   Mendlesham

AIRFIELD DEFENCE

Battle Headquarters

The battle headquarters was an underground office for the direction of airfield defence.

The local defence authority decided which existing building could be adapted for use as a battle headquarters. If no suitable building existed he would recommend the construction of an underground building to drawing number 11008/41. Most were of the sunken type but where there was a high water-table the battle headquarters had to be semi-sunk. In all cases, it was constructed with walls 13.5 inches thick and contained a PBX, office, a room for messengers and runners, and an observation post. Normally, the only part visible above ground was the concrete observation post. This had narrow viewing slits on all four sides.

An Allan Williams steel turret for airfield defence at Arbroath. (Photographed 1991)

drawing no.   11008/41
example   Sawbridgeworth

Pillboxes and Turrets

The retractable pillbox was given the highest priority for airfield defence. It was formed from two large-diameter concrete pipes, one sliding inside the other. Three were installed on the landing areas of grass airfields. When the pillbox was in the closed position, the top of the inner pipe was flush with the grass surface. The inner pipe could be raised by hydraulic means. Defenders could fire through loopholes cut in the pipe.

Other one-man and two-man defence positions on airfields included the Allan Williams steel turret and the single-man Tett turret.

The Allan Williams turret was positioned on the airfield boundary and consisted of curved steel plates welded into a dome-shape and mounted on a curved rail to provide a 360° field of fire. It was entered from a small tunnel on the aerodrome side, which was provided with a sheet steel roof. Inside were a set of handlebars for turning the turret

A sleeping shelter for 32 personnel built to KBC103/40 at the Hook Barrage Balloon Depot. (Photographed 1993; Maurice Cole)

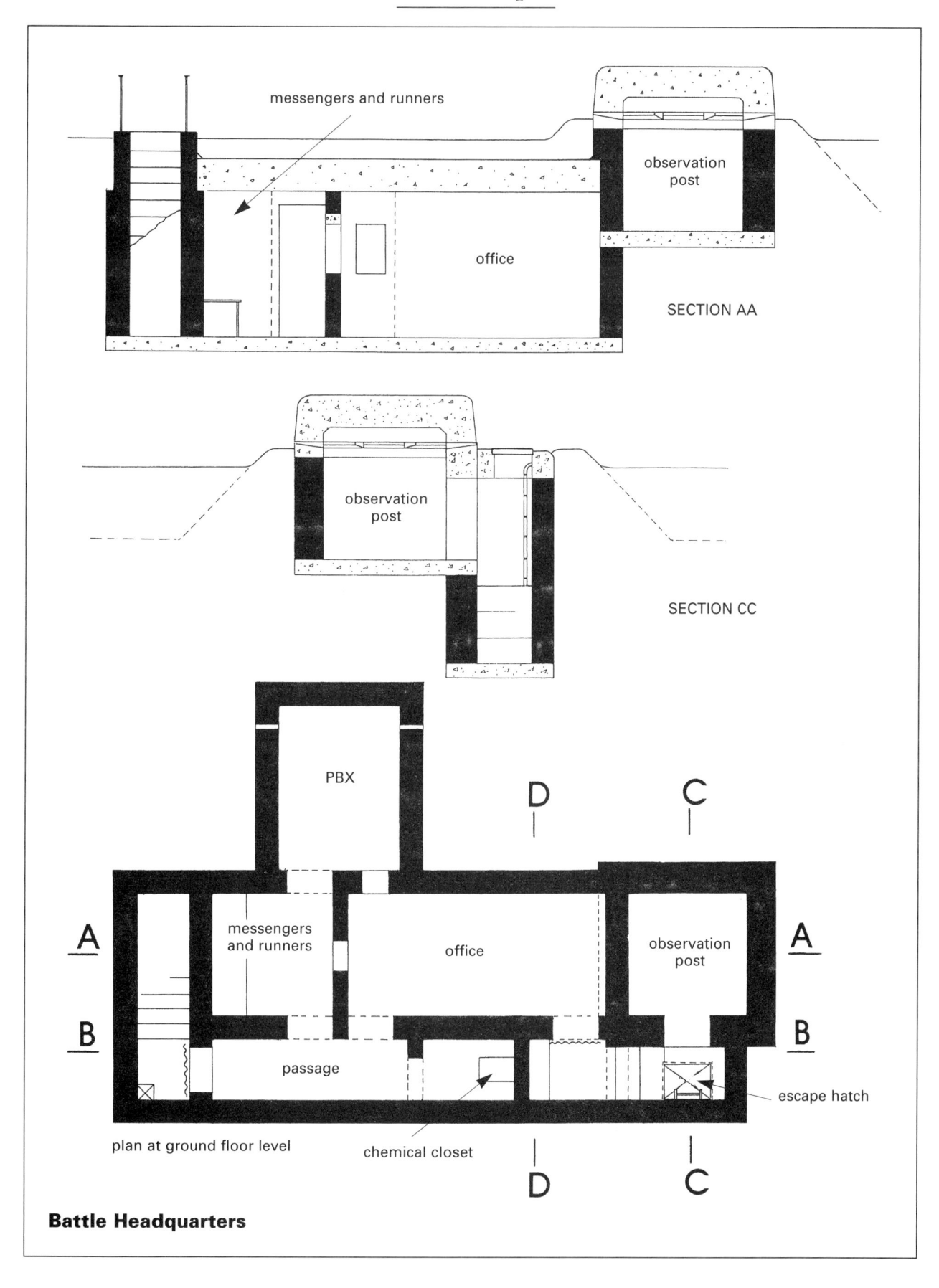

Technical Buildings   61

messengers and runners

observation post

office

SECTION AA

observation post

SECTION CC

PBX

D   C

A — messengers and runners | office | observation post — A

B   B

passage | chemical closet | escape hatch

plan at ground floor level

D   C

Battle Headquarters

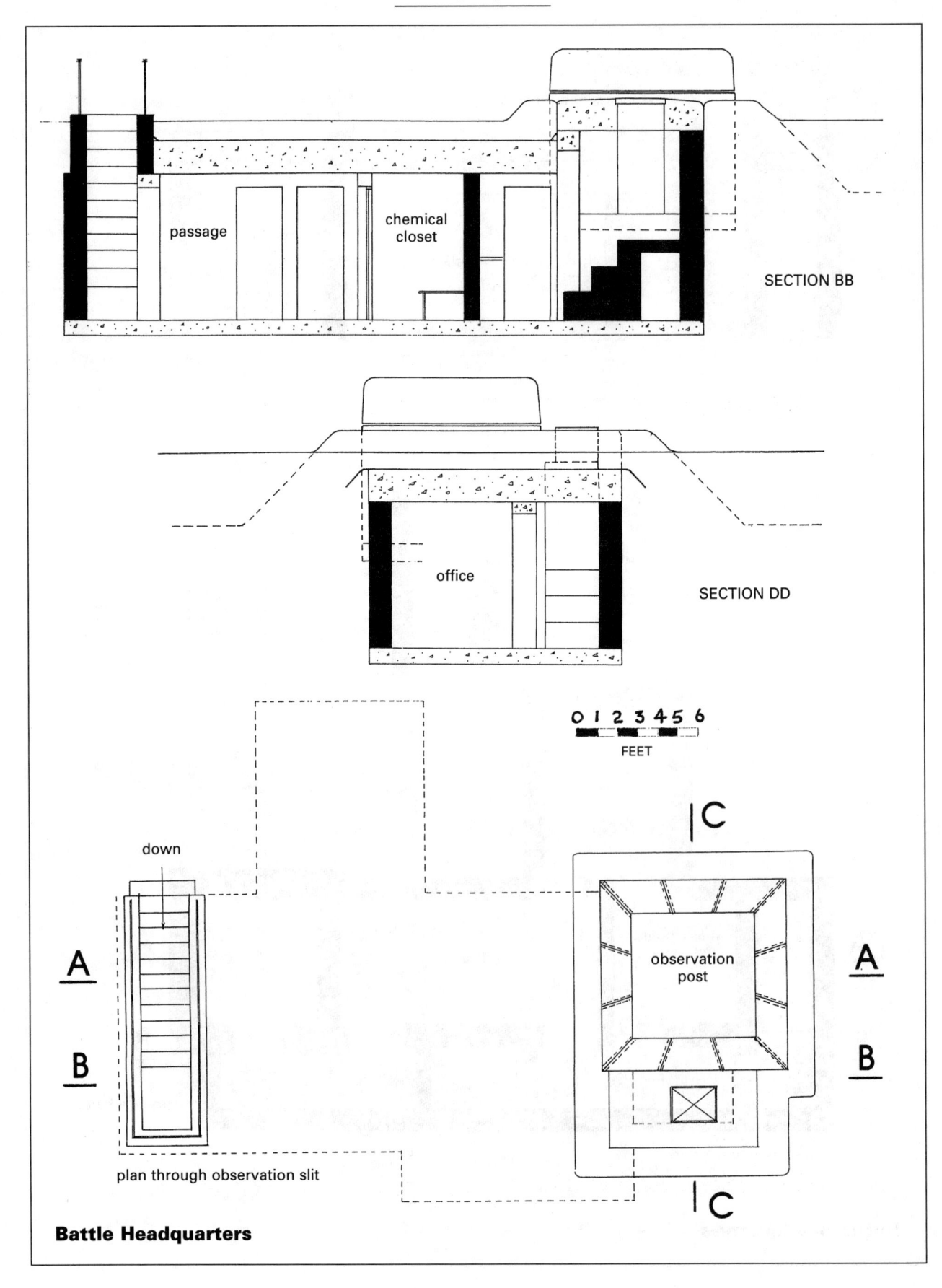

62 *British Military Airfield Architecture*

SECTION BB

SECTION DD

0 1 2 3 4 5 6
FEET

passage

chemical closet

office

down

plan through observation slit

observation post

A — A
B — B
C — C

Battle Headquarters

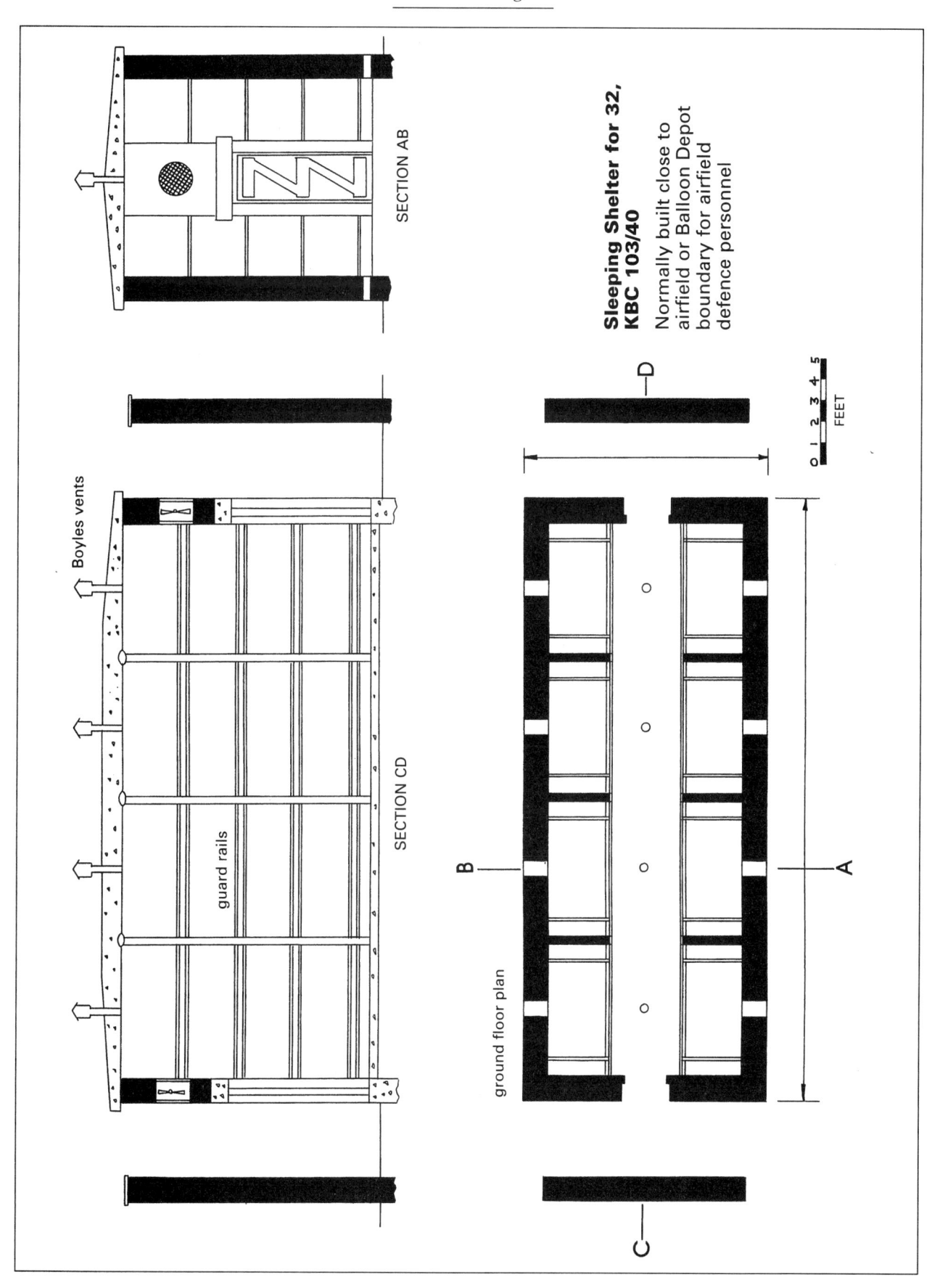

Technical Buildings 63

Sleeping Shelter for 32, KBC 103/40

Normally built close to airfield or Balloon Depot boundary for airfield defence personnel

SECTION AB

SECTION CD

Boyles vents

guard rails

ground floor plan

0 1 2 3 4 5 FEET

Tett turret at Hornchurch. (Photographed 1979)

An anti-aircraft tower at Weston-super-Mare. (Photographed 1990)

to face the desired direction. A fixed bracket was provided for mounting most types of machine-gun of the period.

The Tett Turret was a similar idea but constructed from reinforced concrete. Only 13 inches of the turret were above ground. A loophole was provided for a rifle only. The turret could revolve through 360°, being mounted on a ball-race.

type	retractable pillbox	Allan Williams turret	Tett turret
examples	North Weald	Arbroath, Panshanger, Radlett	Hornchurch

PART 3

BALLOON AND AIRSHIP BUILDINGS

AIRSHIP STATIONS 1909–19

The Defence Committee of the War Office put together a plan in 1909 in which rigid balloons would be given to the Navy and non-rigid balloons to the Army. At this time there was one small dirigible under evaluation at Farnborough with two more expected from France. One of these, *Clement Bayard*, was requested by the Aeronautical Committee of the House of Commons with a view to purchase if it proved satisfactory. On the strength of this, the War Office had built an airship shed on a site behind Hammersmith Hospital next to HM Prison Wormwood Scrubs; the architect was Herbert Ellis, and it was built by R. Moreland & Sons Ltd.

When *Clement Bayard* finally arrived on 16 October 1910, it was manhandled into its shed, deflated and sent to the Government Balloon Factory at Farnborough. The shed was used shortly after for the first flight on 29 October of an airship of British design, *Willows III*. During the First World War, Wormwood Scrubs was used for the production of submarine scout (SS) non-rigid airships (consisting of a modified BE2c aeroplane fuselage suspended beneath a simple envelope of rubberized fabric). In September 1916, the remains of Schütte-Lanz airship *L21* shot down over Cuffley were taken there for detailed examination. The shed was removed before 1930 and all that remains today is the brick wind screen which in more recent times was used as a back wall to a firing range but serves today as perimeter wall to a sports ground. This is now the only surviving airship shed wind screen and deserves protection against demolition.

In 1890, the Royal Engineers' Balloon Factory at Chatham was transferred to Aldershot where it remained until 1905 when it was moved to a new site on the northern edge of Farnborough Common. Among buildings re-erected was an airship shed. When originally built at Aldershot in 1895 it was considered to be very large, but when reconstructed at Farnborough it was discovered that it was too small for an airship on order at the time. Consequently, it had to be raised 10 ft in order to house the new airship. It had a main nave and two annexes with a span of 65 ft and a height of 65 ft. The end of the building was semi-circular in plan. In its greatly enlarged and extended form this became known as 'Beta Shed' and was demolished around 1965.

In July 1909, the War Office invited four structural engineering firms to submit designs and tender for the construction of an airship shed close to the balloon factory at Cove Common, Farnborough. A contract was placed in September with the Cleveland Bridge and Engineering Company of Darlington for a shed with a total length of 360 ft, maximum width of 115 ft (including two workshop annexes) and a roof height of 75 ft. It was constructed of 29 lattice ribs including three in the apse, each being 3 ft 4 in wide and carried on concrete blocks. One end of the building and the roof framing was curved to a radius of 30 ft while the other was entirely open providing a doorway 60 ft wide with 75 ft clear height. The four doors, the subject of an alternative contract, consisted of a steel framework clad with galvanized corrugated sheeting of the same gauge as the building itself.

Eventually there were four sheds at Farnborough including a portable one erected in 1911–12 which, like the 1909 shed, consisted of 14 steel lattice box-section girders with a polygonal (almost circular) roof but also had canted side walls approximately parabolic in shape. Stability was provided by steel wire guide ropes fixed to each frame. This structure was intended to be completely canvas clad but was not very successful as the building was dismantled by 1917; the top half became incorporated in the new foundry and the remaining wall sections were used as the framework for another building. The foundry is now listed Grade 2, while the other building is not listed.

In 1909, Vickers Sons & Maxim Ltd at Barrow-in-Furness were designing and constructing the first British naval dirigible. This was done inside a balloon shed designed and built by Francis Morton & Co Ltd of Hamilton Ironworks, Garston, Liverpool. This shed was built above water with one wall above the sloping pitching of the Cavendish Dock, the other supported by the actual dock bottom. The shed was 600 ft long, 100 ft wide with nearly 70 ft clear height. Steel box-section lattice ribs were spaced at 50 ft centres forming an arch, the inner ribs following a continuous curve; the outer faces were straight for fixing galvanized corrugated sheeting. Two lighter intermediate ribs were also arranged in each 50 ft bay. The shed opened at one end only and was closed by a sailcloth screen secured to vertical wire ropes and opened by hand winches, the screen being furled on the water side of the shed, entirely clear of the opening. The opposite end of the shed was V-shaped in plan with a hipped roof. Timber platforms were provided inside the shed for personnel working on balloon construction.

At the beginning of the First World War, Britain was seriously lacking in rigid airships (a hull and framework made of timber or aluminium alloy, covered with a flexible envelope) and had only a few non-rigid types, (no hull framework). As a result, the only airship sheds of any importance already in existence or being built were: a shed 300 ft by 85 ft and 65 ft high; a shed 355 ft by 60 ft and 75 ft high (Farnborough); a shed 354 ft by 65 ft and 92 ft high; a shed 553 ft by 110 ft and 100 ft high; two sheds 544 ft by 150 ft and 98 ft high. The last two had been, in fact, designed and fabricated in Germany.

The German submarine menace soon emphasized the need for a rapid expansion in airship production and with this airship stations also had to be designed and built. By the end of the war, 61 airship sheds had been constructed.

For operating non-rigid airships against German submarines, suitable sites were found some distance from parent airship stations. Normally, a wooded site was chosen so that airships could be moored outside for several days at a time when not on patrol; the trees offered some protection against wind. Luce Bay was a typical operational patrol station for rigid and non-rigid airships with substations at Ballyliffin, Larne, Machrihanish and Ramsey. Mullion was a typical operational patrol station for non-rigid airships with substations at Bude, Laira, St Mary's, and Toller.

Dalacombe Merechal & Hervieu Ltd were awarded a contract for 16 timber-framed sheds of their own design that were suitable for wooded sites. Although requiring great skill to manufacture, they were very simple to erect, the company claiming it took 40 men just 10 hours to build one. By clever design, the A-frame trestles were erected first at 12 ft 6 in centres (total length 175 ft). Each one was fitted with a worm-driven winch for raising (or lowering) the roof. The central portion of the roof trusses was assembled on the ground including purlins, rafters and canvas covering, and was then raised high enough to fit spandrels at either end. The complete roof section was raised by the winches and locked in place by automatic catches. The trestles were braced together with wire ropes and the complete shed was canvas clad.

Quite often sheltered locations could not be found and sheds in exposed areas were covered with black painted corrugated iron (the reason being that, due to the shortage of spelter during the early part of the war, galvanized corrugated sheeting was not available again until after 1917).

Sir William Arrol Ltd designed and built small sheds that required steel wire guy ropes tied to each trestle to provide the necessary stability. One of these required a sunken floor to give additional headroom, only possible because canvas curtains were used instead of doors.

Another Arrol design had very wide A-frame trestles to spread the load which avoided the need for foundations. The trestles could be partitioned off to provide storerooms. This shed was used for coastal patrol airships. It had a 70 ft clear span, was 220 ft long 70 ft wide. It was similar to those built at Caldale (Orkney) and Cranwell.

Many larger stations had two small non-rigid airship sheds in addition to the main one. They were often positioned to act as wind breaks for airships entering the large shed, such as at Longside. At Cranwell, the smallest was built for SS type airships, 150 ft long and 45 ft wide. It was very similar to a design by Mr E. Marshall Fox. This comprised a series of timber trestles and roof trusses, cut, framed and bolted together on site. Several of this type were built (normally with a length of 300 ft). At least one collapsed during construction due to high winds.

Another clever design was devised by Mr R. G. Sargent of the Admiralty staff. The entire shed including canvas covering could be erected with the aid of winches. This was made possible by having roof trusses, side legs and wall members pin-jointed to each other, and by using one side already erected to build the opposite side.

Some stations such as Luce Bay and Mullion originally had a single permanent shed for non-rigid airships built by A. & J. Main. They were constructed entirely of steel, had a clear span of 110 ft, a clear height of 75 ft, and a total length of 358 ft. Mounted on top of the roof ridge line was an observation tower. They were built with the aid of two 10-ton travelling cranes running both sides of the shed. Although the building at Mullion was removed some years ago, the bulk of it was re-erected as a bus garage in Padstow, Cornwall.

The rapid increase in airship size called for larger designs of shed. The largest in the UK (and the largest building in the country) was the twin-shed (No. 2 shed) at Howden. It was built by Sir William Arrol & Co Ltd, covered an area 754 ft by 410 ft: 8.5 acres including the space occupied by the doors at both ends. Each span had a clear width of 130 ft, a maximum clear height of 130 ft and a clear length of 750 ft. The total weight of the steelwork was 5,208 tons.

A. Findlay & Co Ltd was awarded a contract to design and build the No. 1 shed at Howden. This had a 150 ft clear span, 100 ft clear height and 700 ft clear length. Roof girders were spaced at 25 ft centres and were carried on 98 ft high braced trestles forming 28 bays. Six longitudinal girders were also provided running the full length of the shed. Internal annexes were accommodated within the A-frame trestles, being 35 ft wide, and ran the whole length of the shed.

Normally where two sheds were required at the same time on the same station (as at Pulham) it was more advantageous, despite the increased materials cost, to erect two separate sheds rather than build a twin-shed. This was primarily for safety since an airship on fire in one bay of a twin-shed could easily destroy another in the adjoining bay. Early sheds were designed with hinged explosion flaps of corrugated iron, about 7 ft long, running the full length of the building on both sides; they were hinged at the

Ballon and Airship Buildings

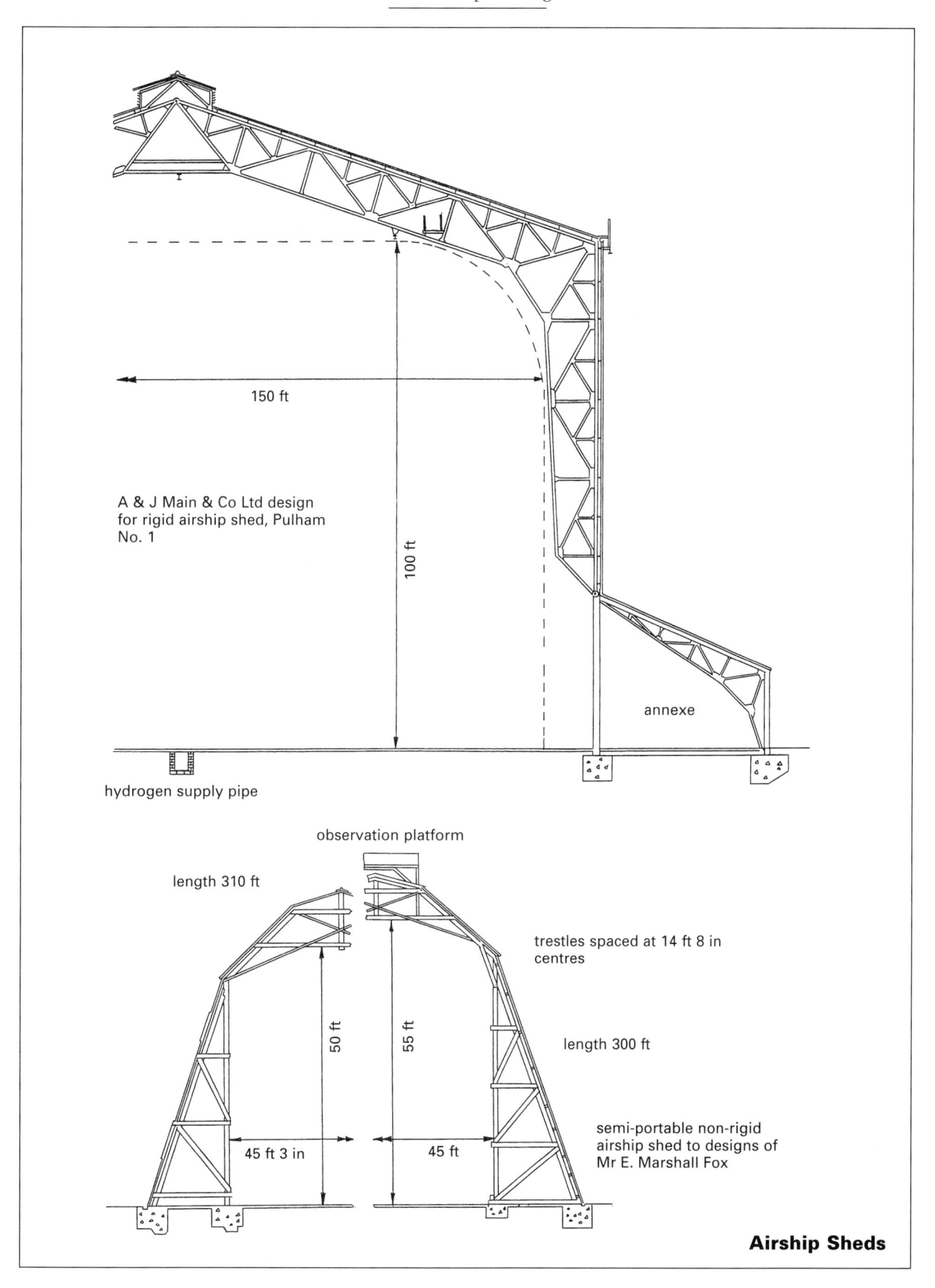

150 ft

100 ft

A & J Main & Co Ltd design for rigid airship shed, Pulham No. 1

annexe

hydrogen supply pipe

observation platform

length 310 ft

trestles spaced at 14 ft 8 in centres

50 ft

55 ft

length 300 ft

45 ft 3 in

45 ft

semi-portable non-rigid airship shed to designs of Mr E. Marshall Fox

Airship Sheds

Airship Sheds

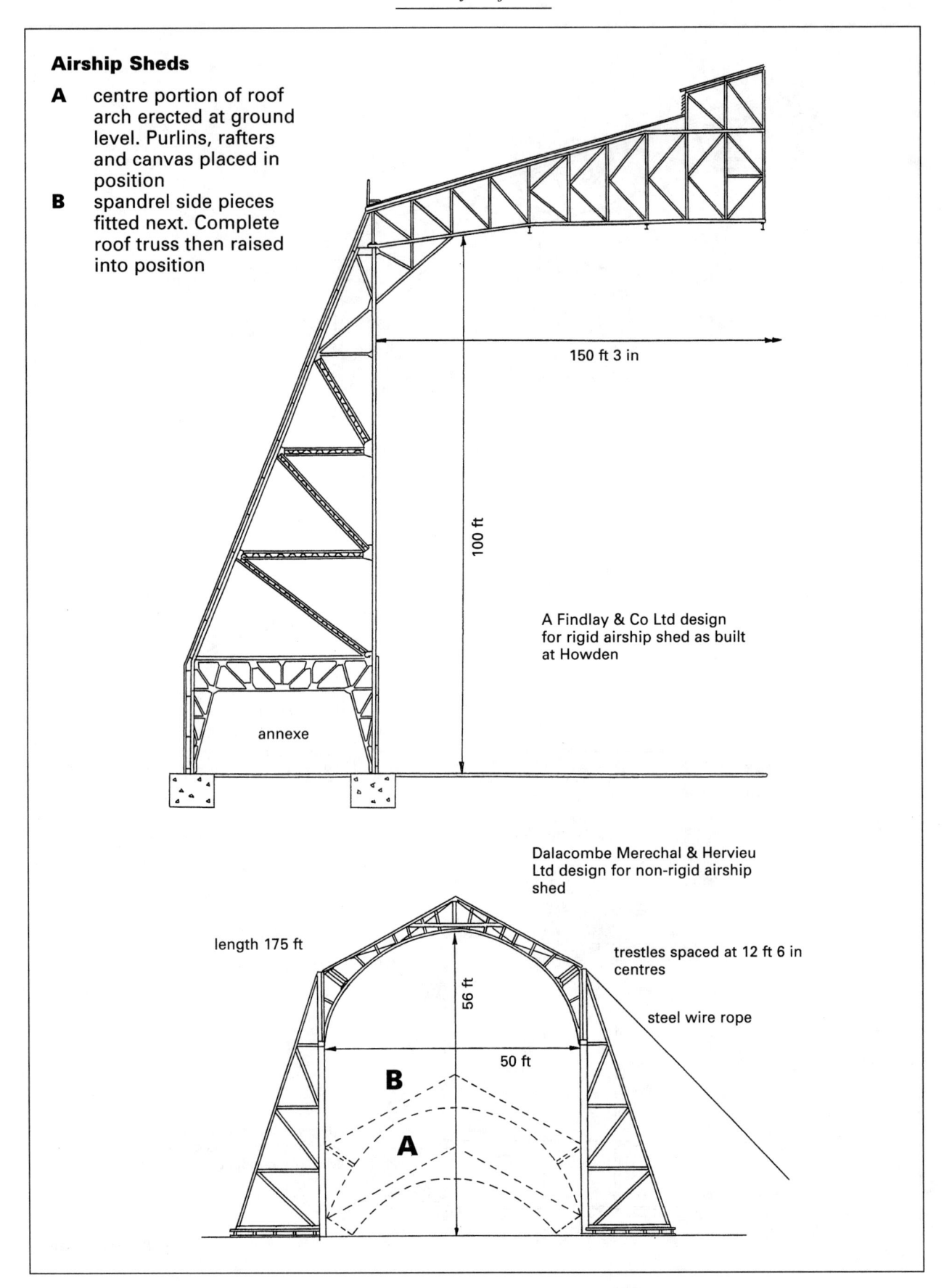

A centre portion of roof arch erected at ground level. Purlins, rafters and canvas placed in position

B spandrel side pieces fitted next. Complete roof truss then raised into position

150 ft 3 in

100 ft

annexe

A Findlay & Co Ltd design for rigid airship shed as built at Howden

Dalcombe Merechal & Hervieu Ltd design for non-rigid airship shed

length 175 ft

56 ft

50 ft

B

A

trestles spaced at 12 ft 6 in centres

steel wire rope

Ballon and Airship Buildings 69

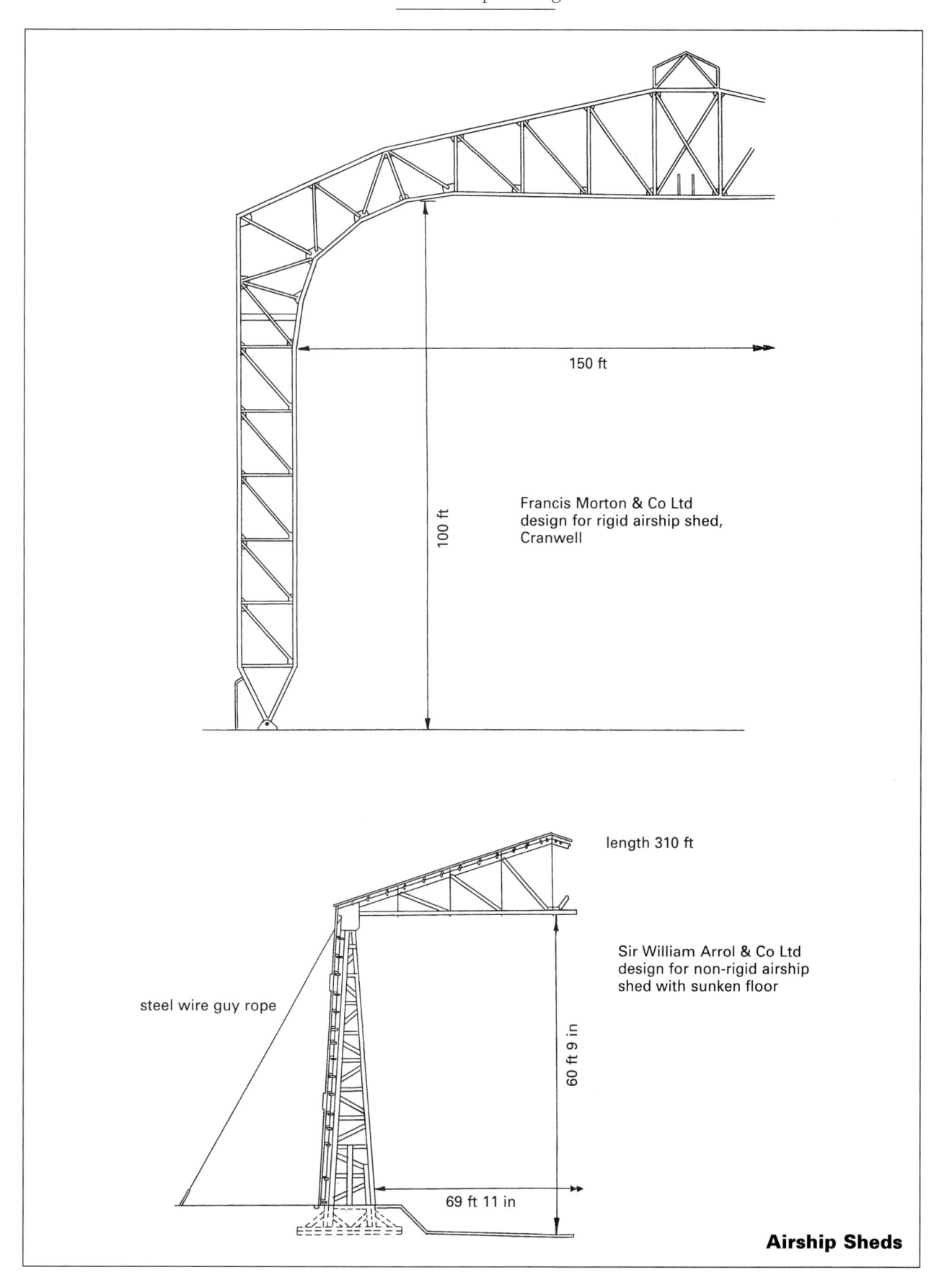

150 ft

100 ft

Francis Morton & Co Ltd design for rigid airship shed, Cranwell

length 310 ft

Sir William Arrol & Co Ltd design for non-rigid airship shed with sunken floor

steel wire guy rope

60 ft 9 in

69 ft 11 in

Airship Sheds

Water-tower at Howden airship station.

bottom and held in place by lead flashing.

A rigid airship, the *R27*, was destroyed by fire in the Findlay shed at Howden. On 16 August 1918, a non-rigid SSZ class airship, the *SSZ23*, was packed ready for transport to America, complete with a new envelope (this was common practice as non-rigids were always supplied with a spare envelope). The American crew decided to present the RNAS with a 'new' unnumbered airship and rigged the old envelope with a spare car. Inside the shed were *R27*, *SSZ38*, *SSZ54*, the packed *SSZ23*, and the 'new' unnumbered SSZ. When the work was nearly completed, the W/T operator checked the W/T set and a spark from his set ignited petrol in the car. The resulting inferno destroyed all the airships except one nearest an open door. The brunt of the explosion was borne by the roof sheeting which opened up, killing a man who was on look-out duty. Much of the internal air pressure was relieved because one of the doors was open. However, the explosion flaps failed to work and as a result all subsequent sheds were built without them.

The main shed at Cranwell was built by Francis Morton. This was a two-pin arched design with pin-joints at ground level. It had a 150 ft clear span, 100 ft clear height and was 700 ft long. Main frames were spaced at 25 ft centres with intermediate lattice frames between 12 longitudinal girders. Annexes for offices, and workshops were built on each side as lean-to sheds. The building was constructed using a 97 ft high travelling stage. This formed a platform from which the centre portions of the roof arches could be assembled.

Sir William Arrol built a shed for the William Beardmore & Co Ltd at Inchinnan near Glasgow. This had a span of 150 ft, a height of 100 ft and was 720 ft long.

MT steel garage at East Fortune airship station. Compare this with the MT garage at Woodsford. (Photographed 1982)

MT garage at Woodsford airship station.

Ballon and Airship Buildings 71

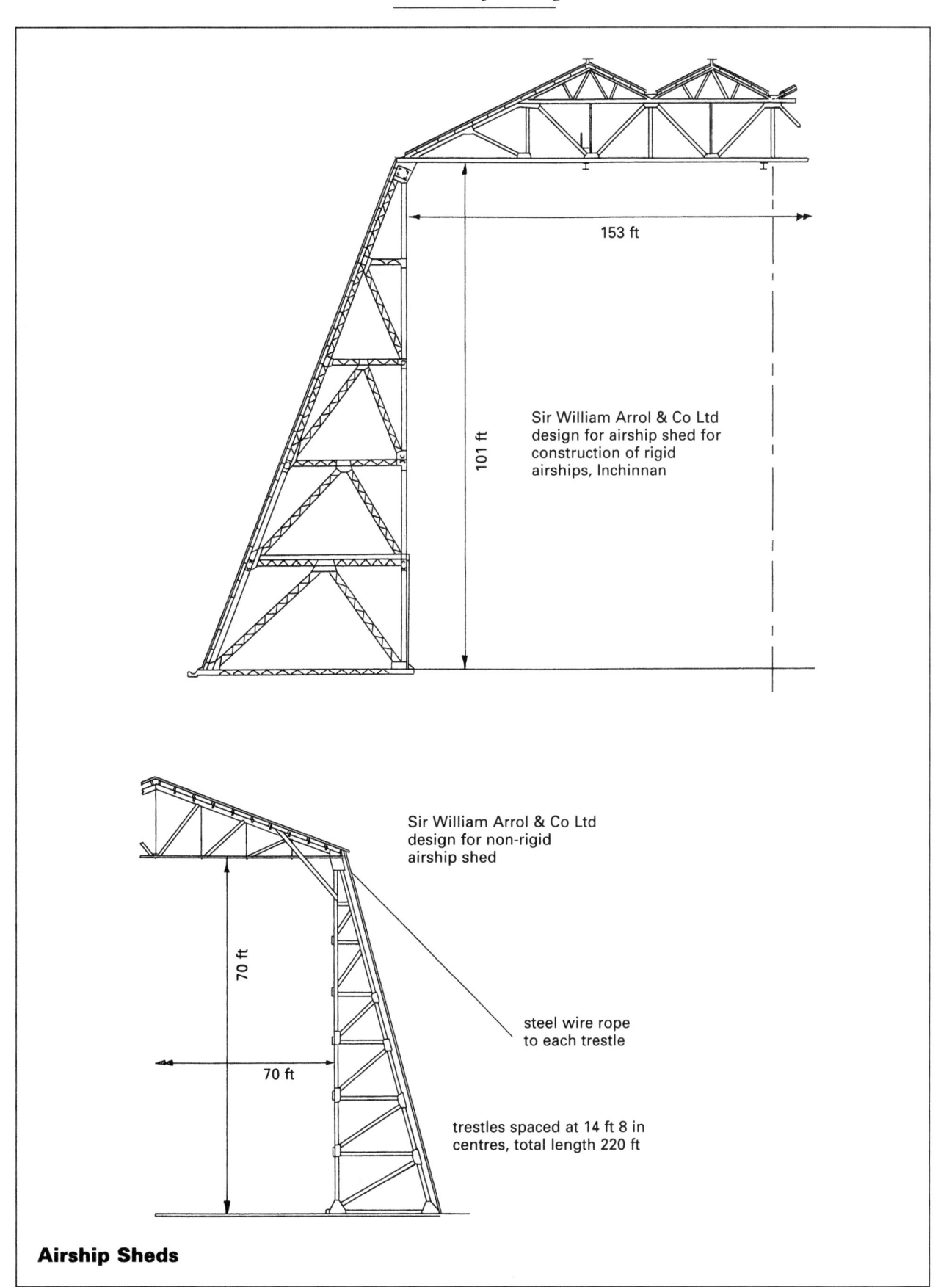

Sir William Arrol & Co Ltd design for airship shed for construction of rigid airships, Inchinnan

153 ft

101 ft

Sir William Arrol & Co Ltd design for non-rigid airship shed

70 ft

70 ft

steel wire rope to each trestle

trestles spaced at 14 ft 8 in centres, total length 220 ft

Airship Sheds

RNAS Training Establishment Cranwell, 1919 showing airship station

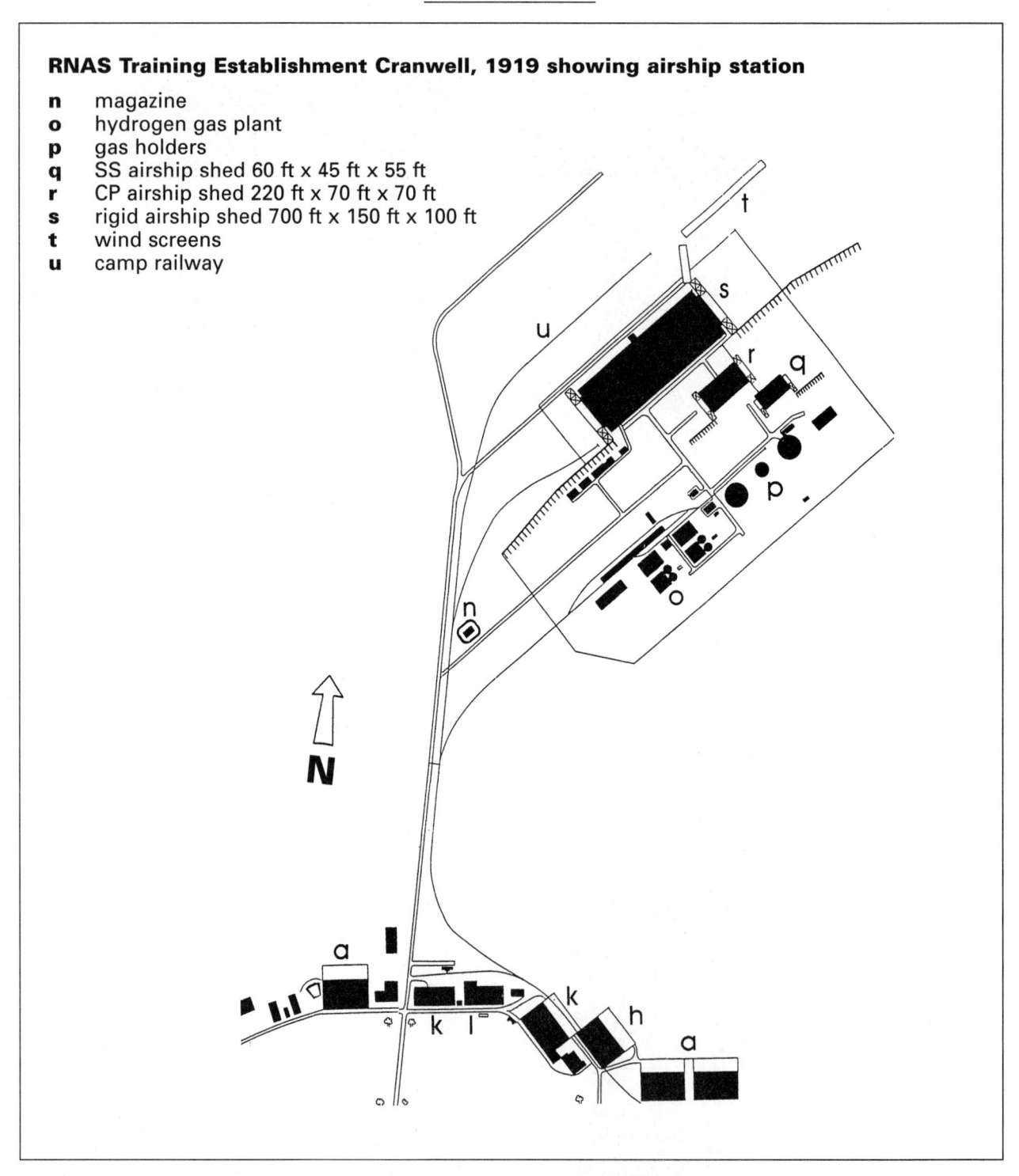

- **n** magazine
- **o** hydrogen gas plant
- **p** gas holders
- **q** SS airship shed 60 ft x 45 ft x 55 ft
- **r** CP airship shed 220 ft x 70 ft x 70 ft
- **s** rigid airship shed 700 ft x 150 ft x 100 ft
- **t** wind screens
- **u** camp railway

The main frames were spaced at 40 ft centres with three intermediate frames. The roof consisted of two half-spans and four complete spans running longitudinally, carried on braced longitudinal and cross girders. Gangways for workers engaged in airship construction were provided on top of the longitudinal girders on the inside of the braced trestles. It was in this shed that work began on the construction of the *R34* on the 9 December 1917, which, in 1919, became the first airship to make a double crossing of the Atlantic.

Originally the sheds were designed with large tanks placed high up in the roof space for the collection of rain water. These were connected by pipes to fire hydrants at ground level. In later designs, roof water was run to waste due to problems with frost damage on the earlier sheds. At these stations, a fire service was provided from an independent reinforced-concrete water-tower. A rare example survives at Howden.

A technical hut at Woodsford airship station. (Photographed 1984)

Vertical screens constructed of timber or steel framing covered with timber boarding or corrugated iron sheeting were built to protect airships from crosswinds when entering or leaving the shed. From 1914, tests were carried out at Farnborough in the 7 ft square wind tunnel using models of airships, sheds and screens. This was to establish the best position for wind screens according to wind direction while the model airship entered the shed. With a wind speed of 20 feet per second, the airflow was shown using smoke and tufts of wool.

Screen size was often similar to the length of a shed. For example, at Cranwell, the main shed had a screen 700 ft by 70 ft at each end. Timber and corrugated iron cladding was far from ideal and the best screens were those covered with close-mesh expanded-metal sheeting. Eventually, screens were abandoned altogether in favour of controlling the airship by the use of claw travellers mounted on rails.

All the parent airship stations were self-contained with many specialist buildings not found elsewhere, as well as the usual living accommodation. The principal buildings were:

- barracks
- officers' mess
- acetylene-generator house
- gasholders
- gas-plant house
- garage
- magazine
- powerhouse
- stores
- water-tower
- workshops

CARDINGTON BETWEEN THE WARS

The original airship shed at the Royal Airship Works, Cardington was built for the Admiralty in 1916–17 by A. & J. Main. At the time, it was the largest clear span shed (180 ft) in the UK and had an overall width of 254 ft, a clear length of 700 ft and a clear height of 110 ft. It was a three-pin arch design, the lower joints being carried on rigidly braced trestles, the lower portion partitioned off to form offices and workshop annexes. Both ends had sliding doors and the approaches were protected against prevailing winds by screens 70 ft high and 700 ft long. The largest rigid airship to be constructed in this shed was the R38, a vessel 695 ft long, 85 ft in diameter with a capacity of 2,700,000 cu ft. Construction of the R38 severely taxed the capacity of the shed. Its design, particularly the positioning of the engine cars, was constrained by the size of shed.

In 1924, the Government decided to build two airships of 5,000,000 cu ft capacity. One of these, the R101, was 720 ft long with a diameter of 120 ft. It was clearly too large for the existing shed which needed to be extended in length by 112 ft and in height by 35 ft. Furthermore, it

The Royal Airship Works at Cardington. (Photographed 1993)

was considered unnecessary to have doors at both ends of the shed. In addition, it was decided to erect a mooring tower so that visiting airships could be berthed outdoors as an alternative to housing them in the shed. In October, a contract was awarded to the Cleveland Bridge & Engineering Co Ltd for the enlargement of the shed. An original idea was to raise the existing structure on hydraulic jacks, but this was abandoned in favour of dismantling it. This had the added bonus of allowing necessary modifications to the original structure to be carried out. The roof was left unaltered and simply raised by increasing the size of the vertical columns. Stability was achieved by new larger raking struts braced to the original rakers. The lengthening was carried out by adding a further four 28 ft bays to the original structure.

The door openings originally had flat tops, the shed being designed to accommodate two airships of the *R33* type, but to accommodate a single airship of increased size the centre section of the door was redesigned with extra height. The new doors were designed to run on two 3 ft 6 in gauge railway tracks to make opening and closing easier. The other end door was removed, dismantled and sent to the factory at Darlington where most of the steelwork was incorporated into a new permanent end.

The work was made possible by the use of a 7-ton steam crane mounted out a 40 ft high steel stage; it was used to erect a travelling stage 120 ft high, 100 ft wide and 80 ft deep on which were mounted two 10-ton steam cranes. The project was completed in May 1926.

In 1924, when it was decided to build the *R100* and *R101*, the Government also agreed to increase airship station facilities abroad. These included a mooring tower designed and built at Ismailia in Egypt. The airship shed at Karachi, India was designed and built by the Armstrong Construction Company Ltd of London, a subsidiary of Armstrong Whitworth. This shed was 850 ft long, with a clear width of 200 ft and a clear height at its centre of 170 ft. It was the largest structure of its kind in the British Empire.

One of the Cardington airship sheds. (Photographed 1993)

The mooring towers built at Cardington, Ismailia, Karachi and St Hubert Airport, Montreal were all very similar, being steel-framed structures 200 ft high with eight supporting columns in an octagonal plan, and 70 ft (across flats) at the base. A 40 ft diameter platform, from which passengers would embark, was 170 ft above the ground. Above this was a circular turret 25 ft in diameter, with a conical roof which housed the masthead and machinery. The tower was designed to cope with a 30 ton pull from an airship in any direction.

A machinery house (which still survives at Cardington) housed three steam winches, each capable of exerting a pull of 15 tons and operated from the passenger platform at the top of the mast. Pumps were installed for pumping ballast water to the airship at a rate of 5,000 gallons per hour, and a 12-inch gas main was provided to supply the airship with gas. A 10,000-gallon petrol storage facility, capable of raising 2,000 gallons per hour to a height of 400 ft, was located inside an underground chamber below the mast.

The St Hubert tower was demolished around 1938 and that at Cardington in July 1943.

Plant for the production of hydrogen was installed at most of the rigid airship stations. Messrs Humphreys Ltd of Glasgow, fitted their Ranes Water Gas, Hydrogen Installation at Cardington in 1917. This worked on the iron contact system where steam was passed over red-hot iron ore to produce the gas. In 1938, ICI altered and enlarged this equipment with parts recovered from Pulham, and a compressor was installed to fill gas cylinders for supplying barrage balloons at different depots and sites all over the country.

Alternative hydrogen-producing plant was the Silicol system (as used at Ismailia). A very rapid chemical reaction occurred when a powdered ferrosilicate was gradually introduced to a chamber containing a strong hot solution of caustic soda. The result was very pure hydrogen which was stored in a gas holder. This system, designed by S. Cutler & Sons Ltd of Millwall, was fairly cheap to install but the chemicals were expensive.

In 1927, the Treasury approved funding for a second airship shed at Cardington. For speed and economy, it was decided to dismantle the existing No. 2 shed at Pulham. On 30 June 1927, a major contract was awarded to the Cleveland Bridge & Engineering Co Ltd for the dismantling, extending and re-erecting. This project was completed and handed over to the Air Ministry on 1 January 1929. The No. 1 shed at Pulham was eventually demolished in August 1948.

The *R100* was authorized in early 1924 for construction by the Airship Guarantee Co Ltd (a subsidiary of Vickers) inside the No. 2 shed at Howden. On 16 December 1929, it made its maiden flight, and was flown to Cardington to take part in trials prior to its historic flight to Canada and back to Cardington. Tragically, *R101* crashed at Beauvais, France in the early hours of 5 October 1930 with the loss of 43 lives. The Government finally decided not to go ahead with further airship development and as a result the *R100* was broken up inside the No. 1 shed at Cardington and sold for scrap in 1931. The No. 2 shed at Howden was demolished in the mid-1930s.

BARRAGE BALLOON STATIONS

A scheme was put forward on 5 September 1917 by Major General Ashmore, GOC London Air Defence Area, for a balloon barrage to protect the capital. His idea was that a balloon barrage consisting of several balloons of the Caquot type connected together by a cable with weighted wire streamers could form an 'apron'. Also, small balloons, each on a single light cable, would be suspended over the rivers Medway and Thames.

The scheme was approved in principal and trials took place at Richmond Park, but unfortunately the five Caquot balloons, joined at the top by a cross cable, broke away from their moorings killing two operators. Further trials with just three balloons proved very successful and on 22 September an order was issued to pilots that balloon aprons were to be established on a line east of Lewisham, east of Plumstead, 1 mile east of Barking, the east edge of Ilford, the east edge of Wanstead and the north edge of Tottenham. No machines were to fly across the lines during operations at a height less than 10,000 ft. The first apron was operating by 6 October 1917 and a request was made for more; by the end of the First World War two aprons were in operation. Major General Ashmore's request that the aprons should be retained during peacetime was turned down and the scheme was disbanded.

Between 1926 and 1928, barrage balloon design was researched. A balloon was made at Cardington, RAW Z1, and another produced by Spencers Ltd was known as the Spencer Z1. Both were unsuccessful, but another balloon, RAW Z2, became the first successful British high-altitude barrage balloon.

In 1929, the AOC-in-C of the Air Defence of Great Britain, Air Vice-Marshall Sir Edward Ellington, recommended that a balloon barrage should form part of the defence of London, and that in the event of war the barrage should be at a high state of readiness. He was of the opinion that the time had come to formulate a definite policy. He suggested that the height of the barrage should be limited to 9,000 ft and take the form of several balloons, suspended on their own independent cables. Experimental work on the design of balloons and cables, meanwhile, continued at Cardington.

After a conference held at the Air Ministry in 1932, approval was given for a low-altitude balloon barrage section to be formed in 1934, but because the balloons and winches were not then available it did not form at Cardington in 1935. Flight Lieutenant Harrison was appointed as First Officer of the Kite Balloon Section and the first balloon designed and built at Cardington for low-altitude work was known as the Low Zone (LZ) Kite Balloon. The first four took part in flying trials there; in May 1935 three were sent to Larkhill to form a barrage flight. Production barrage balloons were just over 62 ft long with a maximum diameter of 25 ft and a capacity of 19,000 cu ft, and filled with hydrogen.

Up to 1938, all balloon operations came under direct control of RAF Fighter Command, but in view of the importance now attached to barrage balloons it was decided that they should have a Command of their own. Balloon Command was therefore formed on 1 November 1938 and Air Vice-Marshall Boyd was appointed Commanding Officer. Balloon training was carried out at No. 1 Balloon Training Unit (BTU) at Cardington and No. 2 BTU Larkhill. Training included three months' driving and three months on balloon handling and wire rope splicing. At the end of the course, trainees took part in a 50 mile run in convoy to inflate a balloon and fly it. In August 1938, it was agreed to open the trade of balloon operator to man new balloon depots being formed around the country. The BTU closed in November 1943, having trained 5,000 RAF balloon operators, a similar number of WAAFs, and approximately 12,000 men and women operator/drivers.

The first balloon depots were planned in 1937 for the defence of London at Kidbrooke No. 1, Hook No. 2, Stanmore No. 3 and Chigwell No. 4. All subsequent depots were based on these designs. Group

The 1932 coupled balloon shed at Larkhill.

No. 2 Balloon Depot, Hook (Chessington), 1945

- **a** winch and trailer shed 2907/37
- **b** balloon sheds 7697/37
- **c** balloon hard standings
- **d** barracks 5170/40
- **e** sick quarters 5950/40
- **f** officers' mess 5169/37
- **g** guardhouse 5172/37
- **h** station headquarters 7779/37
- **i** flagstaff
- **j** decontamination centre 285/39
- **k** institute 5171/37
- **l** sergeants' mess 5170/37
- **m** dining room 5171/37
- **n** squadron offices 5174/37
- **o** MT section 7695/37
- **p** sleeping shelter KBC 103/40

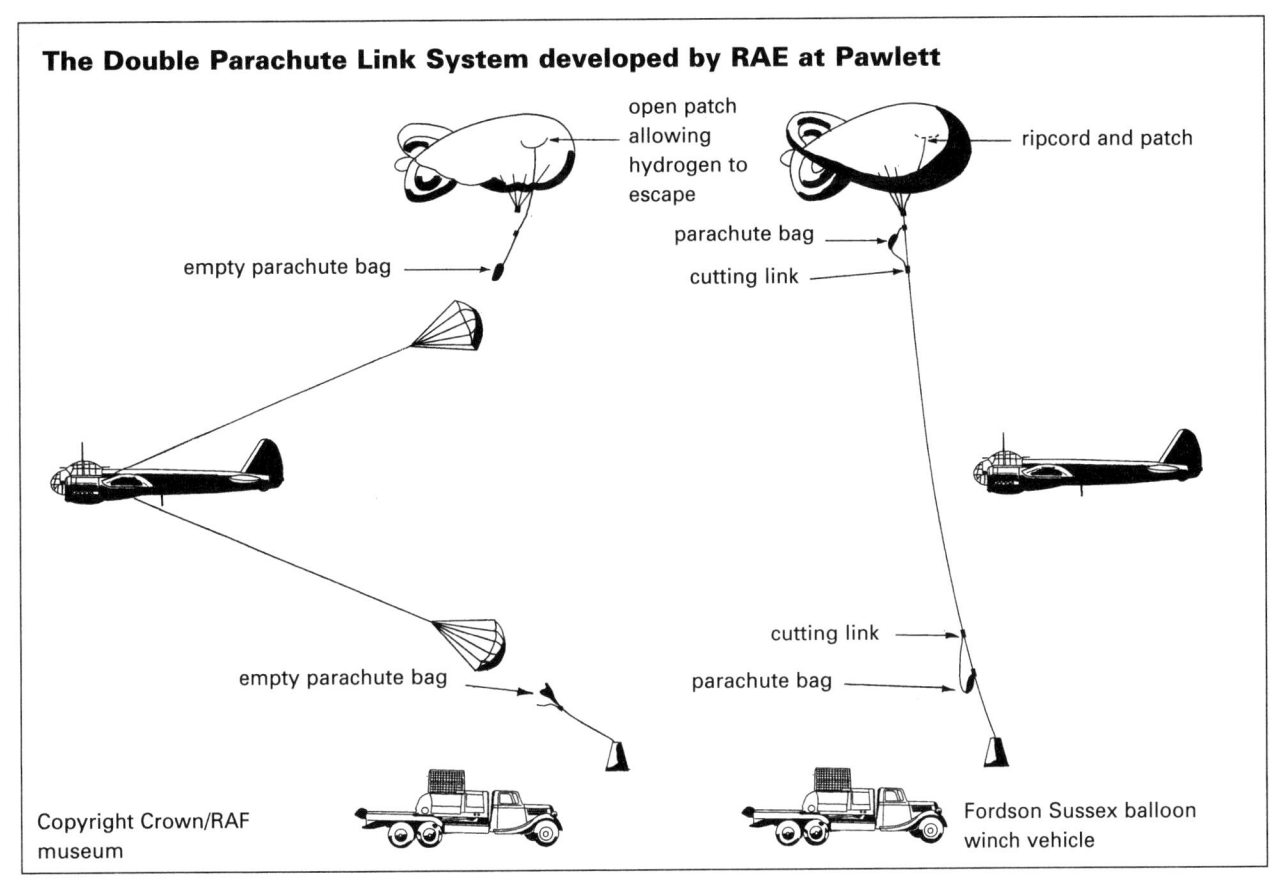

The Double Parachute Link System developed by RAE at Pawlett

Copyright Crown/RAF museum

headquarters were established at or near balloon depots; 30 Group, London; 31 Group, Birmingham; and 33 Group, Newcastle. Altogether 18 balloon depots were built near to city centres around the United Kingdom in 1938–40. Each was responsible for between one and four balloon squadrons, which in turn were based in one or more areas most vulnerable to air attack. These included major cities, ports, naval bases and industrial centres.

Cable-cutting experiments were carried out at Pawlett in Somerset where a huge balloon hangar still survives along with a fabric store and dispersed concrete mooring points. Here various ways of making balloon cables lethal were developed; one called the double parachute link went into production at the end of 1939. The balloon was connected by a single cable to a winch or anchorage point, the cable containing cutting links. A parachute pack was joined to the cable below the balloon and another above the winch. When an aircraft struck the cable, the force of impact sent a tension wave in both directions along it, causing the cutting links to sever the cable at both ends. Meanwhile, the aircraft flew on, taking the cable with it causing the two parachutes to open at the ends of the severed cable, creating a huge increase in drag which caused the aircraft to crash.

The RAF Airfield Construction Service was instructed in February 1944 to build anchorage points to provide a curtain of barrage balloons. This was to be assembled south of London to support RAF fighter and anti-aircraft defences against the threat of flying bombs. It became known as the Diver Balloon Barrage and was nominally sited between Gravesend and Redhill, initially involving 500 balloons. Diver was the code-name given to V-1s. When attacks began, the density was increased and the curtain extended westwards. Altogether some 1,750 Mk X balloons were used. Fitted with two extra cables, they proved very successful. By early 1945, the run-down was

A barrage balloon at Cardington in 1974.

The massive balloon hangar at Pawlett.

A barrage balloon mooring block at Pawlett.

underway and in January 1945 RAF Balloon Command was disbanded.

Accommodation was planned partly in light steel construction for the larger technical buildings and in Type A hutting for other technical and domestic buildings. There were a number of specialist buildings not seen elsewhere: winch lorry and trailer sheds, fabric-rigging shops and packed-balloon stores. The principle technical buildings are described below.

Balloon Sheds

The original four balloon depots were planned with balloon sheds designed by the Air Ministry architect N. S. Bellman to drawing 7697/37 but it is unclear exactly how many were built. They were constructed round a number of standard parts bolted together on site so that wall stanchions and roof ribs were spaced at 12 ft 6 in centres to form a seven-bay shed with a span of 63 ft, a length of 87 ft 6 in and a clear height of 33 ft. Doors were opened along projecting guide-rails and covered with canvas. Two were still extant at Hook in the early 1960s being used by 248 Maintenance Unit, but they have long since been demolished and no others are known to survive today.

The replacement design built by the British Steel Corporation to an Air Ministry specification to drawings 1361/39 and 1566/39 was significantly larger than the earlier shed. It was 100 ft long, with a clear width of 70 ft and a clear height of 50 ft and was built of a number of RSJ-type ribs and hipped roof sections spaced at 25 ft centres clad with Twin Twelve asbestos sheeting and patent glazing panels. The number of sheds depended on the number of squadrons with an additional one for instructional purposes. A three-squadron depot would normally have four; some stations such as Hook only had two (of the earlier design) with space allocated for a further four.

Sheds were built normally in-line with a concrete apron and branches leading off to 110 ft diameter balloon exercising standings, one for each shed.

Today, there are only a handful of surviving BSC sheds;

A balloon shed at Pucklechurch No. 11 Balloon Depot, near Bristol.

the one at Longbenton is used by Newcastle University, and three at Pucklechurch are used by light industry.

drawing no. 7697/37 1361/39 1566/39

Garages

When the first four London balloon depots were planned in 1937, it was thought that each squadron would require 28,800 sq ft for a winch lorry and trailer garage, plus an additional 57,600 sq ft for a workshop and an instructional area. At a three-squadron station, the size of shed or sheds to house them would therefore be very large indeed. At Hook, for example, a two-squadron station had one building 288 ft by 100 ft containing a garage and instructional area, and a further building of similar dimensions containing a garage for the second squadron. All later stations built in and around other cities were planned on a smaller scale. At a typical three-squadron station, such as Norton or Sutton Coldfield, the building was 288 ft by 200 ft. Titchfield, defending Southampton and Portsmouth, housed four squadrons. The building was 400 ft by 200 ft.

Construction was of a series of main rolled steel stanchions spaced at 24 ft centres with intermediate rolled steel stanchions, both supporting a lattice girder carrying 100 ft span roof trusses at 16 ft centres. The side framing (without intermediate stanchions) had 12 ft wide Kinnear roller shutters giving a clear height of 13 ft.

drawing no. 1674/39 1675/39 3433/39

Hydrogen Trailer Sheds

Building length varied from site to site; at Hook and Stanmore it was 120 ft (10 bays), while at Chigwell and Kidbrooke it was 180 ft (15 bays). Built in 12 ft wide bays with a clear height of 13 ft, they had openings on both sides with roller shutters front and rear. Construction was RSJ-type framing, supporting standard 45 ft long steel roof trusses, with walls clad in Twin Twelve asbestos sheeting, the gable ends having a 4 ft wide glazing panel. The roof was lined with Handcraft asbestos tiles.

drawing no. 12936/38

Packed-balloon Stores

The building was 112 ft 6 in by 31 ft, the walls being 13 ft

A balloon shed at Norton No. 16 Balloon Depot, near Sheffield.

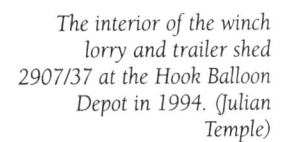

The interior of the winch lorry and trailer shed 2907/37 at the Hook Balloon Depot in 1994. (Julian Temple)

The guardhouse (5172/37) at Hook Balloon Depot. It is a sectional timber Type A hut. (Photographed 1994)

Squadron offices in sectional timber hutting at Longbenton Balloon Depot. (Photographed 1990)

6 in high. Built of RSJs at 12 ft 6 in centres with timber studwork framing supporting Twin Twelve sheeting. The roof was clad with Handcraft tiles. It had four steel cowl-type air ventilators. There were four sliding door openings, one at each end with two on each side wall, served by overhead runway beams that terminated outside the building supported by steel trestles. Packed balloons were received at one end of the building using a block and tackle, stored and then dispatched on request through the other end, again using the block and tackle, and loaded on to a waiting lorry.

Squadron Offices, Stores and Workshops

Originally a single large squadron office, store and workshop building was planned, but on later stations each squadron had its own buildings. They were detached, built in rows behind the winch trolley and trailer shed as at Titchfield, or attached at one end to the squadron balloon shed as at Pucklechurch. The building at Hook (5174/37) was 170 ft long with a span of 52 ft and walls 12 ft 6 in high. The main portion was a fabric shop with a partition separating it from a rigging shop. The office accommodation on the ground floor included rooms for the station adjutant, commanding officer, WCs, and a ready-use store. A staircase led up to five small offices with top lighting from a large roof light.

Construction details are similar to those of buildings on stations later than Hook. They were built of RSJ-type stanchions at 10 ft centres supporting steel roof trusses, timber studwork and standard metal windows between stanchions. The remaining gaps were clad with timber weatherboarding. The roof was clad with Handcraft tiles.

drawing no. 5174/37

PART 4

HANGARS

AEROPLANE SHEDS AND HANGARS 1913–19

The layout and size of Home Defence and Training Depot Stations depended not only on when the station was built but also on the number of flights or squadrons based there. Elmswell, a RFC 6th Brigade Flight Station, for example, was quite small with just two permanent aircraft sheds and a Bessonneau hangar for two Home Defence flights. East Retford, a 6th Brigade Night Training Station, had four 80 ft span general service sheds accommodating two Home Defence squadrons. Training Depot Stations and Wing Headquarters aerodromes such as Scampton had six 80 ft span general service sheds. (Hangars were originally called sheds except in the case of tents which were called hangars; for example, the Bessonneau hangar.)

With the introduction of Anderson Belfast trusses for use on end-opening aircraft sheds, it was now possible to build sheds in multiple spans. The general layout of sheds used on TDS aerodromes was therefore changed to three pairs of coupled sheds; a single-span shed was used by the Aeroplane Repair Section (ARS). Examples of such aerodromes include Andover, Duxford, Feltwell, and Hucknall. This arrangement was continued until the end of the First World War.

Aircraft Acceptance Parks (AAPs) came into being in 1917 to receive aircraft from the factories for flight testing, storage and distribution to operational squadrons. Too numerous to list here, but typical examples included No. 2 (Northern) Marine Acceptance Depot at Brough, adjacent to the Blackburn Aeroplane Company works, for the reception of seaplanes and flying boats from Phoenix Dynamo Ltd, Dick Kerr Ltd, Brush Electrical Ltd, and Robey & Co Ltd. The No. 1 Aircraft Acceptance Park at Coventry was close to the Daimler works for receiving of RE8s manufactured by the Coventry Ordnance Works, Daimler, the Siddeley-Deasy Motor Car Company, the Standard Motor Company, as well as DH9s from the Vulcan Motor and Engineering Company and SE5as from Wolseley Motors. In contrast to the operational and training aerodromes, AAPs were designed with large numbers of aeroplane sheds although at many sites the projected number had to be reduced when the war ended.

The standard AAP hangar was the triple-span general service shed. The first of these to be built had 80 ft spans, such as at Filton (No. 5 AAP) where three sets of triple sheds were built in a row with another set and an Aeroplane Repair Section shed built on another part of the aerodrome. Next came the 100 ft span version at aerodromes such as Bracebridge Heath (No. 4 AAP) and South Shotwick (Sealand). Here again three sets of triple-span general service sheds were provided. Later still, large storage sheds consisting of seven 70 ft span sheds coupled together for the storage of Handley-Page 0/400 aircraft were provided at Aircraft Repair Depots such as Coal Aston (No. 2 Northern ARD) and Henlow (No. 5 Eastern ARD). All are now demolished but a coupled and a five-bay version survive at Netheravon.

Side-opening Aeroplane Sheds

The earliest known aircraft shed similar to the 1913 pattern shed was erected in 1909 at Eastchurch, Kent by William Harbrow for Short Brothers. This became the standard RFC hangar until replaced by the bow-strung truss end-opening sheds of 1916. The layout and position of these sheds was either side by side in a crescent shape with technical buildings behind as at Montrose, or side by side in a straight line following a boundary. Many stations were extended later in the war and quite often new sheds of the end-opening type were built on a detached site well away from the original camp as at London Colney.

They were built as single (Netheravon) or coupled sheds (Montrose) and construction varied from steel frame and steel roof trusses (Catterick) to timber frame and timber roof trusses (Biggin Hill). Wall cladding also varied from concrete blocks (Catterick) or corrugated asbestos sheeting (Biggin Hill) to corrugated iron (Filton). The main ridge line followed the longitudinal axis with two short ridge lines at right angles to the main trusses above the access door openings; each had four timber-framed and timber-clad sliding doors. Timber trusses were of sandwich construction with both principal rafters and tie-beam made from three laminated sections bolted together. The tie-beam, wall posts and principal rafters were supported at both ends of the trusses by timber knee-braces, metal straps and gusset boards. Between tie-beam and principal rafters were diagonal timber compression

RFC 1913 pattern side-opening aeroplane shed at Netheravon.

struts with vertical iron tension bolts. Each truss was cross-braced to its neighbour by timber struts for bracing against strong winds. Along the ridge line were louvred air vents or air cowls. Office, store, dressing-room, and workshop accommodation were in an annexe, with a single-pitched roof, along the rear elevation.

(dimensions apply to all drawing no.)
span	65 ft
length single	160 ft
double	211 ft
clear door opening	58 ft 6 in
clear height	15 ft

description	drawing no.	examples
	84/13, 232/14, 250/15, 251/15	Filton, Netheravon, Montrose, Guernsey (transferred from Leighterton in 1920s)
wireless testing flight shed	25/17–29/17	Biggin Hill
AID shed, Grade 2 listed	34/17	Farnborough
sheds 60, 67, 80 surveyed and redrawn in 1925	1473/25	Catterick

Aeroplane Twin Shed

This was an all timber end-opening (one end only) coupled shed consisting of braced laminated wall posts spaced at 11 ft 3 in centres supporting laminated timber composite trusses with vertical iron tension rods and timber diagonal compression struts. The ends of trusses were anchored to the wall posts; angled bracing was by knee-braces and gusset boards. Walls and roof were clad with timber boarding, and canvas doors opened full width along the front elevation. The opposite gable end had large louvered air vents in lieu of door openings.

The only known examples still in-situ are two pairs at Hainault Farm but although the impressive timber framework is complete, the walls are now of concrete; Brooklands Museum had a few trusses that originally came from Goldhanger and these have now been acquired by a local preservation group who wish to re-erect the shed at North Weald on a site close to the First World War site.

drawing. no	span	width	clear opening	no. of bays	example
56/17	60 ft	11 ft 3 in	15 ft	12	Hainault Farm

Bessonneau Hangar Type H

This was the first standard transportable RFC/RAF hangar and remained the standard until the Bellman hangar was invented in 1936. It was a structure of wood and canvas designed to be re-erected by 20 skilled men in 48 hours.

Bessonneau hangar Type H at Weathersfield.

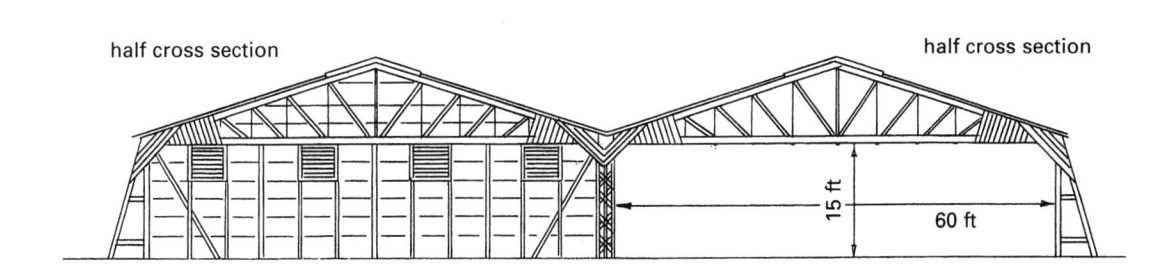

Aeroplane Twin Shed, 51/17

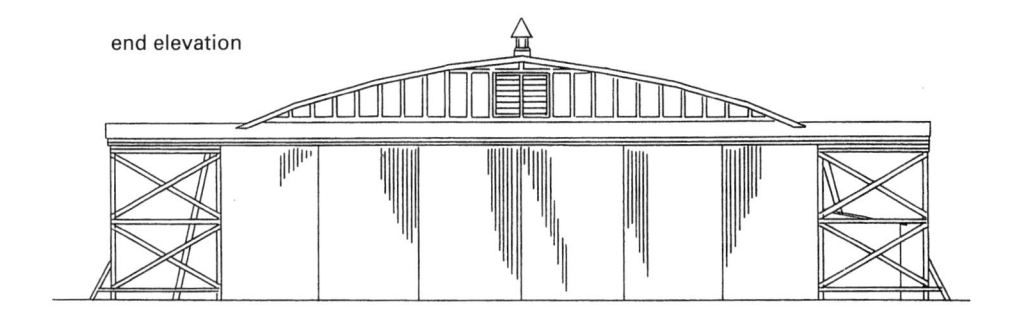

RFC General Service Flight Shed, 146/16

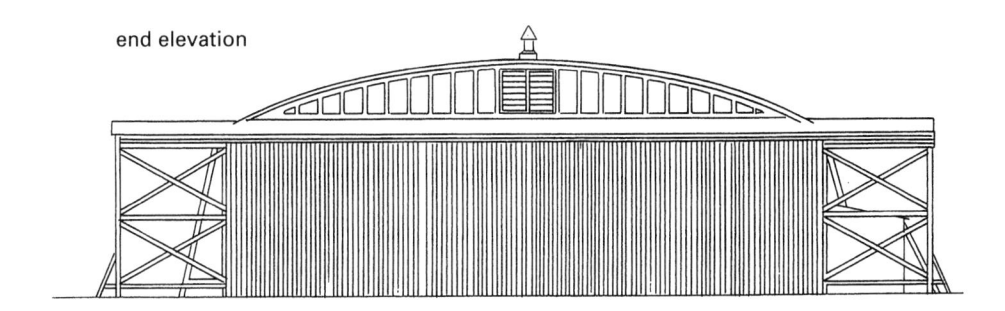

RFC General Service Aeroplane Shed, 68/17

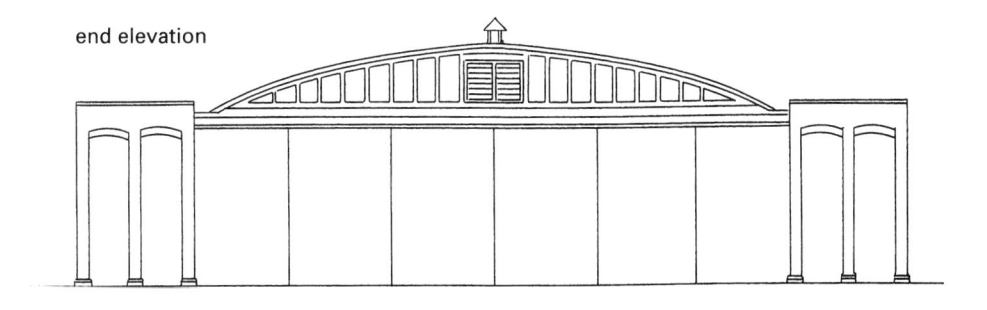

RFC General Service Aeroplane Repair Section Shed (Lympne RFC Dispatching Station), 164/17

A general view of Mount Batten, showing two Admiralty Type F seaplane sheds in their original First World War positions.

Timber A-frame stanchions were spaced at 13 ft 2 in centres supporting timber trusses. The whole hangar was clad with heavy canvas; canvas doors opened one end only.

Almost all RAF Bessonneau hangars have been sold to private owners who have removed them. There are still examples *in situ* at Odiham and Weston-super-Mare.

span	length	clear height	no. of bays
64 ft 10 in	79 ft 7 in	13 ft	6
64 ft 10 in	118 ft 6 in	13 ft	9

Admiralty Seaplane Sheds

The Type F was a 1916 side-opening (one end only) steel-framed seaplane shed consisting of stanchions at 12 ft 10 in centres with alternate ones supported by steel rakers. Roof trusses over the door opening were supported by a lattice girder spanning the width of the opening. Wall cladding was originally of corrugated asbestos sheeting but on some sheds this was later replaced with corrugated iron. Workshop and office accommodation was located in a rear single-pitched roof annexe.

Many of these hangars were removed from former First World War RNAS seaplane bases throughout the 1930s and rebuilt on new Armament Training Schools and Air Observer Schools such Acklington, Evanton, and Sutton Bridge. Wright Anderson & Co Ltd was the main contractor for erecting the F shed at Sutton Bridge.

The Type G was basically a smaller version of the Type F shed built from 1916 on RNAS seaplane bases. This was a side-opening steel-framed shed with a 90 ft long steel lattice girder supporting the main door opening. Normally built with 12 15 ft wide bays with a span of 60 ft. Composite timber trusses similar to the 1916 general service flight shed trusses or steel trusses were used. A workshop could be housed inside a lean-to annexe at the rear.

Type	span	width	length	height	examples
F	100 ft		200 ft	28 ft	Calshot (triple shed – Grade 2* listed), Cranwell, Mount Batten, Rochester
G	60 ft	80 ft 7 in (including annex)	180 ft	18 ft 6 in	Calshot (Grade 2* listed), Lee-on-Solent (2), Mount Batten

General Service Sheds

This flight shed design was the first of a new type of end-

An Admiralty Type F seaplane shed. This was re-erected at Pembrey in the mid-1930s.

Another Admiralty Type F seaplane shed; this one was re-erected at Stormy Down in the mid-1930s.

An admiralty Type G seaplane shed, re-erected at Wimbledon.

opening aeroplane sheds with a characteristic composite curved bow-strung truss roof.

The roof was constructed of 18 timber trusses spaced at 10 ft centres with a span of 80 ft. All trusses had a tie-beam made up of two sections of 9 inches by 1.5 inches timber scarfed together by timber connectors. The upper chord was made from eight lengths of timber giving the truss a roughly curved, polygonal shape. Each length was made from a laminate of three 8-inch by 2-inch pieces of timber, the lengths being joined by a Y-shaped steel plate. One arm of the Y was bolted to diagonal compression struts joining the upper chord with connectors between the two sections of the tie-beam. Vertical steel tension tie-rods also joined the upper chord to the tie-beam. Each truss was cross-braced to its neighbour for resistance to sideways movement, and two longitudinal beams ran the whole length of the shed. The trusses were clad with 1-inch tongued-and-grooved boarding nailed to timber purlins which were protected from the weather by bitumen felt. Along the centre of the roof were four metal air ventilator cowls. Construction of the composite roof truss seems to have ceased by the middle of 1917 and was replaced by ROK roofing (Belfast Truss).

Timber wall posts were also made of laminated sections consisting of three 9-inch by 3-inch pieces bolted together which supported each truss. Timber knee-braces joined the tie-beam to the wall post but later buildings had external angled timber struts for bracing against the wind. Wall cladding was Hy-Rib expanded-metal sheeting nailed to each wall post and rendered both sides with Gunlite or similar sand and cement rendering to a thickness of 2 inches. Alternatively, corrugated iron or timber wallboards covered with bituminous felt were used.

Natural lighting was provided by 5 ft by 9 ft metal windows fitted vertically in each bay except those nearest the shed doors which were cross-braced for added support against the wind.

On each end wall were six timber-framed doors clad with corrugated iron sheeting or vertical timber board. Each door ran along steel guides set into a concrete strip. The remaining floor area was earth and consequently, where these buildings have been demolished, the concrete door runners are sometimes all that remains. Above the doors, projecting out from each side wall, was an angled door guide that also helped to protect the top of the doors from the weather. The projecting door guide was supported by a timber gantry made up of four laminated posts, two at the front and two behind, separated by a gap for three doors at each side of the shed. Both front and rear posts were cross-braced top and bottom. The outer posts were further braced for sideways movement with angle struts. Above the door guide, the front truss was clad with panelled asbestos sheeting and the centre panel was a louvered air vent.

A few buildings had a lean-to annexe along a side elevation covering seven bays. This contained a dressing-room, office, store workshops and a boiler-room. Each room had one 3 ft 6 in wide steel window except for one which had a doorway instead.

This building type is now quite rare.

The construction of the last 80 ft span general service sheds was completely different to that of the earlier type. Timber cladding or cement/Hy-Rib walls gave way to 4.5-inch brick and timber wall posts, while struts gave way to tapering 1 ft 6 in by 4 ft 6 in brick buttresses. Coupled sheds now had wall piers of brick and arches to support the ends of Belfast trusses of both spans rather than timber. Also, brick-built door gantries were constructed to house timber-framed and asbestos-clad door leaves when pushed open and consisted of six brick piers supported two 20 ft high large-radius arches both sides of the door runners.

Single-span ARS sheds retained four large air vents along the ridge line, while coupled or triple sheds were deprived of the natural light from windows along the side walls and instead had pitched skylights.

One side wall of a coupled shed had a seven-bay annexe containing a store; three dressing-rooms and three offices. The opposite side wall had a lean-to workshop annexe covering six bays and a single storeroom. Access to the workshops from inside the hangar was through brick arches. The single-span ARS shed had only one annexe containing a five-bay workshop, office, and boiler-room, with similar brick arches to the workshop bays.

The 100 ft span sheds were the last First World War hangars to use entirely timber for the construction of roof trusses. The width of each bay increased from 10 ft 6 in to 11 ft 6 in and the brick buttresses were enlarged in thickness from 18 inches to 23 inches to support an increase of 5 ft in wall height. Walls were still 4.5 inches wide but the number of bays was reduced from 16 to 15. Hangars with the normal six door arrangement, as built at Eastleigh and Brockworth, had a door gantry similar to the 80 ft span shed with the difference in height (5 ft) being added in brick on top of the arches. Furthermore, the brick piers were joined together by brickwork for the first 5 ft. The arches, unlike on the 80 ft span shed, were of small radius.

A different door arrangement came into use after June 1918; the openings were changed to receive Esavian Type 120 concertina-folding teak doors. Examples included Duxford, Ford, and Aldeburgh. The large brick gantry was removed and brick door stops (L-shape in plan) were built instead. This not only affected aerodromes in the planning stage but also those under construction. At Leuchars, for example, the construction of coupled sheds was well advanced before work had started on the Aeroplane Repair Section shed and therefore the former had doors with flat sheeting while the ARS featured Esavian doors.

Two versions of coupled general service shed were built at Henlow Eastern Aircraft Repair Depot. This design was of similar construction to the 100 ft span general service shed except that it had a Dorman Long steel truss roof and was the last design of this family of hangars.

The width of each bay was increased from 11 ft 6 in to 19 ft but 4.5-inch walls were retained as were the 23-inch

A coupled general service shed at Old Sarum. The single span is 80 ft.

RAF general service shed 2010/18 at Henlow.

A coupled general service shed at Marske. The single span is 100 ft. The shed has brick ends for Esavian folding doors. (Photographed 1982)

brick buttresses. The number of bays was reduced from 15 to nine, making the shed approximately the same length as the earlier general service sheds. The walls of each bay of coupled sheds had four steel window sashes (two on the ground floor and two above), except for end bays which had two windows at first-floor level. The ARS shed had two windows at first-floor level of each bay except the end bays which had a single window both sides.

The ARS shed had an annexe on a side wall elevation covering three bays, containing an instrument repair shop, draughtsmen's office, general office, two other offices, inspection room, and boiler-room. On the opposite side at each end of the building were two 58 ft by 34 ft plane store annexes with pitched roof and Esavian folding doors.

The front and last bays of the coupled shed contained a two-storey annexe with a workshop at ground-floor level with a store above. The single-pitched roof was of the same angle as the roof of the main shed. The centre bay of

Another coupled general service shed with 100 ft single spans. This one is at Eastleigh. (Photographed in 1989)

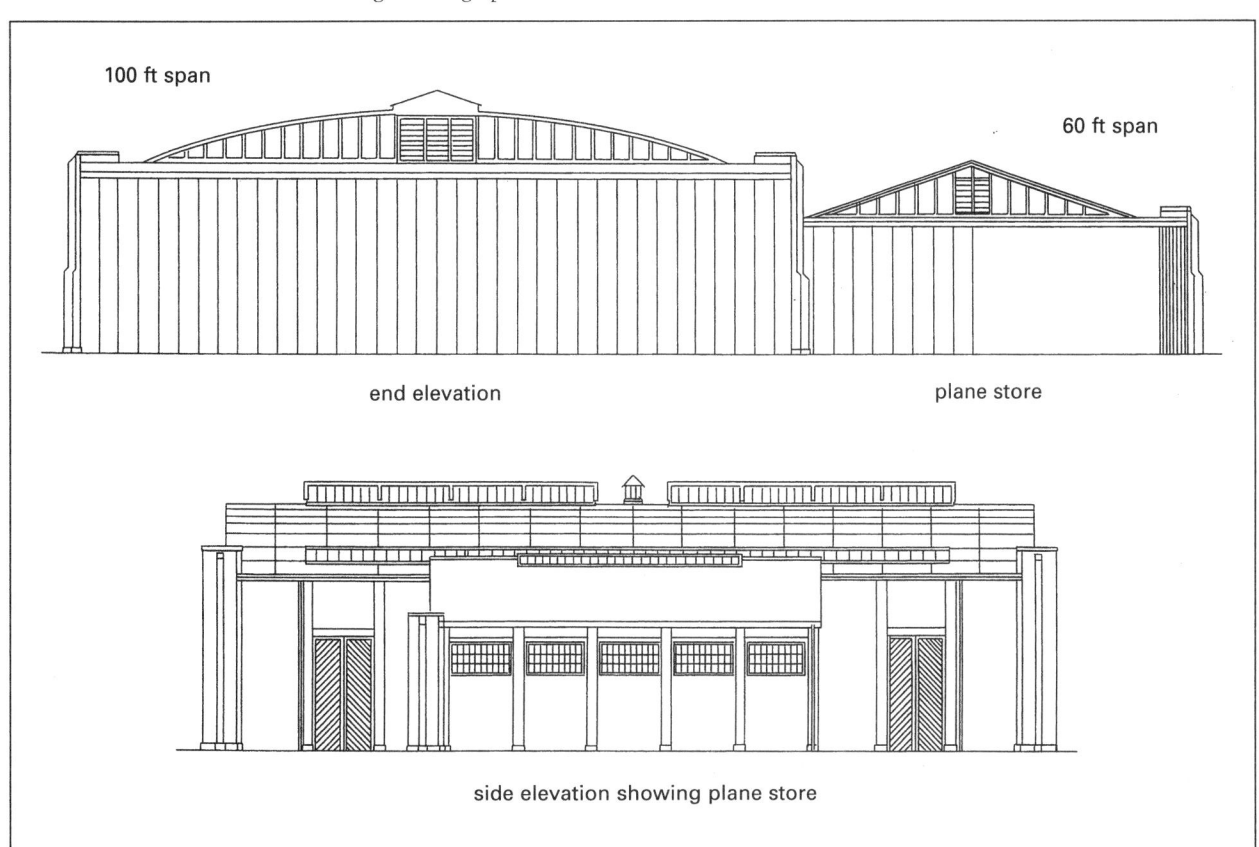

100 ft span

60 ft span

end elevation

plane store

side elevation showing plane store

Aldeburgh Two Squadron Training Depot Aeroplane Repair Section Shed and Plane Store, 584/18

one side wall contained a boiler-room with tall chimney.

Two types of steep-pitched Dorman Long steel roof trusses were used. A special truss was used above the door opening and was suitably braced against the wind while the remaining bays had standard trusses. They were all covered with black-painted corrugated iron sheeting. Dorman Long skylights were fitted along the ridge line with shallow-pitch glazing panels. Each gable end contained a louvered air ventilator in the centre of the gable. The remaining area was clad with corrugated iron. Doors were Esavian folding type or steel-framed with corrugated iron sheeting. The coupled shed at Henlow used the wall of the two-storey workshop and store annexe as a door gantry with a simple brick end-stop similar to that used on Esavian doors.

Few of these aircraft sheds were built because the RAF (as it became in April 1918) had more than enough large-span hangars. Furthermore, many airfields became redundant at the end of the First World War as the RAF reorganized itself to peacetime. There was a hangar of this type planned for the Biggin Hill Wireless Flight but it is unclear if this was ever built.

Belfast Trusses

An advertisement for McTear & Co Ltd published in the Dublin Builder for 1 October 1866 is the earliest known reference to the Belfast truss roof. This early design differed from those used from 1917 on aeroplane sheds in that the lattice bracing between the bowed upper chord member and the lower chord member was arranged as two interlocking fans. The angle of the lattice bars represented setting-out lines (in degrees) worked out from a point where both wall posts at both ends of the truss met the floor to a point on the curved bow. McTear ceased trading in 1903 and the construction of the truss was continued in Belfast by a number of companies. One of these, D. Anderson & Co Ltd, a trader in felt from 1895 and a builder of roofs from 1877, actively marketed the Anderson Belfast truss ROK Roofing in the early 1900s. By 1915, the company was advertising in *Flight*. The first sheds built for aircraft in 1913–14 were at Hamble Point and consisted of a coupled shed, and a single-span shed was built at Calshot, now a Grade 2* listed building. This new type of aeroplane shed was exactly the same size, of the same construction and layout as the earlier 1916 flight shed except that it had a Belfast truss roof instead of the composite bow-strung truss roof.

The Belfast truss was very economical to produce and consisted of a curved laminated upper chord and laminated tie-beam with close-mesh lattice bars set in a criss-cross pattern between the two members. The curved bow was made up of four individual sections of two 3-inch by 3-inch rib sections sandwiched side by side by the lattice bars. The ends of the bow were anchored to the tie-beam by knee-braces and gusset boards which secured the truss to the laminated timber wall posts and angled bracing struts. The trusses were externally clad with 1-inch tongued-and-grooved boarding fixed diagonally and covered with bitumen felt. This was known as ROK roofing.

There were other differences between this and the earlier end-opening shed. Although similar steel window frames were used, they were fitted horizontally and therefore covered the whole width between the wall posts. The outside appearance of the Belfast roof appears to be a perfectly smooth curve whereas the curve of the bow-strung truss roof is roughly polygonal.

Originally both hangar types had earth floors. Later, when a hard surface was laid, a trench was dug from the heating chamber in the boiler-room to the opposite side wall and pipes were laid to distribute heat round the shed.

Three coupled sheds were built at Hendon in 1917–18; two hangars survive today as part of the RAF Museum and are Grade 2 listed buildings. The timber door gantries have been removed and the walls have been bricked up but internal inspection reveals a very impressive structure. Between the two spans of each coupled shed, and supporting the ends of the trusses, are sets of four laminated wall posts. A modern steel-framed bowed roof

The interior of a coupled general service shed at Ford, showing the Belfast truss roof girders.

section connects the original pair of sheds and has timber-framed doors on two side elevations. These are similar to the original main doors of which one set remains.

Clearly the Hendon hangars have many features of an early general service shed such as timber door gantries and laminated-timber wall posts. The brick wall cladding between the wall posts may well be original, which suggests that these hangars represent a development phase between the earlier semi-permanent sheds and the brick sheds built after 1918.

In addition to these sheds, Aeronautical Inspection Department (AID) sheds (127/17) and AID tuning sheds were erected on the north-east side of Hendon aerodrome. Two 480 ft by 100 ft AID sheds, each with six 80 ft span openings were built. Side walls had 20 ft long precast concrete posts and struts. Internal posts between spans were simple cast concrete columns with holes for angled struts supporting the roof trusses. There were no internal walls, just exposed columns. The tuning shed was of similar construction although the precast concrete wall posts were slightly different.

drawing no.	span	length	clear door height	no. of bays	examples
43/17	80 ft	170 ft 9 in			(with Belfast trusses)
44/17	80 ft	170 ft 9 in			(with Belfast trusses)
67/17	80 ft				AID shed (with Belfast trusses)
68/17	80 ft				AID shed (with Belfast trusses)
127/17	80 ft	45 ft			Hendon
142/16–158/16	80 ft	170 ft	20 ft		Yatesbury (3 still extant, Grade 2 listed)
164/17, 165/17, 172/17–175/17					Lympne (with Belfast trusses) Coupled shed (with Belfast trusses)
373/17–375/17	100 ft				
568/18	100 ft	172 ft 6 in	25 ft	15 at 11 ft 6 in centres	Henlow ARS shed
2010/18					Coupled shed

Plane Stores

Later single-span Aeroplane Repair Section sheds had either one (Aldeburgh) or two (Fowlmere and Feltwell) plane store annexes along one side wall. At Aldeburgh, the annexe measured 60 ft by 60 ft with 4.5 inch walls, brick piers, a pitched roof of timber trusses and Esavian folding doors at one end only.

The only known plane store to survive today is at London Colney. This was a detached building and originally had Esavian folding doors but these unfortunately were removed, and it has a new roof.

As the plane store was attached to a side wall, it was necessary to have roof lights on this side only.

A 1916 RFC general service flight shed at Montrose.

A 1914 seaplane shed at Calshot with a Belfast truss roof. It is now a Grade 2 listed building. (Photographed 1994)*

drawing no.	span	length	clear door height	example
584/18	100 ft	126 ft	25 ft	Aldeburgh

Running Shed

In front of the hangars and facing the aerodrome at Aircraft Acceptance Parks was usually a single or coupled running shed. This was a small open (no doors) aircraft shelter consisting of five brick piers spaced at 10 ft centres supporting a course-mesh Belfast-type truss roof. The ends of the trusses and the roof were clad with flat asbestos sheeting.

drawing no.	span (single)	length	clear height
110/17			
175/17	60 ft	40 ft	19 ft 6 in

Handley-Page Sheds

The assembly of Handley-Page 0/400 aircraft was subcontracted to various companies and special storage sheds were designed for Aircraft Repair Depots and Aircraft Acceptance Parks.

The AAP storage shed was intended to house 12 Handley-Page bombers, 10 with wings folded. It was built of 4.5-inch walls with brick buttresses at 12 ft 9 in centres, consisting of five 70 ft span bays, each separated by a 4.5-inch wall with brick piers supporting steel roof trusses; doors opened full width front and rear. Also, two coupled 82 ft 3 in span bays, each with steel-framed trusses, were built against one side wall with side openings of 70 ft so that all openings were on the same elevation. Doors were originally of the sliding type with door gantries of brick, but at Henlow, Esavian folding doors were used.

An end-opening coupled shed (one end only) with walls and buttresses of weathered Bath stone blocks in 12 bays was built at Netheravon. Over each span were standard steel trusses and a special truss was fitted over the front bay. Esavian folding doors opened full width. A five-bay Handley-Page shed is also still extant at Netheravon which, until 1995, was still used for housing aircraft.

drawing no.	span	width	length	clear height	examples
1397/18	70 ft	170 ft	544 ft	30 ft	Coal Aston, Henlow
	44 ft (single)		149 ft (approx)	24 ft	Netheravon

Interwar Hangars

Type A Aeroplane Shed

This was the first of the permanent end-opening hangars of the interwar period. Designed in 1924, it was the largest and became the standard RAF shed until replacement in the mid-1930s RAF expansion period. Built on permanent RAF aerodromes from 1925 until 1940, the number of hangars at each site varied from a single shed at Catfoss to six at Upper Heyford. Some

A Handley-Page aeroplane storage shed at Henlow No. 5 Eastern Aircraft Repair Depot. This was built to store 12 Handley-Page 0/400s.

A coupled Handley-Page storage shed at Netheravon.

half end elevation

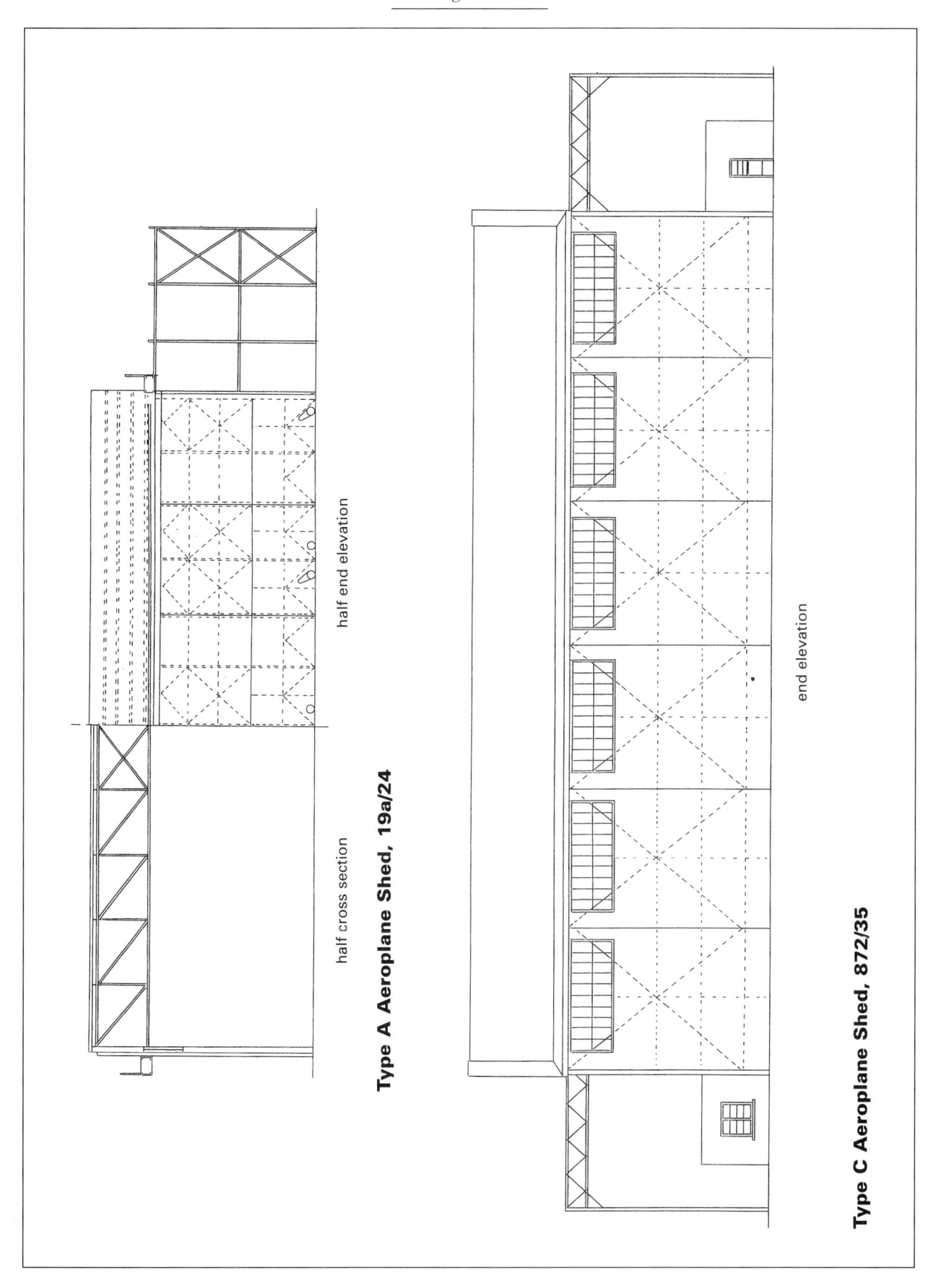

half cross section

Type A Aeroplane Shed, 19a/24

end elevation

Type C Aeroplane Shed, 872/35

A Type A hangar at Abingdon.

A Hinaidi hangar at Chivenor.

stations such as North Weald – one of the first airfields chosen to have Type A sheds – only had two hangars, arranged in a crescent with a gap in the centre for a future shed. Mildenhall's hangars were built to a 1931 contract. The last two hangars were erected around 1940 at Burtonwood and Silloth. A number of different contractors were involved including Herbertson & Co Ltd (Silloth), Nortons Ltd (Tividale), and Wright Anderson & Co Ltd (Mildenhall).

Steel stanchions spaced at 38 ft 4 in centres supported steel-framed roof girders with cantilever gable trusses (ridge and valley) running longitudinally. Steel doors at each end in four leaves opened the full width along door guides supported by braced stanchions. Wall infilling consisted of reinforced concrete 14 inches thick up to a height of 12 ft, then 9 inches thick for another 8 ft with patent Mellows wired glazing above, and finally gable ends of brickwork supported on RSJs. In contrast, the single shed at Silloth was clad with Twin Twelve asbestos cement sheeting except for an 8 ft wide glazing strip.

Workshop annexes with single-pitched roofs were built along the side walls.

drawing no.	span	length	clear door height	examples
19a/24, 564/31, 2355/40	122 ft 5 in	249 ft	30 ft	Bicester, Catfoss, Upper Heyford

Hinaidi Aircraft Shed

This semi-permanent shed was designed by the Air Ministry Directorate of Works in 1927 as a quick and cheap hangar design for stations overseas. To save time and to keep conformity of parts, the structure was based on Admiralty Type F hangars that already existed on former First World War seaplane bases. The basic structure of the old shed was redesigned as an end-opening hangar. They were initially built to supplement existing hangars abroad but were later built at home stations such as Spittlegate and Lee-on-Solent. Meanwhile, many Type F sheds were removed from redundant seaplane bases and re-erected at the new Air Armament Training Schools and Air Observer Schools. The new end-opening hangar, now known as a Hinaidi, was used mainly on new Technical Training Establishments which were being built at Melksham, Hereford, Kirkham, and Weeton.

It was constructed with a system of lattice wall stanchions supporting steel-frame roof trusses with longitudinal bracing. Cladding was normally Twin Twelve asbestos sheeting or similar. The door opened to full width at each end and sometimes there was a single-pitched workshop along one side wall.

drawing no.	span	length	clear door height	examples
1136/27	100 ft	240 ft	23 ft	Chivenor, Madley

Type B Aeroplane Shed

With Air Ministry specifications for new heavy bombers being constrained by existing hangar widths and heights, there was an urgent need for new standard permanent RAF hangars large enough to accommodate future aircraft designs due to enter service.

The standard RAF hangar of the late 1920s was the Type A and it was this basic design that the Air Ministry had to improve. The result was a prototype hangar known as Goliath built at Martlesham Heath in 1929 – its construction was similar to Type A but it was much larger.

It was built with a system of lattice stanchions at 34 ft 4 in centres (4 ft less than for Type A) and intermediate RSJ-type stanchions supporting lattice girders with longitudinal portal roof trusses with ridge and valley gable ends. Wall infilling was of 14-inch reinforced concrete with a strip of patent Mellows glazing above. Six sliding doors at each end opened to full width. Office and workshop accommodation was arranged along the side walls with a steep single-pitched roof similar to the A Type.

Although the Martlesham Heath hangar was a prototype, two more were built in 1934 at Pembroke Dock, and a fourth and final example was erected at Rhu in 1942. The reason why this obsolete design was chosen for these two sites was that its clear height of 40 ft made it ideal for large seaplanes. Like Martlesham Heath, the hangars at Pembroke Dock were built as permanent sheds but that at Rhu was redesigned as a temporary structure based on 1933 drawings. The basic steelwork of all four hangars was the same but the hangar at Rhu was clad with corrugated iron and, like Pembroke Dock, doors opened at one end only.

drawing no.	span	length	clear height	examples
1455/27, 2188/27	160 ft	273 ft	40 ft	Martlesham Heath
454/33, 1414/33–1431/33	160 ft	90 ft	40 ft	Pembroke Dock
4714/41, 154/42	160 ft	120 ft	40 ft	Rhu

Type C Aeroplane Shed

With the many new stations of permanent construction required under the RAF Expansion Scheme, and anticipating the need to house larger aircraft, it was decided that a new standard hangar was required with a clear span of 150 ft, clear length of 300 ft and a clear height of 35 ft. These dimensions would now allow new specifications to be issued to aircraft manufacturers to design heavy bomber aircraft with a wingspan greater than 100 ft. The hangar design chosen to meet these requirements became known as the Type C and after many modifications became the standard permanent RAF hangar.

The first examples were built with the steelwork clothed in brick (or Bath stone) of a class in keeping with the other station buildings as it was appreciated that hangars of such dimensions would dominate both the station and countryside. The designers took public opinion into account, and architectural treatment and style was such that distant views of groups of plain engineering structures were avoided.

Hangars of this type were erected at almost all of the early expansion period stations – both operational and training. Although a height of 35 ft was excessive for fighter aircraft, it was thought necessary in case of a change in the function of the station.

The steel structure was different from aircraft shed Type B, and spacing between lattice wall stanchions was reduced to 25 ft, taking away the need for intermediate stanchions. The wall stanchions supported lattice roof girders which were separated by portal roof trusses. The original 1934 design had traditional gabled roof rafters similar to the previous two sheds, but from 1935 this was changed to a hipped shape. This was exposed above the side walls except at the end bays where the wall was carried above the gabled/hipped trusses. Roof covering consisted of timber purlins and timber boarding with asbestos slates. Walls were initially clad with brick but in 1936, in anticipation of enemy bombing, a change was made to reinforced concrete with hammer dressed or other type of textured surface. Large glazing panels were fitted to each bay for natural lighting. Lifting facilities were provided in the form of four cross runways (two in the centre capable of each lifting 6 tons and one at each end capable of lifting 1.5 tons). Doors arranged in six leaves

Aeroplane shed Type B, 1455/27, 'Goliath' at Martlesham Heath.

94 *British Military Airfield Architecture*

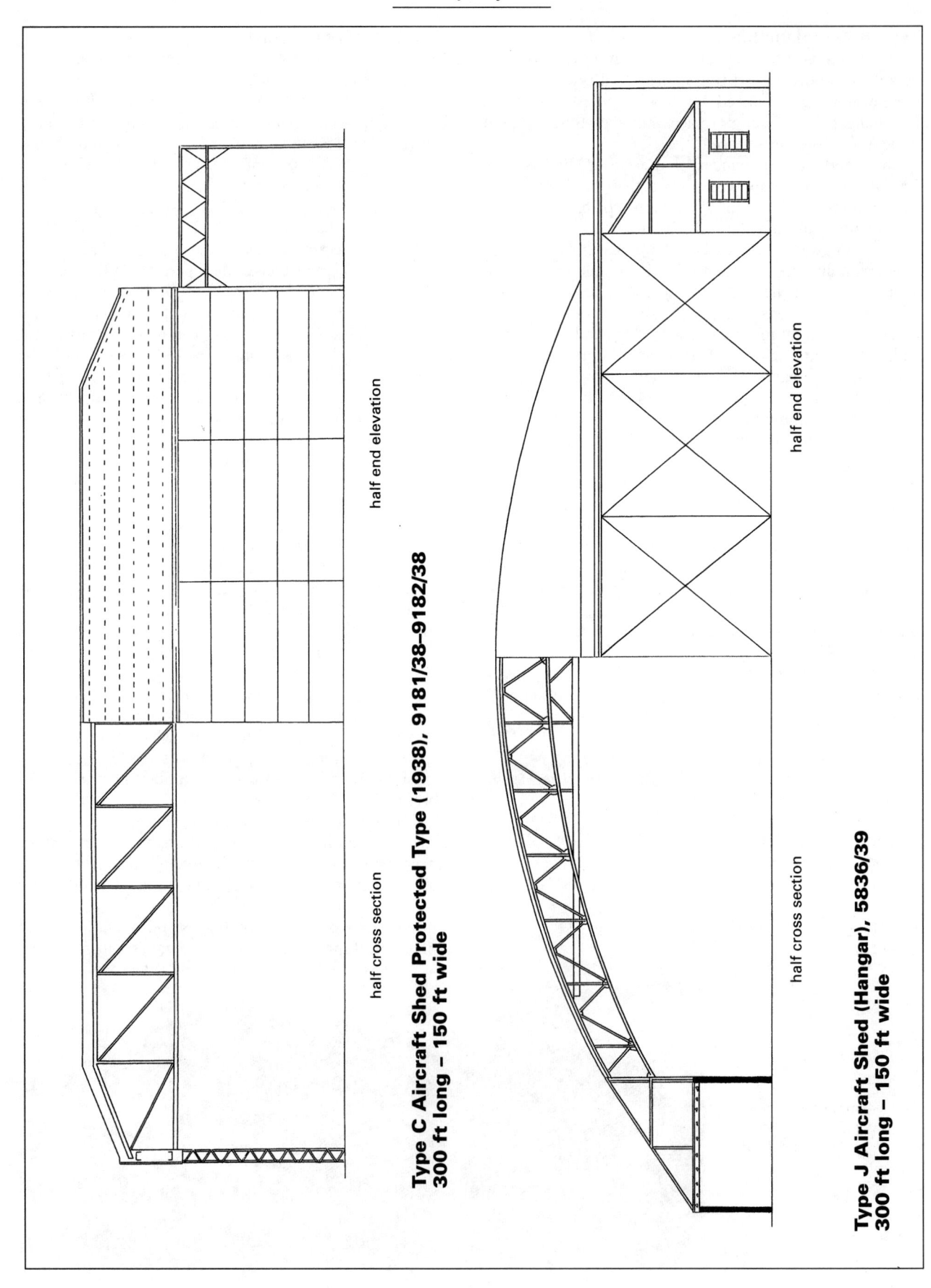

half end elevation

half cross section

**Type C Aircraft Shed Protected Type (1938), 9181/38–9182/38
300 ft long – 150 ft wide**

half end elevation

half cross section

**Type J Aircraft Shed (Hangar), 5836/39
300 ft long – 150 ft wide**

A Type C hangar at Watton.

An early gabled Type C aircraft shed at Gosport. (Photographed 1991)

An austerity Type C hangar at Burtonwood.

were constructed with steel plates on both sides with the cavity filled with gravel to a height of 20 ft to provide protection against bomb splinters.

A typical bomber station had two hangars for each squadron, both identical but differing in the side annexe arrangement. No. 1 shed had two nine-bay annexes, one having a small two-storey portion in the centre for office accommodation. No.2 shed had one single-storey annexe of similar length to the other shed and a six-bay annexe on the opposite side. Most bomber stations had two hangars of each type, but occasionally another hangar was provided. The layout of the annexes along both side walls were designed to serve the day-to-day operations of the squadron using the hangar; this accommodation was far superior to previous aircraft shed designs. Typically, the layout consisted of suites of offices for the squadron, rest rooms for aircrew and ground crews including facilities for heating food, changing and locker rooms, and map and briefing rooms. Also armouries, wireless and instrument workshops, stores, and dope and aircraft equipment stores were all immediately available to the personnel and the aircraft they served.

A major change came in 1938 (8180/38 onwards) when the Type C hangar was redesigned to be more economical on materials with a reduction of 5 ft in clear height to 30 ft. It was sometimes unofficially known as Type C1 but the Directorate General of Works' drawings refer to them as Type C Protected Type. Construction was similar to the 1936 design, but hangars were now built with steel cantilevered roof frames clad with asbestos sheeting exposed above the doors. Wall infilling was of concrete up to a height of 20 ft and the remaining area was patent glazing. Some stations such as St Eval and Wick had unprotected hangars of this type with similar steelwork but Twin Twelve asbestos sheet cladding in lieu of reinforced concrete.

Type	description	drawing no.	span	length	clear height	examples
C	gabled roof	1584/34	150 ft	300 ft	35 ft	Gosport, Northolt
	hipped rafters	872/35, 1581/35	150 ft	300 ft	35 ft	Bicester, Manby
	reinforced concrete	2270/35, 3270/35, 6045/36	150 ft	300 ft	35 ft	Driffield, Upwood, Watton, West Raynham
C1	protected	8180/38– 9192/38 9139/38, 5533/39	150 ft	300 ft	30 ft	Bramcote, Middle Wallop Lossiemouth, Middleton St George

Aircraft Storage Unit Hangars 1936–40

In 1936, planning and construction began on the first five Aircraft Storage Units; eventually 25 were built. They were administered by Maintenance Command, 41 Group and later came under the technical control of the Ministry of Aircraft Production. Their function was to maintain stocks of new and reconditioned aircraft from the factories, carry out routine maintenance, and deliver by air to Home flying units of the Royal Air Force. Packing depots on ASU stations such as St Athan dealt with the dismantling and packing of aircraft for overseas.

ASUs were constructed in areas thought to be safe from enemy aircraft and, as concealment was very important, they were planned so as to make the greatest use of natural features. Most were combined with and shared an airfield with a Service Flying Training School (SFTS) or an Operational Training Unit (OTU) but Kemble and Wroughton were self-contained with their own landing grounds.

The standard ASU layout included a headquarters site with one Type C hangar for the dismantling and erecting of aircraft, and two or four Type D hangars for storage of complete aircraft. Partially dismantled aircraft were stored (with wings removed) in hangars dispersed in four to six groups round the airfield perimeter to avoid having large concentrations of aircraft parked close together. Each group consisted of two or more specially designed storage hangars, the majority being arched semi-circular sheds of three different types. Because of their then unique shape they could easily be concealed from the air by being covered with earth and turf. Access roads to the hangars were constructed to look like farm tracks but in the winter they became impracticable. In 1939, the Air Ministry therefore issued instructions to construct tarmac roads and to camouflage the surface with grey and green chippings.

Most storage hangars were fitted with internal runways running the whole length of the shed and were provided with ½-ton hoists to enable aircraft to be stored 'tails up'. However, this form of storage was abandoned at the outbreak of war in favour of open storage outdoors, dispersed round the airfield perimeter.

A Type D aircraft storage shed at Kirkbride.

A Lamella aircraft storage shed at Burtonwood.

Type D Aircraft Shed

Built at the early ASU airfields (34 hangars at 12 sites), the Type D was constructed with a system of reinforced-concrete columns spaced at 20 ft centres supporting concrete arched ribs and tie-beams carried by suspenders from the arched ribs. Its walls were monolithic 14-inch thick reinforced concrete. Steel doors with six leaves each end were filled with gravel. They opened out into prominent concrete door gantries each side. The earlier hangars had large glazing panels along the side walls and narrow panels along the tops of the doors, but on the last examples built (as at Wroughton), windows were completely omitted.

drawing no.	span	length	clear door height	examples
2312/36, 2313/36	150 ft	300 ft	30 ft	(2) Little Rissington, Hullavington; (4) Silloth, Wroughton

Lamella Aircraft Storage Shed

Known as Lamellendach (segmental roof), lamella construction was developed in Germany in the 1920s for factories and aircraft hangars by Junkers of Dassau. British rights were acquired in 1929 by Horseley Bridge & Engineering Co Ltd of Birmingham which marketed the design as Lamella Construction. The first British arched hangar featuring this form of construction was erected for Henleys (1928) Ltd at Heston Airport between May and June 1930. Taking just five weeks to complete, it had a maximum span of 82 ft, a door opening 62 ft wide and 18 ft high, and a length of 149 ft.

One other version had an arched roof with wall plates carried on girders supported by stanchions. Three hangars were supplied using this arrangement. One at Liverpool Airport is now a Grade 2 listed building. The others were built as part of the Cunliffe-Owen aircraft factory at Southampton Airport.

Lamella construction took the form of a large net-like framework of shallow channel-section standard steel pressings with the ends bent to the correct angle, and bolted together in pairs (a right and left to a left and right). This formed a diamond-shaped web and a lattice arch when assembled with others. Tooling for the manufacture of Lamella roof components was bought and installed in the factory at Tipton. It included a special three-ram 600-ton hydraulic press built by Hollings & Guest Ltd, and, for the manufacture of the webs, a punching and shearing machine built by Henry Pels Ltd.

Civil hangars had longitudinal purlins that supported the outer covering of corrugated asbestos sheeting.

The Lamella aircraft storage shed built to 6953/36 was an arched hangar designed in 1936 and fabricated for the Air Ministry by the Horseley Bridge & Engineering Company as a storage shed for aircraft with their wings removed. No provision was made for tails-up storage so aircraft were simply packed together.

Construction was similar to that described above except that the roof covering was in the form of 0.875-inch steel troughing on which was laid 2 inches of concrete and 9 inches of earth and turf. End walls were 1 ft thick reinforced concrete, with two steel sliding doors at each end giving a clear opening of 40 ft.

drawing no.	span	length	height	examples
6953/36	167 ft	300 ft	35 ft	(4) Kemble; (6) Aldergrove, Brize Norton, Ternhill

(span measured between arch springings at ground level; height measured to crown)

Type E Aircraft Storage Shed

This reinforced 'vibrated' concrete arched shed was designed by the Directorate of Works in 1937. It consisted of concrete arched ribs at 11 ft and 13 ft centres, and cross-beams, the whole framework covered with slightly curved precast concrete slabs cast *in situ* using mobile formwork inside, shuttering on the outside and electric vibrators. End walls were of reinforced concrete columns and beams, with infilling of 5-inch thick concrete. Steel doors at each end allowed a clear opening width of 40 ft at the rear and four leaves at the front gave 60ft. The interior was clad with fibreboard to reduce condensation, and runway beams were provided for storage of aircraft tails-up.

Problems were encountered when trying to keep the earth covering in place but this was largely overcome by incorporating pyramid-shaped blocks of concrete in the vibrated concrete slabs. These contained steel rods to

A Type E aircraft storage shed at Hullavington.

A Type L aircraft storage shed at Llandow.

which steel ropes were attached to form a grid pattern; soil was then built up flush with the ropes which also acted as guides so that soil could be distributed evenly over the whole shed, avoiding any unnecessary stress of the members. Galvanized wire mesh was then laid and secured to the guide ropes. Over this more soil was added and finally turf, giving a total covering of 9 inches.

drawing no.	span	length	height	examples
7305/37	160 ft	300 ft	24 ft 9 in	(2) Brize Norton, Kemble; (6) Hullavington, Little Rissington; (8) Cosford

(span measured between arch springings at ground level)

Type L Shed

In 1939, aircraft production was outpacing storage accommodation and a further hangar design of similar shape and size went into production with the Teesside Bridge & Engineering Co Ltd. These hangars were mainly built at the later ASU aerodromes but were also used to supplement existing storage facilities at Aston Down and Silloth.

Construction was of a series of closely spaced triangular-shaped arches built from pressed steel members welded at the factory into standard units and bolted together on site. After waterproofing, the complete shed was covered in a thin layer of concrete, earth and turf. End walls were constructed of a steel framework clad with dovetailed steel sheeting, which formed the inside face, and reinforced concrete 12 inches thick on the outside. Sliding steel doors at both ends gave a clear opening of 70 ft.

drawing no.	span	length	clear door height	clear opening	examples
5163/39–5165/39	167 ft	300 ft	25 ft	70 ft	(6) Edzell, Hawarden; (7) Lossiemouth; (8) Lichfield; (9) Kinloss

(span measured at floor level)

Type J and Type K Sheds

Designed by the Air Ministry Directorate of Works and built by Sir William Arrol & Co, these were basically the same; one was for the maintenance of aircraft on operational airfields (Type J), the other (Type K) for the storage of aircraft on ASU stations.

Probably the first operational station to have a Type J was Middleton St George which, although planned under the 1939 M Scheme expansion along with several other airfields such as Lindholme and Topcliffe, was far from being completed at the outbreak of war. It was therefore caught in the transition between permanent and temporary hangar accommodation. Here a single austerity Type C was provided but other hangars of this type were cancelled in favour of a single Type J and by this time the T2 was in production, so two hangars of this type were

A Type J hangar at Dumfries.

Hangars 99

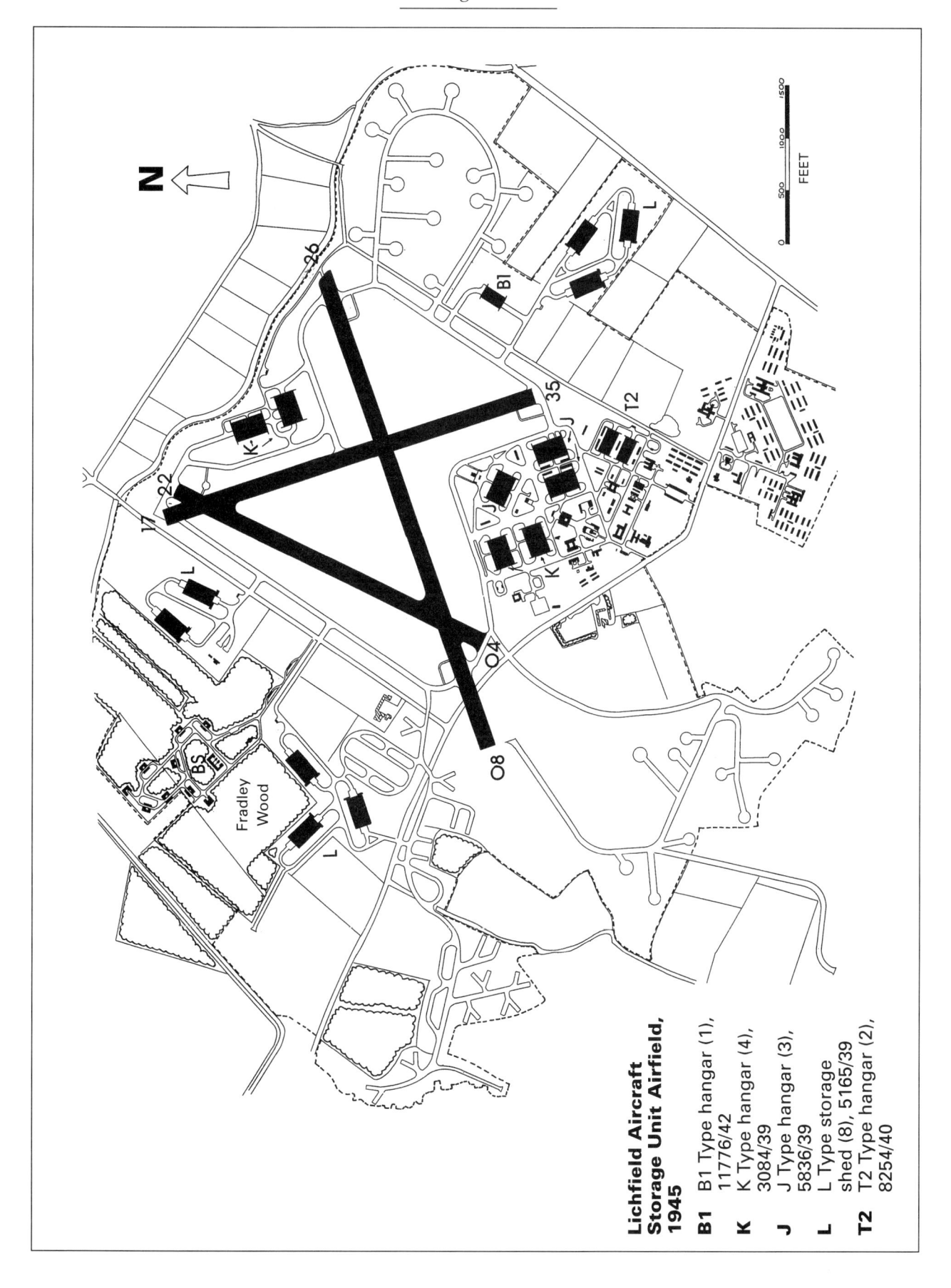

Lichfield Aircraft Storage Unit Airfield, 1945

- **B1** B1 Type hangar (1), 1776/42
- **K** K Type hangar (4), 3084/39
- **J** J Type hangar (3), 5836/39
- **L** L Type storage shed (8), 5165/39
- **T2** T2 Type hangar (2), 8254/40

A Type K aircraft storage shed at Burtonwood. (Photographed 1982)

also provided. Had the station been planned slightly later it would have had two Type Js similar to other stations planned at the end of 1939 such as North Luffenham and Waterbeach. The last stations with non-dispersed layouts and temporary accommodation, such as Chipping Warden and Elsham Wolds, only had a single Type J with additional hangars provided in the form of two T2s.

The last of the aircraft storage units such as Dumfries, Hawarden and Lichfield were planned and commenced in 1939. They had several Type K storage sheds at Dumfries and Hawarden had one Type J shed, while Lichfield had three.

The only real difference between the two was that the Type J had lifting tackle runways the width of the span, while Type K had a slightly different structural roof arrangement to support runways the full length of the shed. Type J had annexes running both sides of the shed which were used as office and workshop accommodation and therefore had a large number of windows; the Type K had similar annexes but being only used for storage did not require many windows.

Constructed of a series of steel columns spaced at 16 ft 8 in centres there were 18 bays supporting arched steel trusses. Parts of the upper members were exposed as an open framework above the annexes built along the side walls. Special trusses carried 1.5-ton runways at each end, and two 6-ton runways were located in the centre of the shed. Roof covering was of 0.25-inch thick mild steel plates and the gable ends were clad with corrugated iron. Sliding steel-framed and steel-clad doors at both ends opened out along door guides supported by end frames.

Annexes were of brick or concrete and subdivided into offices and workshops.

drawing no.	clear span	length	clear height	examples
5836/39–5844/39	150 ft	300 ft	30 ft	(Type J) Goxhill, Snaith, Swanton Morley
3084/39				(Type K) Burtonwood, Hawarden, High Ercall, Lichfield

TRANSPORTABLE HANGARS

During the First World War and for some time after, the only successful transportable hangar design was the Bessonneau. This could be very quickly erected and secured to provide adequate shelter for a few small aeroplanes. But with postwar increases in the number and size of aeroplanes, the need for larger transportable accommodation soon became apparent. The Air Ministry therefore issued a specification in 1936 covering the dimensions and requirements for a light transportable shed for use in war. It had to be end-opening with doors at both ends, be capable of mass production and have interchangeable parts to permit rapid erection and dismantling with minimal permanent foundations. This specification was submitted to various designers and eventually two different designs were chosen.

An example of each was erected at two demonstration sites (airfields) in the north-east: at Thornaby an Air Ministry design was built (later to be known as the Bellman hangar) and at Usworth a Callender Cable & Construction design was built (later to be known as the Callender-Hamilton hangar). Eventually, in 1938, the Bellman design was chosen as the standard Air Ministry wartime transportable shed but Callender-Hamilton hangars were also purchased in small numbers for RNASs until superseded by a new hangar type in 1943.

Bellman Hangars

This was designed in 1936 by the Directorate of Works' structural engineer, N. S. Bellman, as a temporary hangar capable of being erected or dismantled by unskilled labour with simple equipment and to be easily transportable. Commercial manufacturing rights were acquired by Head Wrightson & Co of Teesdale Iron Works, Thornaby-on-Tees. By November 1938, 10 had been supplied to Russia!

The hangar was constructed on a unit system of rolled steel sections, both walls and roof using the same standard units joined at the junction of wall and roof by a standard corner unit. The time taken for 12 men to erect the hangar at Thornaby, including levelling the ground, laying door

A Bellman hangar at Halfpenny Green.

A Bellman hangar at Chivenor.

tracks, erecting the steelwork, and fitting oiled canvas doors, was 500 man-hours. Two light jib derricks made of timber poles were required to erect the fabricated vertical and side members. The roof trusses were assembled on the ground before being lifted into position.

As a result of the bad winter of 1937 when a number of Bellman hangars at Thornaby were damaged after a heavy fall of snow, production Bellmans were modified slightly to have steel-framed and steel-clad doors. During the period 1938–40 some 400 hangars of this type were built. They proved to be invaluable in the early part of the war. They met an increasing demand not only to supplement existing permanent hangars but also to provide the total hangar requirements for many temporary Armament Training, Elementary Flying Training and Air Navigation Schools.

Sheds were purchased in bulk and in 1938 a central storage depot was established at No. 3 MU at Milton, Oxfordshire. The parts for 40 Bellmans were stored in two specially built Bellman sheds for issue in the event of war. When all the hangars had been dispatched, the two sheds were used for storing spare parts.

drawing no.	clear span	length	clear height	no. of bays	example
5498/36–5500/36, 959/37, 960/37,	87 ft 9 in	175 ft	25 ft	14 at 12 ft 6 in centres	
8349/37	87 ft 9 in	105 ft 10 in	25 ft		RNAS Bellman

Callender Hangars

Using their previous experience of designing Callender-Hamilton bridges and electric pylons for the Central Electricity Board, Callender Cable & Construction took up the challenge to design a new end-opening transportable hangar to meet the Air Ministry specification sent to several structural steel companies. This led to a new unit construction hangar to be manufactured by Painter Brothers of Hereford in 1937.

The new design consisted of a steel framework fabricated from 10 ft long and 5 ft square box-section girder ribs at 20 ft centres. Vertical stanchions supporting shallow-pitched roof girders were fabricated from 10 ft and 15 ft lengths of similar cross-section. The main features of the design were lightness, low cost, standardization of parts, bolted connections to facilitate erecting and dismantling, and all parts were protected against corrosion by hot-dip galvanizing to a weight of 2 oz per sq ft (thus eliminating the need to paint the framework).

The Air Ministry arranged wind-tunnel tests on a model of the proposed shed at the National Physical Laboratory at Teddington, with a wind speed of 80 mph. This produced a pressure of 17 lb per sq ft on the side wall facing the wind and a maximum upward roof pressure of 22 lb per sq ft. This data was used in the design to provide a minimum safety factor of 1.5 on the elasticity limit of the steel.

Extensive tests were carried out by Painter Brothers using a unique lattice girder testing plant. Forces were applied to a single rib and gradually increased to represent a severe overload, simulating various wind pressures,

A Callender-Hamilton hangar 17346/40 at East Fortune. It is 17 ft high.

A Callender hangar to drawing 6637/37 at Burscough. It is 25 ft high. (Photographed 1982)

A T2 hangar to drawing 3653/42 at Tarrant Rushton. (Photographed 1981)

without distortion to the framework. Tests were also carried out to investigate the behaviour of the rib when loaded with snow. As a result of these satisfactory tests, the Air Ministry ordered a complete hangar of 90 ft span, 185 ft long with a clear door height of 25 ft. The shed was built at Usworth. It was mainly clad with corrugated iron but doors were canvas, and oiled fabric was used for eaves and gables. Eventually, eight hangars of the original design were ordered by the Air Ministry in 1938. In 1940, more hangars were purchased but these had a reduced clear door height of 17 ft.

drawing no.	clear door opening span	length	height	example
6633/37	90 ft	185 ft	25 ft	Usworth
17346/40	90 ft	185 ft	17 ft	Madley
17348/40				Barrow
17346				Atcham
17384				

Type T Hangars

By 1940, with the rapidly increasing development of aircraft, it became obvious that the Bellman shed was obsolete. As a result, the Air Ministry, in collaboration with Teesside Bridge & Engineering, developed a series of sheds known as Type T. The first design was the T2 and like the others in this family was of standard steel-fabricated units of welded-and-bolted construction covered with galvanized corrugated iron, 22-gauge for the roof and 24-gauge for the walls. The original 1940 Type A design had roof sheeting fixed with the overlapping portion cranked above its neighbour using angle-iron purlins and U-shaped bolts. This method was discontinued from 1942 in favour of fitting commercial corrugated sheeting with the overlapping portion fitted flush using the same angle-iron (fitted the opposite way up) and hook bolts.

After a development period of two years involving several minor design changes, the T2 became the standard

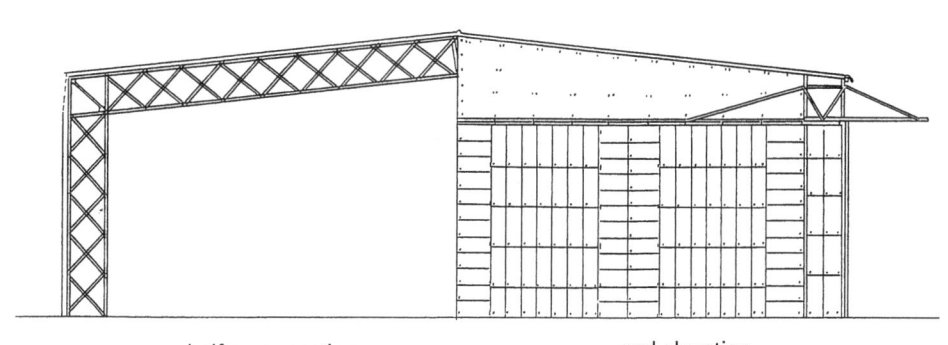

half cross section   end elevation

Callender Unit Construction Hangar with canvas doors, 6637/37

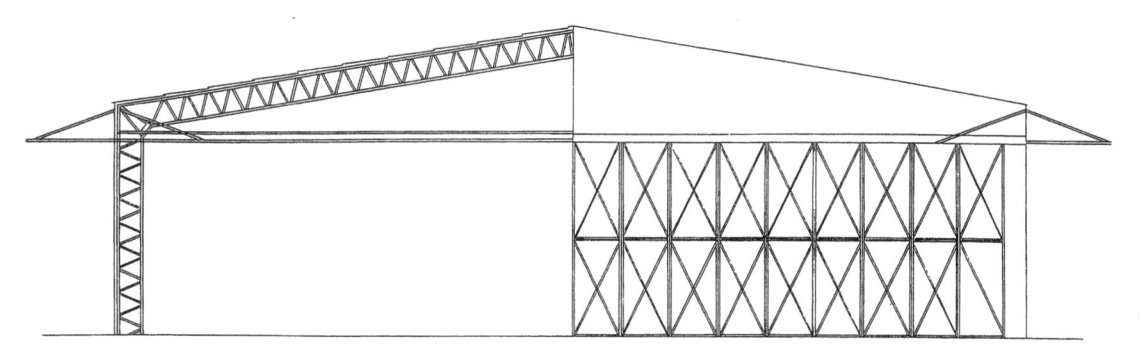

T2 Transportable Shed, (cranked sheeting), 8254/40

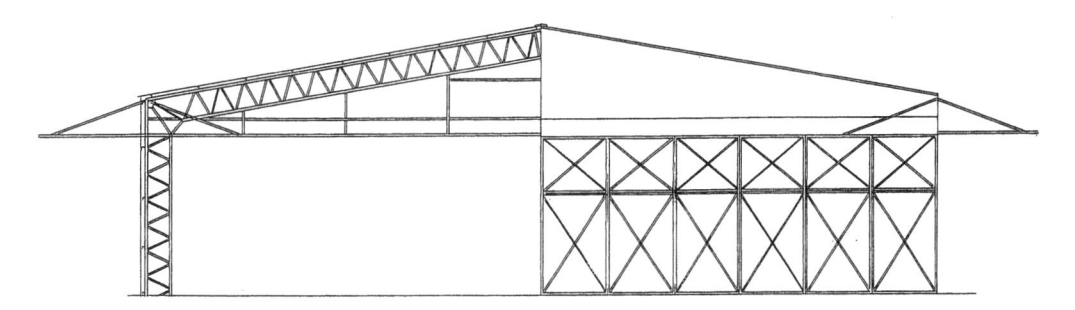

T1 Transportable Shed (14), (commercial sheeting), 19ft clear height, 9659/42

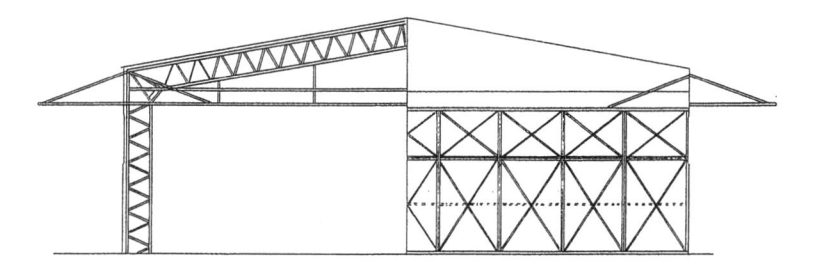

T3 Transportable Shed, (commercial sheeting), 3505/42

A T3 hangar at Topcliffe.

	description	drawing no.	span	clear length	clear height	no. of bays	examples
T1		7541/41					
T1	special cranked and punched roof sheeting	7557/41	90 ft 4 in	175 ft	19 ft		
T1	similar to the 7541/41 but commercially sheeted	9658/42, 9659/42					Babdown Farm, Bibury Condover, Long Newton
T2 Type A	cranked sheeting	8254/40	113 ft 6 in	239 ft 7 in	25 ft	23	Finmere, Framlingham, Goxhill, Keevil
T2	cranked sheeting	7512/41	113 ft 6 in	135 ft 5 in	25 ft	13	Crosby-on-Eden, Weston Zoyland
T2	commercial sheeting	3670/42	113 ft 6 in	135 ft 5 in	25 ft	13	Scatsa
T2	commercial sheeting; most common T2	3653/42	113 ft 6 in	239 ft 7 in	25 ft	23	Eye, Foulsham, Grove, Riccal
Heavy Duty T2	twice as many wall stanchions and roof trusses; extra side bracing	4306/41				46	
Heavy Duty T2	extra side bracing; projecting door rails supported by braced trestles; sheeting painted black	5215/42		135 ft 5 in		26	
Heavy Duty T2		5216/42		239 ft 7 in		46	
T2 Marine Craft		809/44	54 ft 3 in	73 ft	19 ft		
T3	earlier shed may have had cranked sheeting; other details similar to T2 with commercial sheeting but trusses spaced at 12 ft 6 in centres.	16245/41, 3505/42	66 ft	75 ft	19 ft		Risley

temporary hangar for the Royal Air Force during the Second World War. A total of 906 were built for RAF stations at home and abroad.

Type S Hangar

Designed and built by the Teesside Bridge & Engineering Co, these were small hangars built mainly on RNAS airfields for folding wing aircraft. They were constructed of RSJ-type stanchions spaced at 12 ft 6 in centres supporting roof girders of similar cross-section. Cladding was 24-gauge corrugated iron sheeting; sliding doors were provided at one end only and opened out supported by door guides carried on steel trestles. The only difference between them was that the second type had a length of 70 ft consisting of two additional 10 ft bays.

Type	drawing no.	span	length	clear height	examples
first Type S	12819/40	60 ft 5 in	50 ft	20 ft	Campbeltown, Henstridge, Easthaven, Stretton
second Type S	1527/42, 3621/42				

Main Hangars

The first hangar designed and built by A. & J. Main of Glasgow was a small RNAS workshop and dispersed maintenance hangar with doors at only one end. It consisted of a series of A-shaped wall frames spaced at 7 ft centres supporting steel trusses and was clad with

A Main hangar at Lee-on-Solent. (Photographed 1993)

A Main hangar used as a workshop at Burscough. (Photographed in 1982)

A Pentad hangar at Stretton. (Photographed 1982)

corrugated iron or asbestos sheeting.

The later Mainhill Type B was constructed of a series of A-wall frames spaced at 15 ft 5 in centres supporting roof trusses clad with corrugated iron sheeting, and lined inside with asbestos sheeting. Steel-framed doors opened at both ends.

Type	drawing no.	clear span	length	clear door width	clear door height	examples
Type A		60 ft	70 ft, 84 ft	55 ft	17 ft	Burscough, Inskip
Type B	195/53	105 ft	165 ft		26 ft	
Admiralty	46691/41, 2198/42					Lee-on-Solent, Yeovilton

Pentad Transportable Hangar

This was an all-steel end-opening RNAS hangar with canted sides designed for aircraft with wings folded, and consisted of box-section wall and roof girders spaced at 14 ft 3 in centres. Normally it was 13 bays long and clad with corrugated iron sheeting.

drawing no	span	length	clear height	examples
3304/43	105 ft	185 ft	25 ft	Culdrose, Yeovilton

Blister Hangars

The blister hangar was designed by architects and consulting engineers Norman & Dawbarn and William C. Inman of Miskins & Sons who filed UK patent applications 31,002/39 and 32,529/39 in respect of the hangar. The blister hangar was a small arched-type of dispersal shed for the storage and maintenance of aircraft with small wing-spans.

There were three main types: a standard blister of timber construction; an Over Type of light welded-steel construction; and an Extra Over Type also of light welded-steel construction.

The standard blister hangar consisted of a series of arched ribs made of timber, spaced at 5 ft centres. These were made up of several rib units bolted together to form an arch. They were supported on wooden bearers and restrained on each side by vertical posts. Wooden floor platforms (decking) were laid over the bearers inside each side wall and timber purlins were clad with continental-pattern steel sheeting. Quick-release canvas curtains at each end formed conical tent coverings giving additional floor space. The hangar did not require any foundations, being anchored by T-irons staked into the ground. Aircraft were parked on the earth floor, and any stores or tools were kept on the timber decking.

Miskins steel-framed blister hangars were developed to provide hangars of greater span and were made up of a series of all-welded steel rib sections bolted together to form the arches. Spaced at 7 ft 6 in centres, they were

The remains of the canvas curtains on a Miskins blister hangar at Panshanger.

The exposed framework of a Miskins steel blister hangar at Fordoun.

A Fromson Massillon hangar to drawing 3752/43 at Dunino.

joined by steel ties and purlins of timber or steel and carried commercial corrugated iron sheeting. These were the Over Type and the Extra Over Type.

The construction of Dorman Long blister hangars was completely different from the Miskins type. They only had three RSJ-type arched ribs made up of four sections spliced together, each separated from its neighbour by a series of I-section purlins. Unlike the Miskins hangars, the ribs were bolted to foundations.

Type	drawing no.	span	length	height	examples
standard	12497/41	45 ft	25 ft	14 ft	Panshanger
Over	12512/41	65 ft	45 ft	19 ft 10 in	Overton (2), Heath Alton Barnes (6), Ayr (8)
Extra Over	12532/41	69 ft	45 ft	20 ft 4 in	Horne (4), Ayr (9); Annan, Thornaby Castle Camps, Kingscliffe
	13087/41				
Double Extra Over	9392/42				Banff
Dorman Long	4630/42	71 ft 9 in	45 ft	20 ft 6 in	Brunton, Sawbridgeworth

Fromson Hangars

The four-bay type was a small arched hangar built by the Canadian company Fromson of Byfleet, Surrey. Similar in appearance to a Miskins blister hangar (but without curtains), it was used only as a storage shed on RNASs. The bays were 17 ft 6 in wide.

The Massillon was the same as the four-bay type but was used for storing aircraft with small wing-spans. The sliding steel doors opened out on to projecting guide rails.

Type	drawing no.	span	length	clear door height	clear door opening	no of bays	examples
Massillon	3752/43	57 ft	70 ft 87 ft	17 ft	53 ft		Dunino, Eglinton, Maydown
	3971/43	57 ft	70 ft	15 ft 6 in	16 ft	4	Abbotsinch

MINISTRY OF AIRCRAFT PRODUCTION HANGARS

The Ministry of Aircraft Production funded the design and construction of a series of standard prefabricated buildings for the maintenance of aircraft on operational bases, Aircraft Storage Units, and Satellite Landing Grounds, and at aircraft factories. These were to supplement existing hangars.

Types A and B

Types B1 and B2 were large aircraft repair hangars

A Type B1 hangar to drawings 11776/42–11781/42 at St Athan.

A Type A1 hangar at Hamble.

mainly built on operational bomber bases. They were designed by T. Bedford Consulting Engineers and met the requirement to repair damaged heavy bombers on their own airfields (rather than transport them by road to repair centres). Single B1 hangars were eventually erected at nearly all operational bomber bases and were manned by civilian repair parties under the control of MAP. B2 hangars were a smaller version of the B1 and were erected on aircraft factory sites rather than operational airfields.

B1 and B2 hangars were constructed from a number of stanchions spaced at 15 ft 2 in centres supporting roof trusses, a single 5-ton runway being installed. Cladding was normally black corrugated iron. Total cost including foundations and erection was £8,770.

A1 and A2 hangars were smaller with stanchions at 14 ft 7 in centres and had a 2-ton runway. They were mainly built on aircraft factory aerodromes. The total cost including foundations and erection was £5,120.

Type	drawing no.	span	length	clear door height	examples
A1		95 ft	175 ft	18 ft	
A2	454/43			16 ft	
B1	11776/42–11781/42	120 ft	227 ft	27 ft	Bardney, Barkston Heath,
B2			20 ft 6 in	20 ft	Catfoss, Pocklington

Robins Hangars

The Type B (Robin) was a small dispersal hangar found at ASUs and SLGs. Many were often camouflaged as farm buildings. The two main contractors were Dawnays and Redpath Brown.

The structure consisted of A-frames spaced at 12 ft 6 in centres supporting steep-pitched roof trusses and clad with corrugated iron. The doors opened at one end only into projecting door guides supported by outriggers. Foundations were only required for the steel framework, the remaining floor area often being compacted earth. In 1943, the total cost per hangar, including foundations (frame only), delivery, and erection, was £875.

At most ASUs, a complicated network of connecting tracks led from the airfield perimeter track to dispersal areas, which contained a complex system of concrete hard standings, and beyond to several dispersal fields. Robin hangars were often erected along hedge boundaries in these fields and many can still be seen today; there are, for example, about six dispersed around both Kemble and Wroughton.

The Super Robins Type A hangar was similar to the Robin but it was larger. The framework of the Super Robins was entirely different from that of the Super Robins Type A. It consisted of RSJ-type stanchions as opposed to prefabricated A-frames. It was normally six bays long with trusses spaced at 12 ft 6 in centres. The total cost in 1943 including foundations (framework

A Robins Type B hangar at Abbots Bromley.

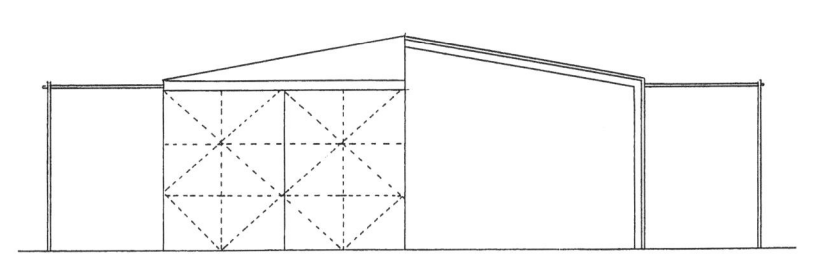

end elevation   half cross section elevation

Transportable Hangar Teesside Type S, 12819/40

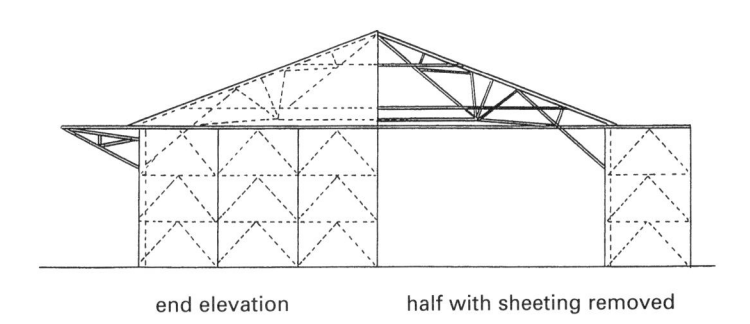

end elevation   half with sheeting removed

Super Robins, 6910/43

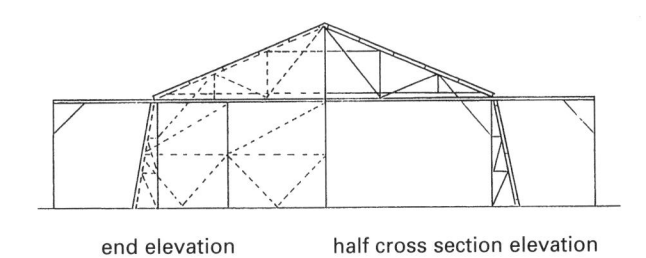

end elevation   half cross section elevation

Robins Type B, 2204/41

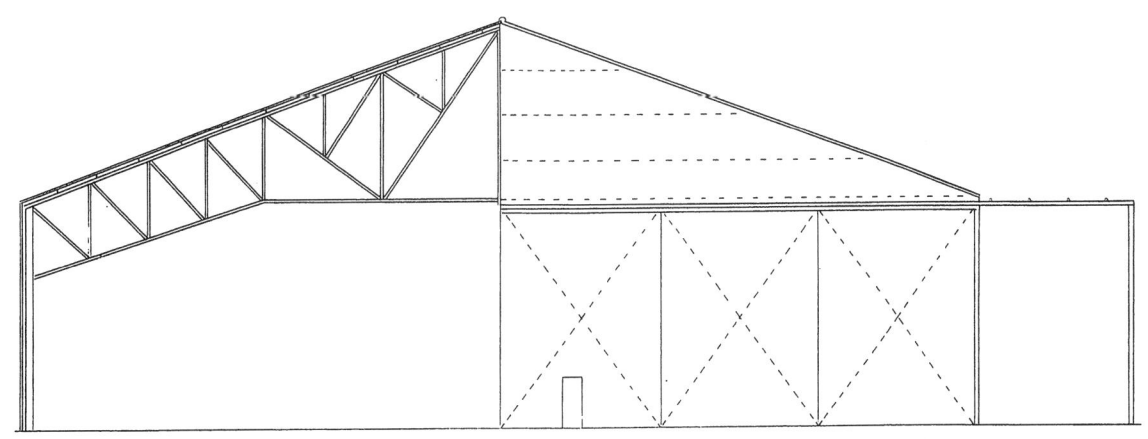

end elevation   half cross section elevation

Type B1 Hangar, 11776/42–11781/42

A Boulton & Paul VR2 hangar at Stormy Down.

only), delivery and erection was £1,370.

Type	drawing no.	span	length	clear door height	examples
Super Robins		60 ft	75 ft	17 ft	Hinton-in-the-Hedges
Super Robins Type A	2243/41	60 ft	72 ft	14 ft	(aircraft factories) Leavesden, Woodley
(Robin) Type B	2204/41 (Dawnays), 6874/43, 6875/43 (Redpath Brown)	44 ft	62 ft 6 in	14 ft	Aston Down, Black Isle, Hatfield (aircraft factory)

MISCELLANEOUS TYPES

Butler Combat Hangar

Also supplied as a stores building, this hangar type was designed and produced by the Butler Manufacturing Company of Kansas City, USA. Supplied in kit form for on-site assembly by Engineer Aviation Battalion Personnel, the hangar version featured box-section girders and was clad on the inside with canvas. The stores building had rigid frames and beams bolted together to form a 40 ft span. In the Second World War, the hangars were constructed at a limited number of USAAF airfields, but considerably more stores buildings were erected postwar on USAF airbases such as Alconbury, Bentwaters, and Weathersfield.

examples Kingston Bagpuize (2), Kingscliffe, Little Staughton

Type VR1 and Type VR2 Hangars

Boulton & Paul of London and Norwich designed and built a series of hangars for aircraft factories and RAF Armament Training Schools in single span (VR1) and coupled forms (VR2).

Both hangars were similar but the VR2 essentially consisted of two single-span sheds built side by side without a dividing wall; both sides were supported by lattice girders carried on stanchions. Roof trusses were spaced at 12 ft 4 in centres supported by lattice-type wall stanchions. Steel-framed doors opened at one end only into outriggers supported by trestles. Cladding was normally corrugated asbestos sheeting.

Type	drawing no.	span	length	clear door height	examples
VR1	4178/44	100 ft	150 ft	20 ft	Ringway
VR2		100 ft (x 2)	150 ft	20 ft	Moreton Valance, Squires Gate

PART 5

CONTROL TOWERS

MILITARY AIR TRAFFIC CONTROL

Despite civil air traffic control being developed between the wars, it was practically non-existent on military aerodromes and was limited to the activities of the duty pilot. His essential equipment consisted of only a note book, a quantity of pyrotechnics and, on occasion, a radio. A report issued by Air Commodore Leackie in 1937 recommended that the 'watch hut' be redesigned and enlarged, manned by an officer with the authority to direct aircraft in the air, prevent departure if weather became unfavourable, and redirect aircraft if the airfield became congested.

In December 1937, the AOC-in-C Bomber Command suggested the opening of Military Area Control Centres similar to the civil Area Control Centres at Croydon, Heston, Manchester West (Barton), and Portsmouth to control *en route* traffic. In January 1938, the responsibility for organization and administration was vested in Bomber Command. The RAF selected 12 officers for air traffic control duties. They were posted to Uxbridge for a short training course, then to Croydon airport for practical experience. Having completed their training, the new flying control officers were paired off to set up Regional Control Organizations and posted to six airfields selected for their strategic importance: Abingdon, Boscombe Down, Leuchars, Linton-on-Ouse, Mildenhall, and Waddington. In September 1938, Flight Lieutenants Bell and Bullmore were posted to Boscombe Down. Their watch office was a converted First World War hut situated half way along the line of general service aeroplane sheds. They set up office with the aid of four civilian clerks and some W/T equipment.

During the early part of the war it became necessary to expand the control of aircraft at all RAF stations and this became even more apparent as the bomber offensive gathered momentum. As pilots could not be spared, large numbers of civil controllers were drafted. This was soon recognized by the Air Ministry as being a specialist job and selected officers in the Special Duties branch of the service were posted in May 1941 to form the new Regional Control School at Brasenose College, Oxford. Some 40 controllers a month graduated from here, which transferred to Watchfield at the end of 1941 and became known as the Flying Control School. It was administered by the RAF but manned by civilian staff of Air Service Training Ltd. In 1946, the school's name changed to School of Air Traffic Control and remained so until the unit was combined with the Central Navigation School at Shawbury in February 1950 to form the Central Navigation and Control School.

Regional Control aerodromes, later to be called Type 1 aerodromes were equipped with a system of boundary lights, an illuminated landing T, a landing strip 1,300 yd by 400 yd complete with contact lighting and the Standard Beam Approach (SBA) blind landing system. This equipment was installed at all of the Regional Control airfields and was an adaptation of the Lorenz system operating on VHF radio frequencies and manufactured by Standard Telephones & Cables. The greatest difficulty a pilot had to contend with when approaching an aerodrome was landing in fog. Navigational skill and D/F bearings could get him over the top of the aerodrome but if fog obscured the ground his most difficult task was still ahead. A directional wireless system was developed in Germany by Lorenz AG of Stuttgart. The first installation in 1934–5 was at Templehof, Berlin, and the first airport in the UK to use this system was Heston in 1936.

Ground equipment consisted of three ultra-short wave transmitters, while the aircraft carried two receivers in addition to the standard wireless set for direct communication with the control tower. In principal, when an aircraft was on the best line of approach, a continuous note was heard by the pilot in his headphones. A deviation from this path was indicated by the signal changing to either dots or dashes depending on to which side of the path he wandered. The zones of dots and dashes were spread progressively from the ground beacon at angles of 60° from the correct approach line and could be heard up to 15 miles away at 1,500 ft. About 8 minutes were needed for the approach, which would begin about 12 miles out. The final glide was started when the aircraft arrived over the first marker beacon at about 1,000 ft and roughly 2 miles from the airfield.

In September 1936, the Lorenz system was evaluated at Farnborough for possible use on RAF stations, but it was not until early 1939 that the RAF began to train pilots in its use. A school was set up at Mildenhall under the command of Squadron Leader Blucke using Anson Mk I *L9155*. In July 1939, the Blind Approach Training and Development Unit was formed at Boscombe Down, one of the first stations to use the new equipment consisting of T1122 and T1123 transmitters.

It was considered essential that contact lighting should be installed at aerodromes with SBA but as there were manufacturing problems with the toughened glass lens, only 35 stations had been equipped with SBA by October 1941. Only 80 per cent of Bomber Command airfields were suitable for SBA because the requirement required a 10-mile straight approach to the main runway without crossing another SBA beam. Normally the outer marker was positioned 10 miles out, a middle marker at 2 miles and an inner marker at 250 yd from the runway. Some stations such as Middleton St George and Thornaby had beams for a south-west approach instead of the usual north-east approach because this avoided the industrial conurbation of Teesside. Many aircraft, such as Beaufort, Blenheim, Hudson, and Liberator, did not have enough room in the cockpit for the SBA receivers. The system was unsuitable for fighter aircraft for the same reason.

Identification friend or foe (IFF) was invented by scientists at Bawdsey Manor. Its primary function was to enable radar operators to recognize friendly aircraft. First introduced at the beginning of the war, the older types of IFF used a system of direct interrogation. Aircraft were fitted with IFF transponders which swept a particular frequency band. When the ground station transmitted a signal of an appropriate frequency, 'interrogating' the aircraft's IFF, the transponder detected it and 'answered' the interrogation. Radar working at the same frequency detected the IFF response for a fraction of a second each time the transponder swept the frequency band. Therefore, for most of the time the radar display showed a normal echo, but every few seconds this echo increased in amplitude for an instant. Echoes showing this periodic increase were identified as friendly.

Later equipment used an indirect interrogation system, in which radar used to interrogate IFF was provided with a subsidiary set called the 'interrogator'. This was of a relatively low power so it could only detect the relatively strong pulses from the aircraft's IFF but not the normal aircraft echo. Radar beacons of the IFF type could also be used as navigational aids such as homing or beam approach beacons (BABS).

From February 1941, the RAF began the installation of another radio set for aircraft and the watch office control room. This was a small TR9D HF short-range radio set to help aircraft in distress. It included a simple transmitter/receiver working on a fixed frequency of 6.44 MHz. It had a useful range of 10 miles and the scheme was given the code-name *Darky*.

The idea was that an aircraft lost and in trouble could make a *Darky* call ('Darky–Darky–Darky') which would be heard by the nearest *Darky* station which would then give assistance. In the autumn of 1942, it was decided by the Director General of Airfield Safety to extend *Darky* to include 45 ROC posts (extended to 50 in 1944) in areas where RAF coverage was poor. Each ROC *Darky* post was allocated to a parent RAF station and maintained a listening watch from sunset to sunrise.

Flight Lieutenant Bullmore was instrumental in obtaining 1,200 surplus searchlights from Anti-Aircraft Command. These were supplied to RAF stations to form 'canopies' of searchlights at airfields. The objective was to make the airfields easier to find in poor visibility, and especially in low cloud. Cloud penetration of three lights to form an equilateral triangle was found to be very effective, but a shortage of personnel sometimes meant that only two could be manned. When this happened the lights were located on the left-hand side of both ends of the runway in use. The light at the upwind end projected its beam vertically, whilst the other projected its beam towards it at 45°. This scheme was allocated the code-name *Sandra*.

Another 107 searchlights were installed at Royal Observer Corps posts located where there were large gaps between airfields. In 1941, the standard procedure for an aircraft in distress to obtain a searchlight homing was to circle for at least 2 minutes, fire that day's combination of coloured lights and send a succession of dots on the navigation lights (later amended to the switching of navigation and downward recognition lights).

Any searchlight detachment seeing these signals, or on the order from control, would expose the beam horizontally for 30 seconds in the direction of the selected airfield. In order to catch the pilot's attention, the beam was elevated to 45° and depressed three times in succession. Finally, the beam was left horizontal for a further 30 seconds.

The complete sequence was repeated until the aircraft flew in the correct direction; the beam was then kept on for 2 minutes as a horizontal pointer.

The Post Office and Standard Telephones & Cables installed the first RAF multi-channel telegraph system of the Defence Teleprinter Network (DTN) for Fighter Command on 31 March 1939 for operation between Uxbridge, HQ of 11 Group, and the Faraday building, London. The system was known as stop-start telegraphy. It used coded seven-hole ticker-tape which was sent and received at + 80 volts and – 80 volts (up and down). It ran off the 250-volt mains supply with a 110-volt motor which had a governor preventing the speed exceeding 3,000 rpm. Most stations were issued with Teleprinter Type 7b, Equipment Table DTN2000, Rectifier 22 (for the 110-volt motor), Rectifier 26a (for signalling power), and Bell Type 546a. The day-to-day maintenance was carried out by RAF personnel on the station but major faults were repaired by the local GPO engineer. Most control towers had two teleprinters, one for Met reports and one for communications. At other locations such as group HQ there could be up to 20.

The starting procedure required an operator at one end of the line to press a button to operate the 110-volt motor. He then pressed the space bar which operated an electromagnet at the receiving end of the line to start the teleprinter there. With a conventional typewriter set of keys in front of him, he would then press 'figs D', indicating the code 'who are you?'. He held this down until a code returned, which could be, for example, 'Q BIN' (Binbrook) or 'Q NCT' (North Coates). This ensured that the receiving station was operative. Should a reply be required he would press 'figs J' which operated the Bell Type 546a under the table. This attracted the attention of the operator at the receiving station who would then reply. When the messages had been passed, the operator would again press 'figs D' and wait for the return code –'Q BIN' if the receiving station was Binbrook – thus confirming that the line had been connected all the time the messages were being sent and that both teleprinters had been working at the same speed. Occasionally the line may have been disconnected, thus breaking the transmission. Although the operator at each end had to manually start the teleprinters, the actual signalling power was never switched off.

The Met teleprinters in control towers were only operated 'on broadcast' which meant that once a code had been sent to the machine it would switch on and receive information. It did not have the capability to transmit a code to the originator.

A broadcasting system was first introduced at RAF stations in the early part of 1940. Its purpose was to pass operational instructions rapidly, clearly and simultaneously to personnel stationed at aircraft dispersal points. Essentially the system comprised microphones placed at the main operational centres, including the operations block, control tower and battle headquarters. The microphones were connected to the speech broadcasting building which housed the amplifying equipment. From here, cables ran to the loudspeaker units situated around the airfield.

Certain operating regulations were necessary to minimize accidents on or in the vicinity of airfields. Accidents could happen during taxiing, be caused by obstructions such as vehicles or breaches of discipline, and aircraft could collide when landing, taking off or in the approach. The senior flying control officer was directly responsible to the station commander for the local control of aircraft based permanently or temporarily on the station.

Normally, two flying control officers were on duty, one responsible for aircraft on approach, the other responsible for aircraft in the circuit. The senior flying control officer was responsible for marking out all bad ground, controlling the activities of contractors working out on the airfield, and for the marking and daily checking of obstructions. All relevant information was kept up to date on a site plan of the airfield kept in the watch office. Each runway was identified on the plan by its QDM number; the runway in use was indicated by an arrow. Usually an NCO inspected the airfield twice daily, and once before dusk prior to the commencement of night flying. A vehicle was made available for this purpose, which was also used to tow the runway caravan and fetch meals for the night duty staff.

The FCO made sure that all obstruction lights were in place and suitably hooded to prevent observation from above, and that aircraft were not parked in line with a recognized take-off and landing strip or within a distance of 200 yd either side. He delegated an airman to be stationed at the up-wind end of the runway in use throughout the daylight hours to control aircraft or vehicles moving across the end of the runways. At Thorney Island, for example, an airman was stationed inside a caravan positioned on the grass triangle between the intersecting runways because there was a public road across the airfield to the church and officers' mess at West Thorney. He was equipped with a telephone connected to the tower, binoculars, and a loud hailer to warn anyone near the active runway to stay clear when it was about to be used.

On grass airfields, the FCO detailed the flarepath party to load up a lorry with portable lighting equipment kept in the NFE store. Also on board the lorry was a large 'cotton reel' drum of telephone cable. This would be gradually unwound as the lorry progressed along the landing strip while distributing the portable lighting. The cable was for communication between the airfield controller and the FCO. The FCO was responsible for the duty flight, who looked after the reception and parking of visiting aircraft, and the supervision of the airfield controller.

The mimic diagram in the control room was in the form of a free-standing unit or designed to be mounted on a wall. The diagram was about 2 ft 6 in square showing the layout of the runways and taxiways, with a mimic representation of all lighting on and surrounding the airfield. As each airfield lighting circuit was energized, the corresponding lamps on the mimic display lit up, confirming that the correct switching sequence had been carried out. This allowed the FCO to see at a glance the set-up of airfield lighting.

The airfield controller (aerodrome control pilot) was positioned on the airfield to the left of the downwind end of the runway in use. On grass airfields, he usually sat inside a portable makeshift windbreak – normally a wooden box with handles and a rooftop astrodome. On airfields with hard runways, a special caravan was placed on a concrete hard standing.

His duties included placing the landing T to mark the runway in use. He controlled the traffic on the perimeter track in the vicinity of the runway in use, and the movement of vehicles requiring to cross the downwind end of the runway. He could refuse a pilot permission to land if the aircraft still had its undercarriage up, or if there was danger of collision. He could refuse to allow an aircraft to leave the marshalling point or to take off if to do so would obstruct an aircraft approaching to land. Any breaches of discipline were reported to the FCO, including the use of non-standard signals or unusual aircraft movements.

He was provided with two signal lamps, one red and one green, a Very Pistol with red cartridges only, binoculars, the letters and colours of the day, direct telephone or R/T communication (sometimes both) with the FCO, an airfield site plan, and a landing T.

Pilots established R/T contact with the FCO before leaving dispersal and listened in. Having left the dispersal, the pilot taxied towards the marshalling point where he waited for permission from the airfield controller to turn on to the runway. Permission was indicated by an intermittent green lamp signal, refusal by a steady red lamp signal. More care was needed on grass airfields and pilots were required to keep a sharp look out for aircraft landing. Final permission to take off was given by a steady green lamp signal. An intermittent red lamp signal directed at an aircraft on the runway indicated that the aircraft was to be immediately taxied clear of the runway.

If a pilot on approach was refused permission to land by a steady red lamp signal (temporary refusal) or an intermittent red lamp signal, he had to open up the throttle again and rejoin the circuit unless he considered this to be dangerous in which case he simply completed his approach and landed. Having landed, the pilot taxied at a safe speed to the perimeter track. On a grass airfield, the pilot brought the aircraft to rest and then turned 90° to port, and after completing his cockpit drill, the pilot made sure visually that his aircraft would not cut across the path of another; he then taxied to the airfield perimeter. On grass SFTS airfields, pilots taxied directly downwind after having received an intermittent green lamp signal from the airfield controller.

The rules for control did not apply to fighter aircraft under scramble conditions. Under such circumstances, the movement of all non-operational aircraft was prohibited until the airfield was clear.

For night flying, a blackboard in the control tower displayed the layout of the flarepath, the position of the marshalling point, the locations of obstructions and bad ground with lighting details, the positions of dispersed aircraft, and the direction and strength of the wind. This was consulted by all pilots and marshalling personnel. When R/T was not fitted, aircraft left the dispersal according to a pre-arranged programme or on the receipt of instructions from the FCO. Navigation lights were switched on while taxiing unless there was a possibility of intruder activity, when resin lights were used. Rear gunners carried a torch as an additional safeguard on the ground.

On receiving instructions, pilots taxied to the marshalling point, using the blue and amber taxiway if the airfield was equipped with airfield lighting Mk II, or on a similar track laid out with blue glim lamps. At the marshalling point, the pilot carried out the necessary cockpit drill and then requested permission from the airfield controller by signalling his distinguishing letter on the downward identification lights before he could go on to the flarepath. Permission to proceed was given by repeating the distinguishing letter in green, refusal by repeating in red. Final permission to take off was given by a steady green lamp signal.

On a hard runway airfield, the FCO ordered the lead out lights, the fog funnel lights at the upwind end of the runway to be switched on when the pilot received permission to take off.

When landing, normal R/T procedure was used or a combination of R/T and visual landing procedures. A pilot requested permission to land by signalling his distinguishing letter on the aircraft upward and downward identification lights. The airfield controller gave permission as described above and the pilot acknowledged this instruction by keeping his identification lights on. If for any reason a pilot was refused permission to land, he circled the airfield at 2,000 ft, or at a height instructed by the controller, until permission was given to land.

Aircraft landing on a runway then taxied to the end of the runway unless there was a runway intersection which was used if it provided a shorter route to the dispersal or marshalling point.

Air Traffic Control Signals

Ground-to-air signals were usually displayed in the signals area near the control tower on civil and service airfields. They warned pilots about the prevailing conditions and the precautions to be taken when landing and taking off. Other methods of signalling from the ground to air (or vice versa) included W/T, R/T, the firing of pyrotechnics, Morse code signals flashed on a lamp, and flags.

The majority of signals were, however, displayed horizontally on a black-coloured concrete signal square edged with a white border, 1 ft wide with internal sides measuring 40 ft. Vertical symbols or flags displayed on a signals mast were for pilots of aircraft within the manoeuvring area of the airfield.

A red square with sides 10 ft long indicated that special rules for air traffic in the vicinity of airfields open to the public were not in use. This signal was permanently displayed at RAF stations. Superimposing a diagonal strip on the red square indicated that temporary obstructions existed, that the airfield was partly unserviceable, and that special care was required when landing. This was probably one of the most frequently used ground signals during the war, displayed when contractors were repairing runways or grass cutting.

Superimposing a yellow X on the red square indicated that there was a total landing prohibition. This was usually used when the runway in use was obstructed and for some reason the other runways could not be used. Two yellow parallel bars on the red square showed that only emergency landings were to be made and that care should be taken as there were no emergency services available. This was once a common sight on redundant airfields on Care and Maintenance.

The landing T was first used during the First World War. A white T of regulation size was installed by the airfield controller at the end and to the left of the runway in use. It was laid parallel to the runway and indicated the direction of landing. Another T was displayed in the

Ground Signals at RAF Stations

Signal	Meaning
	Temporary obstuctions signal
	Detachable black cross bars indicated that landing and take-offs were only to be made on runways
	Total landing prohibition signal
	A separate landing area for light aircraft
	Emergency landings only
	Bombing practice signal
	Landing T
	Airfield subjected to a gas attack
	Change to right-hand circuit
	Airfield subjected to a gas attack; aircraft not allowed to land
	A white dumb-bell indicated that the airfield was unserviceable except for runways and taxiways

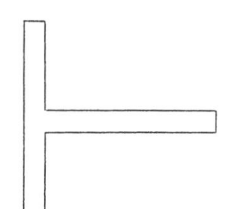

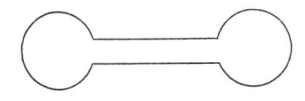

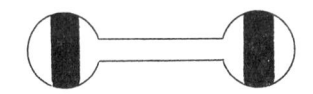

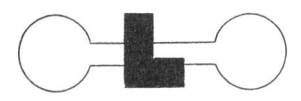

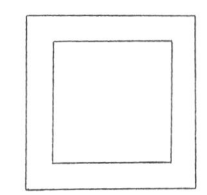

Signals Associated with the Signals Mast

A red diamond on a white square, a red diamond on a white flag

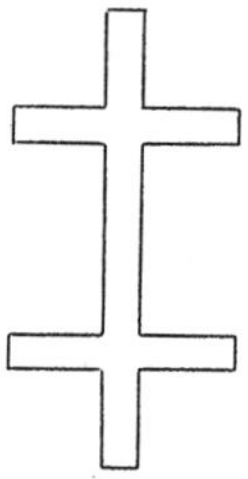

A double white cross used in conjunction with two red balls hoisted on the signals mast

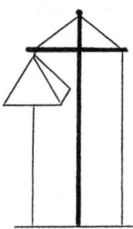

A large yellow pyramid hanging from the signals mast. There was no equivalent horizontal signal for the signals square

A white flag on the signals mast indicated full dual and solo flying

A black flag indicated 'no flying today'

A black and white horizontally striped flag on the signals mast indicated dual flying only

Air Traffic Control Signals Not Associated with the Signals Area or Mast

Marshalling Point – the 2 ft square yellow board with the runway number in black numerals

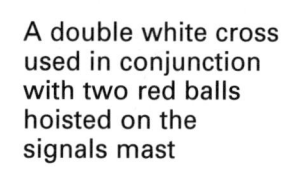

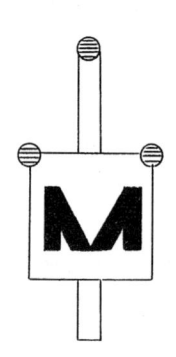

The board displayed at the marshalling point of grass airfields

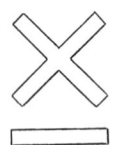

Airfield abandoned signal

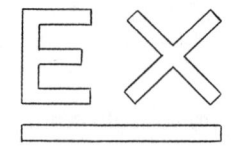

Explosives stored on disused runway

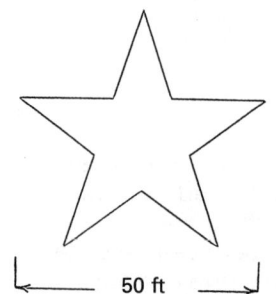

On grass airfields this indicated that aircraft must take off on the left and land on the right

signals square. Sometimes due to a change of wind direction or because special exercises were taking place, it was necessary to change from the normal left-hand circuit to a right-hand one. When this happened, a red right-handed arrow was used in conjunction with the red square signal. A green flag was hoisted on the signal mast, indicating to those on the ground that a right-hand circuit was in force. A red flag was hoisted when the normal circuit was restored.

A white dumb-bell indicated that the airfield was unserviceable except for runways and taxiways. Landing and taking off were only to be performed on the runways; aircraft were not allowed to use the grass surface at all. This was frequently used when grass airfields had new concrete runways laid and there was a risk of aircraft becoming bogged down on the grass surface. Superimposing a detachable crossbar on each of the circular ends of the dumb-bell indicated that landing and taking off were only to be performed on runways but aircraft could turn on to the grass surface for taxiing purposes. Certain grass areas at some airfields were set aside for light aircraft to avoid the delay caused by slowly taxiing light aircraft on a long concrete runway. There was a separate landing area for light aircraft indicated by white corner markings.

When bombing practice was being carried out, a white hollow square was placed in the signals square or in the centre of the landing circle (as at Eastchurch). In the 1930s, an arrow pointing to the bombing target was situated near the watch office. Pilots who wished to land at an airfield with this signal displayed kept a sharp look-out for aircraft bombing or diving and avoided the target area. The target to be bombed consisted of a solid white square with sides 15 ft long; at some stations a chalk silhouette of an aircraft was also used.

A red G on a triangular white background indicated that the airfield had been subjected to a gas attack. Aircraft could land but were to taxi to the upwind edge of the airfield and remain there until further notice. A red G with a red strip underneath on a triangular white background indicated that the airfield had been subjected to a gas attack and that aircraft were not allowed to land.

A red diamond on a white square displayed from the signals mast (replacing the red square in a corner of the signals square), or a red diamond on a white flag, indicated that permission must be obtained before joining the circuit or before starting to taxi or take off. A white double cross indicated that glider flying was in progress. This was used in conjunction with two red balls on the signals mast. A single yellow cross was used to indicate the cable dropping area. A single black ball hoisted on the signal mast and a white cross on the ground indicated that parachute dropping was in progress. When these signals were displayed, pilots were not to taxi, take off, or land. Pilots already in the air were to fly to a distance not less than 2 miles from the centre of the airfield and to a height of not less than 1,500 ft.

A large yellow pyramid with sides 6 ft across hanging from the signal mast indicated that a standard beam approach landing was in progress. A white flag on the signals mast indicated full dual and solo flying was in progress (Flying Training Schools). A black flag on the signals mast indicated 'no flying today' (Flying Training Schools). A black and white horizontally striped flag on the signals mast indicated dual flying only (Flying Training Schools).

At junctions of runway and taxiway the marshalling point was indicated by a solid white line, 1 ft wide, painted across the taxiway at right angles to the centre line and 225 ft from the nearest runway end. A 2 ft square yellow board with the runway number in black numerals was also displayed 225 ft on both sides of the runway and 75 ft from the outside edge of the taxiway. They indicated the point on the taxiway where pilots had to halt their aircraft, make any last minute checks and await the go signal from the airfield controller's green Aldis lamp.

A similar board bearing a black letter M was displayed at the marshalling point on grass airfields. Both types of board could be illuminated by three 15-watt blue pigmy lamps connected to the flarepath circuit. They also acted as a guide at night for taxiing to the correct end of the runway.

When the airfield was finally abandoned, the signals square and windsocks were removed. A white X with arms 60 ft long and 5 ft wide was painted on the ends of the runways, indicating the airfield had been abandoned and that no landing should take place except in an emergency. Runways at some disused airfields had a white bar painted beneath the cross to indicate that the airfield had been inspected within the last six months and found to be serviceable for emergency use. After the war at a few abandoned airfields, explosives were stored on the disused runways. Here a white letter E was painted beside the white cross. No landing was to be attempted at these airfields (an example was Attlebridge). A white five-pointed star on grass airfields indicated that the airfield was divided by an imaginary line and aircraft must take off on the left and land on the right

The site of the airfield's main windsock was marked by a 20 ft diameter ring, 1 ft wide. Each dispersal area was identified by illuminated indicators. Each indicator was a tin-plate box 9.5 inches square by 13.5 inches high with holes drilled into it in the shape of a digit designating the dispersal number. In practice, the indicators were made from discarded 4-gallon petrol cans and 15-watt pygmy lamps. At certain airfields, to enable the control tower to be located at night, a panel displaying an illuminated letter C was used. This was installed vertically, the C being outlined by a single row of 30 40-watt blue lamps mounted on a timber framework and shielded so that they could not be seen from above.

When the control tower was not manned, the ground signals had still to indicate the correct state of the aerodrome. Therefore the landing T was covered or removed from the runway and signals square, and the 'land emergency only' signal displayed instead. The runway control caravan was removed as were the QDM boards.

The First Buildings

The first standard design of office for the duty pilot (later to be called the watch office) appeared in 1926. Before 1926, the only references made to buildings of this kind were to the 'control tops' built above door gantries of general service sheds at Beaulieu and Bircham Newton from 1918, but their exact function is unclear.

The watch office for the duty pilot 2072/26 at Hendon, photographed shortly before its demolition in 1989.

On the right is the watch office for the duty pilot 2072/26 at Netheravon. The building on the left is a later addition. (Photographed in 1994)

The office for the duty pilot 2072/26 with a flarepath trolley shelter at Upavon. A later extension was built in front of the shelter to a similar style to that of the office for the duty pilot. (Photographed 1993)

The watch office on bomber stations was a small bungalow with a bay window on the front elevation; a similar office served as the duty pilot's office, a station having one or other but not both. The style of the casement and whether it was free-standing were the only differences between the offices. There were two main rooms, the duty pilot's office and a rest room, both heated by fireplaces built back-to-back. Construction was of unrendered cavity brick walls with a pitched roof of timber purlins and rafters clad with diamond-shaped asbestos tiles. At some stations, such as Martlesham Heath, Upavon and Upper Heyford, a flarepath trolley shelter was built against a side wall in the same style as the existing building. It was simply an open-plan garage 14 ft by 12 ft. Possibly, only three survive today: Gosport, Netheravon, and Upavon.

Sharing the same drawing number as the watch office at bomber stations, the fighter version was a much larger building to include a pilots' room. It was a semi-detached building. The watch office portion was similar to the bomber station version, having an office with a bay window at the front with a rest room behind. Between here and the pilots' room was a heating chamber, WCs, and corridor. The greater part of the building was used for pilots' accommodation. This included a rest room with a large dormer window. The only other room was for the storage of lockers. It made sense that fighter stations should have a combined watch office and pilots' rest room where pilots could relax while waiting for a scramble; and after a mission they reported to the watch office.

The building was built of unrendered brick cavity walls and a steel-framed pitched roof clad with diamond-shaped asbestos tiles.

At Tangmere, instead of having a combined watch office and pilots' room as described above, pilots of two squadrons were relocated to the ARS shed. Here, two large locker and rest rooms were created covering five bays of the shed, 20 ft wide, with the use of studwork and matchboard inside both ends of the shed so that the hangar doors had to be permanently closed. Officers and clerks of the three flights of a squadron were now housed inside the south annexes of aircraft sheds Nos 1 and 2.

A watch office with tower 1959/34 at Odiham.

The detached watch office was therefore a conversion of an old flight office located on the airfield side of aircraft shed No. 2. This consisted of a brick-built structure with cavity walls and a close-coupled roof. The entrance was roughly in the centre of the front elevation and led into a lobby area. A bay window was added to the watch office itself. The only other room was a rest room. Heating for both rooms was provided by a pair of fireplaces built back-to-back. Another entrance at the front gave access to a fuel store.

It is believed that this building along with the aircraft sheds were destroyed during the Battle of Britain. As a result, a temporary watch office was located in a small room on top of the fire tender garage until the new control tower was built.

The original 1930s' watch office at Halton, now demolished. (Photographed 1977)

Type	drawing no.	length	width	examples
watch office	1072/26	61 ft	20 ft	Bircham Newton, Gosport, Hendon, Hornchurch, Mildenhall, Netheravon, Northolt, Upavon, Wittering
duty pilot's office	2072/26			
watch office	1597/27			Tangmere

Permanent Buildings 1934–40

Watch Office with Tower

A major change in building design took place in 1934 with the invention of the two-storey watch office, known as the watch office with tower (1959/34). This became the standard Type design for aerodromes both at home and abroad, replacing all previous designs. Its shape resembled a child's toy fort, consisting of a large (approximately square in plan) ground floor 28 ft by 22 ft with a flat roof, built either without a tower as at Hornchurch (2062/34) or more commonly with a central observation tower.

The ground floor served as the watch office for the duty pilot at the front with large casement windows spanning the whole width of the building, a spiral staircase connected with a room on the floor above. Ceiling height here was only 6 ft and could only be used for storage and to get access to the roof. The staircase led up to the observation room, from where a fairly good all round view was possible although at some stations the rear view was poor because of the close proximity of the hangars. A cat ladder gave access to the roof of the observation tower.

Construction of 1959/34 was in unrendered cavity walls, 15 inches thick for the ground floor and 11 inches thick for the tower. A combination of load-bearing walls and cased steel beams in a square pattern supported the weight of the tower. A change in construction from permanent brick to all concrete came after 1936 with drawing number 207/36. This was in keeping with other technical buildings including Type C hangars. The precast concrete walls of both the main building and the tower were 10 inches thick and internally lined with pioneer blocks. The tower supported by four reinforced-concrete up-stand beams, comprised eight reinforced-concrete columns with walls cast *in situ*.

With the outbreak of war and the subsequent construction of hard runways, it was found at many stations that the existing watch office was now in the wrong position. Therefore a new building built to the latest Type design was constructed well away from hangars and other buildings so that now the ends of runways could be seen. With a new watch office, some of the original buildings were demolished, including those at Burtonwood and Upwood, but some were retained, such as those at Odiham and Watton.

An alternative idea, where the position of the building was satisfactory but the observation tower was still too small for the installation of airfield lighting control equipment, was to remove the tower and build a larger control room to 4698/43. The new extension took up two-thirds of the roof space with a gallery area in front. Access was from the spiral staircase repositioned against an outside wall, or from a new external brick-built staircase.

Another bizarre idea was to retain the tower and build a new control room around it. This strange idea happened at Bassingbourn. The new extension was built above the existing parapet wall of the main building up to the level of the tower windows. A balcony was added to the front elevation and supported by scaffolding. Later, a new signalling penthouse was added on top of the original observation tower. The observation tower can still be seen today in the former control room.

The watch office 207/36 at West Raynham once had a tower but it was removed and replaced by a new control room 4698/43. (Photographed in 1993)

drawing no.	1959/34	1960/34	207/36
examples	Bicester, Bircham Newton, Catterick, Felixstowe, Odiham		Wattisham, Watton

drawing no.	4698/43
examples	Cosford, Cranfield, Hemswell, Leconfield, West Raynham

(all still extant)

Chief Instructor's Block

This was built from 1936 on Service Flying Training Schools including those combined with Aircraft Storage Units. The original drawing 5740/36 was for a single-

The watch office and chief instructor's office for Service Flying Training Schools at Little Rissington. (Photographed 1984)

storey wing either side of a central tower similar to 1959/34 only much larger. Although aerodrome site plans of all five stations state this drawing number, they were all extended at first-floor level of each wing in slightly different ways.

The tower contained the watch office on the ground floor, staircase, and a rest room above with the observation room on the second floor. Each wing had an office for either the chief flying instructor and his assistant or the officer commanding and his assistants. Clerks were accommodated in two offices at the rear and WCs were located both sides of the main entrance at the rear of the building.

Construction was of brick cavity wall or Bath stone (Hullavington) with concrete floors and precast concrete stairs.

drawing no.	length	width	examples
5740/36	53 ft 4 in	39 ft	Hullavington, Little Rissington, Shawbury, South Cerney, Ternhill

Watch Office with Meteorological Section

The watch office with meteorological section was designed in 1939 for RAF Regional Control Organization airfields. For the first time, serious thought was given to a building for the future requirements of air traffic control, large enough to accommodate the development of airfield lighting control equipment. Furthermore, the basic design had to be adapted to conform to the current emergency. Buildings constructed during wartime were of a less permanent nature but there was no compromise in standards of room arrangement and size of building.

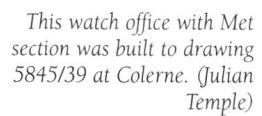

This watch office with Met section was built to drawing 5845/39 at Colerne. (Julian Temple)

This watch office with Met section 2423/39 was built in timber at Wick. (Photographed 1991)

A watch office with Met section 518/40 and 8936/40 at Holme-on-Spalding Moor.

All new aerodromes under construction in the period leading up to the beginning of the Second World War had a watch office with the meteorological section in all-concrete construction (2328/39). By 1940, on stations with two Type J hangars supplemented by T2s, the technical accommodation and watch office with meteorological section were built in permanent brick and concrete (5845/39). Almost simultaneously, on new parent stations built with a single Type J, two T2s and temporary brick technical accommodation, the watch office was built in temporary brick, concrete, and timber.

Both concrete and permanent brick buildings were similar in appearance, being designed on modern lines with a large proportion of the front elevation covered with double-glazed metal-framed folding or pivoted windows. The control room had typical 1930s' curved return windows which was both attractive and functional. The watch office on the ground floor extended forward and supported the balcony above. This was finished with radiused corners, and large number of closely spaced balustrades and rails round the edge, again typical of the period.

The 2328/39 design was built entirely of reinforced concrete. The walls were 14 inches thick, heavily reinforced with steel bars especially round the windows and beams which were all cast *in situ* using plywood shuttering. At roof level, it had a concrete parapet wall all the way round the edge. The 5845/39 design had brick cavity walls 15.5 inches wide, reinforced-concrete columns, reinforced-concrete up-stand roof beams, and a concrete slab floor and roof. It had a brick parapet only on the front elevation, the remaining area having steel balustrades and railings.

Room arrangement was typical for all designs. The main entrance was on the right hand side of the staircase at the rear of the building (the left hand door was a hydrogen gas cylinder store) and this led into a hall and staircase. The right hand side contained WCs, while on the left was a meteorological store. A corridor to the front of the building passed the duty pilot's rest room on the right and led to a passageway (to exit the building). Opposite here was the forecast room which also led to a teleprinter room. The front of the building was the watch office; here in one corner was a pyrotechnic cupboard which was

Control Towers

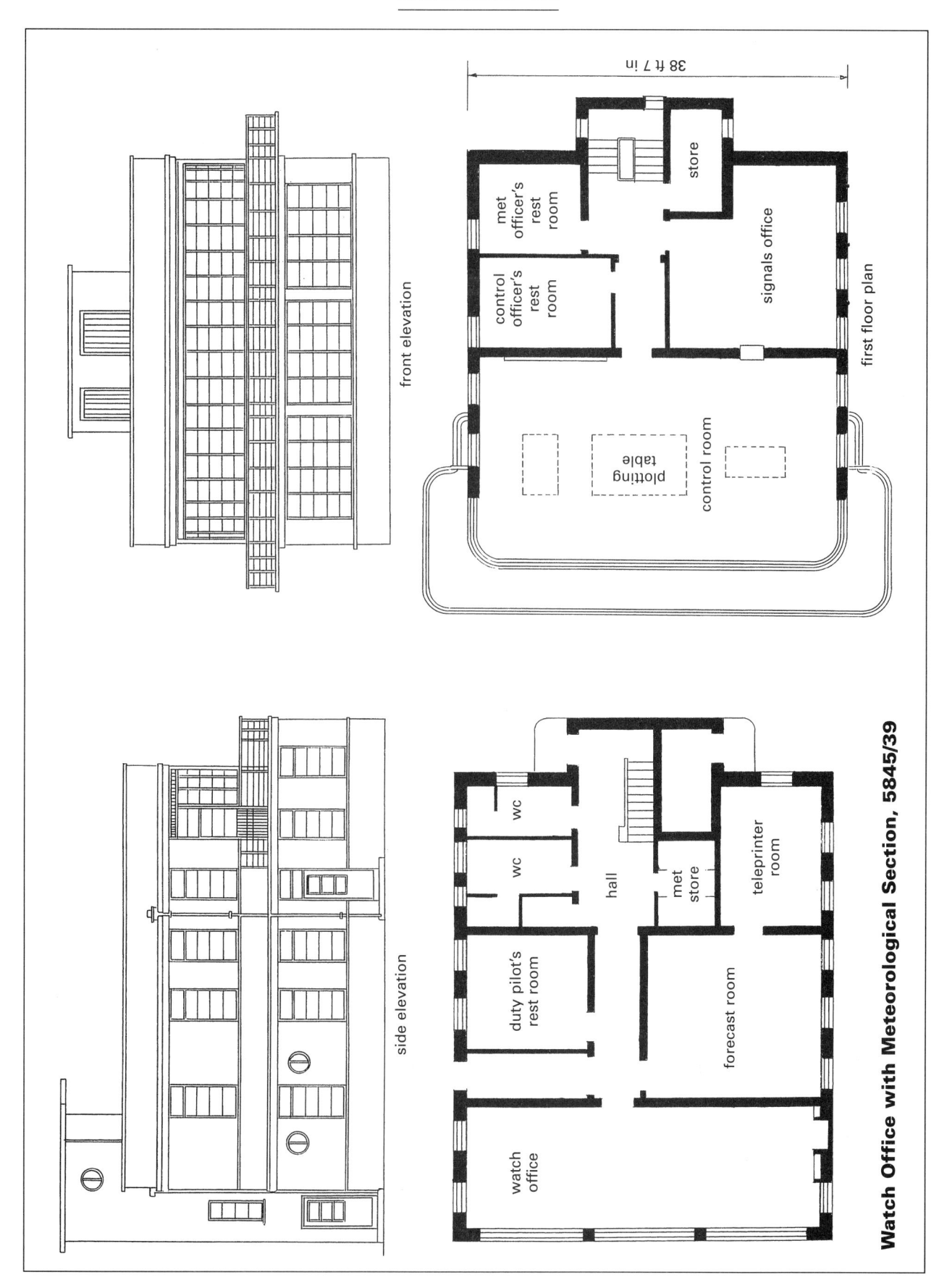

front elevation

side elevation

first floor plan

- met officer's rest room
- control officer's rest room
- store
- signals office
- control room
- plotting table

38 ft 7 in

- wc
- wc
- hall
- met store
- teleprinter room
- duty pilot's rest room
- forecast room
- watch office

Watch Office with Meteorological Section, 5845/39

typically stocked with wing-tip flares, white and green signal cartridges, powder charges for location signals, friction tubes for location charges, and rockets or signal charges.

On the first floor, at the rear, were three rooms: the meteorological officer's bedroom, the control officer's rest room, and the signals office. The front half of the building was taken up with the control room. All the ATC equipment was located here, including the Lorenz control board and later the airfield lighting control board, the airfield lighting mimic display table, the aerodrome state board, and the plotting table. The staircase continued to the roof and balloon-filling room.

Drawing numbers 518/40 and 8936/40 were based on 2423/40 except that construction was in rendered 9-inch solid brick walls, part timber and reinforced-concrete floor, and an all-concrete roof. Originally 518/40 called for an all-timber floor, roof, and staircase but the acute timber shortage in 1941 dictated a redesign so that only the control room and balcony were made in timber. As a result, the deviation drawing 8936/40 was used in conjunction with 518/40 on all buildings. At Ibsley, the builders went one step further and built the complete first floor and balcony in concrete; this may have been the last to be built.

Some airfields were planned in permanent construction but were of timber hutting. At these airfields, the watch office was also built in timber (2423/39), for example, Wick. Despite postwar modifications, at first glance this building looks like a typical 518/40 brick-built watch office. Not until you approach it can you see that it is, in fact, built entirely of timber. This is the only surviving example. It was reclad in 1968 and the original windows replaced. Not much is known about its construction except that it was built to a slightly better standard than a Type A sectional hut, with timber-framed walls clad with rebated weatherboarding. Floor and roof were timber-framed and timber-boarded units supported by RSJs.

drawing no.	2328/39	5845/39	2423/39
examples	Binbrook, Bramcote, Coltishall, Leeming	Abingdon, North Luffenham, Swanton Morley, Syerston	St Eval, Wick

drawing no.	518/40, 8936/40
examples	Andreas, Goxhill, Bottesford, Rednal

SECOND WORLD WAR TEMPORARY BUILDINGS

In contrast to the watch office designs described above for Regional Control stations, contemporary fighter and bomber satellite airfields had to make do with vastly inferior building designs. As the war progressed, and as air traffic control developed, it became necessary to carry out major structural modifications to existing buildings or, in some cases, abandon them altogether and build new structures to the latest standard design.

Bomber Satellite Station Watch Offices

This watch office was originally designed to be similar to a standard 18 ft span, 60 ft long temporary brick hut with one end used as a watch office, the centre portion as an operations room and the rear third as a crew briefing room. After June 1941, buildings already completed became known as the Type A.

All new structures built to a new standard were known as Type B. Type A buildings were then structurally altered to bring them up to the same standard as Type B. This phase of the rebuilding programme of Type A buildings involved the operations room and included the provision of a PBX, a speech broadcasting installation and a teleprinter room. The PBX part was built at right angles to the main structure, creating a T-shaped building in plan. The walls were increased in thickness to 13.5 inches, and a flat reinforced-concrete roof was added. On top of this, a pitched roof was built using brick spandrels to blend in with what already existed above the watch office and crew briefing rooms.

New Type B buildings were 78 ft long with the operations room built in the centre and the PBX in the same plane as the rest of structure. As with all operations rooms, this section of the building was perfectly sealed against a possible gas attack with gas-tight doors and airlocks. Today, this part can easily be identified by the tapering narrow slit-like windows.

The next rebuilding phase, around 1942, included the addition of an observation room extension. This involved removing the pitched roof above either the operations or PBX depending on where the new extension was to be added. Brick walls 9 inches thick with large window openings on all sides and a flat concrete roof were built above the load-bearing walls of the rooms below. Entrance to the observation room was via a steel ladder (Blyton), using the blast wall outside the entrance to the teleprinter and PBX to support a landing. Alternatively, a brick staircase (Kirmington) could be provided. In both cases, a parapet wall was built offering some protection to personnel from attack by enemy aircraft. Other local variations included retaining the pitched roof above the watch office and the old crew briefing room (Ingham), and increasing the wall thickness to support a reinforced-concrete roof (Tibenham). A combination of both can be seen at Edge Hill.

Also at this stage, half of the crew briefing room became a kitchen, and half WCs. A corridor was built connecting a new crew briefing room in temporary brick (Long Marston) or more commonly in 24 ft span Nissen hutting. This building was built open plan with a raised dais at one end and a blackboard fixed to the rear wall which the assembled aircrew faced during a briefing. An example of

Control Towers 125

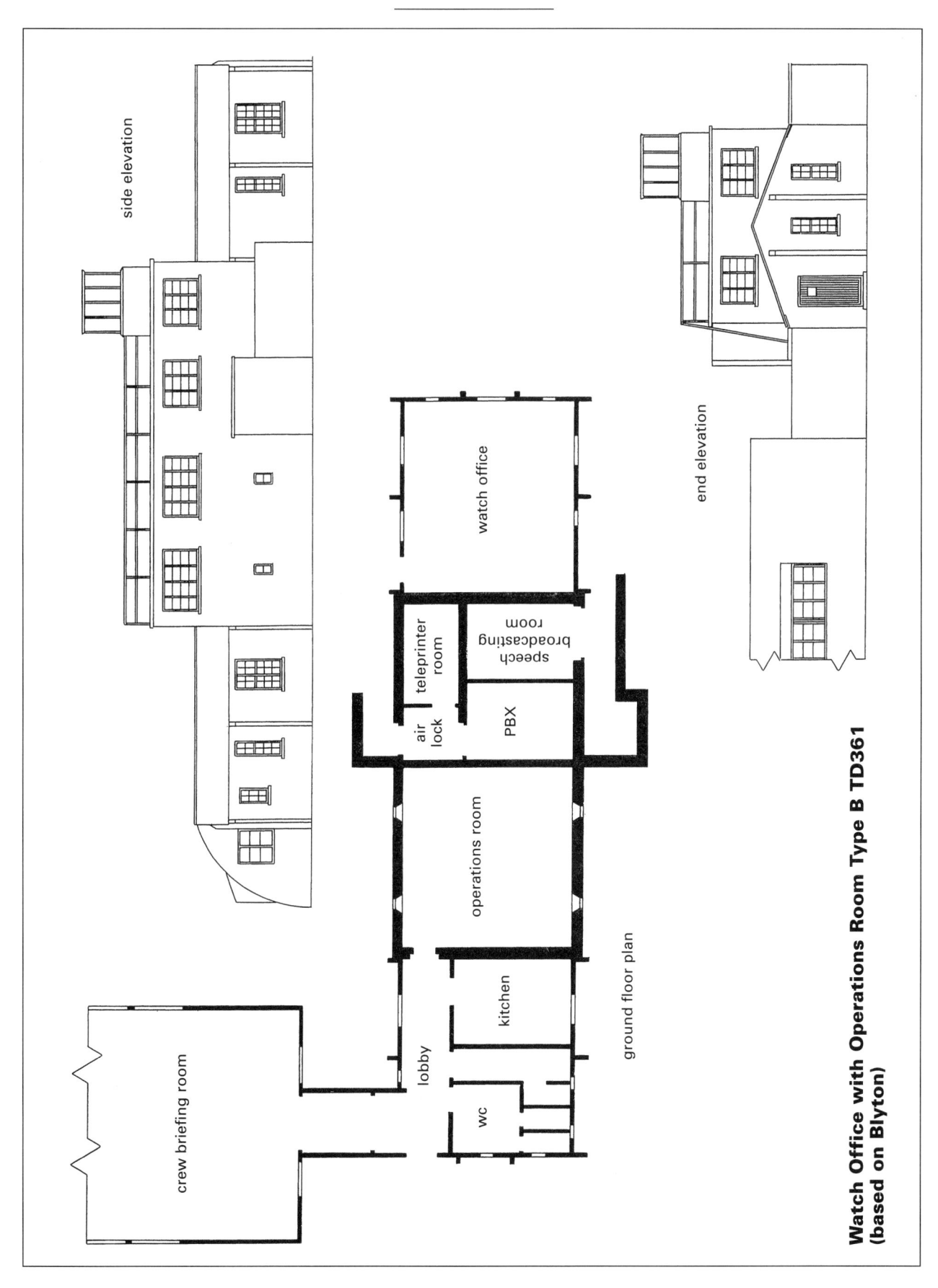

Watch Office with Operations Room Type B TD361 (based on Blyton)

side elevation

end elevation

ground floor plan

- watch office
- teleprinter room
- speech broadcasting room
- air lock
- PBX
- operations room
- kitchen
- lobby
- wc
- crew briefing room

The watch office with operations room 7345/41 and 13079/41 at Seighford to which an observation room was added. (Photographed 1984)

this can be seen at Seighford.

It is interesting to note that the operations room and its ancillary rooms, including the new crew briefing room Nissen hut, were very similar to the operations room complex 13023/41 and 13742/41 built on a few bomber OTU satellite stations which had a different design of watch office.

At many bomber satellite airfields, such as Seighford, the building in its phase 2 form proved perfectly adequate for local airfield control and therefore did not require further structural modifications. But an improvement was implemented at some stations, such as Attlebridge and Bungay, in the form of a Uni-Seco control room (5966/43) which was simply anchored to the roof of the observation room.

The watch office with operations room 7345/41 and 13079/41 at Rufforth. The Seco huts 4702/43 accommodated signals, and teleprinter, and a rest room.

At those airfields with extended hard runways and were upgraded to the Class A standard, there were two options: abandon the existing watch office and build a new one to the latest design in a better position; upgrade the existing building. Where the existing building was retained, the size of the observation room could be doubled to become a control room. This was achieved by building against the end wall of the observation room and above the load-bearing walls of the room below. The observation room end wall was removed to create a large control room. On the roof, a signalling penthouse was built in one corner and tubular railings were fitted round the edge of the roof. Close to the penthouse were QDM (runway heading) boards (1358/44) corresponding to the runway in use. Also at this stage, a new operations block was built on a dispersed administration site to drawing number 288/43.

A design to similar standard as 12779/41 but on a smaller scale became the standard RAF bomber satellite watch office from September 1941, superseding the watch

A watch office and operations room 7345, 13079/41, and 4170/43. The framework on the roof on the right was for runway heading boards.

Bomber satellite station watch office 13726/41 at Enstone. (Photographed 1978)

office with operations room. A similar operations block to that belonging to the original bomber satellite watch office design was built as a detached building (13023/41) on a dispersed administration site. Construction was similar to 12779/41. Like 12779/41, large windows in the watch office and control rooms were bricked up and replaced by narrow-framed windows, this time to drawing 15683/41. Furthermore, the majority of the remaining buildings were modified to receive windows of an intermediate size similar to 343/43.

The internal arrangement was similar to the night-fighter design 15684/41. The main entrance was at the rear with a corridor leading to the front. Immediately on the right was a precast concrete staircase. Opposite here were two WCs, one for officers, the other for airmen. Opposite these was the meteorological office. Then came the switch room, opposite which was a rest room. The corridor terminated at the entrance to the watch office. Upstairs was an L-shaped corridor leading to storeroom, signal office and controller's rest room. The corridor finished at the control room with access to the balcony and roof via a steel stairway.

An additional control room in Seco construction was sometimes built on the roof but this was a rare addition.

drawing no.	15898/40, 15956/40, 17821/40	7344/41	7345/41
Type	A	phase 1 A rebuild	B

drawing no.	13023/41	13079/41	13726/41
Type		phase 1 B rebuild	
examples	Bardney, Cottam, Turweston		Bardney, Enstone, Castle Coombe, Chipping Norton, Nuneaton

drawing no.	15683/41	4170/43
Type		phase 2 B rebuild
examples	Thorpe Abbotts, Cottam	Blyton, Grafton Underwood, Ingham, Waltham

Very Heavy Bomber Station Control Tower

Perhaps the most impressive of the RAF wartime-designed watch office/control towers was the design 294/45. Airfields, such as Sculthorpe, subsequently designated as very heavy bomber stations, had to be developed to standards in excess of normal Class A operational stations. They were all closed after 1945 to have their main

Very heavy bomber station watch office at West Raynham. (Photographed 1993)

runways increased to 3,000 yd by 100 yd and their subsidiaries to 200 yd by 100 yd. Part of this modernization programme included the construction of a modern control tower to 294/45. Sculthorpe reopened in December 1948.

This was the first RAF building to be designed with an airfield control room (later to be called the visual control room or VCR). The basic structure was three stories with a single-storey annexe, leading off from a side elevation, containing the airfield services such as the fire station and NFE store. Construction was of a steel frame with unrendered red facing-brick cavity walls. Floors and subfloors were of precast concrete of the Seigwart type, supported on RSJs and cased steel beams. Flooring was tongued-and-grooved timber boarding.

The main entrance consisted of a single-storey lobby which led into a large hallway with a corridor running to the front of the building. At the rear of the hall were stairs. To the left of here were the WCs and hydrogen store. Along the corridor, the first room contained the GPO apparatus. Opposite here was the rest room for visiting crews and a kitchen. Next to the GPO apparatus was the signals apparatus. Then came the battery and power room. On the opposite side and next to the visiting crew's rest room was the meteorological rest room, and finally a compressor and switch room.

The annexe contained a fire party rest room, ambulance and crash tender drive-through garages, and NFE store at right angles to the garages containing a goose flare trolley, glim lamp trolley and illuminated landing T.

On the first floor, there was a similar arrangement of hall and corridor with WC above to those on the ground floor. Immediately in front of the hall was the operations and planning room containing a large plotting table and map wall. On the right was a small meteorological store and large forecast room with access to the teleprinter room. At the front of the building were offices for the CO, navigation officer, Wg Cdr plans, and meteorological officer.

On the second floor, a small landing contained a balloon-filling room with a supply of hydrogen in cylinders in the storeroom on the ground floor. The whole of the second floor was taken up by the ACR and a small office for the senior flying control officer, located above the WCs on the floors below. In an area partitioned off at the rear of this large room were five R/T monitor cubicles. Equipment in the approach control room included the airfield lighting mimic display board and a plotting table large enough to cover 100 square miles. There were pneumatic tubes for communication with other rooms connected with the forecast and airfield control rooms. Steel doors on each side gave access to a concrete balcony, and timber stairs gave access to the airfield control room; the main staircase led to the roof.

ACRs were required to provide a 360° view, have angled glazed windows to cut down on glare, and had to be large enough to accommodate the control desk and airfield lighting control panel and to allow plenty of room for the continuing development of this equipment. The design of the ACR on this control tower type was more than capable of meeting these requirements.

The ACR was octagonal in plan, 20 ft 6 in across flats with a height of 8 ft 6 in. It was framed with RSJs, and clad on the outside with mild steel sheeting and had double-glazed window units. The centre upper windows were top-hung opening sashes, but were so heavy that they took two people to open them. The roof was also glazed, each section consisting of seven sheets of glass. It was quite crude-looking and resembled a greenhouse. At West Raynham, this window glazing has been painted over and a false ceiling of acoustic tiles has been added. Access to the roof of the main block was via a steel-framed sliding door which was frequently very difficult to open.

Today, the control tower at West Raynham looks rather neglected, the ACR is rusting away and most of its equipment has been removed, although the airfield lighting control panel is still *in situ*. The approach control room is now subdivided into offices and some of the second floor is unsafe due to fire damage. The NFE store, crash tender and ambulance station have been bricked up and have been used as offices for the fire section, which, with security, occupied the ground floor of the main building. A new fire station was built adjacent to the NFE store in the 1960s. New control towers have replaced those at Lakenheath, while at Sculthorpe the building has been boarded up.

drawing no.   294/45
examples   Sculthorpe, West Raynham

Fighter Satellite Station Watch Office

Built on fighter sector and satellite stations, this was a small single-storey structure with just one room (15 ft by 15 ft), containing a pyrotechnic cupboard, and built of rendered 9-inch brick with a flat reinforced-concrete roof. The single entrance was located at the rear, protected by a traverse wall with a chemical WC at one end. The view from the watch office was very limited: three windows at the front and a single window on each side wall, the rear being blind because of the traverse wall.

Mainly as a result of the construction of hard runways and the installation of airfield lighting, the first stage in extending this building was the addition in 1942 of a switch room 1536/42 and ME 3651/42. This extension was built against a side wall and here the incoming mains cables connected with switchgear, fuse-box, and main distribution board for airfield lighting, watch office lighting and electric heating.

At certain airfields, such as Stapleford Tawney, the grass airfield was retained and the watch office did not require further modification. But at airfields that now had hard runways two options were open: retain the existing building and develop it; or abandon it and build another to the latest Type design in a better position. Most were abandoned and the design of the new building depended on how the station was to be developed. For example, Cark had a 12096/41, Calveley 12779/41 and 343/43, Longtown a 13726/41, and Fearn had a four-storey naval

The fighter satellite station watch office at Winfield.

type. The original building was then relegated to other uses, such as fire section office (Lulsgate), battery-charging room (Culmhead), or balloon-filling hut (Calveley).

Where the existing building was retained and developed, one idea was to build a new observation room on top of the concrete roof of the watch office. This was designed with a large number of windows on all four sides, giving a good view of the runways and the approach. Examples were at Dale and Matlask, but even these two were eventually replaced by new structures.

From October 1942, at day fighter OTU satellites and fighter satellite airfields that were to be converted to forward fighter satellite stations, a new two-storey extension was built to 7332/42. The new extension was built against the opposite side wall to the switch room in rendered 9-inch brick, and consisted of two 15 ft square rooms, one above the other. The original watch office was converted to a signals office, and the pyrotechnics cupboard was removed and rebuilt in the new observation room. The gap made by the loss of the pyrotechnics cupboard was made larger and a door inserted to gain access to the new NFE storeroom. Access to the roofs of the old and new structures was by a steel ladder. Tubular steel railings were fitted round the edge of the roof.

One last alternative, was the addition of a Uni-Seco control room anchored to the concrete roof; this was done at North Weald and Lympne to 5966/43.

drawing no.   14383/40, 17658/40, 18441/40, 3156/41
examples   Balado Bridge, Kinnal, Montford Bridge

Night-Fighter Stations Watch Office

All buildings in this group had similar structural characteristics to 12096/41 but not all stations were used for fighter operations. Walls were 13.5 inches thick, supporting a reinforced-concrete floor, balcony, and roof. The roof and balcony were reinforced with down-stand beams and curiously the roof was further reinforced with an up-stand beam running the width of the building above the control room.

The rear was practically blind except in some cases for a small window on the ground floor opposite the staircase. Originally, on the front elevation, there were six large windows of similar size, but smaller frames were fitted

The watch office at Elvington before restoration.

Detail of artwork on the rear wall of the watch office at Elvington. (Photographed 1979)

where appropriate to the deviation drawing 16560/41, although it was a rare modification; an example is Scorton. The only access to the roof was by a steel ladder fixed to the rear wall, but later another was sometimes fitted to the balcony, similar to those on later building designs.

A rear main entrance led into a lobby area and corridor. On the left was a staircase, underneath which was the switchgear. Opposite the staircase and storeroom were WCs, and next to these was a rest room. The corridor then turned right towards an exit. After the store was a meteorological observer's office. The last room was the watch office which took up the whole width of the building. On the first floor, an L-shaped corridor gave access to the controller's rest room and to a storeroom on the right; opposite these was a wireless operators' room containing three cubicles. The control room took up the front half of the building with one wall having three hatches, each connected to the wireless operators' cubicles. Curtain rails were fitted to the ceiling to enable the room to be blacked out.

Some airfields, such as Coleby Grange, had a steel-framed additional control room to 10413/42 which was built on to the concrete roof.

This design soon became obsolete and was replaced with a design of the latest standard. The superseding design was similar in size, appearance and internal arrangement to the standard bomber satellite station watch office 15683/41. Not so obvious was its method of construction, which was quite different. Nine reinforced-concrete columns and beams with walls 13.5 inches thick provided the load-bearing structure that supported the reinforced-concrete floor, balcony and roof. Long narrow windows were provided for the control room, while the watch office had shorter windows. The internal arrangement was the same as that for the watch office built on bomber and OTU satellite stations from September 1941 onwards.

drawing no.	12096/41, 16560/41, FCW 4514	15684/41
examples	Church Fenton, Bradwell, Grove, Woolfox Lodge	Winfield

Training Schools Watch Office

Civilian operated Elementary Flying Training Schools also had accommodation designed by the Directorate General of Works and a combined watch office and chief instructor's office based around a typical 18 ft span, 40 ft long temporary brick hut. The main difference between this design and a brick hut was that the front elevation had two bay windows, one for the watch office and the other for the chief instructor. The entrance was at the rear which led to a corridor connecting all rooms. The watch office room had a pyrotechnics cupboard in one corner.

Air Gunner Schools (AGS) and Air Observer Schools (AOS) normally had a 24 ft span Nissen hut, which was 36 ft long (14525/41, 2846/42) with two bay windows, or 48 ft long (13739/41, 1534/42) with three bay windows, one each for the chief flying instructor's room, the commanding officer's room, and the watch office.

drawing no.	641/41	14525/41, 13739/41	2846/42, 1534/42
type	EFTS	AGS	AOS
examples	Halfpenny Green, Shellingford, Wolverhampton		

Watch office for night-fighter stations 15684/41 at Winfield.

Watch office and chief flying instructor's office 641/41 at Shellingford. (Photographed 1989)

Watch Office for all Commands

This was designed as a result of the requirement to standardize the design and layout of the watch office on OTU stations and later extended to all operational airfields. Eventually it became the most common building type used for air traffic control during the Second World War. It was a two-storey structure, approximately square shaped (35 ft by 33 ft 6 in) built in 9-inch rendered brick except for the front elevation which was 13.5 inches thick. The flat roof, balcony and first floor were of reinforced-concrete slabwork, with the control room floor battened to receive timber floorboards.

Between 1942 and March 1943, these were constructed using 12779/41 as the working drawing. This allowed for very large windows for the watch office and control room. But at some airfields, such as Kimbolton and Rougham, a deviation drawing (15371/41) was issued which required the large windows to be bricked up and made good to receive narrow window frames so that all windows had the same size frames. This may have been carried out because of night operations.

Most remaining buildings were modified to drawing 343/43 where the original large windows were removed and smaller frames fitted, the consequent gap being filled

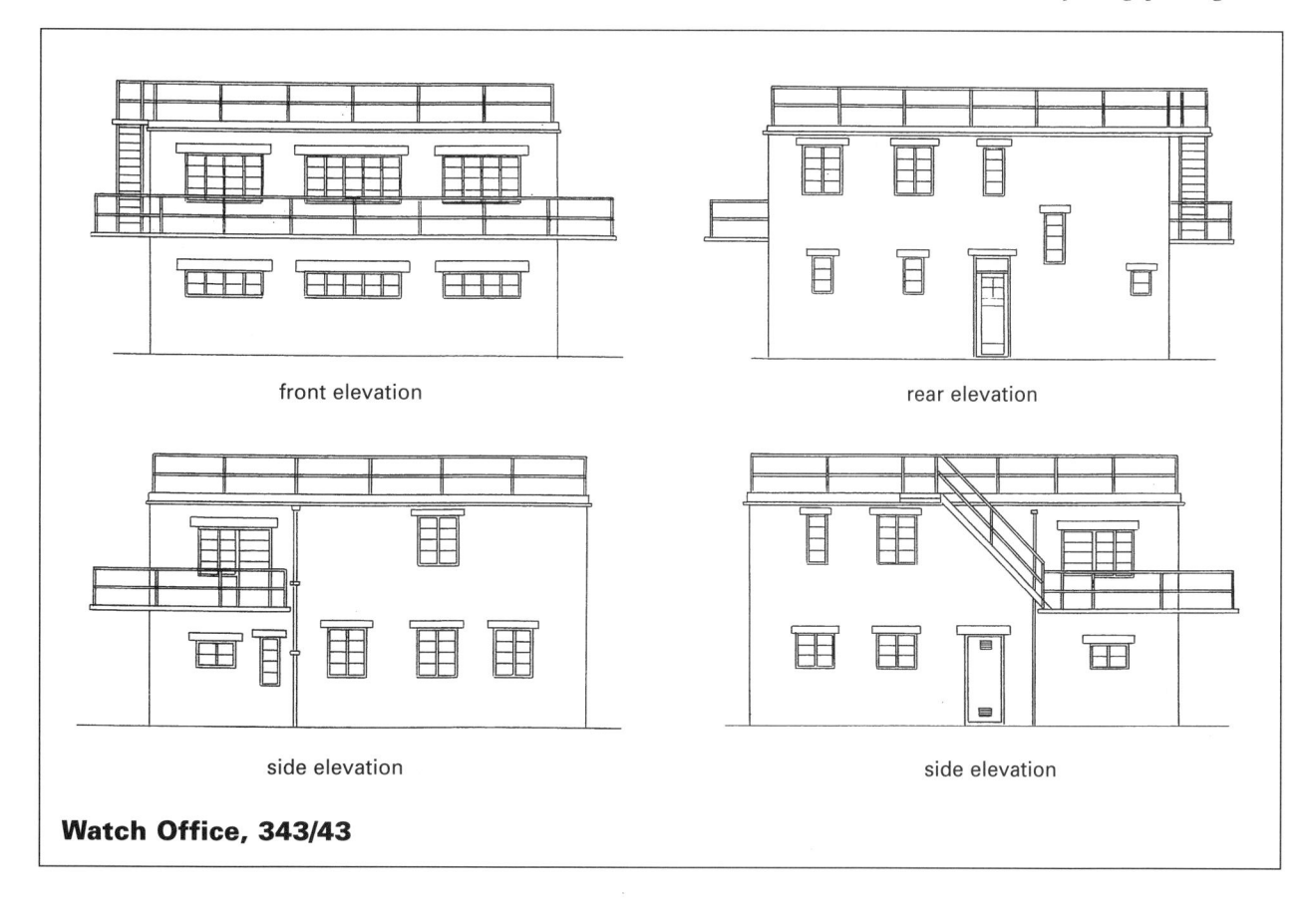

front elevation

rear elevation

side elevation

side elevation

Watch Office, 343/43

Watch office 343/43 at Woodbridge. (Photographed 1993)

The Kimbolton watch office 12779/41 and 15371/41. (Photographed 1977)

Watch office 12779/41 and 343/43 at Bentwaters. (Photographed 1994)

with straight-joint brickwork. Today, it is possible to see evidence of this practice where original window sills have been left *in situ*, a few courses below the new sills. The outline of the former frames can sometimes be seen where the straight joint in the brickwork has been exposed by the cement rendering falling away. Looking inside the building, you can sometimes see where the gaps between the new and old frames have been filled with 9-inch brickwork instead of 13.5-inch brickwork of the original.

All new buildings constructed after 1943 were built from scratch to this latest standard and some of these have a longer central window in the watch office room than the earlier buildings. The main entrance at the rear led into a central corridor with rooms on both sides, with staircase on the right. Further along the corridor were WCs, and opposite here and the staircase was the meteorological office. In here, behind a partition, was the teleprinter connected to the DTN. Beyond the WCs and on the same side was the switch room, the only access being from outside. Opposite here was the duty pilot's rest room and office, the last room being the watch office at the front of the building. The staircase led up to the first-floor landing and corridor. The first room was the controller's rest room, and opposite this and the stairs was the signals office. The front half was taken up with the control room; this had a small portion partitioned off for the PBX. Two exits, one each side, led to a balcony. On one side, a steel stairway gave access to the roof.

Some buildings had an additional control room in Seco construction anchored to the roof. Although none survive, replicas have been built at East Kirkby and Framlingham. Similar brick or concrete additional control rooms were also built at a few sites such as Alconbury and Stretton. QDM boards were usually mounted on towers made from tubular-steel, sometimes erected above the additional control room. The boards were hinged in two leaves and operated by a rope from roof level when a new runway heading was required.

drawing no.   12779/41, 343/43
examples   Alconbury, Bodney, Bruntingthorpe, Culmhead, Matching Green, Tholthorpe

ROYAL NAVAL AIR STATION CONTROL TOWERS

The majority of RNAS control buildings were built by the Royal Marine Engineers to standard designs and were all based on a common ground floor plan (38 ft 3 in by 30 ft 3 in). This forward thinking idea involved three control tower types, each designed to suit the role of the station. The idea was that one, two, or three floors could be built above a common ground-floor plan, either in the form of a new building or on to an existing one with only two floors, should the station be extended later in the war. The basic two-storey structure was built at Dunino while three-storey buildings to drawing 3860/42 were built at Anthorn and Grimsetta. The most common type, consisting of four stories, was built at locations all over the UK, including Abbotsinch, Dale, Culham, East Haven, and Hensdridge.

The latest building to be demolished was at Sydenham in early 1995 but others survive at Burscough, Fearn and Inskip.

Construction of the walls was in a mixture of solid brick, cavity brick, and reinforced concrete, with the air watch office being built of reinforced concrete or wood.

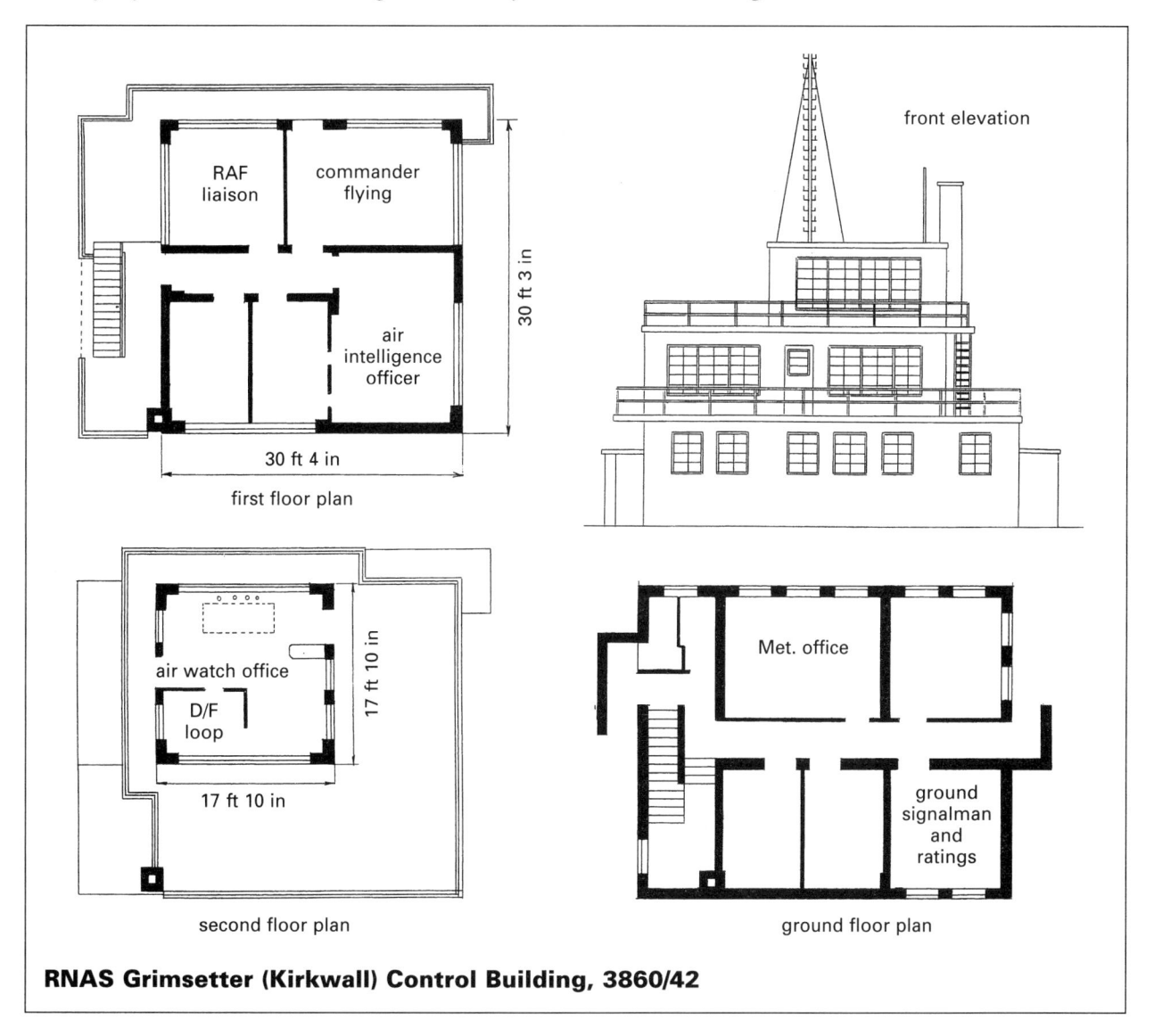

RNAS Grimsetter (Kirkwall) Control Building, 3860/42

RNAS Lee-on-Solent Control Building, 566/42

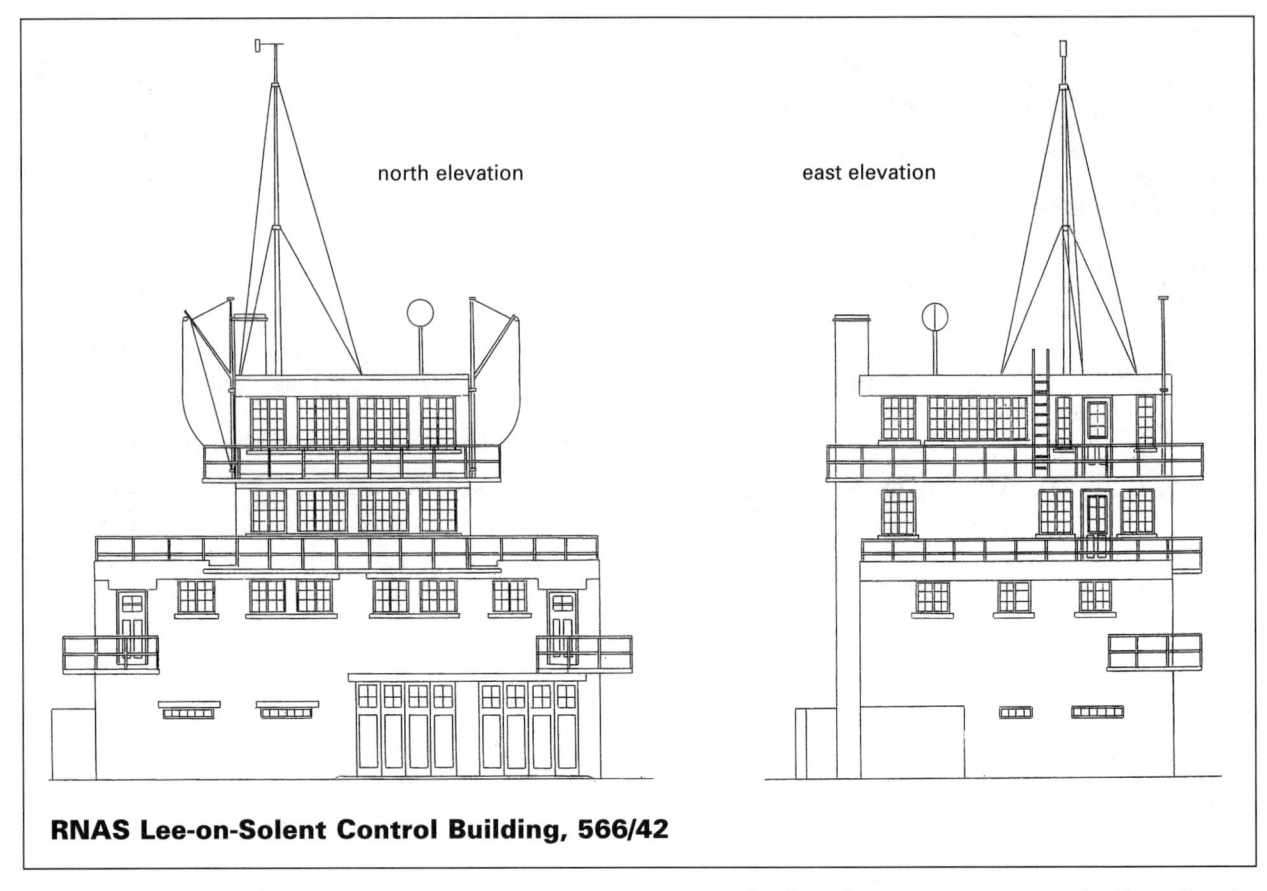

north elevation

east elevation

The control tower at Lee-on-Solent, designed by M. C. Broad of the Civil Engineer in Chief's Department of the Admiralty, was far superior to contemporary RAF watch office designs. The original idea was to have a single multifunctional two-storey building (45 ft 10 in by 28 ft) with a ground floor containing airfield services such as ambulance and crash tender garages, and duty crew room. The first floor was made up of offices for the meteorological officer and commander flying, and a further two floors were provided in the form of a central tower for the offices of air traffic control. The shape of the building resembled the existing watch office with tower (1959/34) at Lee-on-Solent, but was somewhat larger, suggesting perhaps that the architect was

RNAS control tower at Fearn. (Photographed 1992)

RNAS Lee-on-Solent Control Building, 566/42

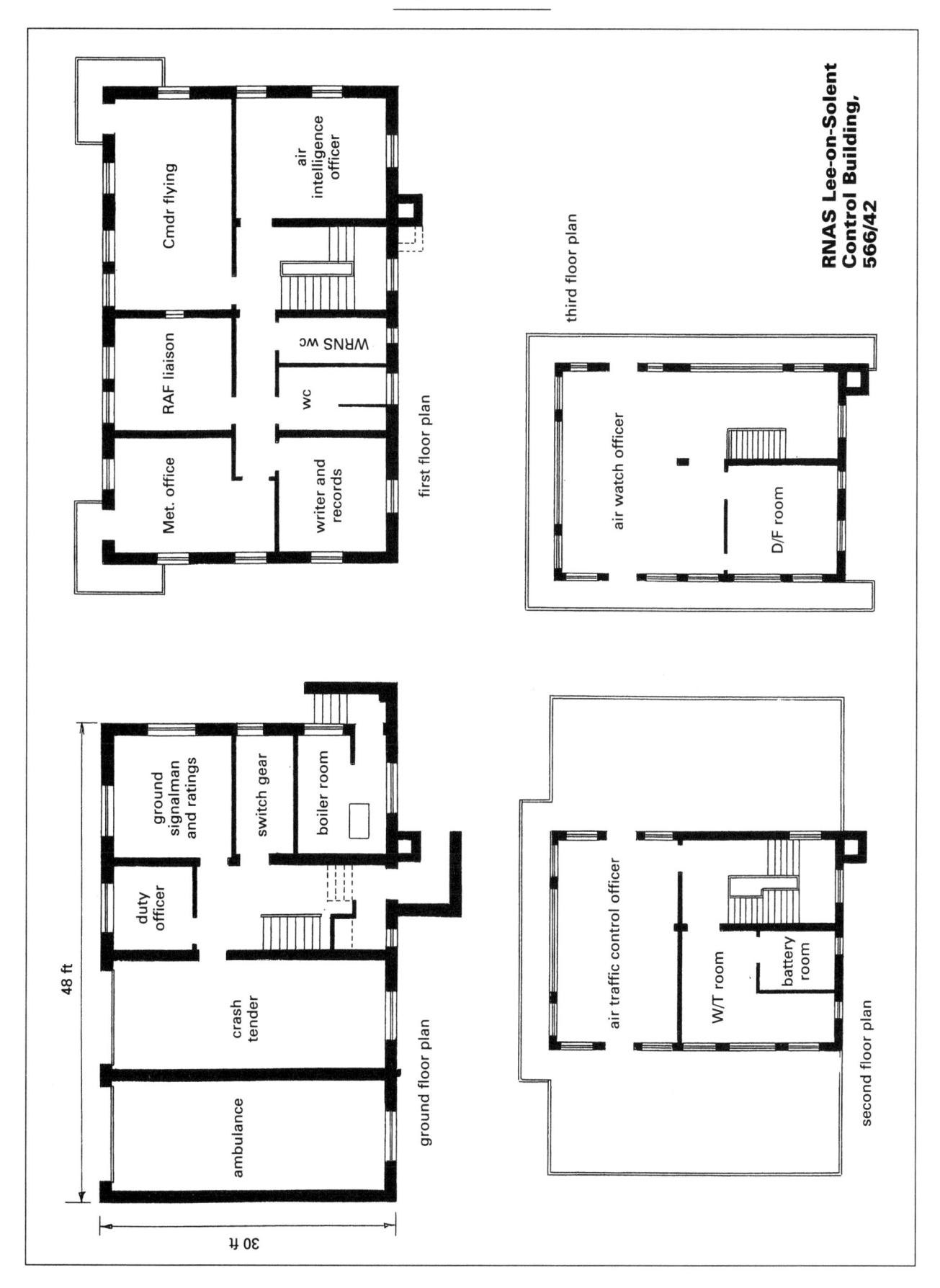

RNAS control tower at Arbroath. (Photographed 1990)

The control tower at the 3rd Base Air Depot (Station 597) at Langford Lodge, County Antrim photographed in May 1995. (Bill Haggan)

influenced by the earlier structure.

After 1943, the structure was redesigned at second-floor level to include a larger ATC office. This was achieved by building above the roof space so that the second floor was the same width as that below, but the air watch office above was retained in its original form. Another major extension took place in 1950–1 when a new meteorological office, designed as a single-storey annexe, was built against a side wall. The new extension was the same width (28 ft) as the existing building and 71 ft 6 in long, with walls of permanent construction and a flat concrete roof.

The ambulance garage on the ground floor became a crash tender garage. The original crash tender garage was subdivided to become a reception area with an entrance in the front elevation in one half. At the rear was a new battery room. The main entrance was at the rear with a lobby and staircase, and the boiler-room. The duty office was at the front along with the ground signalmen's and ratings' rest room which was renamed the duty crew room. The switchgear room next to the boiler-room became a parachute store.

The first floor comprised office accommodation for the commander flying and the intelligence officer; this became the chart room. The RAF liaison room was renamed the SMO office, while the meteorological office was retained. A records office became a meteorological plotting room. WCs were also provided at this level.

Originally, the second floor was 20 ft 7 in by 28 ft and consisted of a small ATC office, a battery room, and W/T room, with a flat roof each side. Later, when this floor was extended, the ATC office was made larger, a new FDO office and W/T office were added, and the former battery room (batteries were now charged on the ground floor) was made larger, incorporating part of the original W/T room.

The air watch office and D/F room on the third floor originally had a balcony running round three sides. When the second floor extension was added, it was only necessary to have the balcony on the front elevation. On the roof was a D/F loop and anemometer mast.

drawing no.		3860/42		AL15/42–AL21/42, 566/42
storeys	2	3	4	
examples	Dunino	Anthorn, Grimsetta	Abbotsinch, Dale, Culham, East Haven, Henstridge	Lee-on-Solent, Machrihanish, Ronaldsway (Isle of Man)

PART 6

SYNTHETIC TRAINING

AIRCREW TRAINING

A new organization for the initial training of pilots and observers was established in November 1939. At seaside resorts, properties such as holiday camps were requisitioned to be used as Initial Training Wings, and Aircrew Reception and Dispatch Centres for recruit training. This was in the form of physical and barrack square drill as well as elementary instruction in signals, navigation, the theory of flight, and map reading.

Training for pilots was in four stages. The first stage was conducted at the Initial Training Wing (ITW) where basic training and the theory of flight were taught. Second stage was the Elementary Flying Training School (EFTS), first

Hixon Dispersed Sites (part) showing position of instructional site

- **IS** instructional site
- **a** instructional block 12881/41
- **b** gunnery crew and procedure centre 9116/41
- **c** Link trainer for two trainers 8112/41 (2)
- **d** turret instructional building 11023/40
- **e** building for three AML bombing teacher/teachers 1739/41
- **f** W/T operational instructional centre 12944/41

formed in 1934 to undertake the *ab inito* training of regular RAF pilots. These schools were operated by civilian companies under contract to the Air Ministry. The design of all buildings came under the scrutiny of the Directorate of Works. Here, training consisted of more advanced theory and basic flying on simple training aircraft right up to the stage of cross-country flights and basic aerobatics. The third stage was the Service Flying Training School (known initially as an FTS and later as an SFTS) where more advanced trainer aircraft were flown; here trainees gained their wings. The final stage was the Operational Training Unit. At a multi-engined bomber OTU the pilots met up with navigators, wireless operators and air gunners from their specialized schools.

A new class of aircrew known as the air observer came into being in 1935. Air observers were trained in bombing and gunnery at No. 1 Air Observer School at North Coates Fitties which opened in 1 January 1936. By 1937, it was decided that all observers should be trained in navigation to the same standard as pilots and the AOS course was extended to include navigational training. In November 1938, No. 2 AOS was formed at Acklington and, by the outbreak of war, nine civil Air Observer Schools were operating on a similar basis as Elementary Flying Training Schools.

Typically, training included more advanced map reading and signals, and long navigational flights over the sea and above cloud. After graduating, the pupils went to a Bombing and Gunnery School, corresponding to the SFTS, for the next stage of their training.

Before the Second World War, Flying Training Schools turned out pilots who, in theory, were ready to be posted to operational squadrons but they still needed to become familiar with the aeroplane with which the squadron was equipped. An operational squadron could ill afford time for the training of new aircrew. At first, to combat this problem, Group Pools were established in September 1939 from which operational squadrons could draw replacement aircrew as required. But the demand for fully trained aircrew led to the creation of Operational Training Units. The first of these were located on existing late expansion period aerodromes but purpose-built OTU stations were later constructed with detached instructional sites.

The training at an OTU was in effect a postgraduate course as all aircrew were qualified to wear their appropriate badges: pilot's wings, the single wing of the observer, the air gunner's badge. Crews were formed and trained together, being taught to work on the actual type that they were to fly in an operational squadron.

At the beginning of the war, top priority was given to the construction of purpose-built OTU airfields. The rapid development of aircraft during the war brought with it a need for synthetic aids for training in flying, navigation, bombing, and gunnery. A school was set up at Elstree, Herts to train instructors in the use of these synthetic training aids.

Instructional Site
Under the Second World War dispersal system, the instructional site on OTU airfields was located between the administration site and the main communal site. The buildings on this site contained all the necessary synthetic training aids dedicated to the role of the station. Typically, the following could be included on an instructional site.

- Link trainer
- gunnery and crew procedure centre
- W/T operational instruction centre
- synthetic navigation classroom
- Hawarden trainer
- modified Haskard range
- modified Hunt range
- panoramic trainer
- turret trainers
- elementary deflection teacher
- Edmonds deflection trainer
- Fisher front gun trainer
- torpedo attack trainer
- Air Ministry bombing teacher
- camera obscura
- anti-aircraft dome trainer (ground-to-air)

There were others besides these. Operational bomber stations, and to a lesser extent fighter stations, contained a selected number of synthetic training buildings located on the technical site.

LINK TRAINER

The Link trainer provided a cheaper alternative for training pilots in instrument flying than flying actual aircraft. The trainer was invented in 1929 by Edwin Link, an American organ manufacturer, and it was first introduced into the UK in 1936 when a company called JVW Ltd was set up at Aylesbury to handle sales installations and maintenance.

Fitups Ltd of Manchester won a contract in 1940 for the manufacture of a synthetic trainer for the RAF to the designs of Raymond Myerscough Walker. This basically consisted of a circular cubicle in the centre of which was a Link trainer. The first of the new trainers was installed at Burnaston (Derby Airport) where there was already a trainer room, the four walls of which were painted to resemble various landscapes. The cubicle was circular, 20 ft in diameter and 10 ft high, acting as a cyclorama. It was made of curved timber sections and timber frames covered with fibreboard on which was painted a landscape with various features as seen from an altitude of about 2,000 ft. The function of the painted landscape was to present, realistically, the various climatic and geographical features which a pilot would encounter. This included mountains with the level horizon lost, a city with a smoke pall obscuring the horizon, and mist over the sea (visibility nil). About 30 of the trainer units were erected at the Initial Training Wing at Hastings and had to be dismantled and transferred to Torquay when the Wing was evacuated. Similar installations were supplied to several university flying clubs.

The most common type of Link trainer used during the war was the Type D2 which was introduced in 1942, superseding the D1. The first to be manufactured in Britain was Type D4; these were made under licence from 1950 by Air Trainers Ltd, who succeeded JVW in 1946, and had originally purchased war surplus RAF trainers from the Ministry of Supply for reconditioning and resale at home and abroad.

The wartime Link trainer comprised a fuselage approximately 7 ft long of timber frame construction covered with plywood or canvas. Powerful bellows enabled the device to simulate basic flying movements similar to pitching, banking, and turning of a real aircraft. Early machines had wings, tailplane, and fin with corresponding control surfaces. The cockpit closely resembled a typical single-engined aircraft of the period, with the usual six basic instruments plus compass, radio, rudder pedals, and control column. Any changes in flight attitude were indicated by the instruments and the relevant control surfaces. Night flying could be simulated by placing a detachable hood over the cockpit; stormy conditions could be created by means of a 'rough air device'.

Connections led from the trainer to an instructor's desk where a small three-wheeled trolley called a 'tracking crab' (automatic recorder) reacted to time and rate of movement of the fuselage. One of these wheels, known as an idler wheel, acted as a pen recorder and traced an accurate course on to a map of the countryside over which the 'pilot' was supposed to be flying. The instructor's desk had a duplicate set of instruments which enabled him to assess the pilot's flying ability.

By using Link trainers under the control of a fighter operations room, it was possible to show a number of pupils how an operations room was used. In addition, pupils could be trained in R/T procedure under simulated blind-flying conditions, when the fighter controller directed operations by R/T communication. The exercise required the use of a fighter controller, a plotting table with two plotters, four Links, each with an instructor, a number of loud speakers, and R/T sets.

On each Link table was set out a map of the area where they were supposed to be flying, and on the plotting table was an enlarged map of the same area. The movements of each Link were reported to the plotters on the operations table over a land line by each instructor at his Link table. Two of the Links were used as friendly fighters and two as raider aircraft; the controller directed the friendly aircraft to intercept the raiders. One plotter looked after the friendly aircraft and the other the two raiders.

The typical procedure for a ground-controlled approach exercise was as follows. The two raider Links were given a specific target and a route to fly; for example, 20,000 ft, air speed 150 mph, at 020° for 5 minutes, 060° for 3 minutes, 020° for 2 minutes, and 040° for 5 minutes. This course was drawn on the maps on the Link tables, relative to the two raiders. The controller was not told any details about the chosen course. The pupils in the raider Links then flew blind on these courses and the movements of the crabs on each of their Links were plotted by the plotter in the operations room.

The two pupils playing the 'friendlies' relaxed in an adjacent room. The controller then gave the command 'Scramble' over the loudspeakers and instructed the pupils to climb to 20,000 ft on a course and air speed to be flown. With the movements of all four crabs plotted on the operations table, the controller directed the friendly fighters by R/T to obtain an interception.

A number of these early 'flight simulators' still survive; the Air Training Corps still have a few which are used for cadet training, some apparently in full working order, albeit prone to breakdowns and shortage of spares. Preserved examples may be viewed at the Museum of Flight at East Fortune, near Edinburgh, and at the RAF Museum, Hendon.

Buildings

Expansion period buildings accommodating Link trainers were sited with the axis of the trainer and instructor's desk aligned north–south so that the cockpit compass and the maps were aligned. With the desk at the southern end of the room, the instructor, facing north, looked directly over the desk at his maps and the trainer. The concrete floor of the room had to be perfectly level, so that the cockpit instruments functioned correctly.

Permanent buildings on expansion period aerodromes, such as 1762/39, were single-bay structures with flat reinforced-concrete roofs (protected type). Alternatively, double-bay buildings with flat or hipped roofs were used.

A three-bay Link trainer building 4188/42 at Matching Green.

side elevation

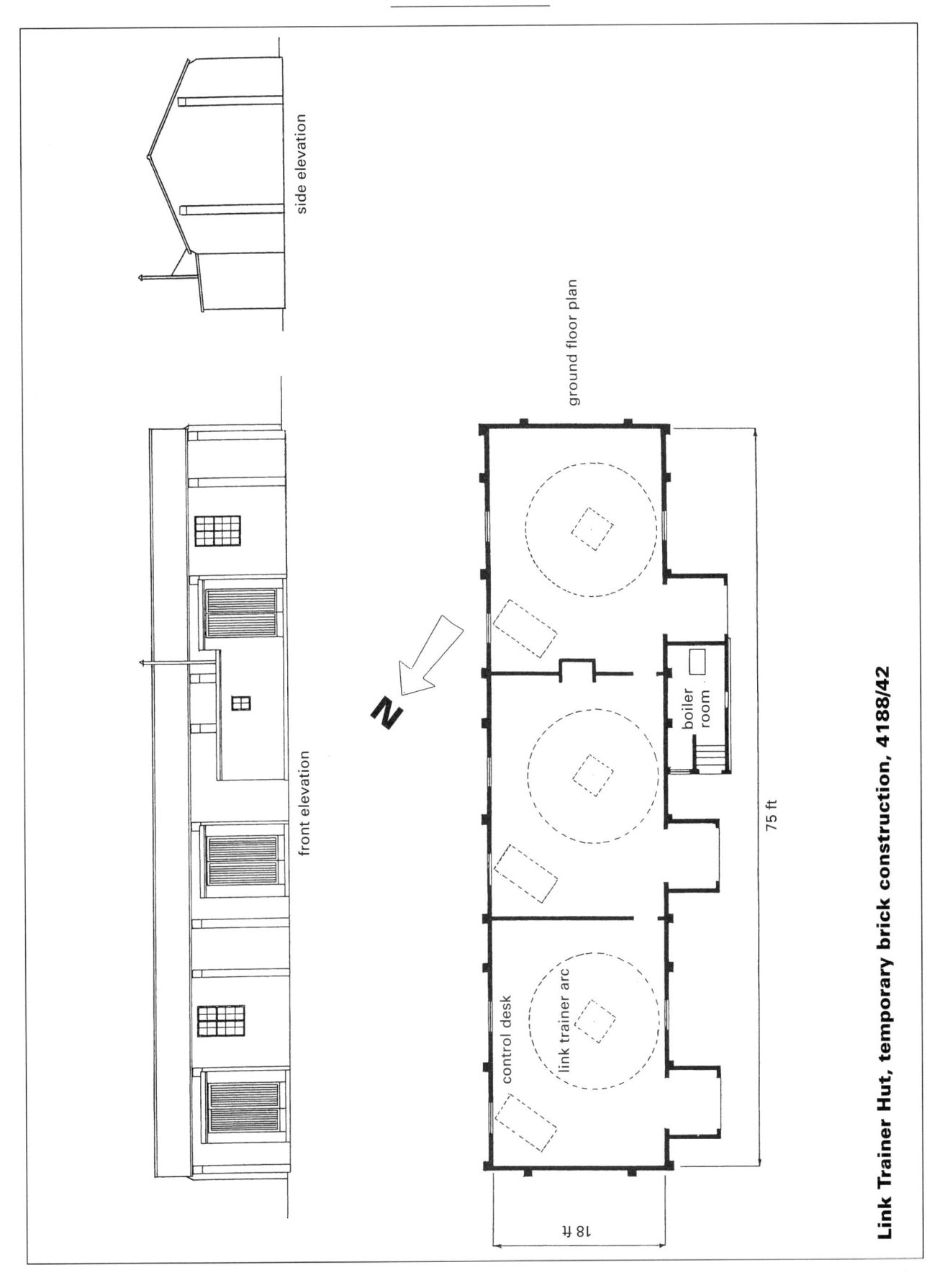

front elevation

ground floor plan

boiler room

control desk
link trainer arc

75 ft

18 ft

Link Trainer Hut, temporary brick construction, 4188/42

Hipped roofs were steel framed, clad with tiles. Cavity brick walls were 11 inches thick. The wall separating the two bays was a half-brick wall. Each bay was 25 ft square and each had an entrance lobby, the doors in the centre of the front elevation. Several of these buildings still survive, including one at Manby.

Drawing 7790/40 was a temporary brick building with between one and four rooms, each 25 ft by 18 ft. A single entrance lobby on a corner of the front elevation served all rooms. Similar buildings were built on some training airfields yet were attached to the rear of the watch office; good examples of these can be seen at Jurby and Halfpenny Green, whilst detached buildings are still extant at Atcham and Bottesford.

Later wartime buildings (10040/41 and 4188/42) were sited in blocks or groups depending on site conditions, usually with a maximum of four units in one block or group. In some cases, there was a combination of both as at Lavenham.

drawing no.	1762/39	7790/40	10040/41, 4188/42
examples	Middleton St George, Manby	Halfpenny Green, Jurby, Atcham, Bottesford	Lavenham

drawing no.	2548/42	10039/41
examples	Alton Barnes	Babdown farm

GUNNERY AND CREW PROCEDURE CENTRE

The object of the crew procedure known to aircrew as 'grope' was the efficient training of aircrew on the ground, simulating as far as possible by synthetic means the conditions of actual operations. The building used as the gunnery and crew procedure centre, or airmanship hall, depended on the date of construction. The early OTU stations had a large purpose-built temporary brick structure, while later stations had a Marston shed or any other suitable large building such as an aircraft hangar.

The use of display material to enable pupils to learn easily from what they saw or read was of paramount importance. Striking posters and air diagrams that dealt with all aspects of handling, fuel consumption, and abandoning and ditching drills were all displayed. Quite often, an artist stationed on the camp would paint posters directly on to the wall; a super example of this can be seen inside the airmanship hall at Turnberry.

The layout of the building and the way the instructional fuselage and other equipment was displayed was very important. The intention was to impress pupils with the importance of thoroughly knowing their aircraft.

Instructional Fuselages

The most important ground training aid in gunnery and crew procedure centre was the instructional fuselage in the dummy ops and fuselage room. The fuselage was permanently jacked clear of the ground, with tail secured to eye-bolts in the floor. Motors and pumps were provided to raise and lower flaps and undercarriage. Stands for instructors to demonstrate the operations of hydraulic, fuel, and pneumatic systems were also provided.

A system of cockpit drill was devised to test a pupil's knowledge of his aircraft. This drill included:

- the main points of the exterior of the aircraft, and of the interior up to the pilot's panel
- pilot's preliminary check before starting the engines
- starting the engines by the fitter or pilot
- action in the event of an air-intake fire when starting up
- warming up and testing engines
- taxiing and preparing to take off
- take-off and climb, undercarriage up
- cruising and gliding
- preparing to land, approaching and landing
- 'going round again'
- use of hydraulic emergency services
- action in the event of engine failure
- taxiing and stopping engines
- abandoning the aircraft by parachute
- ditching drill
- dinghy drill

In addition to this drill procedure, it was necessary for the pupils to practise certain exercises blindfolded. These included:

Gunnery and crew procedure centre on the instructional site at Mullaghmore, County Londonderry photographed in September 1981. (Ernie Cromie)

- finding the controls and instruments by touch
- taking off and climbing
- circuit, approach to land, and landing
- hydraulic emergency devices; operation
- action in the event of engine failure
- 'going around again'
- abandoning aircraft

Another trainer consisted of a fuselage mounted on two pillars. The aircraft's instrument panel was fitted with working instrumentation to simulate actual flying. The crew under instruction sat in their normal positions in the fuselage.

It enabled crews, under the supervision of a qualified instructor, to carry out synthetic training exercises, including action in the event of engine fire, fuel or oil failure, ditching, crash landing, parachuting, and R/T and W/T procedures. Controls for the operation of fuel cocks, throttle levers, flaps, dinghy release, bomb doors, and fire extinguishers were all connected to microswitches or potentiometers to represent the real things. With the selection of a few switches on the instructor's control panel, any number of problems could be simulated; for example, engine fire warning lamps could be illuminated or oil pressure warning lamps could be operated.

examples   Charterhall, East Fortune (blister hangar), Eshott, Tealing

Fighter Control Trainer

This was for training crews in the use of a standard system of reporting the position, type, and range of enemy aircraft about to attack. The crew took up their normal positions inside an instructional fuselage (Blenheim) and reported on silhouettes of enemy aircraft which appeared in various positions on the hangar walls. Silhouettes were placed inside lighted boxes and were wound up and down on wires. Different ranges could be achieved with cards of different sizes. The gunner reported the position and aircraft type by normal communication with a controller who advised him.

example   Bicester

W/T OPERATIONAL INSTRUCTION CENTRE

Drawing number 12944/41 depicted a block of two buildings in 30 ft span Nissen hutting. The larger of the two consisted of 19 bays with a total length of over 115 ft. The entrance lobby led into a hall and connecting corridor to the smaller Nissen hut which had 14 bays and was nearly 85 ft long. The rooms in the main hut included a general W/T instruction room, crew briefing and conference room, directing room, and D/F navigation trainer. This room had five cubicles in brick, each with viewing panels for pupils under training, and a larger cubicle to house the epidiascope. The screen was 25 ft away in the viewing hall. The other Nissen hut contained a W/T instruction classroom, a Harwell box room, (large enough for six Harwell boxes), a battery-charging room, and a W/T instruments room.

drawing no.   12944/41
examples   Bruntingthorpe, Hixon, Silverstone, Tilstock

D/F Navigational Trainer

Shortly after the outbreak of the Second World War, a scheme for training bomber crews was conceived and put forward to the Air Ministry by Mr P. Adorjan, Technical Director of Rediffusion. His idea was that the aircrew – pilot, navigator and wireless operator – who had already received individual specialized training in their respective duties should be brought together in a synthetic trainer in the form of a cubicle or, in some cases, the fuselage of the aircraft.

With the help from equipment controlled by an instructor the crew could 'fly' a course similar to that which they would fly in a real aircraft. The cubicle was fitted with all the essential equipment of an aircraft for wireless navigation and, for the pilot, a compass. Six or more cubicles could be used at the same time. The crew were connected to the instructor by R/T, over which he could send typical messages while on 'ops' and reproduced different kinds of interference liable to occur during a real flight.

It was possible to give crews practice in operating procedure, including wireless and celestial navigation, and could teach the crew how to fix their position by these methods. Aural and visual effects such as glimpses of land or sea below them were reproduced. Stars were simulated by means of spots of light reflected on mirrors, and sounds and light effects produced the impressions of enemy searchlights, flak, and bomb bursts. The crew worked against the clock which could be regulated to operate at one and half times normal speed.

Before going into their cubicles, the crew were briefed in exactly the same manner as if they were going on an operational flight. They then retired to their cubicles and, except for wireless contact with the instructor, were cut off from the outside world until the 'flight' was finished. The duration was usually reduced to one-third of an operational flight, and the presumed height was 10,000 ft. Each member of the crew did his job exactly as though he was in the air. The words 'take-off' appeared on the screen, and the clock was set. The navigator plotted his course and the wireless operator, with his D/F loop, got 'fixes' every so often, and the pilot kept an eye on the speed of the 'aircraft' and the compass bearing. Occasionally, the instructor changed the view on the screen, the new image only appearing for a short while. In the time the new image was on the screen the crews had to identify it and check their course.

Sometimes, when a landmark should have appeared, the picture was changed to ten-tenths cloud and the flight continued by dead-reckoning. As the target was approached, the pictures were almost obscured by shining the searchlights, making it difficult for the crew to see the picture. Furthermore, a series of tiny pinpoint flashes

144 *British Military Airfield Architecture*

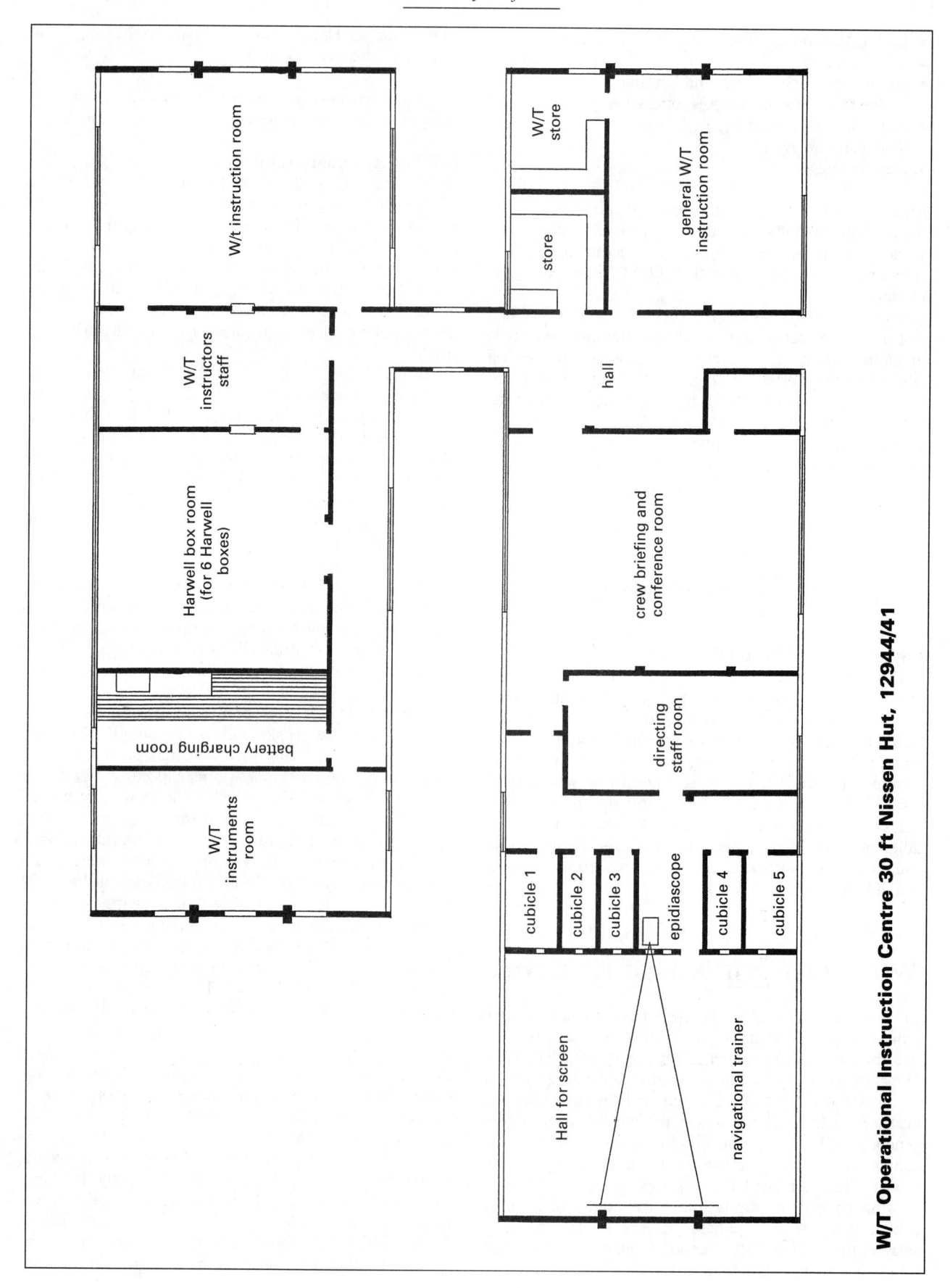

W/T Operational Instruction Centre 30 ft Nissen Hut, 12944/41

Synthetic Training 145

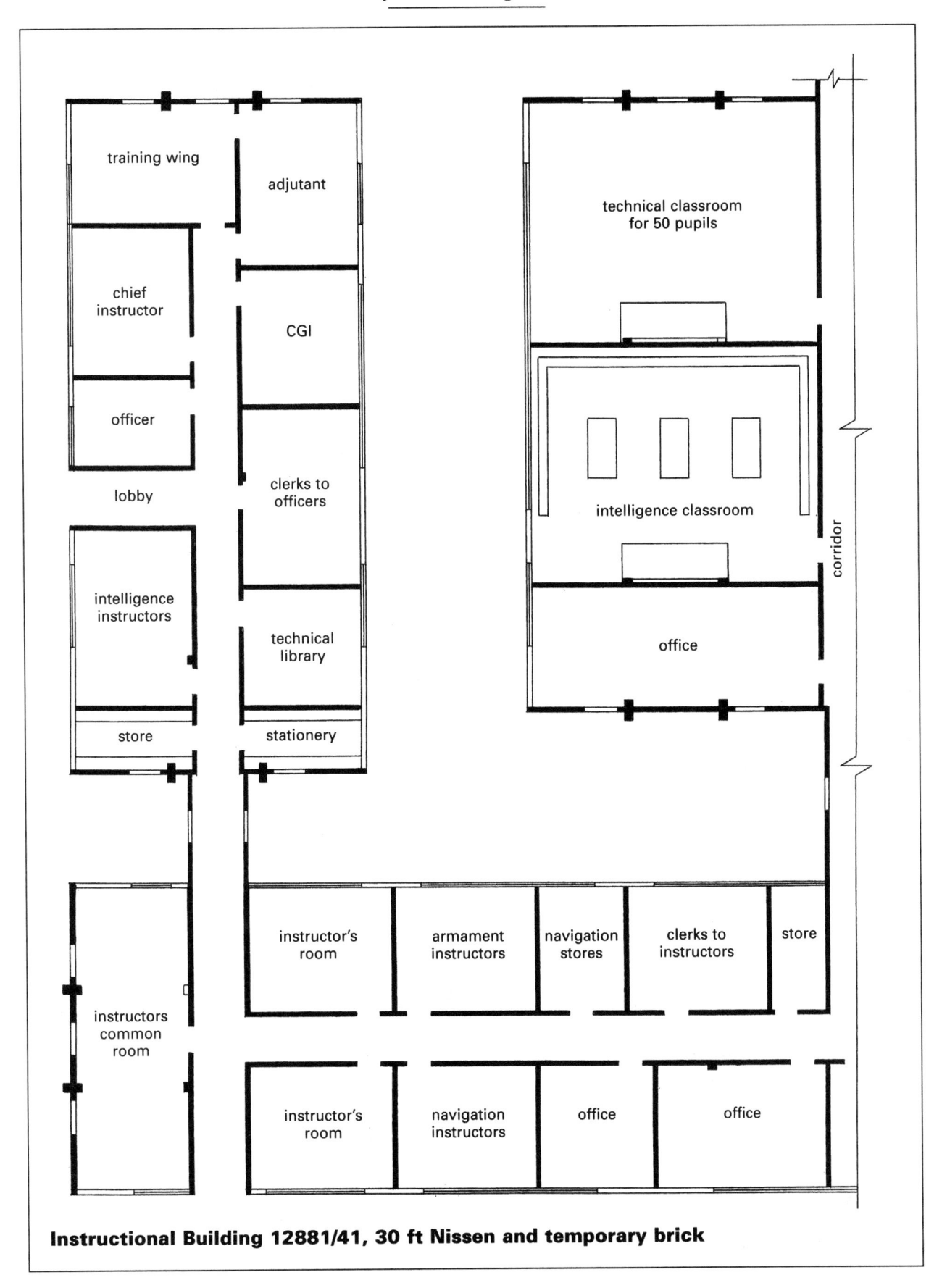

Instructional Building 12881/41, 30 ft Nissen and temporary brick

Instructional Building, 12881/41

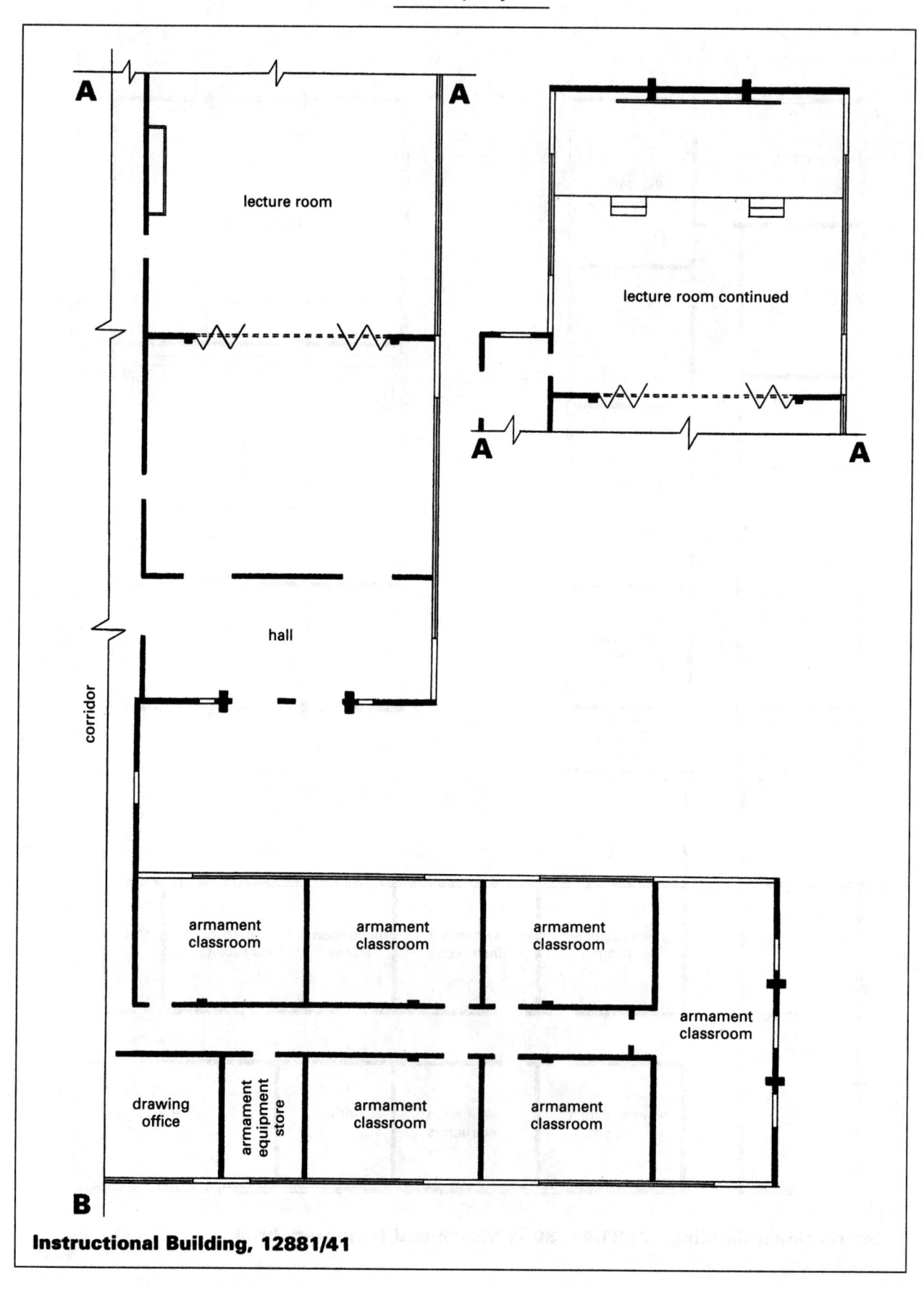

Navigational Trainer Type 3

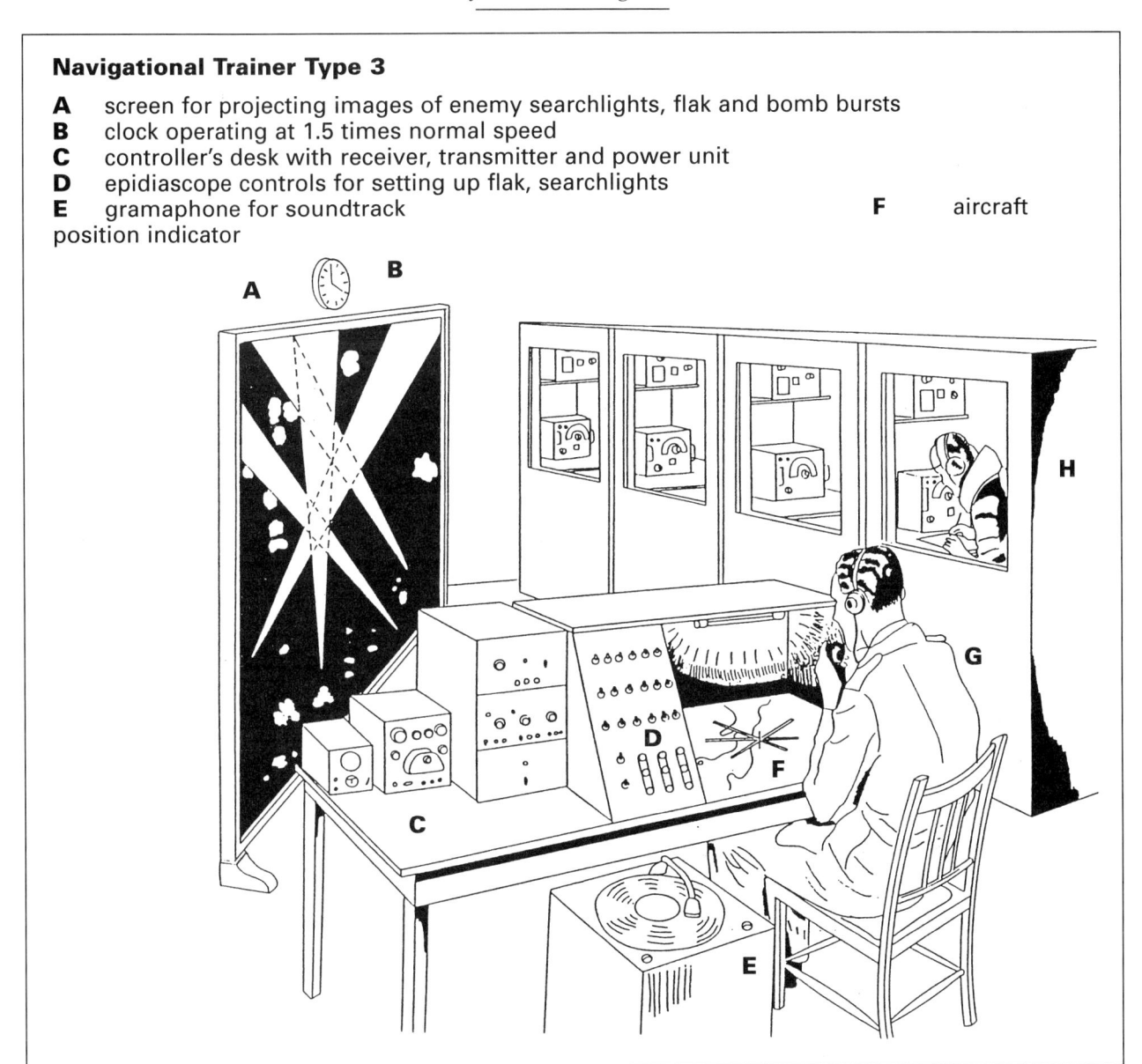

- **A** screen for projecting images of enemy searchlights, flak and bomb bursts
- **B** clock operating at 1.5 times normal speed
- **C** controller's desk with receiver, transmitter and power unit
- **D** epidiascope controls for setting up flak, searchlights
- **E** gramaphone for soundtrack
- **F** aircraft position indicator

appeared on the picture to imitate gun flashes thus creating a complete illusion of a bombing run.

The apparatus was installed in what was termed the 'grope' room. Five or more aircrews could be given individual and simultaneous training by a single instructor. The crews were accommodated in separate training cubicles, each representing a separate aircraft.

Harwell Box

This W/T trainer consisted of a wooden box in which the pupil sat. It was fitted with all the appropriate radio equipment. Signals were fed down a line, simulating the actual reception conditions, and a system of homing beacons was also provided so that he could take bearings. This trainer was quite useful for teaching intercommunication skills and the use of the D/F loop. Bearings and homings, D/F loop manipulation, maintenance of W/T equipment, frequency changing, fault finding, and communication with ground W/T D/F stations could all be practised.

To add some realism to the drill while carrying out a drill procedure suggested by the instructor, a loudspeaker played a continuous roar of desynchronized engine noise.

examples   Carew Cheriton, Madeley, Staverton

SYNTHETIC NAVIGATION CLASSROOM

This was a purpose-built detached temporary brick building containing a large classroom for training and teaching all aspects of navigation by synthetic means. One end of the building had a flat roof with two glazed astro-hatches. Below these, were raised platforms for the use of an astroscope. This was a device used to teach pupils about the swinging of a magnetic compass using an astro compass when the sun or stars were visible.

Synthetic Navigation Classroom, temporary brick construction, 2075/43

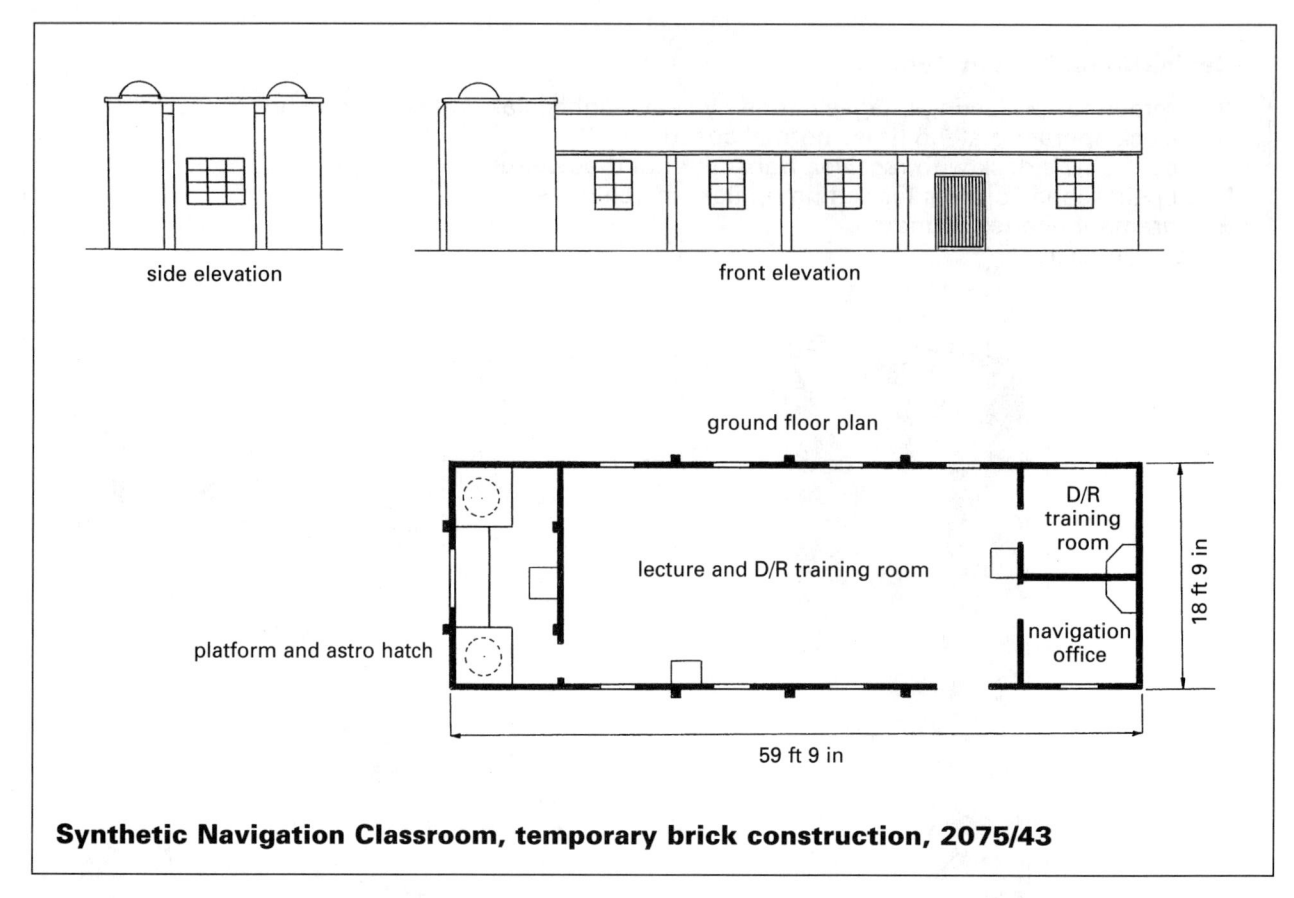

drawing no. 2075/43
examples Eye, Mepal, Saltby, Spanhoe, Tempsford

Hawarden Trainer

The idea of the Hawarden trainer was to simulate as realistically as possible the procedure of an operational flight from a state of readiness in the crew room to the completing of a combat report at the end of a flight. The procedure was to carry out the correct cockpit drill, intercept and get within range, keep a constant look-out for enemy aircraft to avoid being shot down, the homing procedure, and interception.

The aircraft was a centre section of a Spitfire fuselage mounted on trestles and positioned so that there was a minimum of 60 ft between the pilot's head and the end wall of the building. Behind him was a sector controller with R/T communication. The rear of the fuselage had a series of lights corresponding with cockpit instrumentation such as flaps up/down, undercarriage up/down, IFF, compass, and guns so that the instructor knew instantly which cockpit drill had been carried out.

Interception, range estimation, aircraft recognition, and throttle control exercises were all carried out on a model aircraft attached to an overhead rail in front of the pilot. When the throttle was in the cruising position, the model was stationary (both model and Spitfire flying at the same speed). Opening throttle caused the model to move

Synthetic navigation trainer 2075/43 at Strubby.

backwards; its speed varying with the opening of the throttle (Spitfire catching up with the model). Closing the throttle caused the model to move forward, away from the fuselage (Spitfire losing the model).

A canvas screen at the end and along the side wall of the hut was painted with a cloudscape. Hostile aircraft were hidden behind movable clouds. The pilot had to react quickly when a cloud was removed or a Klaxon sounded to represent hostile machine gunfire.

drawing no. 12896/41
examples Annan, Eshott, Milfield, Tealing

MODIFIED HASKARD RANGE

The modified Haskard range consisted of a model landscape which was used for a variety of purposes, not only by aircrew but also by the Army. The range could be easily constructed from materials found locally; the models were available from the Defence Research Studios, Netheravon. Some of the uses to which the trainer could be put included training observers to pinpoint their position with the aid of a map or photograph, training in air observation for ground artillery using a map, training in air reconnaissance under ground battle conditions, and training in R/T communication procedure from ground to air.

The range consisted of a model landscape a minimum of 12 ft square. The landscape was painted on sacking

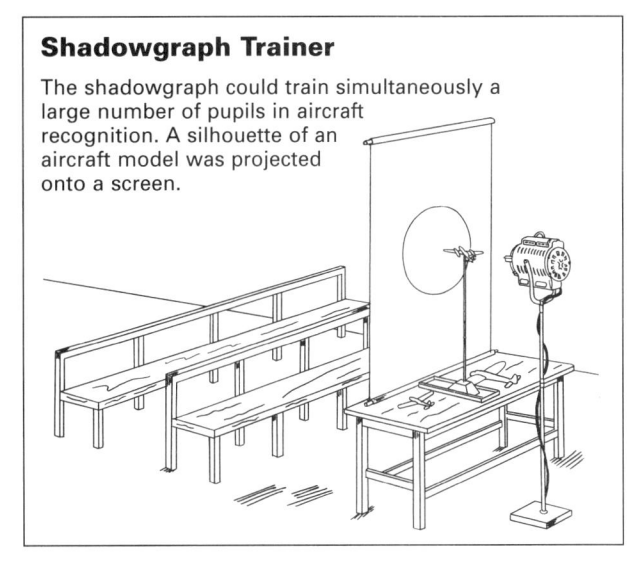

Shadowgraph Trainer

The shadowgraph could train simultaneously a large number of pupils in aircraft recognition. A silhouette of an aircraft model was projected onto a screen.

supported by a wooden frame about 4 ft from the ground. Hedges, houses, bridges, and other salient features were fixed to the sacking. Model anti-aircraft batteries, tanks, and railways could be placed on the landscape, and were made to move with magnets moving underneath the sacking. Small pygmy lamps were used to simulate gun flashes. A grid layout was marked on the floor underneath, with part of the landscape traced on it so that the markings on the ground corresponded with the landscape directly above. With the instructor underneath

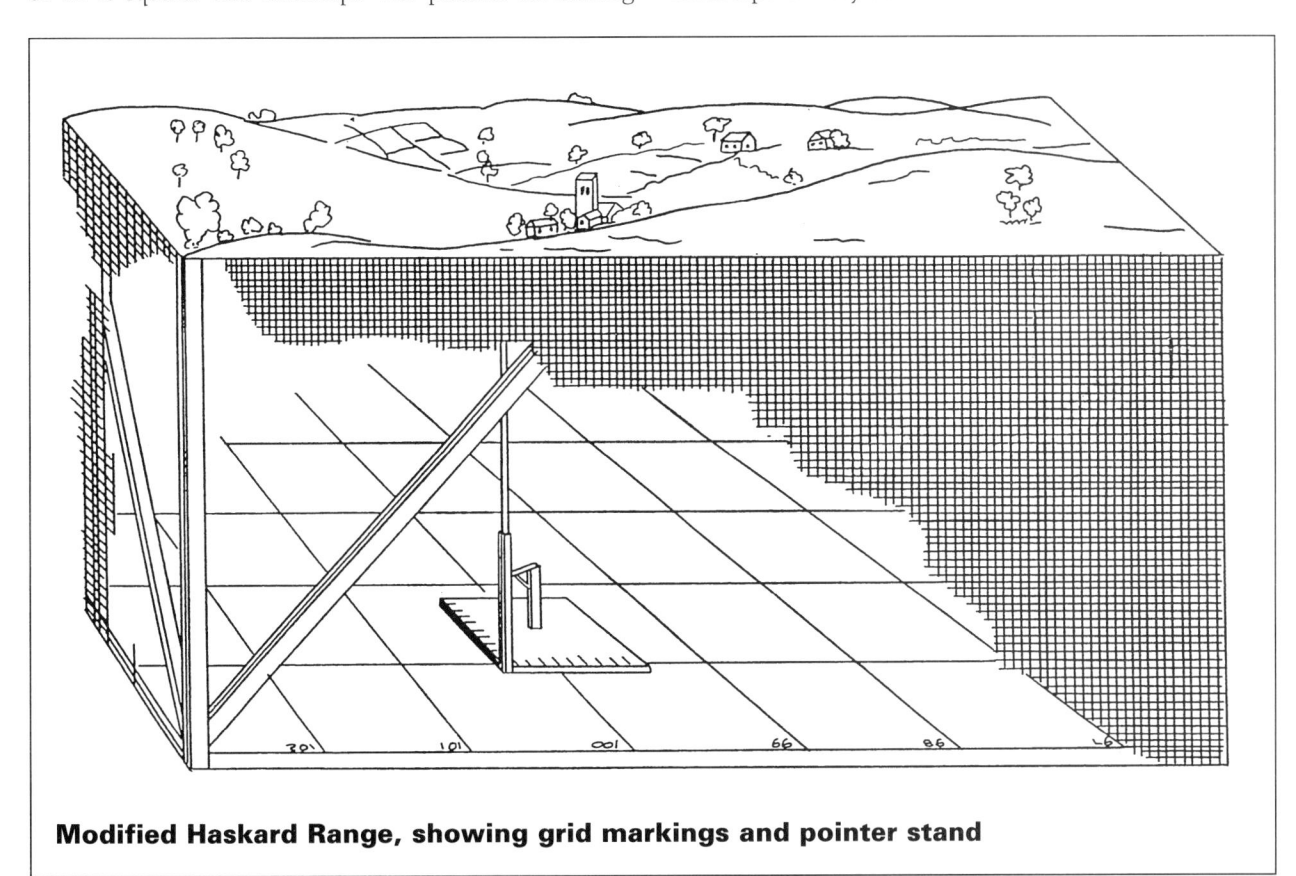

Modified Haskard Range, showing grid markings and pointer stand

the model and with the aid of a pointer stand to show the instructor where the target was, he simply blew puffs of smoke (from a cigarette) through the sacking to produce the effect of shell bursts.

The observer was positioned on a raised platform, so that his eye was well above the landscape, and to one side of it so that he saw the model at an angle as he would do if he was flying over the area.

One example was at Hawkinge. It is thought that this model was used in the planning of the British evacuation of Dunkirk in 1940; the building was demolished in 1993. The remains of another are at the Museum of Flight at East Fortune where the model landscape still survives in storage.

MODIFIED HUNT RANGE

The Hunt range was intended to teach aircraft recognition with the aid of models seen at different ranges and altitudes. The pupil sat on a bench and faced a large mirror. Behind him, at the rear of the building, was a cyclorama in front of which was a turn and bank turntable and a carriage for straight and level model aircraft. An electric motor (purchased from Carter Brothers of Romford) propelled the models across the cyclorama for the pupil to identify. An elaborate system of lights, dimmer switches and coloured screens (obtained from Strand Electric, Covent Garden, London) could simulate different weather conditions and create a realistic illusion of a typical wartime air-to-air situation.

The images of the flying aircraft were seen by the pupil in the mirror. The mirror was highly polished and distortionless. It could be set at different distances (up to 14 ft) away from the pupil by a winding it along a metal track to give the impression of range.

The Hunt range was mainly set up in a 16 ft span Nissen hut or a temporary brick building. The range was built at quite a number of airfields.

drawing no. 15/42, 661/42
examples Atcham (Nissen hut), Bibury, East Fortune, Ludham (Laing hut), Southam, Windrush

PANORAMIC TRAINER

The panoramic trainer was housed inside a large building such as an aircraft hangar. A backcloth was stretched round a semicircular frame. At one end was a large tripod carrying a large-radius lattice girder which ran on a rail fixed to the semicircular frame. The end of the girder was supported by the tripod so that it could rotate about the arc of the backcloth. Running its length was an endless chain with various aircraft models suspended from it.

Instructional gun turrets were wheeled in and the models set in motion along the arm. With a turret positioned close to the pivot point of the arm, the model presented a no-deflection head-on or tail target. Range estimation was checked when pressing of the gun trigger; the aircraft stopped and the range scale from the turret could be read off from a scale fixed to the radius arm. This trainer was also useful in checking aircraft recognition, turret manipulation, aiming, and reporting.

TURRET GUNNERY TRAINING

In the late 1930s, the Air Ministry developed a trainer for teaching air gunners how to report the correct position of enemy aircraft. This was achieved inside a darkened hangar where illuminated silhouettes of aircraft were exposed in quick succession on the walls. The silhouettes showed red for port and green for starboard, and gunners were taught to call out the colours when reporting to the pilot. The spotlight trainer consisted of free guns mounted on Scarff rings or a power-operated gun turret mounted on top of a steel frame with the gun pointing at a hemispherical target screen. When the gunner pressed the trigger a spotlight appeared on the wall where his shot would have struck. An instructor standing below with a powerful hand-held projector shone a figure of an enemy aircraft on to the wall and manoeuvred it so that the gunner could follow and shoot at it with his spotlight. The equipment was manufactured by Nash & Thompson; 130 trainers being built.

With the assistance of two representatives from the Air Ministry, namely Squadron Leaders Swayne and Heath, the National Institute of Industrial Psychology developed an improved method of turret training using a similar hemispherical target screen, and demonstrated a rough mock-up to Air Ministry Officials on 16 July 1940. An official demonstration was held on 27 November at West Freugh to representatives of both the RAF and the Admiralty. At the end of the year, Stanhope Engineering of Cricklewood was awarded a contract to manufacture 40 trainers, now called the turret gun sighting trainer (TGST).

A later design called the standard free gunnery trainer (SFGT) was very similar to the TGST except that cams used for moving the projector were dispensed with; instead, the operator had to follow a diagram showing the required movement of the aircraft image on the screen. Stanhope Engineering went on to make 341 SFGTs.

The TGST used a hydraulic-operated Frazer-Nash Type 16 turret. Above this was a cam-operated projector. In addition to the projector, there was a floodlight mounted on gimbals which illuminated the whole screen, and a diffuser merged this light with the general screen illumination. A vignette (consisting of a metal plate on a rod) was placed in front of the floodlight, blanking off the centre of the floodlit area. A corresponding vignette (a plate with a rectangular aperture in it) was placed in front of the projector allowing the projected film to fill the aperture with an image of a dark aircraft against a light background.

The turret in the tower was fitted with a graticule projector to show the point being aimed at on the screen; the gunner looked through the hood of a free gun reflector sight Mk IIIa fitted with a yellow filter to mask the yellow future position spot (invisible to the trainee but not to the

Synthetic Training 151

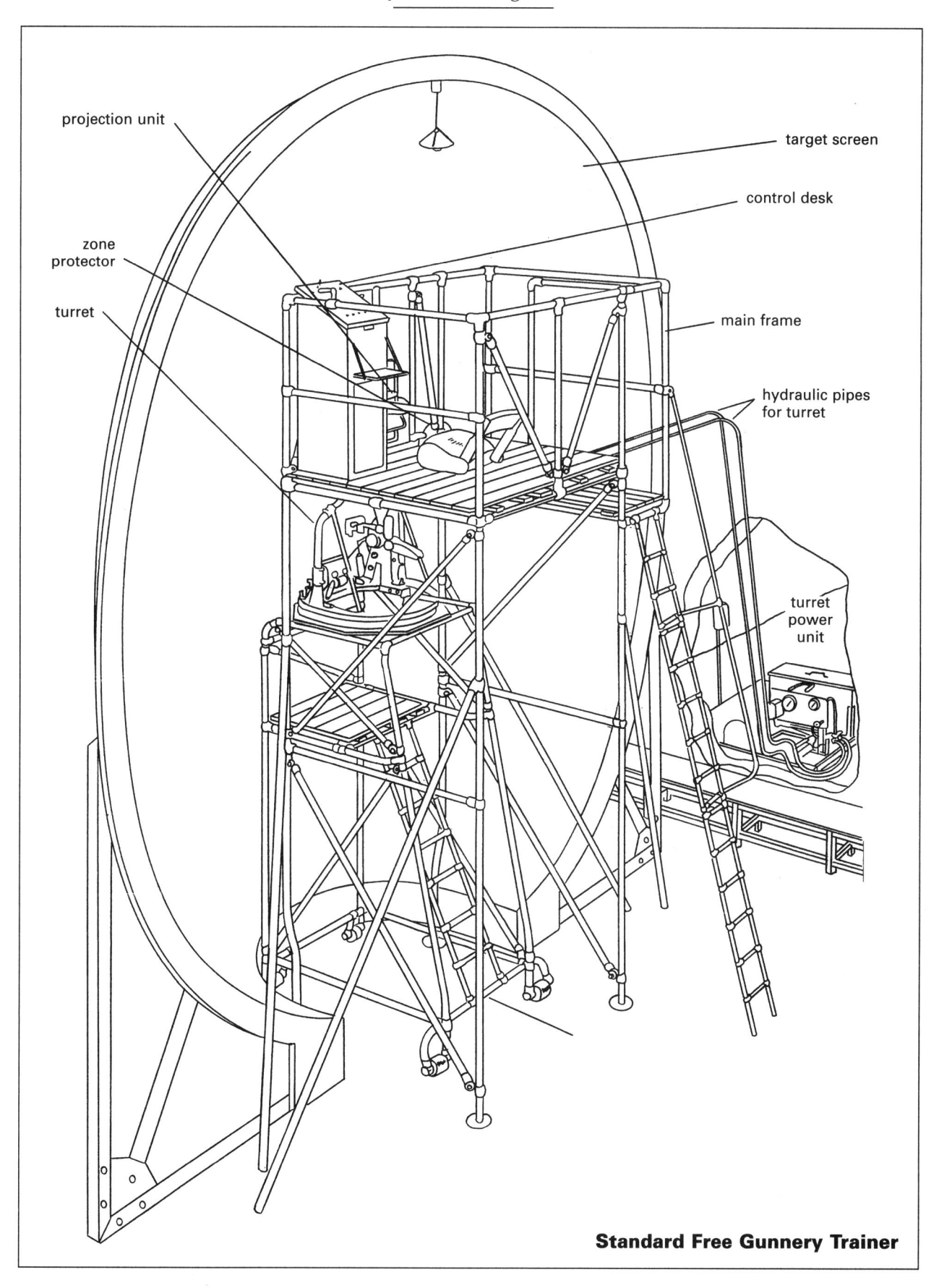

Standard Free Gunnery Trainer

instructor and therefore was an aid to help judge the accuracy of the pupil). The instructor recorded the number of hits on a hit recorder. The gunner heard the sound of his own aircraft engines and the sound of his guns when he opened fire. Films manufactured by Technicolor consisted of images of Me 109s, Me 110s and He 111s for attacks for front or rear turrets.

Typical target films included attack 1A and attack 5. Attack 1A filmed was from a rear turret. A Me 109 was sighted flying on a parallel course at 1,800 yd range, 15° off the stern on the starboard quarter. The fighter turned in towards the bomber until flying at right angles to its course, then came back until his guns were bearing on the bomber. The fighter continued to attack the aircraft closing to 50 yd before breaking away downwards and to the right. The speed of the bomber was 250 mph while that of the fighter was 300 mph. Attack 5 was filmed from a front turret. A Me 110 was sighted at 3,000 yd range, 500 ft above bomber. The Messerschmitt closed, making a sighting allowance, and finally broke away to climb above the bomber.

In the SFGT, the pupil sat inside a mock-up of an aircraft gun turret mounted on a steel frame at such a height that the eye of the air gunner was approximately level with the centre of curvature of the screen. This gave the impression that he was flying, surrounded by open sky, and to further the illusion, cloud formations were projected and a realistic sound track was played. The turret frame was positioned inside a larger main frame which was fixed to the concrete floor. On the main frame, a platform directly above the turret contained the target presentation projector, zone projector, control desk, and a seat for the instructor.

The Frazer-Nash Type 16 turret with an electrically driven power unit or a Boulton Paul Type C Mk IIa turret with a motor generator set could be used. The turret was fitted with a projector unit mounted on a dummy gun. Its movement was controlled by the turret controls. This would project an image of a ring-and-bead pattern similar to the Mk III free gun reflector sight. If the Frazer-Nash Mk Ia or the Boulton Paul Mk Ib trainer was used, a gyro gun-sight (GGS) dummy sighting head and GGS projector unit were used instead of the Mk III reflector sight. The pattern of the fixed and movable graticules of a GGS were projected on to the screen instead of the ring and bead of the reflector sight.

A 16 mm Ensign projector for presentation target was mounted above the platform of the main frame in such a way as to allow both sideways and vertical movement. The projector was loaded with an endless roll of film. There also was a mechanism for measuring the expenditure of ammunition. This automatically stopped the projector when the pre-set ammunition 'supply' was exhausted. The operator controlled the movement of the projected image of the attacking aircraft.

The air gunner manoeuvred the turret in the same way as he would a turret in an aircraft during an actual attack. When he recognized the target and had taken into account any deflection needed to hit the target, he pressed the trigger. This was noted by the instructor who pressed a button on a hit recorder. A pointer moved round a dial and recorded the number of hits until his supply of ammunition was used up.

A special training film was available for use with the gyro gun-sight. This consisted of a disc image that could change the size of its circumference. The exercise was performed with the disc tracking around the screen at different speeds. The air gunner had to track and range the target, then position a ring of diamonds to calliper the span of the target by moving the turret's pedals. He followed the target by keeping it within the image of the moving graticule and varied the size of the graticule as the size of the target varied. The operation of the gun trigger was noted by the instructor who pressed the hit recorder button to register the score.

A night attack training attachment could be used instead of the film projector to project the attacking aircraft image on to the screen. This attachment simulated night attacks to enable air gunners to practice searching for targets.

Group Captain Alfold was associated with the development of an arc-type trainer at Jurby on the Isle of Man. His screen was cylindrical, about 10 ft high with a diameter of 90 ft. He projected aircraft images on to the screen and could have as many as 12 turrets training at the same time. By July 1942, he had perfected the trainer and was supplying it to various RAF commands.

The main advantage of the multiple free gunnery trainer, as it was to become known, was that it enabled a large number of air gunners to be simultaneously trained in turret manipulation. Air gunners learned the use of the Mk IIc GGS, how to synchronize eyes, hands and feet, and intercommunication procedures and crew drill. They could also learn about the motions and attitudes of the GGS during movement of the turret. Another major advantage was it could be constructed locally. As a result, they varied in size depending on what materials were available. A large building such as a Type C hangar was required. The equipment consisted of a number of turrets, target presentation apparatus, an operating platform, a semicircular target screen, a control desk and GGS.

A spotlight animator was used for initial training of air gunners in ranging and tracking. It projected on the screen a line of light which increased in length. Each pupil positioned the line in the centre of the graticule of the GGS by operating his turret controls as the light moved across the screen. When using target film, the pupil operated his turret controls to position the target in the centre of the graticule so that two diametrically opposed diamonds of the graticule just spanned the wings of the target.

Buildings

The Type A turret instruction building on late expansion period airfields had a steel framework, externally clad with corrugated asbestos sheeting and lined internally with flat sheets of plasterboard. It had one, two, or three bays, each partitioned off from the others by timber

Synthetic Training 153

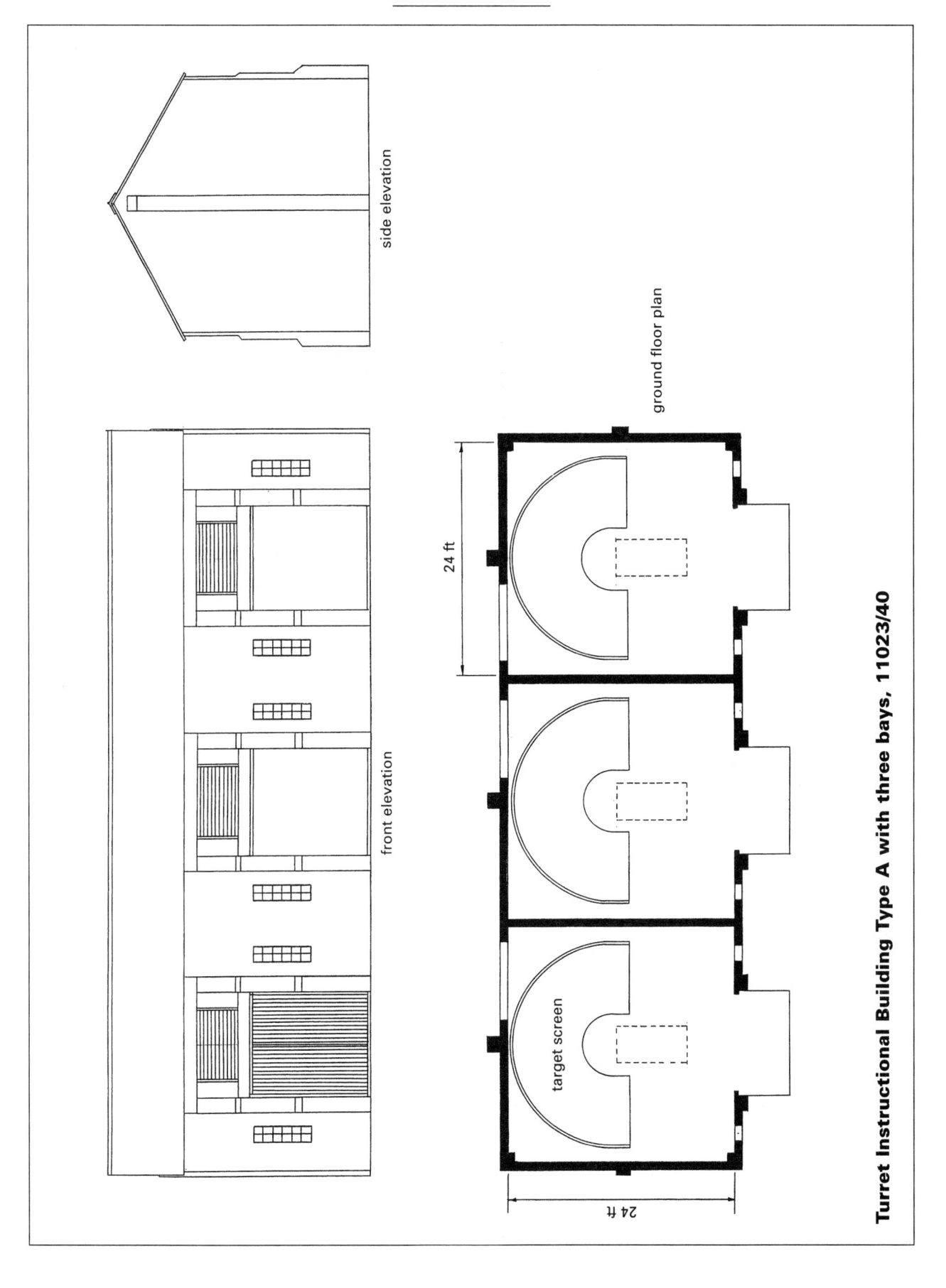

side elevation

front elevation

ground floor plan

24 ft

24 ft

target screen

Turret Instructional Building Type A with three bays, 11023/40

studwork of plasterboard with slag wall infill. Each bay had an off-centre entrance with double doors large enough for access with a turret trolley. The roof was constructed of steel trusses clad with corrugated asbestos sheeting. The ceiling was plasterboard. Each bay was equipped with a hemispherical plaster target screen. Frazer-Nash, Bristol, and Boulton Paul turrets were used in conjunction with the Nash & Thompson spotlight trainer.

The Type B building was of similar construction to Type A but was never intended to have a target screen. The first bay was a repair shop with two sets of doors. At the rear was a workbench. The next three bays were instructional rooms, and the last was divided by a partition to form an instructor's office. Each of the five bays measured 20 ft square.

Drawing number 11023/40 (Type A) was the most common design of SFGT building until it was replaced with a totally different building type. It was built with 9-inch thick brick walls, laid fair face; most were not cement rendered. The entrance was in the centre of the front elevation, on both sides of which were brick buttresses supporting reinforced-concrete lintels above and below large louvered air vents of timber. A concrete ramp led up to large timber doors to allow the trolley turret frame to be manoeuvred in and out of the room. The roof was constructed of steel trusses externally clad with corrugated asbestos sheeting and internally lined with plasterboard. The ceiling was not flat as in 3550/39 but followed the angle of the roof. This was necessary in order to allow room for the screen because the walls were shorter than on the earlier design.

As the turret required a power supply, hydraulic or electric, a power house to keep the noise to a minimum when the equipment was operating was required. This was simply built against a side elevation and normally quite small, just large enough to house the equipment.

Most were built as single-bay buildings, but some were double-bay buildings with extra bays built side by side. There were also a few buildings, constructed after 1942, consisting of both a turret trainer and an AML bombing teacher built to drawing number 633/42; they were built back-to-back. Although they are now rare, an example still stands at Tatenhill.

The final building design used to house the SFGT was a straightforward and economical conversion of an enlarged over type blister hangar. This was 82 ft 6 in long and had a radius of 60 ft with a maximum height of 20 ft. There were two basic designs: 7316/42 which had one or two 9-inch brick gable ends, and 1111/43 which had steel gable walls made from 24-gauge black-painted corrugated iron sheeting supported by steel stanchions and angle framing.

In the centre of the hangar and bolted to the concrete floor was the target screen, this was quite different from the earlier hemispherical type as it was made of Gyproc wall boards painted with white distemper. The screen was supported by a timber framework. It was flat and curved (non-hemispherical), 16 ft high with a radius of 33 ft. No screen is known to survive and the only evidence today are the rag-bolts left in the concrete floor following the line of the screen. An example can be seen inside the building at Little Walden.

Various airfields still have this building type still *in situ* and they are often mistaken for aircraft hangars. Their postwar uses vary from farm equipment stores to small grain silos.

A Type A turret trainer 11023/40 at Arbroath.

drawing no.	11023/40	11023/40	3550/39
Type	A		B
no. of bays	1	3	
examples	Mount Batten	Bicester, Odiham	

drawing no.	11023/40	11023/40	7316/42
Type	A		
no. of bays	1	2	
examples	Rougham, Hemswell, Melton Mowbray	Haverfordwest, Silverstone	

drawing no 1111/43

Surviving Target Screen at Sleap

The only known screen to survive is at Sleap in Shropshire, in a combined AML bombing teacher and turret trainer to drawing number 633/42; the screen was built to drawing number 1588/41. The building is completely devoid of doors, roof or window glazing and so is completely open to the elements. It is remarkable that it has survived under these conditions for so long. When first seen in 1984, it was in very good condition. Unfortunately, more recently (1993), a large portion of the screen has been removed. Despite this, the target screen could still be renovated if anyone was willing to take on such a project.

When surveyed in 1984, evidence was found on the concrete floor of the fixed tubular steel main frame that once supported the control desk and target presentation apparatus. The 20 ft diameter screen was found to be made from a fibrous plaster or hair-bound lime and sand which was plastered on to hemispherical Hy-Rib expanded metal sheeting.

A large steel frame supported the screen against the walls and floor. It is quite often impossible to find evidence of this framework, or the power house. The explanation can only be that, in such cases, the building never had a target screen but was used for the static instruction instead.

ELEMENTARY DEFLECTION TEACHER

This gave fixed-gun fighter pilots ground training in estimating the aiming allowances necessary when attacking enemy aircraft. A base board was mounted on trestles; at one end was a white screen where a model aircraft could be set in any desired direction. At the opposite end of the base board was a sighting unit. This consisted of a pilot's reflector gun-sight Mk II, controlled by a hand-grip and a periscope spotlight. The spotlight was also controlled by the hand-grip with the aid of a linkage which allowed it to indicate the correct deflection allowance when the firing button was pressed.

The pupil aimed at the model aircraft through the gun-sight and pressed the firing button after allowing for the correct amount of deflection. If the aim was correct, the spot of light would hit the target aircraft. The spot of light was 2.5 inches in diameter, representing a normal fighter machine-gun grouping at the ranges covered by the teacher, to the same scale as the model aircraft. If, however, the aim was incorrect, the position of the spot of light relative to the nose of the target aircraft indicated the amount of deflection error.

EDMONDS DEFLECTION TRAINER

This was for the training of fighter pilots in aircraft recognition, range judging, and deflection shooting, using a standard Link trainer. This was fitted with a reflector sight and spotlight, and was operated by firing a button on the control column. A 1:48 scale aircraft model joined to a graph board was positioned 6 ft 6 in from the ground, mounted on a trolley with castors and positioned at some distance from the Link. Arcs of circles from the pivot point of the Link were painted on the floor at intervals of 37.5 inches, representing ranges from 150 yd to 600 yd at 50 yd intervals.

The pupil flew the Link to 'attack' the model which moved to simulate an aircraft under attack. When the pilot considered he was in range, he pressed the trigger in short bursts and the beam of light from the spotlight registered on the graph. The instructor immediately read

A target screen at Sleap.

off the range from the arcs on the floor and the errors shown on the graph.

drawing no. 4188/42
examples Calveley, Long Newton, Tealing

FISHER FRONT GUN TRAINER

A 22 ft diameter steel track (1051/43), some 11 ft from the floor, was fixed to a steel supporting framework. Hanging from the track was a 1:72 scale model aircraft. In the centre of the room below the circle of track was a Link trainer fitted with a spotlight and a reflector sight.

The instructor set the model aircraft in motion and altered, from a control cabinet, the angle of the model to simulate a flight path round the room. Suspended below the model was an arm which was kept parallel to it and at the same level as the spotlight in the front of the Link. Fixed to this arm was a photo-electric cell positioned at a scale distance of 250 yd for a speed of 200 mph. The pupil in the Link trainer took into account the angle of deflection and pressed his firing button, sending out a beam of light to hit the photo-electric cell, ringing a bell or operating a ticker-tape machine to record the hit.

The building housing the trainer was of temporary brick construction, 28 ft by 25 ft. On the front elevation was a lobby and boiler-room, giving it an appearance similar to a Link trainer hut.

drawing no. 10839/42
examples Annan, Calveley, Crosby-on-Eden, East Fortune, Errol, Eshott, High Ercall, Milfield

TORPEDO ATTACK TRAINER

The torpedo attack trainer (TAT) was a sophisticated

device that provided instruction in the use of the F director system of torpedo attack on various types of ship within a simulated 'attack' environment. Prior to the introduction of this system, torpedo aiming was on the 'aim off' principle. The torpedo was released with the aircraft pointing at a position ahead of the target, the pilot estimating the track of the target ship, just like deflection shooting at any moving target. There were some very basic aids to help the pilot. For example, the Swordfish was fitted with a bar and bulb sight fixed to the centre-section struts; the bulbs were a known distance apart along the bar and tables were used to establish the range of the ship. But there was always the possibility of an aiming error due to factors which were difficult to judge using this crude sight.

Range was the most difficult to estimate. Range estimation was effected by the angle of the bow. The appearance of the ship changed as the angle of the bow changed; the smaller the angle the shorter the length of the ship which had the effect of making the ship appear much further away. It was also difficult to estimate the ship's speed. The pilot had to recognize the type of ship he was attacking as this would give him a fair indication of its top speed; the theory was that a ship under attack would be making its best speed. The size of the secondary bow wave also helped in estimating the ship's speed; the faster the ship the further back the bow wave. When these two waves merged, the ship was going at full speed. The amount of wake could also help.

The F director, a computer in the aircraft, was fed with information by the pilot. The director in turn fed settings to the torpedo, calculating the amount of deflection required. The aircraft was positioned straight at the target ship, thus eliminating sighting error and the torpedo headed off at an angle after entering the water.

An attack with Barracuda torpedo-bombers, involved

The epidiascope of the torpedo attack trainer at Crail.

The target screen of the torpedo attack trainer. On the floor is the tubular ring on which the effects lanterns were mounted.

three aircraft (the number of aircraft could be any multiple of three) in line-ahead flying at right angles to the target ship's track, aiming to cross her bows. The attack began with a shallow positioning dive; the dive brakes were then applied to go into the steep attack dive. The aircraft were all at the same height during this operation. At a few hundred feet, they turned in, again together (in nautical parlance a Blue Turn), so that they were running at the target in line abreast. At this point, dive brakes were raised and the aircraft flew level, and the settings on the F director controls adjusted as necessary; the target ship's speed was set to the known performance of the vessel, and the bow angle was corrected. When the ship started to turn, as a ship under attack always did, the 'avoiding action' was entered. The aircraft had to be straight and level with no roll or pitch since any error would affect the aim of the torpedo.

At this point, one aircraft would have the target head-on and the other two would have a shot on the bow. All three would drop their torpedoes, though no hit was expected from the head-on shot. If the pilots had got everything right, the other two would hit; the F director was that good. Getting everything right was difficult, which was why so much training was needed.

Practice without a torpedo (attack, light, torpedo, or ALT) was the first stage, learning to estimate range and height dropping a smoke bomb. Bearings from the target ship, readings from the F director, and the aircraft camera film were used to score the attack. Then followed attacks with a dummy torpedo (ADT), and finally attacks with a real torpedo or 'runner' fitted with a 'blowing head' (ART).

At the beginning of the Second World War, because of the fear of bombing raids on our cities, cinemas and theatres were shut. The companies who had relied on supplying theatre equipment had to seek alternative work.

The firm of Fitups Ltd of Manchester (later to become Watts & Corry) was in 1940 operating jointly with the north of England branch of Strand Electric (later to become Rank Strand Electric). The staff of these two companies included joiners, scenic artists, draughtsmen, engineers, and electricians. They were versatile in their approach to finding suitable work. Representatives were sent to the Air Ministry to try and obtain camouflage work. Unfortunately, this was not available but a contract was won for the design and manufacture of painted scenic cycloramas for Link trainers.

As a result of the experience gained while building this equipment for the RAF, Fitups was asked by the Royal Navy for their co-operation in the design and development of a trainer for the instruction of pilots in the techniques of torpedo attack on ships at sea. After a lot of discussion and trial and error, the result was a circular (in plan) cyclorama, 44 ft in diameter, 23 ft high, and curved at the top and bottom. The structure consisted of heavy timber formers covered with expanded-metal sheeting, plastered to provide a smooth surface. The lower portion of the target screen was painted to represent the sea and the upper portion was painted off-white to allow various sky effects to be projected on to it.

When the prototype trainer was completed it was demonstrated for the approval of an impressive assembly of senior officers. Commander Flying occupied the Link for the demonstration exercise and the contractors made sure he registered a hit. As a result of the successful demonstration both FAA and RAF acquired trainers for UK airfields, and later for overseas stations. Eventually the company was asked to adapt the trainer for the instruction

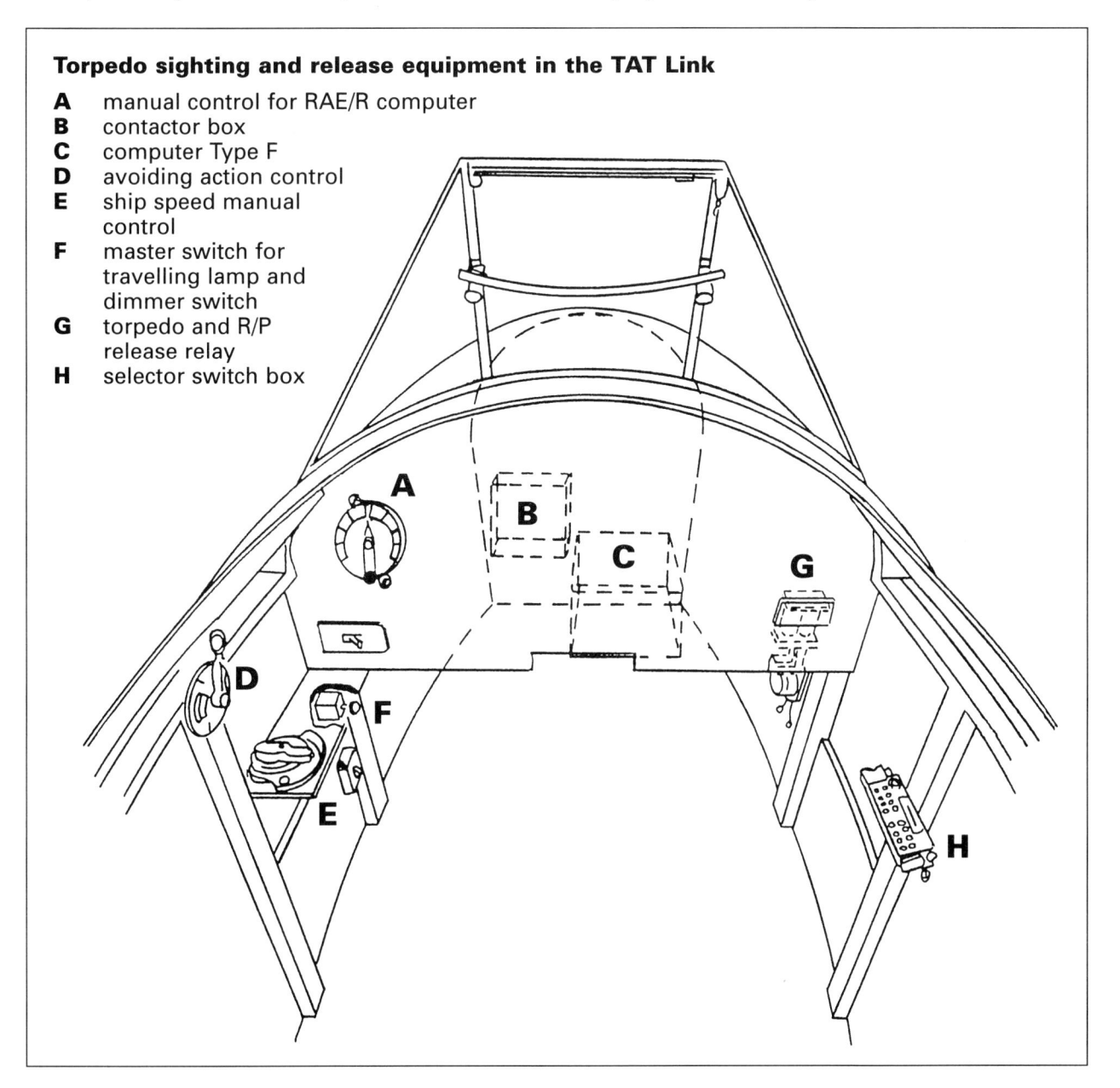

Torpedo sighting and release equipment in the TAT Link

- **A** manual control for RAE/R computer
- **B** contactor box
- **C** computer Type F
- **D** avoiding action control
- **E** ship speed manual control
- **F** master switch for travelling lamp and dimmer switch
- **G** torpedo and R/P release relay
- **H** selector switch box

158 *British Military Airfield Architecture*

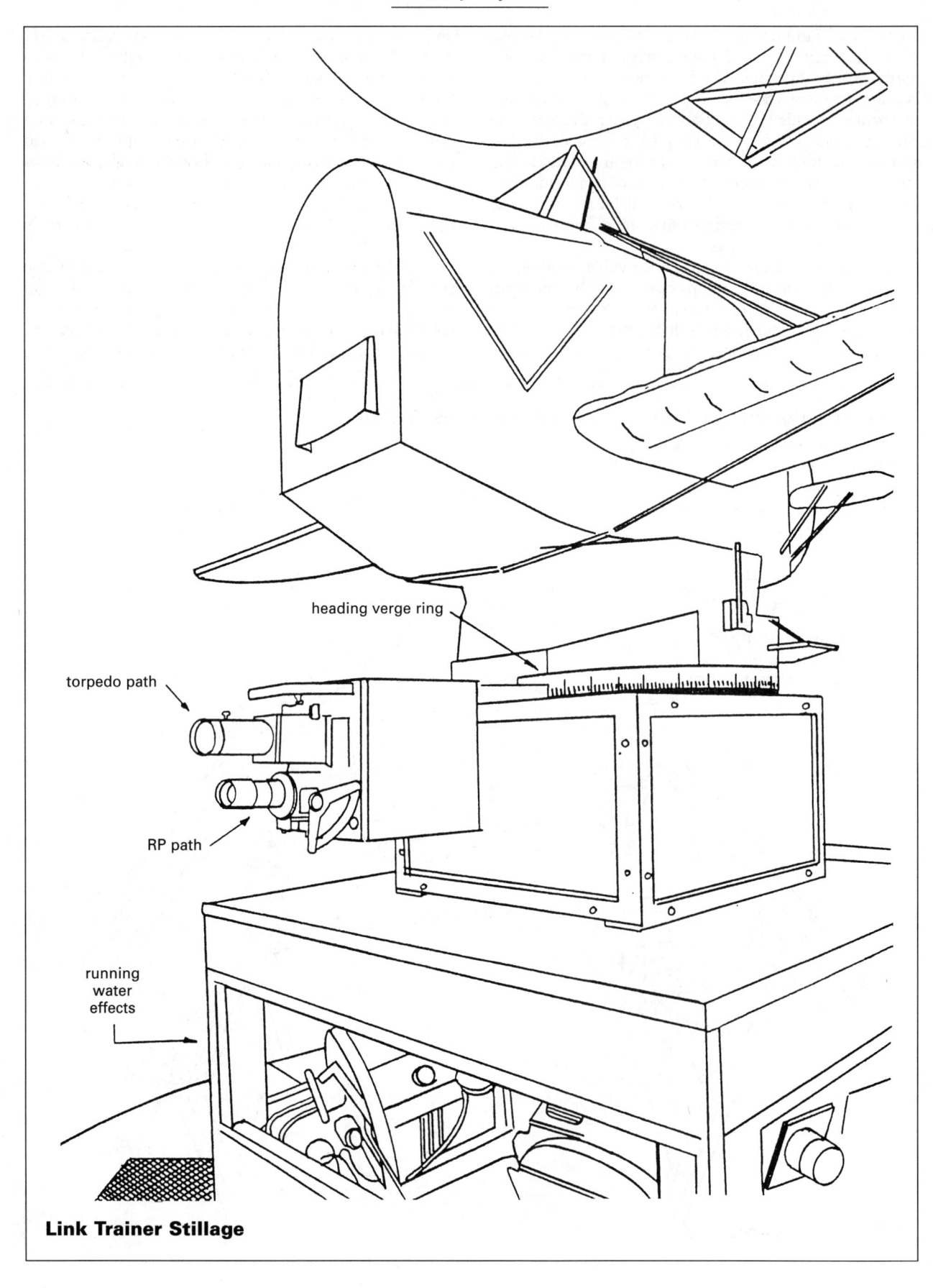

torpedo path

RP path

heading verge ring

running water effects

Link Trainer Stillage

of destroyer, MTB, and submarine personnel. All of these trainers required the design and construction of suitable units to replace the Link. The submarine trainer required the most complicated unit of all as it incorporated a replica of the control room complete with periscope and conning tower.

Another trainer designed on similar lines to the TAT was the operational crew trainer. Its object was the instruction of pilots in observing and reporting the success of gunnery attacks. The pilots of four Link trainers in separate cubicles were able to observe bombardment of a shore installation by ships. The target was a model diorama constructed on a rotating turntable which moved to simulate the view seen from an aircraft flying on an off-shore figure-of-eight course. The instructor selected the shell bursts at random by push-buttons on a mimic control panel, and at 'night' simulated flares could be 'dropped' over the target.

Buildings

The TAT building at Arbroath was built to drawing number 1697/42 and consisted of a steel-framed square-shaped building with walls having a clear length of 50 ft and a clear height of 23 ft. Steel roof trusses were bolted to RSJ stanchions and clad with corrugated iron. Cross bracing of the roof trusses was arranged to give support to a steel frame to carry the weight of a moving projector. A motorized ventilator fan provided cooling air for the projector equipment.

The centre of the building consisted of an approximately spherical cyclorama (target screen). In the centre, was a Link trainer mounted on a raised platform. Part of the effects apparatus was mounted under it. External to the target screen was a control room. A small window was set into the side of the screen to allow the instructor to see the action. The instructor controlled the silhouette and lighting effects.

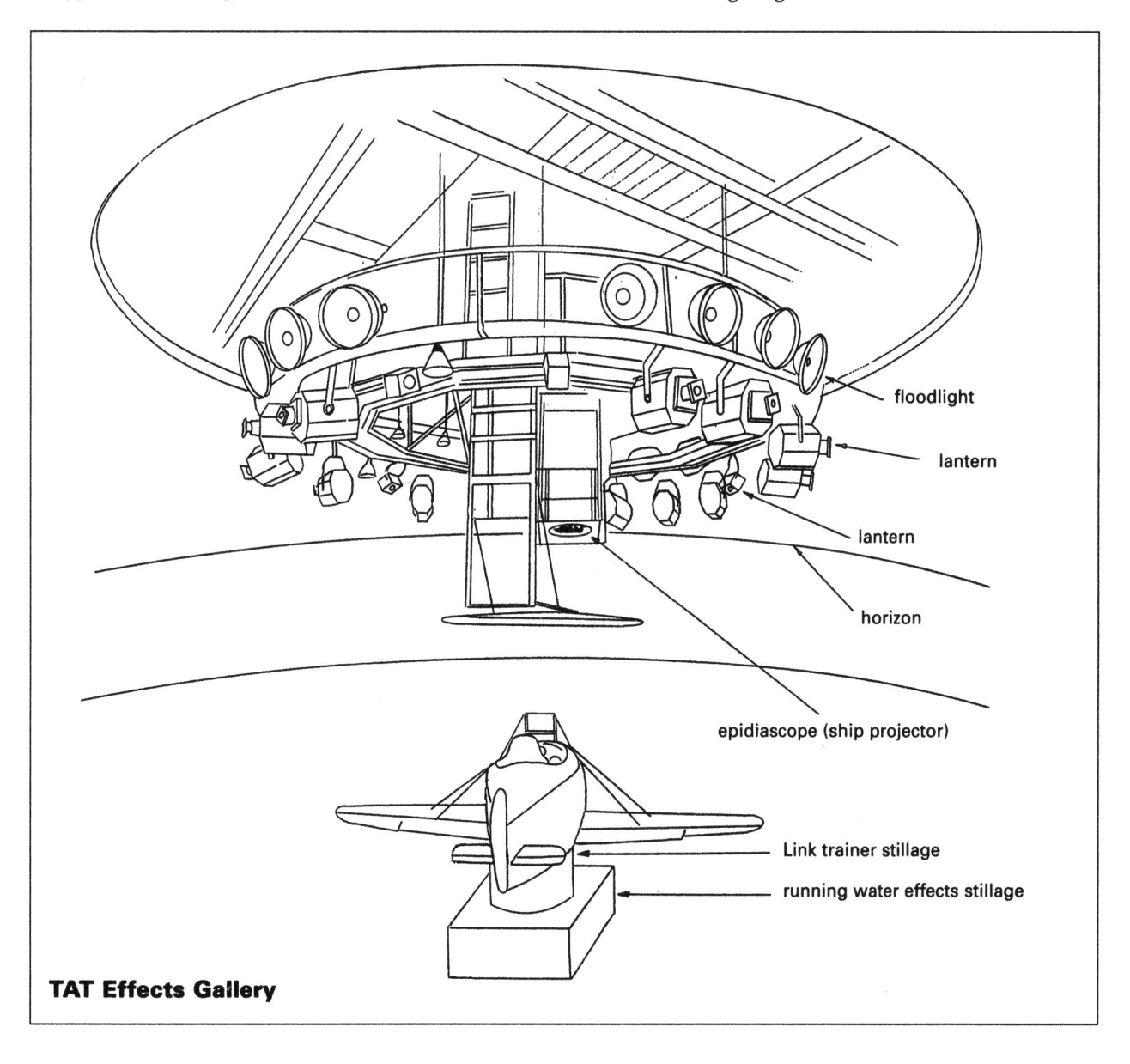

TAT Effects Gallery

Hanging from the platform above the target screen was the main effects gallery consisting of a large-diameter tubular ring from which were suspended 43 lanterns. These were fitted with coloured filters; light blue for fleecy clouds, dark blue for stormy clouds, and 'sunset' (orange) for daylight conditions. In fact, nine different effects could be obtained by varying the brightness of individual lanterns or groups of lanterns to create the required effect. There was a dimmer bank with a number of push-buttons labelled according to the effect each produced: dark night, searchlight, bright night, moonlight, sunset, misty day, overcast day, fine day, and target test. Each switch operated GPO-style relays according to the selection mode. Rheostats increased the power to the stage lighting and the lamps shone on the screen with increasing brightness until the limit switches operated at the appropriate selection, producing a bright day or whatever effect was required.

An additional lighting feature was the representation of flying close to the surface of the sea. This could be achieved by transparent rotating discs of glass; the lamps were automatically switched on when the Link trainer came down to a simulated level of 30 ft as recorded by the altimeter in the cockpit. Another lighting feature was flare illumination of the target, achieved by rotating a white-painted irregular plate behind the model ship in the epidiascope. Switching on the lamps illuminated the plate and the target was seen as a silhouette.

In the centre of the floor in front of the screen was a Link trainer on a raised dais some 4 ft from the floor. The Link had a number of special modifications. Normal Link trainers were only capable of 15° of climb or dive, but the TAT Link was able to pitch 25° in both directions. Other modifications included an extended nose, no canopy, and fitting a torpedo F sight. This was controlled by a circular plate, divided into red and green halves, with a pointer representing the target ship. On this was set the estimated angle of the bow. There was also a 'ship's speed' control and an 'avoiding action' lever.

The Link was driven in the same manner as all trainers of the era. The outputs went to a tracking crab (this one had no idler wheel) and was connected to another crab by a rack and pinion. The second crab represented the target ship. Both crabs sat on a sand-blasted glass-topped table in the control console. The relative position of the aircraft crab to the ship crab was monitored by the instructor. Furthermore, this relationship produced signals which were used, via a magslip device, to drive three ARL oil motors which in turn drove the epidiascope in its vertical arc and its horizontal axis (up to 270°), and the lens system so as to enlarge or diminish the size of the image of the model ship projected on the screen.

The ship's steering and speed were controlled by the instructor from a control console. The movement was fairly slow so as to represent the inertia of the ship, but avoiding action could be taken by fast manipulation of a control. The disposition of the two crabs and their movements with respect to each other was the essential part of the training.

The projector or epidiascope was mounted from the top of the building and was used to project the image of the ship on to the screen. It could rotate to move the ship image round the screen, tilt to take into consideration the height of the aircraft, and vary the size of the image to conform to changes in true range. The aspect of the target image changed when the ship changed course, when the angle on the bow changed, and when the line of sight differed from the horizontal. The model ship, made of brass and built to a scale of 1 inch to 100 feet, was between 3 and 5 inches long and fitted to a spindle, round which the projector rotated, and was mounted upside down on the axis of the lens system. With the use of high intensity lamps and moving lenses, images of enemy vessels could be projected.

The trainee sighted the ship as a small white object on the horizon, except when 'dark night' was selected and a flare button was pressed, in which case the image of the ship was shown as a silhouette. In all cases, when the aircraft was manoeuvred in accordance with the procedure described above, the ship image moved in a logical sense, moving up the screen as the aircraft dived, presenting a deck view to the pilot and a changing profile as the aircraft turned in. As there was no wake, the speed and possible avoiding action were given. The trainee used his F sight to get the correct angle to allow for drift and other variables as the ship took avoiding action and eventually he 'dropped' his torpedo. At this point, the target froze and the pilot took the necessary evasive action to avoid the attentions of the ship's gunners. A white line of light was shown on the screen representing the track of the torpedo. The target ship was then set in motion again and moved for a time equal to the duration of the torpedo run when it stopped. If the target ship stopped on the line of light, a hit was recorded. An assessment was then made by the controller to determine the success or failure of the exercise.

The TAT building at Crail consists of a large brick-built structure with two small windows, and thus more or less devoid of natural light to allow the simulation of various weather conditions using artificial light. The roof was constructed of steel trusses clad with corrugated iron sheeting, three air ventilators being located along the ridge line. Attached to the rear of the building is a boiler house complete with boiler and tall chimney, and at the front is a power house and entrance porch.

The interior of the building is dominated by the target screen; once inside, the sheer size becomes apparent as your eyes get accustomed to the darkness. The screen is hemispherical with a small section missing for access. This differs from other TAT target screens (at Arbroath, for example); a doorway built into the screen wall pivoted about a central hinge point, the upper portion outward, the lower portion inward. When closed, this screen was a complete hemisphere. Another version had a passageway below floor level, with stairs to a trapdoor giving access to the Link trainer.

The screen at Crail has a maximum internal diameter of 40 ft. The curvature in profile blends in with the floor where the internal diameter is 29 ft. The line of the horizon can still be seen painted on the screen some 6 ft from the floor. It is not clear what method was used to construct the screen. One theory is that the timber framework was erected to the correct radius, which was then clad with wooden laths or expanded-metal fabric to form the profile which was then plastered with sand and cement. The timber framework behind the screen can still be seen and each section is numbered for correct assembly. Originally it was clad with hardboard, most of which was found on the floor.

Lying on the floor in front of the screen was a large piece of apparatus identified by reference to AP 2655C as the epidiascope (target presentation equipment). It consists of a large metal hood inside which are eight 120-ampere 22-volt lamps which were probably aircraft landing lamps, each bulb mounted inside reflective hoods below which are two filter packs. Protruding from the epidiascope is a central shaft with a large reduction gear wheel which is located behind a thick-section metal plate. The other side contains a bearing. The shaft ends inside the hood, driving brass cogs. About midway up the upper section are two electric motors (probably 'range' motors) driving a common rod. This rod is connected to a sprocket which probably once had a bicycle-type chain attached to it connecting another sprocket now missing. The rear of the large metal hood is a counterbalance weight. There are several electric sockets (two-pin) and four main hoses containing electric wiring. A large frame at the front contains the focussing rail and a large lens carriage plate. Right at the front is another plate with a large serrated edge ellipse of unknown function.

Also found on the floor in front of the screen was a large-diameter tubular frame which once held the stage lighting equipment. On the floor is a conduit pit for the power supply to the Link trainer and the control console. Unfortunately, the console was missing as was the raised dais for the Link trainer. A ladder gave access to a timber catwalk above the target screen which was supported by RSJs. From here, steps led down to a small platform which may have been used for access to the epidiascope in order to change the model ship when another class of target vessel was required.

drawing no.   1697/42
examples   Arbroath, Crail

AIR MINISTRY LABORATORY BOMBING TEACHER

The AML bombing teacher was originally designed in 1925 at the Air Ministry Laboratory (hence AML) at Imperial College, London. It enabled bomb aimers to be trained in the use of the course setting bomb-sight in a realistic representation of operational flying.

Inside the AML bombing teacher, the concrete floor was made perfectly flat with a screed. A white circle 18 ft in diameter was painted on it. The walls and rest of the floor were painted matt black. Stairs led up to an L-shaped landing which, when fitted with a bomb aimer's platform and equipment, represented the fuselage of the aircraft. At the forward end of the landing a course setting bomb-sight and compass were mounted. The 'pilot' sat with a rudder bar that was connected to the controlling mechanism on the projection floor above. Further along the landing were stairs to the projection room. This floor had a square hole in its centre, above which was a box to raise the controlling mechanism and projector to the correct height so that the image seen on the floor below was to the correct scale. The controlling mechanism was manufactured by Vickers Armstrong and was originally known as the Vickers Bygrave bombing teacher.

The teacher provided a photographic representation of a section of 'ground' as would be seen from an aircraft. The projector of the mechanism consisted of a 500 candlepower Point-o-lite lamp with a two-lens condenser system and a short-focus lens. A 12 ft square aerial photographic mosaic of the ground was projected from a 10-inch square slide and was seen on the ground floor of the building. This represented about 900 square miles although only 4 square miles were visible at any one time. The scale of the transparency was about 1:22. Very fine detail was not possible, but sufficient detail was shown for the recognition of ground marks as seen from a height of 8,000 ft. A 1-inch diameter circle was marked on the floor of the screen representing the trail point. Concentric circles were drawn round the trail point so that bombing errors could be determined; for example, at 8,000 ft, 3.5 inches represented a 100 yd of error.

A flight effect was obtained by the movement of the projected image in any direction. The idea was that the 'fuselage' was fixed and the 'ground' moved relative to it. Provision was also made for the correct change in drift and ground speed with a change of course.

A 14-inch diameter rotating table was driven via a chain by a motor. This was controlled by the rudder bar operated by the pilot. When the rudder bar was moved, a change of course took place on the projected image. Another motor traversed the slide in the desired direction by means of lead screws which gave the effect of the aircraft flying at approximately 90 mph. Two friction-driven tables on the circumference of the rotating table were rotated by chain drives connected to the traversing motor. This produced a wind speed effect on the course of the aircraft.

The pilot regularly altered course upon receipt of instructions from the bomb aimer who calculated wind direction and strength as if on a real mission. After he had sighted on the target, and if the bomb-sight had been correctly set, the target travelled from his line of sight to the trail point in the same time as it took for the 'bomb' to fall. Bomb release started a timing mechanism. After a time equal to that taken for the 'bomb' to fall and hit the target, the apparatus stopped. At the moment of the 'explosion', the target should have been inside the trail point. The difference between the two showed the amount of error.

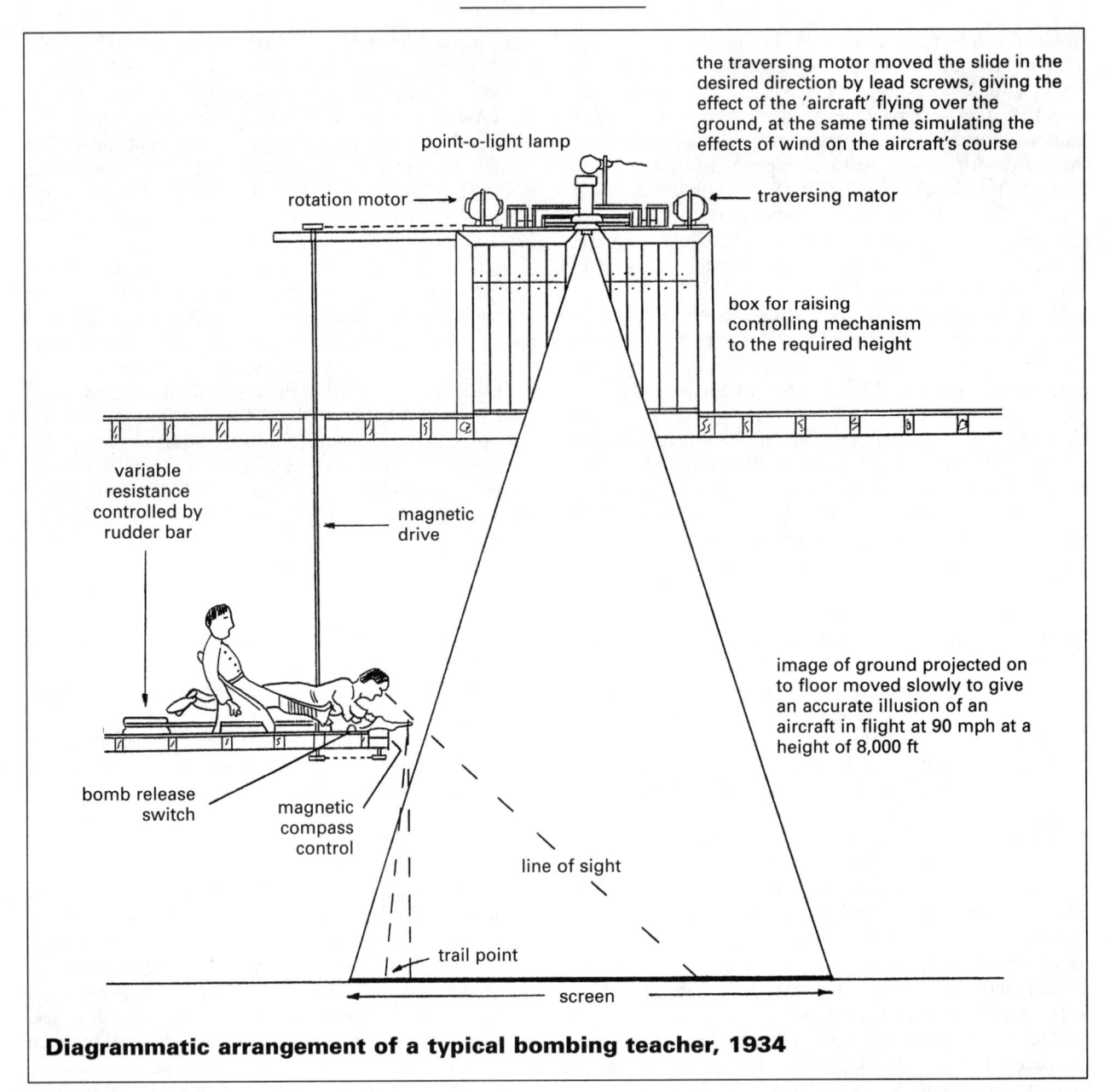

Diagrammatic arrangement of a typical bombing teacher, 1934

(labels on diagram:)
- point-o-light lamp
- rotation motor
- traversing motor — the traversing motor moved the slide in the desired direction by lead screws, giving the effect of the 'aircraft' flying over the ground, at the same time simulating the effects of wind on the aircraft's course
- box for raising controlling mechanism to the required height
- variable resistance controlled by rudder bar
- magnetic drive
- image of ground projected on to floor moved slowly to give an accurate illusion of an aircraft in flight at 90 mph at a height of 8,000 ft
- bomb release switch
- magnetic compass control
- line of sight
- trail point
- screen

Buildings

The earliest known drawing numbers were 2103/26 and 69/27. This design remained largely unchanged until 1938. It was a two-storey detached building (approximately 13 ft square in cross-section) of sectional timber frame construction (similar to a Type A hut), with a flat or pitched roof clad with cedar wood weatherboarding. A small and narrow projecting extension at first-floor level supported by timber posts contained a landing area and stairs to the projection floor above.

None is known to survive today but a brick building based on this design is still extant at Crail.

At bomber aerodromes built during the expansion period, the AML bombing teacher was part of the armoury building complex. It was situated in the centre of the rear half of the two-storey section of the building. Access to the AML was from the main entrance lobby and hallway which led to a staircase that connected the screen floor, some 4 ft 6 in below ground-floor level, to the bomb aimer's landing and led to the floor containing the projection room. The staircase also gave access to a photographic room which shared the first floor of the armoury with the projection floor of the AML.

The bombing teacher within the armoury was constructed of 9-inch thick brick walls, with the projection floor and landing of reinforced concrete. The screen area was 13 ft square. The bomb aimer's landing projected into the workshop area of the armoury.

Early wartime buildings to 47/40 had similar dimensions to those of earlier detached designs but incorporated a few modifications. They were built of

An AML bombing teacher 47/40 at Snaith.

AN AML bombing teacher 6301/42 at Melton Mowbray.

cement-rendered brick. The narrow landing was retained but a storeroom was added beneath it. A flat timber roof was used instead of the pitched roof. Where more than one trainer was required the buildings could be built with more than one bay to accommodate them unlike the earlier design which could only house one trainer.

A much larger and improved design superseded 47/40, constructed on new airfields in 1942. This new building, 1739/41, was constructed in 9-inch brick and had a shallow pitched roof using standard 18 ft span steel trusses supported by internal brick piers. The trusses were clad with corrugated asbestos sheeting and lined inside with fibreboard. Attached to the entrance elevation of single-bay buildings was a boiler house and fuel store complete with 30 ft high chimney, giving this building design the appearance of a small house. Those buildings with more than one bay were electrically heated. New buildings had a boiler house between the two bays on the front elevation. After 1942, new buildings were built to 6301/42 with reinforced concrete instead of timber for landing and projection room floors. Furthermore, steel ladders and tubular steel guide rails replaced timber ladders and rails. A set of timber doors at the floor level of the projection room on the front elevation were common to 1739/41 and 6301/42 designs. After 1943, new buildings built to 937/43 had a window instead of doors.

Wigtown also had a four-bay building. It was unusual because two of the bays were similar to 47/40 with a flat roof while the other two were similar to 1739/41. Undoubtedly, the airfield at Errol had the building with the most bays (six), three bays in a row and another three built back-to-back.

The final building design 633/42 came in late 1942. This consisted of a combined AML and turret trainer built side by side. Some were electrically heated while others

A pair of twin AML bombing teachers at Dumfries.

164 *British Military Airfield Architecture*

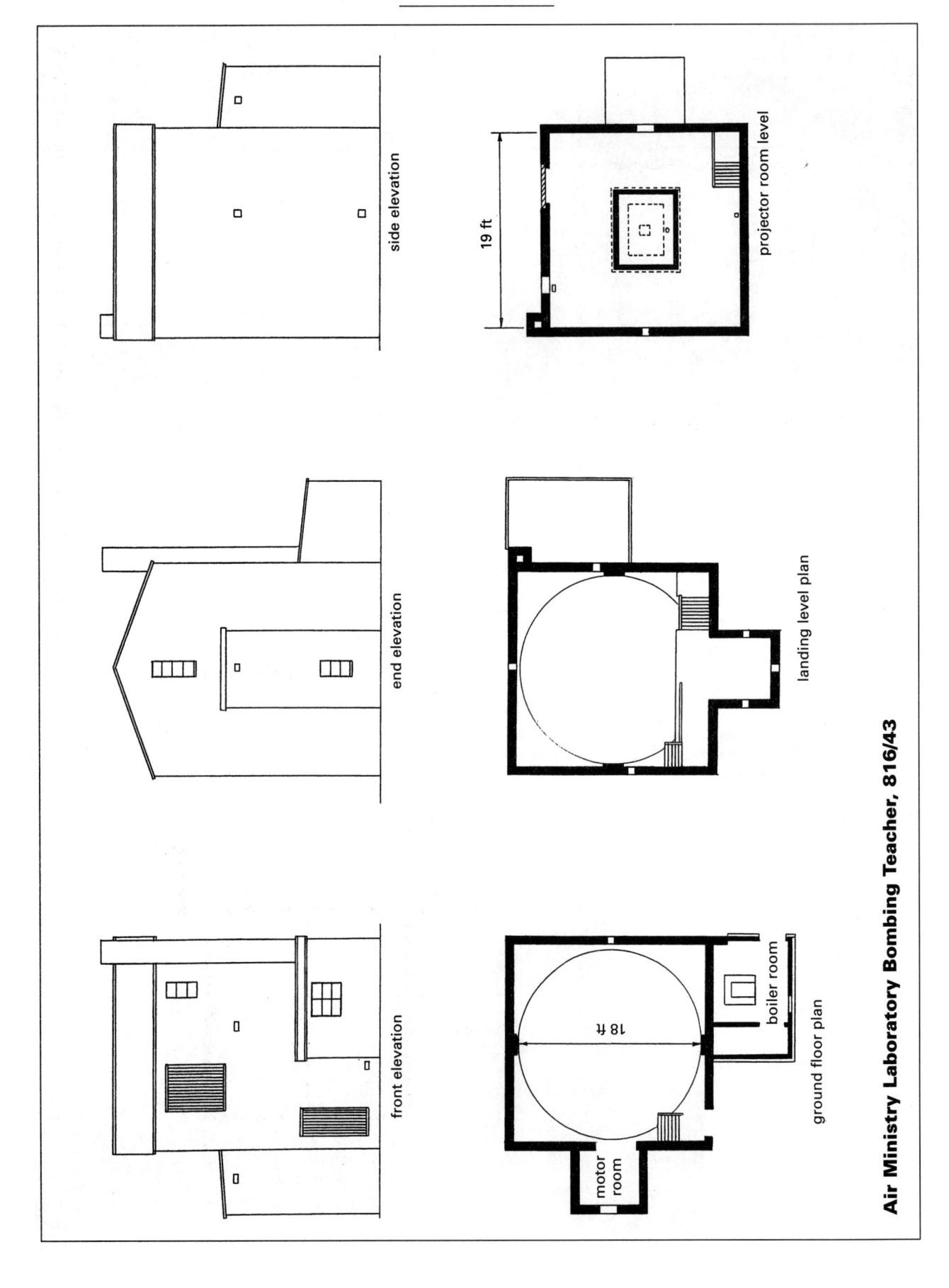

Air Ministry Laboratory Bombing Teacher, 816/43

Turret Instructional Type A and AML Bombing Teacher, 937/43

SECTION AA

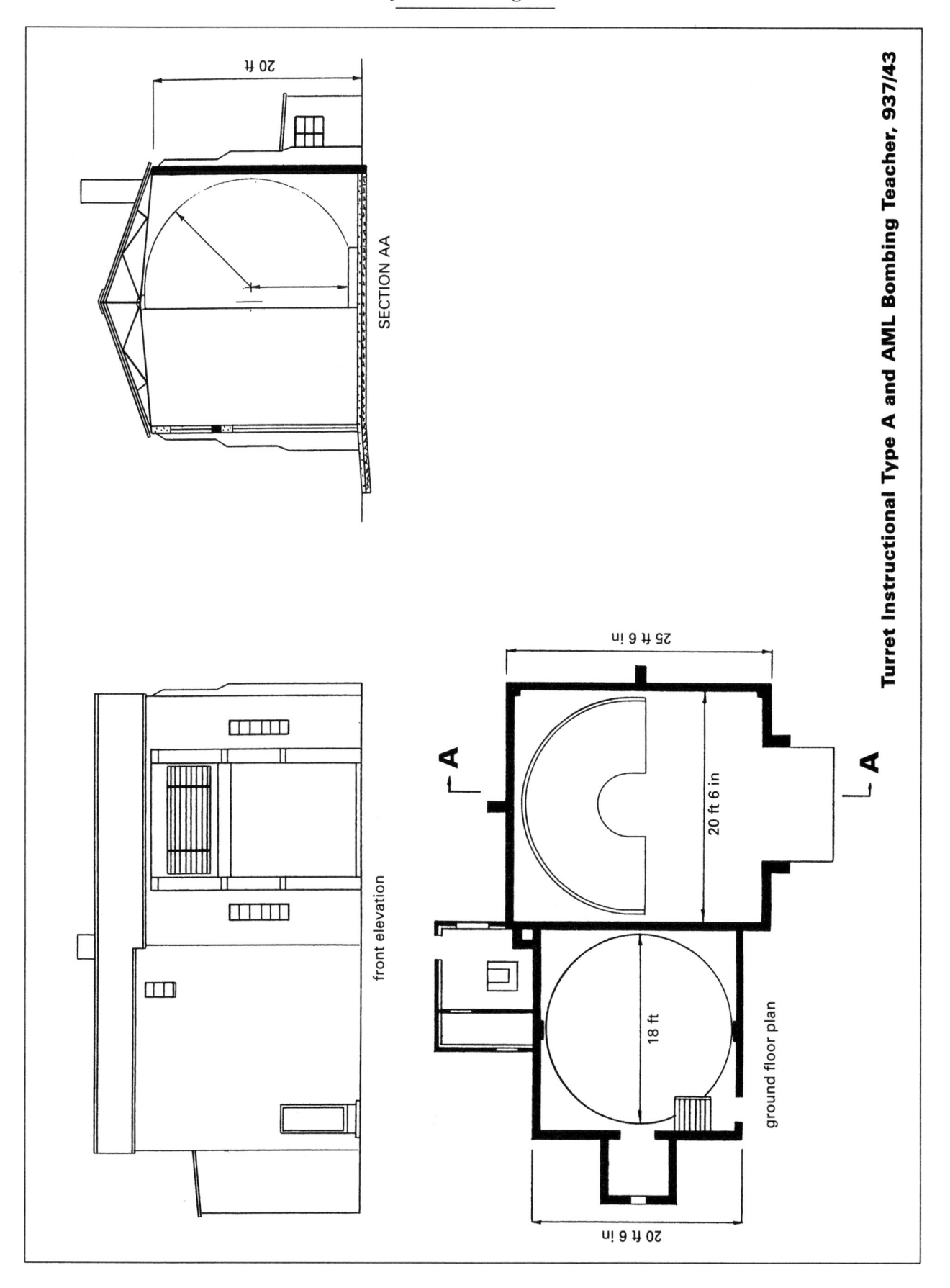

20 ft

front elevation

ground floor plan

25 ft 6 in
20 ft 6 in
18 ft
20 ft 6 in

were heated by a boiler house built against the rear wall of the AML. Later drawings like 937/43 were for minor alterations only.

drawing no.	2103/26, 69/27	7616/37	47/40
examples (no. of bays)	Old Sarum, Montrose, Wittering, Evanton	Bassingbourn, West Raynham, Watton	Holme-on-Spalding Moor (1), Dumfries (2)

drawing no.	1739/41, 6301/42	633/42
examples (no. of bays)	Dumfries (2 back-to-back), Silverstone (1 behind a pair), Haverfordwest (4, a pair behind a pair)	Finmere, Oakly, Seighford

CAMERA OBSCURA

The camera obscura was an early device for the checking of a pilot's ability to fly straight courses, find wind speed and direction, and for the simulation of level bombing. In the roof of the camera obscura was a glass lens through which the image of the aircraft was projected on to a table. The release of an imaginary bomb was indicated by the flash of a magnesium bulb fitted to the aircraft. From the position of the image in relation to the focal centre and fixed target position on the table, the operator could tell where the bomb would have fallen.

There were two types of camera obscura: a portable type and a fixed type. Because of the mobility of the portable type, it could be used for tactical training exercises during which the bombing of unfamiliar targets could be practised. The fixed camera obscura was a purpose-built structure or part of a multifunctional building, such as the station headquarters at Bicester or the station armoury of the early expansion period. All camera obscuras had to have a clear all-round upward view and were built in a position where they could be seen easily from the air.

Drawing number 3391/35 was a sectional Type B hut, 20 ft long and 10 ft wide, with walls of timber unit construction with an almost-flat roof of joists, boarding and felt. Directly below the sliding cover in the roof was a concrete platform with four oak posts fixed to the concrete. This allowed for the accurate positioning of the table, tripod and lens.

Another building type was of permanent brick cavity wall construction with a precast concrete roof. The walls and ceiling were painted with matt black distemper as the room had to be in complete darkness.

drawing no.	299/26	483/28	527/31
examples	Castle Bromwich	Boscombe Down	Catterick, Mount Batten

drawing no.	3391/35	3569/37	23/40
examples	Cottesmore, Honington, Montrose, Upwood	Gullane, Penrhos, Stormy Down	Cranage, Millom

ANTI-AIRCRAFT DOME TRAINERS

The first documented trainer was a prototype built by Colonel G. F. Haszard, who served in the Royal Marines from 1914 to 1934, and Brigadier Vere Ronald Krohn of the Royal Artillery. In 1926, as Gunnery instructors at an Army Anti-Aircraft School at Biggin Hill, they built their miniature anti-aircraft range. This used basically the same principles as the dome trainers devised by H. C. Stephens.

The aircraft image was projected by hand and the burst of the shell was indicated by a still projector when the trigger was pressed. Only silent film was used although attempts were made to create separately generated sound. This equipment was manufactured by the Admiralty Research Laboratory. Haszard and Krohn took out a UK patent for their invention, No. 273,385 granted in 1926, and later defended actions be brought by others who

The camera obscura at Filton. (Photographed 1993)

Synthetic Training 167

claimed to have invented the dome trainer.

In late 1939, while in a cinema watching a newsreel on AA gunners in training, Henry Christian Stephens conceived the idea of using films to train AA gunners. With Commander Pigou, he visited the anti-aircraft department at the Royal Navy's School of Gunnery, HMS *Excellent*, at Whale Island, Portsmouth. The head of the Anti-Aircraft Department, Commander Campbell, reported the idea to his superiors and was eventually permitted to start development. Stephens was posted to HMS *Excellent*. Technicolor Ltd of Harmondsworth, Middlesex were brought in on the discussions.

In November 1940, it was decided to build a half-dome with a diameter of 25 ft inside an existing building, the old squash racket court at Whale Island. Target film was shot of actual aircraft using the Eastney ranges at, Portsmouth. By mid-January 1941, however, the design was changed; the dome was now to be cylindrical and vertical up to a height of 5 ft, with the dome wall only starting to curve above this. This was so that the aircraft image viewed from the floor would appear optically correct to a trainee operator. The production quarter-sphere dome had a radius of 10 ft or 20 ft. Initially, the domes were of steel and plaster construction. Later, timber domes of 20 ft diameter were built for the RAF.

The aircraft image could be projected by 16 mm or 35 mm equipment on to a gimbals-mounted mirror which could traverse up to 180° and elevate up to 90°. It reflected the image on to the projection surface of the dome. The movements of the mirror were controlled by

An anti-aircraft dome trainer 73/42 at Burtonwood.

A 40 ft diameter wooden dome trainer without its exterior cladding. (RFD Ltd)

two-man dummy gun sighting unit

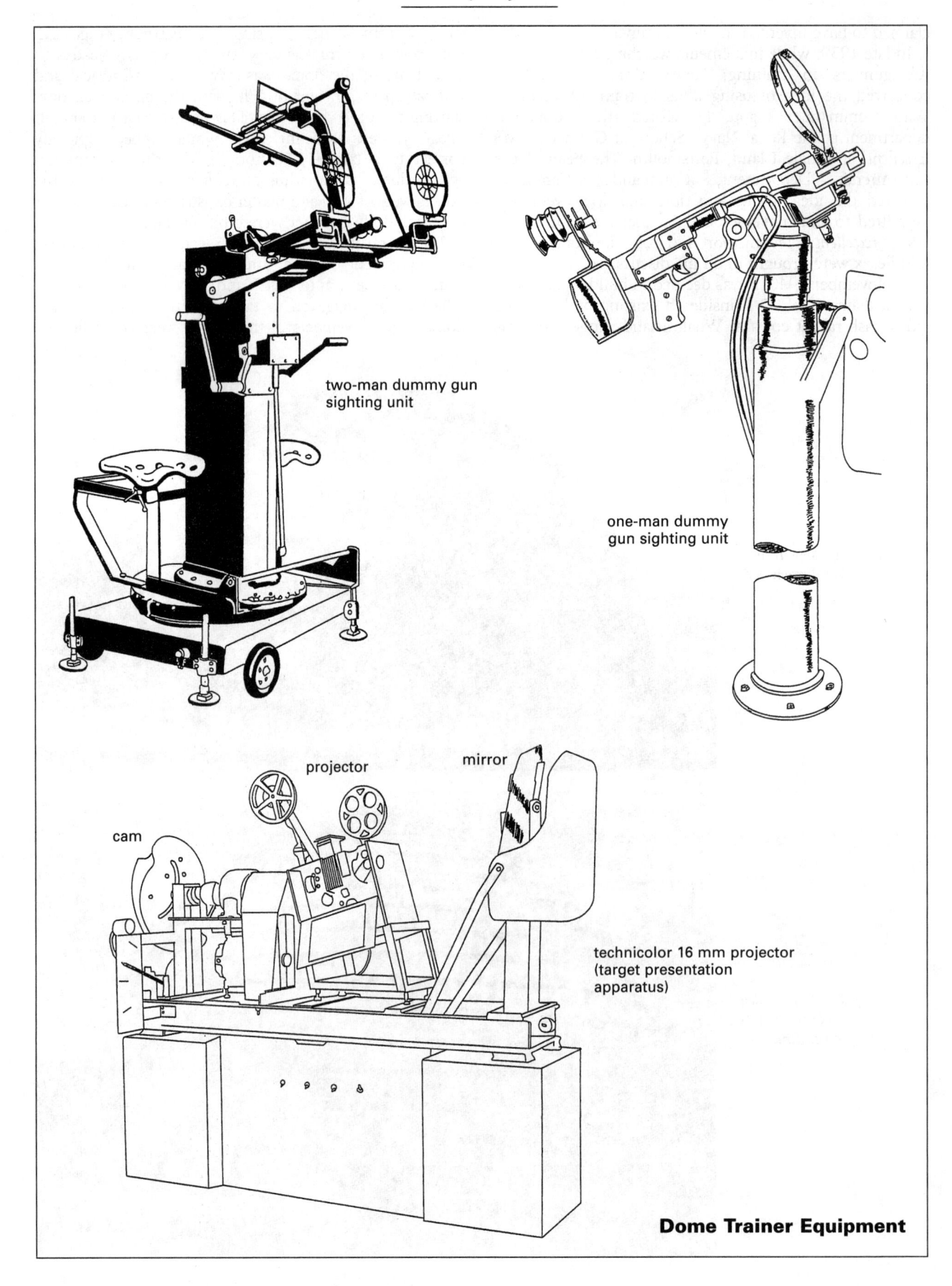

one-man dummy gun sighting unit

cam

projector

mirror

technicolor 16 mm projector (target presentation apparatus)

Dome Trainer Equipment

three cams (elevation, traverse, and one for indicating the range) driven from the projector motor via a reduction gearbox. The cams were changed when a new target film was required. Films were produced by Technicolor by a system of model photography and were used both on Stephens domes and Portobell domes.

To show the correct aim-off point (future position), a yellow spot or line was added to each frame of the film so that when projected, the aircraft image appeared with the yellow future position spot in front. This spot could be easily made invisible to the gunner by his wearing tinted spectacles or by looking through a yellow filter in front of the sights. The trainee used simple dummy guns which had controls similar to real weapons but were less bulky. To show where the gun was being aimed, a gun-sight projector shone a graticule on to the dome wall, which represented the actual point at which he was aiming. The idea was that when the graticule coincided with the future position spot, the instructor could see at a glance if any hits were on target.

A more realistic effect was achieved on early domes by having the wall surface painted blue. Later, a fluorescent tube was used to flood the whole surface with low-intensity blue light to help create the illusion of distance and of being surrounded by cloudless sky.

When the gunner opened fire, an amplifier produced a sound simulating a weapon firing at close range. With the Lewis gun, if the trigger was pressed continuously, the firing would continue for 5 seconds, then stop. This represented the time it took to empty a small ammunition pan on a Lewis gun. Aircraft noise was recorded on the soundtrack of the film so that full sound effects continued throughout the 'attack', allowing the pupil to get accustomed to the noise of the attacking aircraft.

The 20 ft diameter timber dome provided training with the ring and aperture gun-sight normally found on short-range weapons used for the defence of airfields against low-level and dive-bombing attacks. Only half of the dome surface was used as the target screen, the other half being covered with a sound-absorbent material to reduce echoes.

The one-man sighting unit consisted of a 5 ft pillar on which was mounted a dummy gun with a ring and aperture sight, a gun-sight projector, and a trigger. The dummy gun could be moved in azimuth and elevation. The gunner trained the sighting unit on the target aircraft image projected by 16 mm equipment on the spherical surface of the dome. An image of the gunner's sight ring was projected on to the dome surface so that it could be seen by the instructor and other pupils. If the gunner was aiming correctly, the centre of this sight image appeared on the yellow line just in front of the aircraft image, with the edge of the ring on the nose of the aircraft.

The Trussed Concrete Steel Co Ltd designed and constructed a concrete dome adopted by the Air Ministry in January 1942 as drawing number 73/42. The building was 25 ft high, 40 ft in internal diameter, and built on a 5 ft high vertical wall base. The framework was welded-steel longitudinal and lateral members forming a great circle arc. This was fabricated in the factory to strict tolerances before dispatch to the various airfields. On site, a light metal lathing (Hy-Rib) was wired to the framework inside and out to support the poured concrete during construction, also serving as reinforcement for the shell. The wall thickness was 4.5 inches. The rough key provided by the Hy-Rib mesh and protruding concrete was then plastered inside to form the screen and cement rendered on the outside. Between the wall and floor was a plaster and Hy-Rib coving. The specification for camouflage was either a tar spray coating with chopped heather or tar and stone chippings.

On one side of the single entrance lobby was a cloakroom and on the other was a ventilating plant room. These were separated from the training area by a partition of welded rods clad with Cabolts Quilt for soundproofing and wire netting. Inlet and exhaust ports for the plant equipment were located above the doorway and are often mistaken today for loudspeakers. The initial contract was for 25 dome trainers. The first three were built at Bovingdon, Hook, and Hornchurch. Approximately 40 were eventually built in the UK but only a handful survive today.

During 1940–41, Charles Stanley Bell was serving as an instructor at HMS *Glendower*, a training establishment set up at the former Butlin's Holiday Camp at Pwllheli in North Wales. Here he experimented with different ways of training anti-aircraft gunners. One method was known as the range and deflection teacher and consisted of a target aircraft model suspended on a wire which ran between two posts about 30 yd apart. A manually operated pulley controlled its speed of travel. The models were 1:80 scale and relative speeds of up to 70 mph could be achieved.

On a visit to RAF Penrhos, Bell was impressed by the spotlight trainer and as a result devised a similar set-up using an ornamental clam previously used in the holiday camp. The clam became an upright target screen for trainee gunners to practice deflection shooting at a moving aircraft image produced by a hand-held stills projector. In late 1941, Bell visited Whale Island to see the Stephens dome trainer. He found the equipment to be too bulky and the dome structure too complicated to construct. Eventually, he was given permission to redesign the equipment and method of construction. Together with Gerald N. Pritty, who owned the Midlands engineering firm, Caxton Metal Production Ltd, he refined the equipment and replaced the 35 mm projector with a 16 mm projector and generally reduced the size.

Two methods of construction of the dome structure were considered. Use of a wooden former over which concrete was poured was rejected outright. The idea of an inflatable envelope over which concrete was poured to form the dome was adopted instead. Bell visited the RFD company at Godalming which was engaged in the manufacture of barrage balloons for the Ministry of Supply. While there, the works manager, Charles Fellowes, suggested the simpler idea of making the device in one piece, including the floor, by inflating a complete fabric structure. Bell was taken inside a barrage balloon

Portobel Dome

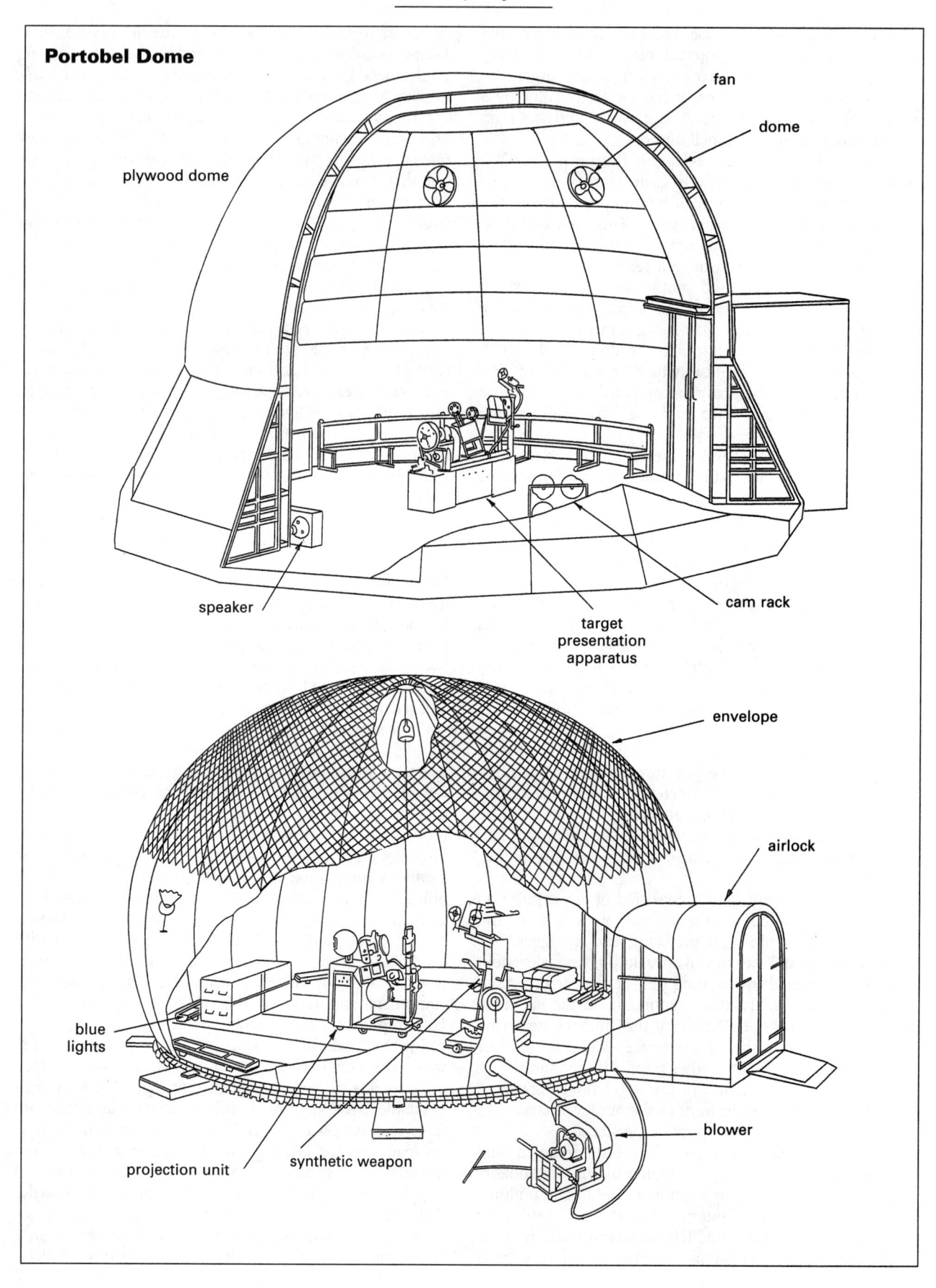

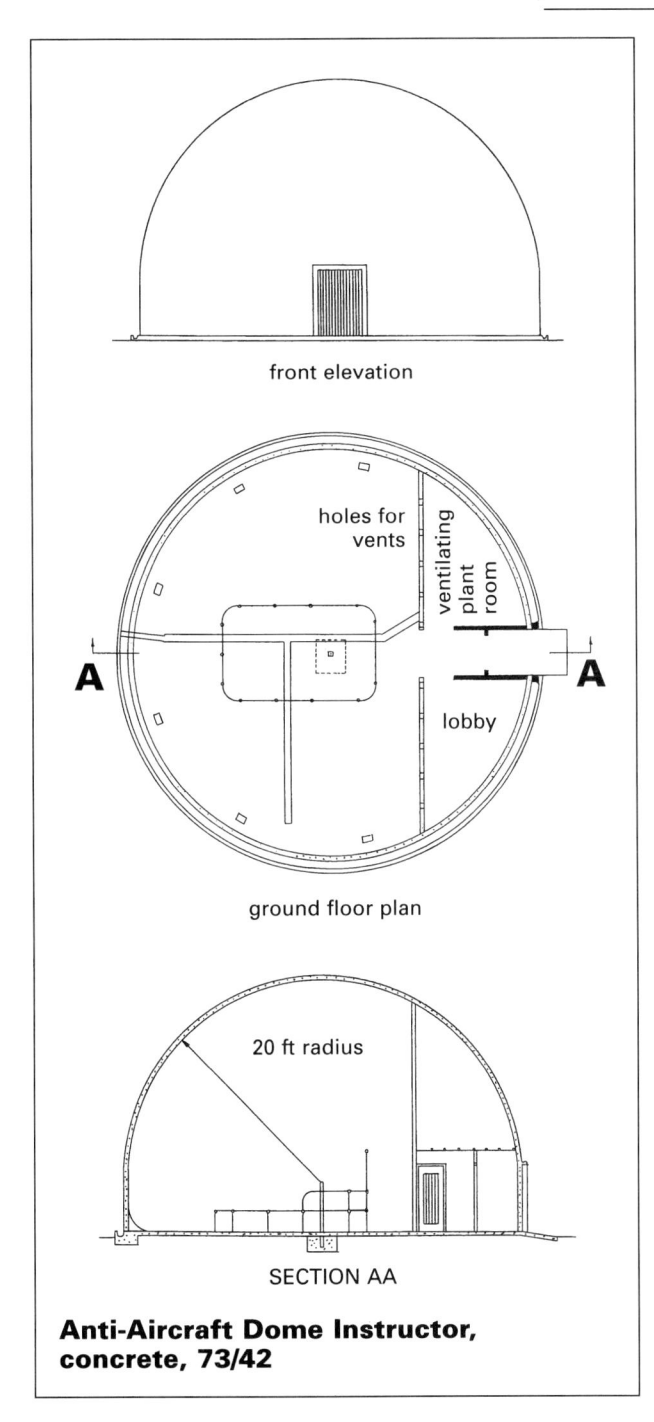

where women were applying patches to the inner surface. It immediately became obvious that he could dispense with concrete altogether and use an inflatable dome instead. This had the added advantage of being portable, and together with the scaled-down equipment, was a very attractive proposition.

RFD developed the first inflatable dome with the floor as part of the hemisphere to form a sealed envelope made of two-ply balloon fabric. Only a low pressure was needed to keep it inflated which was provided by an air-blower. Excess pressure could escape through pressure relief valves. The first inflatable dome was demonstrated on 6 May 1942 in the presence of representatives from HMS *Excellent*.

After the successful demonstration Bell formed a company CB Projections (Engineering) Ltd at Cranleigh, Surrey. A contract for two domes was placed by the Admiralty on 12 May 1942. Bell filed a patent application for the portable dome trainer on 1 October 1942, which became UK patent No. 586,870. Eventually, a further contract was placed for 110 Portobell (the trade name) domes although the contract was terminated after only 88 trainers had been delivered. The internal equipment was subcontracted to Gerald Pritty's company, the manufacture of the domes to RFD, and the target films to Technicolor.

In 1948, RFD obtained a manufacturing licence from CB Projections and marketed the RFD Portobell Gunnery Trainer Mk II. Between 1948 and 1951 RFD sold a large number of 30 ft diameter Portobell dome trainers to the Royal Navy and the Ministry of Supply, as well as Sweden, Finland, Iceland, and America. In 1951, Bell sold CB Projections to De La Rue; RFD paid royalties to this company until 1956 when RFD acquired all the rights to the Portobell gunnery trainer. Around 1956, the construction of Portobell 30 ft fabric domes was replaced by timber and plywood portable domes of 40 ft and 60 ft diameters. This new design consisted of a series of wood-framed sections bolted together and covered both inside and out with hardboard. The RFD Group continued to manufacture dome trainers until the early 1980s when the manufacturing rights were taken over by Ferranti International (Simulation and Training).

drawing no. 73/42
examples Langham, Mildenhall, Pembray, Shoreham, Wyton (all surviving in 1995)

PART 7

DOMESTIC BUILDINGS

Domestic accommodation on First World War aerodromes was split into three main groups: officers' mess and quarters; regimental institute and men's barracks; and the women's camp or hostel. Normally, the men's quarters were separated from the women's hostel by the officers' quarters. Officers' quarters were made up of:

- bath house and WCs
- mess
- living quarters (cabins)

Regimental buildings could include:

- barrack huts
- drying room
- men's bath house
- men's WCs
- NCO pilots' ablutions and WCs
- NCO pilots' mess
- NCO pilots' quarters
- regimental institute and cookhouse
- regimental stores
- YMCA

Buildings were arranged in Army fashion of blocks or groups in neat rows so that the men's quarters were planned with ablutions, barrack huts, and regimental institute together in the same group. Officers' cabins were usually on both sides of the officer's mess with the mess facing a tennis court or some other open aspect.

The women's hostel included:

- ablutions
- bath house
- dormitory blocks
- kitchen
- WCs

In some cases, these were linked together by corridors, the whole complex being fenced off.

Like technical buildings, the domestic buildings were mainly of temporary brick with piers at 10 ft centres, but other forms construction of the prefabricated type were also used. Typically, these included the Adrian (98 ft by 27 ft), the Armstrong (huts and tents), the Detchet (60 ft by 16 ft), the Nissen Hospital hut (60 ft by 20 ft), the Tarrant Mk I (60 ft by 20 ft) and the Tarrant Mk II (60 ft by 16 ft).

Despite the limitations inflicted by the 10 Year Rule on defence expenditure in the 1920s, there was a limited amount of modernization carried out on domestic accommodation at those stations selected as permanent RAF aerodromes. The most significant change to domestic buildings was the invention of the two-storey barrack block for RAF stations. In contrast to rows and rows of detached huts and the inconvenience of separate barracks, WCs and bath houses, airmen had the luxury of having all sanitary facilities under the same roof as the barrack room for the first time. The revised standard layout meant that domestic buildings for airmen were planned round a square, with barrack blocks, dining-room/cookhouse and institute arranged round the perimeter of the parade ground. The officers' mess and quarters were built away from the main domestic quarters, usually with landscaped gardens and uninterrupted views of the countryside.

New domestic accommodation built on aerodromes, such as Bicester and Upper Heyford, were often constrained by existing Air Ministry boundaries, and the increased number of technical buildings had to be separated from the main camp. With the original boundary running along a main road, it became necessary to purchase land on the other side of the road for the domestic accommodation. If however, the station was on a new site, such as Suttons Farm (later to be renamed Hornchurch), it was easier for the planners to arrange most of the domestic accommodation together with the technical buildings, providing more of a secure and compact layout.

The new domestic buildings included:

- barrack blocks
- dining-room/cookhouse
- gymnasium
- married quarters for all ranks
- institute
- officers' mess and quarters for single officers
- sergeants' mess

- squash racquets court
- station sick quarters

The planning of domestic accommodation on expansion period aerodromes was in keeping with the technical buildings and based on a series of standardized Type designs. Therefore all new stations had similar standard accommodation, the positioning of which was adapted to suit each site. Furthermore, existing established stations were quite often extended with buildings of the same Type designs as the new stations. The layout now was of a compact type where all buildings, both domestic and technical, were built together on the same site without being split into two groups by public roads.

One of the most significant changes to domestic buildings in the expansion period was that the sergeants were no longer expected to be accommodated in barrack blocks. Instead, the sergeants' mess was designed as a two-storey building with sergeants' quarters located on the first floor, and in two attached wings.

Domestic accommodation on a typical expansion period aerodrome such as Upwood included:

- barrack blocks
- decontamination centre
- dining-room/cookhouse
- institute
- married quarters for all ranks
- officers' mess and quarters
- sergeants' mess and quarters
- squash racquets court
- station sick quarters and annexe

Married quarters for officers, warrant officers, sergeants, and airmen were redesigned to get away from the influence of the 1920s' Army style. Married airmen's quarters were planned in blocks of four or six houses. The blocks were designed with separate sitting rooms and kitchens, unlike the older designs where these two rooms were combined. Separate bathrooms and WCs were also provided. Married officers' quarters were designed to fit in well with the locality and particular care was taken to provide for the comfort and convenience of servants. Married quarters for all ranks were centrally heated from the station hot water supply system.

At the outbreak of war, austerity measures had to be applied to those stations still not completed and the construction of married quarters was discontinued.

Under the wartime dispersed layout system, where domestic accommodation was separated from the technical site, communal buildings were grouped together in a number of detached sites. As an aid to concealment,

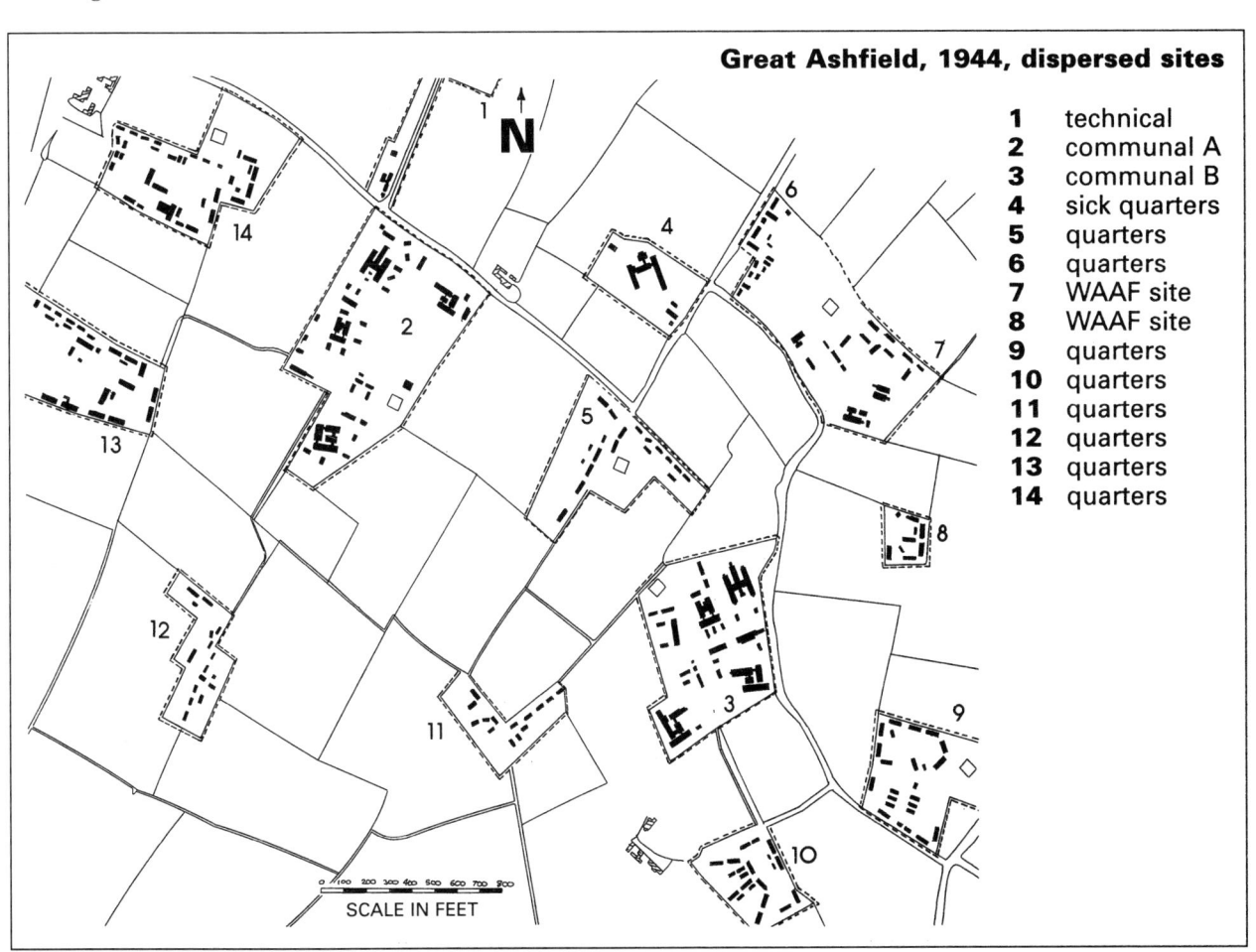

Great Ashfield, 1944, dispersed sites

1	technical
2	communal A
3	communal B
4	sick quarters
5	quarters
6	quarters
7	WAAF site
8	WAAF site
9	quarters
10	quarters
11	quarters
12	quarters
13	quarters
14	quarters

buildings were laid out asymmetrically, with no discernible pattern. As far as possible, huts were sited to follow the lines of hedges or the perimeters of woods. Furthermore, important structures required for the running of the station, such as the high-level water tank and the house for the stand-by set, were also located away from the technical area on the main communal site.

Although every airfield and its domestic sites were unique, they all followed a similar pattern. At Shipdham, for example, there were 14 dispersed sites consisting of a sick quarters, two RAF communal sites, one WAAF communal site, six RAF dormitory sites, two WAAF dormitory sites, and two sewage works. Shipdham was designed and built early in the war when the policy was that WAAFs should have their own communal sites. By 1942, this was changed so that on new airfields WAAFs shared RAF communal sites and separate WAAF communal buildings were omitted. WAAF dormitory sites were retained and as a result of this change in policy RAF communal accommodation was increased to cater for WAAFs.

Temporary airfield communal sites contained buildings of specialist function including:

- decontamination centre
- dining-room/cinema
- grocery and local produce store
- gymnasium/church/cinema
- high-level water tank
- NAAFI
- ration store
- squash racquets court
- stand-by set house
- tailor's, barber's and shoemaker's shop

In addition, there could be:

- airmen's WC block
- airmen's shower block
- boiler house
- commanding officer's quarters
- education block
- officers' baths and WCs
- officers' mess
- sergeants' mess
- sergeants' showers and WCs

If there was more than one communal site these would constitute communal site No. 2.

In contrast to the peacetime barrack block with its own sanitary facilities, wartime buildings constructed on RAF living sites contained separate quarters with detached WCs and ablutions. A single site could have as many as 25 barrack huts, each sleeping up to 24 airmen, and WC blocks built close by in the ratio of one WC block to three barrack huts. Other buildings on the same site could include officers' quarters (five), with accompanying ablutions and WCs, and sergeants' quarters (five) with adjacent ablutions and WCs.

WAAF Communal sites, before 1942, contained:

- barrack huts
- bath, WC and ablution block
- decontamination, ablutions and laundry block
- dining-room and sergeants' mess
- institute and sergeants' recreation room
- NAAFI
- officers' quarters and mess
- WAAF sick quarters

WAAF Dormitory sites could have quarters for up to 20 sergeants and airwomen with separate ablutions, bath house and decontamination blocks.

BARRACKS

The earliest permanent barrack block design for RAF stations was also the largest, housing a staggering 512 men in four rooms on each of two floors and eight NCOs in four rooms on both floors. The blocks were built at Cranwell to drawing number 26/19 which was the first building to have ablutions, drying rooms and dormitories all under one roof for airmen. The building was arranged roughly in an H shape, with two two-storey wings both sides of a central entrance hall. Ablutions and WCs containing 36 showers/foot baths and 22 WCs were housed inside a central single-storey annexe between the two barrack wings and connected to them by a corridor.

Construction was of a steel frame and permanent brick with a slate-covered steel-framed roof. Each barrack room was 24 ft wide and 120 ft long; the total area covered by a single block was 117 ft 6 in by 291 ft 10 in. Heating was via boilers housed in an underground chamber in the ablution annexe.

All six barracks along with all of the East Camp at Cranwell were demolished some time ago.

Perhaps the most important barrack block design was that for a group of three-storey buildings built in 1920 at Halton Park under the Home Defence Scheme. These were the first modern barracks and were to influence barrack design for the next 18 years. Each block had a similar square-shaped central unit complete with an architectural feature façade containing entrance hall, stairs to upper floors and the barrack rooms arranged in wings each side. Also, ablutions, drying room and WCs were all located in a rear annexe giving the complete building a characteristic T shape in plan view. The basic architectural central feature was adopted on the majority of RAF Home Defence Scheme barrack designs until 1932 when it was replaced with another style of central feature. The classic T-shaped barrack design was retained until 1938 when it was replaced with Type H designs.

The Halton Park barrack blocks each accommodated four sergeants, six corporals and 126 airmen. Each floor contained two barrack rooms 20 ft wide and 66 ft long, both with 21 beds and one corporal's room. Sergeants' and flight sergeants' bedrooms were located each side of the staircase but with one room on the ground floor used as a switchboard room.

Home Defence Scheme two-storey barrack block designs of the 1920s (640/22, 641/22, 99/23–109/23 and 507/23) built on former First World War aerodromes, such as Martlesham Heath and North Weald, all had a similar central architectural feature to that found on the three-storey barrack blocks at Halton Park. Again, the central unit contained the main entrance hall and staircase with an NCO's bedroom each side of the hall on both floors. The entrance was set back from the bedrooms so that at eaves level they formed two false towers, each with its own hipped roof cutting into the main roof. The central unit also contained the ablution annexe at the rear and this was retained for all designs. Standard barrack rooms of different lengths were simply added each side of the central unit to form Types A to E.

At Gosport, six Type E barrack blocks were the first to be protected against incendiary bombs and were possibly the only examples with flat roofs built of steel decking. They were built in 1928 and were followed in 1934 by a similar but smaller block.

Construction of the walls was similar to contemporary barracks but with the exception of internal brick piers to support large-section RSJs supporting hollow steel deck flooring and roof.

Type E barracks to 746/27 were for three NCOs and 80 airmen, while 396/33 was for four NCOs and 56 airmen; both designs had flat steel roofs. Drawings 447/32–450/32

The central entrance of the barrack block Type C 104/23 at North Weald. (Photographed 1982)

A barrack block Type C 104/23 and 230/27. (Photographed 1982)

A barrack block Type C 548/28 at Biggin Hill. (Photographed 1993)

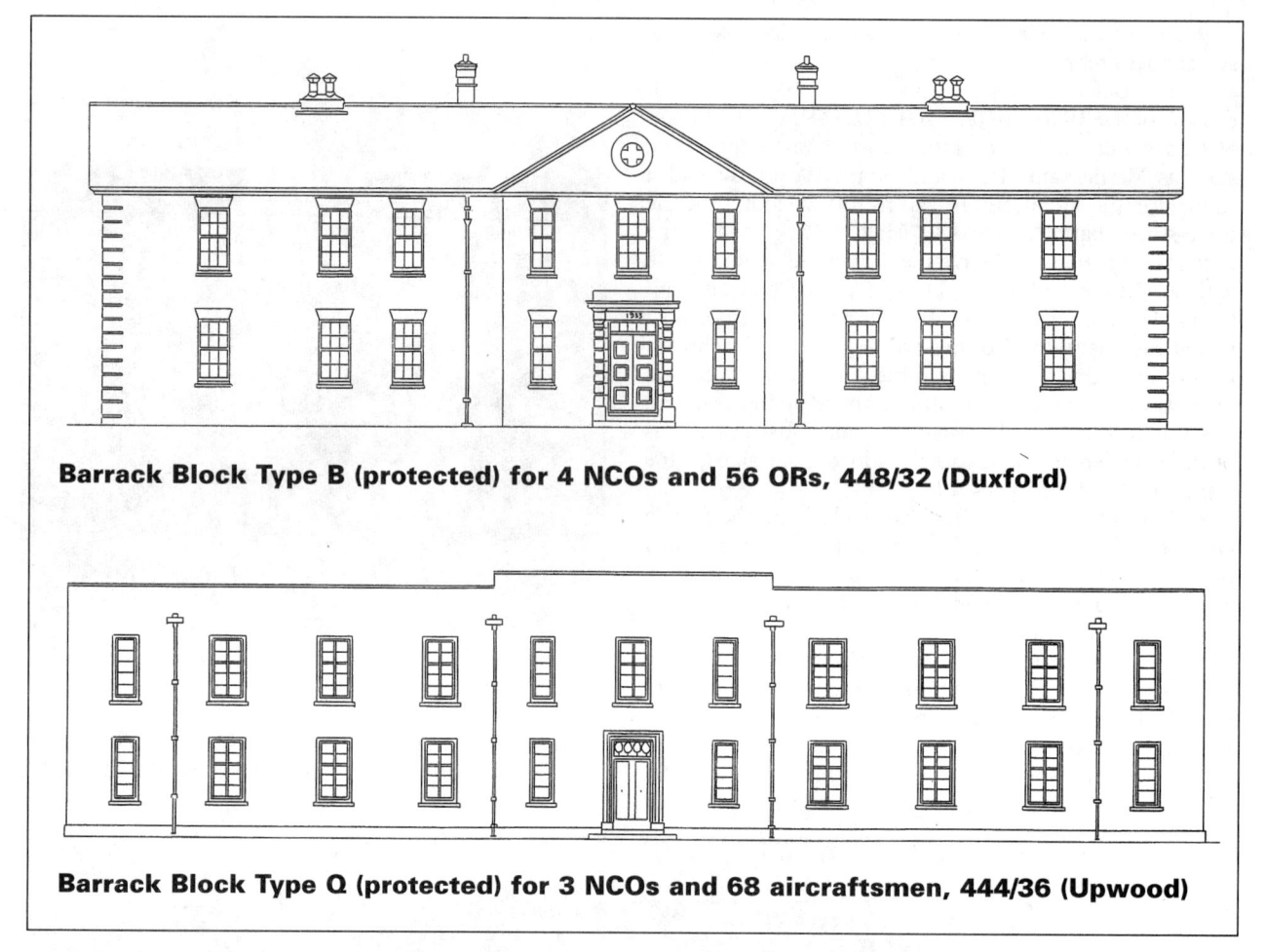

Barrack Block Type B (protected) for 4 NCOs and 56 ORs, 448/32 (Duxford)

Barrack Block Type Q (protected) for 3 NCOs and 68 aircraftsmen, 444/36 (Upwood)

were for some of the last designs of barrack block before the expansion period incorporated a new design of central unit entrance with a gable roof cutting the main gable at right angles. This was also a protected roof design but this time with steel trusses clad with slate; it had an asbestos ceiling and a concrete floor. Type B barracks to 447/32–450/32 were for four NCOs and 56 other ranks.

The designs of the expansion period adopted a simple symmetrical Georgian style without a central feature. The first barrack designs (Types P, Q and R) of 1934 had hipped roofs. After 1936, anticipation of the effects of aerial warfare, led to modifications to provide protection against light incendiary bombs. Eventually, new drawings were prepared for barracks with flat reinforced-concrete roofs which were otherwise the same size and layout as the earlier expansion period designs; these designs therefore were also known as Types P, Q and R.

Heating and hot water supplies were from the district

A three-storey barrack block at Mount Batten. (Photographed 1993)

Domestic Buildings 177

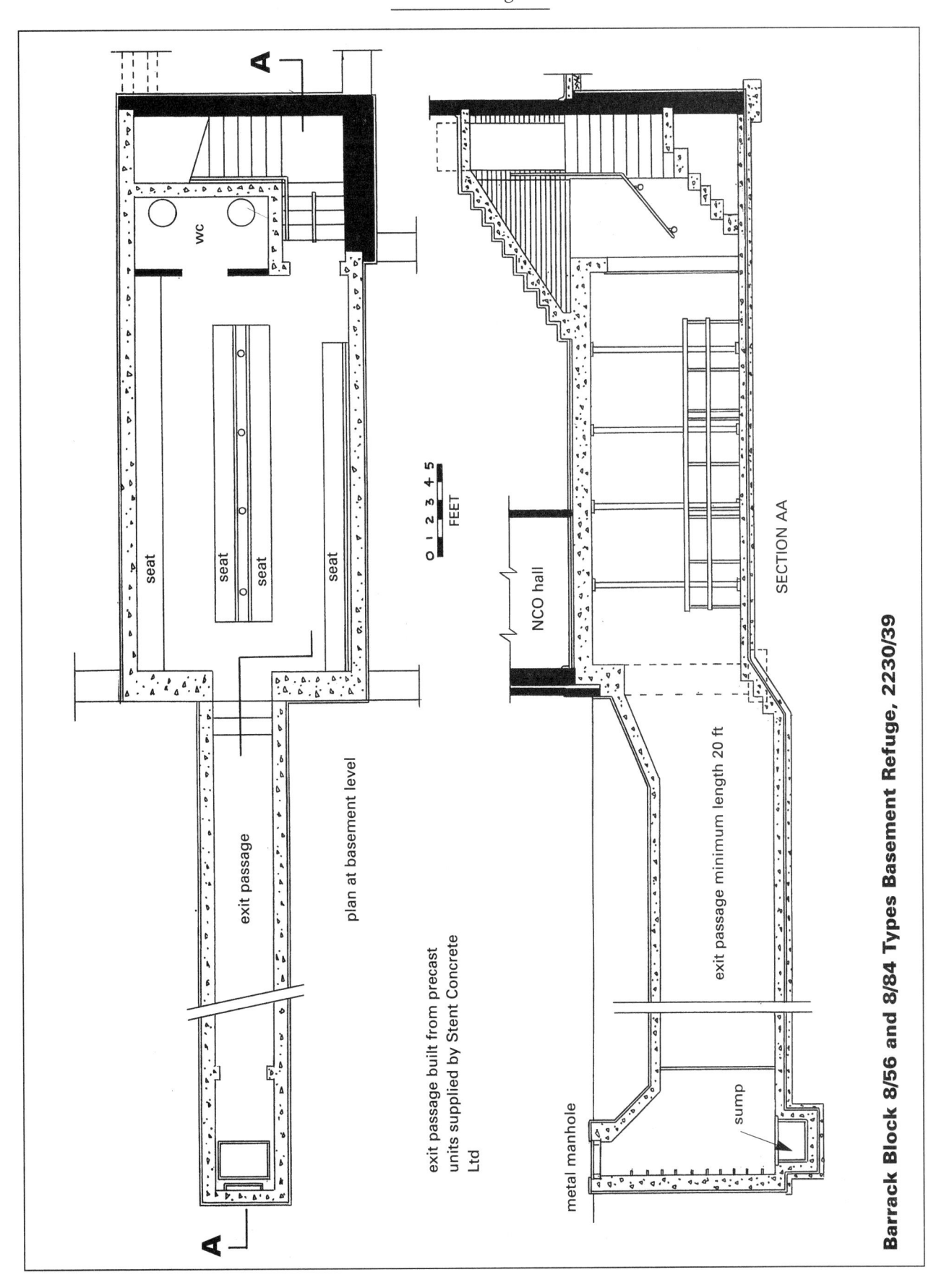

Barrack Block 8/56 and 8/84 Types Basement Refuge, 2230/39

heating installation. Sanitary fittings were of modern design and of high standard. Barrack rooms had hardwood floors, walls were plastered to a high finish and painted in bright colours.

A number of improvements came about in 1938 under the L Scheme of the expansion period when it was decided that the floor area per man in barrack rooms should be increased from 60 sq ft to 67 sq ft. There was also a reduction in room height from 10 ft to 9 ft and a reduction in the number of men per room to a maximum of 12. The provision of a sitting room for entertainment, such as listening to the radio and reading, was added. A utility room for cleaning equipment was also included. All these improvements led to the design of Type H blocks with both flat and pitched roofs. Buildings of this type were erected at all the later expansion period stations and to supplement existing accommodation on older stations.

Included in the design of H blocks was an underground air-raid shelter (2230/39) located in a basement directly below the hall and NCO's bedroom. A steel door and a flight of steps below the staircase led to a room 11 ft wide and 20 ft long. Enough seating was provided for 40 airmen and a WC was provided. A narrow escape passage 25 ft long and built of Stent precast concrete blocks led via a steel door and vertical ladder to an exit well clear of the building. At the outbreak of war, the sitting room became a barrack room and the temporary luxury of 67 sq ft of floor area was greatly reduced to accommodate the increase in personnel now posted to a wartime RAF station.

There were four designs of H block: design 8/56, protected roof and hipped roof versions; and design 8/84, protected roof and hipped roof versions.

drawing no.	26/19	746/27	447/32–450/32
example	Cranwell	Gosport	Abingdon, Biggin Hill, Tangmere
drawing no.	396/33		

Type	drawing no.	accommodation NCOs	ORs	ORs per room	examples
A	640/22 641/22	3	48	12	Hornchurch (1) Filton, Upper Heyford, Martlesham Heath
B	99/23–109/23	3	56	14	Biggin Hill, Northolt
C		3	64	16	Hornchurch (3)
D	507/23	3	72	18	Tangmere
E		3	80	20	

The Type A room was 32 ft 9 in x 22 ft.

Barrack Block (protected) 8/56, 11589/38, front elevation

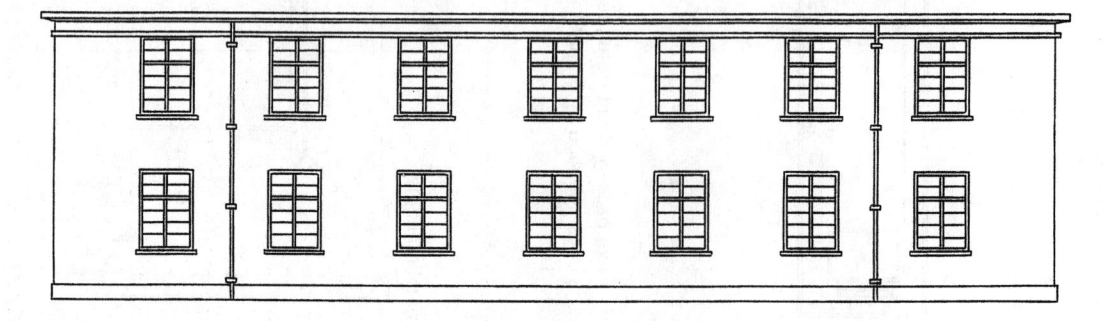

Single Sergeants Quarters for 34 (protected) 14557/39, west elevation

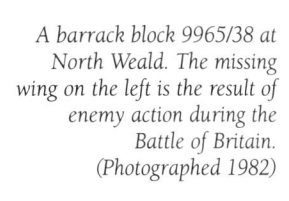

A barrack block 9965/38 at North Weald. The missing wing on the left is the result of enemy action during the Battle of Britain. (Photographed 1982)

Type	drawing no.	accommodation NCOs ORs room size	roof design	examples
P	2363/37	4 52	hipped	Little Rissington
Q	582/36	4 68 57 ft x 20 ft (17 beds)	hipped	Upwood (4), Feltwell
	444/36		protected	Little Rissington
R	2277/34	4 84 20 ft wide	hipped	Cranfield, Feltwell, Marham
	2357/36		protected	Bircham, Newton, Upwood
8/84	1132/38–1137/38	8 84 39 ft 9 in x 21 ft (12 beds)	protected	Bramcote, Ouston, Cottesmore
	9965/38–		hipped	North Weald
8/56	11587/38–11592/38	8 56	protected	
	11595/58–11600/38	25 ft 10 in x 21 ft (8 beds)	pitched	Bassingbourn, Bircham, Newton, Ouston

SERGEANTS' MESS AND QUARTERS

On early First World War 6th Brigade flight and squadron stations, sergeants had their own quarters, separate ablutions, and mess. Towards the end of the war, on Training Depot Stations, NCO pilots had their own quarters. Postwar, it became RAF policy for sergeants and airmen to share barrack blocks (the sergeants having separate bedrooms) but retaining their own mess. This was changed during the expansion period as a result of the increase in number of sergeant pilots and led to a complete redesign of the sergeants' mess. This now included quarters over the mess and additional accommodation in the form of extended wing blocks.

Early sergeants' messes were single-storey buildings. One such design, 341/20–346/20, of which two were built at Halton, was for 36 sergeants. This design was of great character with two heavy-mullioned bay windows on the front elevation, hipped roof of timber trusses clad with timber boarding and slates, and an impressive main entrance containing a semicircular fanlight and canopy above double doors.

Inside, the interior was richly decorated with moulded picture rails, salt-glazed bricks, moulded skirting, architraves, and plaster cornices in the main rooms, including an Arts and Crafts style inglenook fireplace recessed with a small grate. Mess rooms included billiard room with bay window, reading and writing room which

The sergeants' mess built to 191/24 and 2897/35 at North Weald.

also had a bay window. Kitchen, cook room, scullery, meat room, and beer cellar were all located at the rear.

A single-storey permanent brick building intended to accommodate between 15 and 40 members was built to 191/24. The projecting gable end of the billiard room cut the main roof line. The billiard room had a decorative semicircular arch above a three-light window, with a herringbone bond brick infill. The mess room had a bay window. This style was similar to 107/23 sick quarters.

Construction was in 11-inch cavity brick walls with timber trusses carrying slates. The entrance to the building was by the side of the billiard room. On the left was a reading and writing room, and a turn to the left along a passage led to the mess. (The mess could be made larger as there was only a movable partition separating it from the reading room). Kitchen, scullery, and store were all behind the mess, and beer cellar, WCs and liquor store were all behind the billiard room, with a yard separating the two. A bell system allowed staff in the kitchen to respond to calls from the front entrance, billiard room, reading room, or mess.

In 1935, it was decided to increase the membership capacity of these buildings to 55 by constructing extensions. The bay window of the mess and the top of the gable were removed and replaced with double doors. A new mess room (40 ft by 20 ft) was built perpendicular to the original, the new projecting gable matching the billiard room end in every way, making the building symmetrical. The original mess became an ante-room.

At Duxford, at the beginning of the expansion period, a new combined sergeants' mess and quarters was planned for a vacant site to the west of the camp but was not completed until 1939. The old sergeants' mess became a corporals' mess until 1942/43 when the building was extended yet again, with the arrival of the Americans, to become an additional officers' mess, this time for 113 members. The former mess room became an ante-room, the mess president's office, and a new entrance hall. From the hall, a passageway led to a new mess room built in temporary brick construction (70 ft by 28 ft). A further 40 ft were added to supplement the kitchen facilities to include a washing-up area, servery, larders, food preparation area, and staff changing rooms. At the far end, a boiler-room was also added.

In addition, at Duxford, a detached temporary brick building was built nearby. This functioned as a card and writing room.

The mess and quarters building of the protected roof design came in two sizes, the larger one having a mess for 170 sergeants while the smaller version could only cope with 116.

The part of the building with facilities for members was, in plan, an inverted T shape and consisted of an ante-room on one side of the entrance hall, and WC with cloakroom, and a billiards room on the other. The entrance hall contained stairs to the quarters above and the hall led to an inner hall with corridors connecting the wing blocks containing additional sergeants' quarters. Beyond the inner hall was the mess room with the servery, kitchen, and scullery all located in an annexe on the left-hand side which with the mess room was a single storey. The first floor contained 14 or 17 bedrooms (depending on which drawing number was used) arranged each side of a central corridor along with a bathroom, a cleaning room, and a drying room.

As with the 1938 Type H barrack blocks, an emergency refuge was provided, the entrance to which was in the hall. This led to a shelter and an escape tunnel with an exit at a point well clear of the building.

Used in conjunction with these designs was a pair of blocks, built close to each side of the main block and at right-angles to it. They were connected to the main block

Sergeants' Mess, 191/24, with extension for 55 members 2897/35 (Duxford)

Sergeants' Mess and Quarters, 116/14 (Wyton), 7859/38

Domestic Buildings 181

by a corridor. Each block contained 17 bedrooms in a similar arrangement to the first floor of the main block.

drawing no.	341/20–346/20	191/24	7858/38
example	Halton	Bicester, Duxford, Hornchurch, North Weald, Upavon, Upper Heyford	Bassingbourn, Honington, Wyton

drawing no.	11527/38	14557/39
example		Swinderby

OFFICERS' MESS AND QUARTERS

During the First World War, there was no standard design of officers' mess. Aerodromes had their own individual styles, often being influenced by other buildings on the station. Sometimes, an existing building was requisitioned; at Biggin Hill, a house called 'Koonowla', and owned by the Victoria Hospital for Sick Children in Chelsea, was used until it burnt down in 1925. Very often, officers' cabins or quarters were linked by corridors to the mess, as at Farnborough, or were built in two neat rows each side of the mess block, overlooking landscaped gardens, as at Netheravon. The position of the mess building was obviously very important as many were built with commanding views of the countryside or overlooking the aerodrome. The majority were single-storey buildings but the officers' quarters (68/18) at Uxbridge RFC Armament School, designed by the Royal Engineers, was a two-storey structure with a characteristic mansard roof and contained 16 bedrooms for officers with one room on each floor for servants.

A very impressive prefabricated structure was erected at Netheravon in 1914. Along with many buildings here, it was built in Mock Tudor style, being faced with roughcast asbestos sheeting framed in timber. Above a projecting entrance gable, is a large plaque depicting the RFC wings and motto *per ardua ad astra*. This building is now listed Grade 2.

The main entrance of the officers' mess at Netheravon. (Photographed 1994)

The oldest officers' mess in existence and still used for its original purpose is at Farnborough and dates from 1912. Although it is an impressive building, it is doubtful whether it could be listed on account of its modern double-glazed windows.

Perhaps the most impressive officers' mess (for 94 members) and quarters (for 75) of the 1920s was that built at Gosport in 1929 to a series of drawings from 450/28. The main block was a two-storey brick-built structure with a central projecting entrance gable with Portland stone quoins surrounding the doorway and a Portland stone canopy with wrought iron railings with a

The officers' mess at Netheravon dating from about 1914. (Photographed 1994)

The officers' mess at Farnborough dating from about 1912. (Photographed 1994)

The officers' mess at Upavon dating from about 1913. (Photographed 1994)

feature 'RAF' incorporated into the scroll work.

The ground floor of the main block consisted of a card and writing room on one side of the hall; one the other side was the ante-room. Upstairs had a central sitting-room above the main entrance with a number of bedrooms each side. The hallway led to the mess room immediately behind the main block. Further officers' quarters were located in two-storey wings located each side of the main block and connected to it by a corridor.

General improvements during the expansion period included providing a more intimate 'club' atmosphere, better methods of service with bigger serveries, and good quality fittings of modern design. Improvements to single officers' quarters were made in the form of one or two floors above the mess and in attached wings. Built-in wardrobes were provided, and rooms were subdivided to provide separate bedrooms and sitting rooms. Lavatory basins, shelves, mirrors, and WC fittings, with hot and cold running water were in every room.

Type B was a single-storey red-brick neo-Georgian style building designed by S. Bullock. It was the standard officers' mess on expansion period aerodromes and was

The officers' mess 1524/25 at North Weald for 40 officers.

Officers' mess Type B 2290/343–2292/34 at Swanton Morley. (Photographed 1984)

intended to accommodate 36–45 members. The main block consisted of a south-facing E-shaped structure with corridors, one each side connecting two accommodation wings (east and west). The impressive main entrance consisted of a projecting porch with three two-ring arches, leading to a large plywood-panelled hallway and cloakroom. Facilities included billiard room, mess, and ante-room, all located in the wings of the main block. The kitchen facilities were located in a flat-roofed annexe between the main block and a two-storey servants' dormitory block that also functioned as a scullery.

Single officers' quarters were located in L-shaped wings, one each side of the main block (east and west). One version, 3043/38, could cater for 44 (22 in each block), and another could cater for 34. Senior officers had large rooms, each subdivided into a sitting room and bedroom, while junior officers just had single rooms.

Construction of the roof included steel trusses with hipped gable ends. Ceilings were plastered on to Hy-Rib steel mesh sheeting, and the roof cladding consisted of Smith's patent tile slabs, offering protection against the effects of incendiary bombs.

drawing no.   68/18, 450/28, 2290/34–2292/34, 3043/38

AIRMEN'S DINING-ROOM AND INSTITUTE

The cookhouse of 1923 was a single-storey red-brick structure with an impressive queen-post timber truss supporting a slate roof and a ridge-mounted large lantern light running the length of the building and supported by brick gable ends. Inside, the main source of natural light was from above as it was quite often surrounded by other structures such as the dining-room. The main dining-room was built in brick but quite small and often had to be extended with timber hutting.

A combined dining-room and institute was built in 1932 at Duxford in the same architectural style as contemporary barrack blocks, and faced the parade ground. It accommodated 291 corporals and airmen in a two-storey combined dining-room and institute with two projecting entrance blocks, one each end, with a pitched roof cutting the main ridge at right angles (a feature found on expansion period dining-room/institutes). Each entrance led into a hallway with stairs to the upper floor and access to the airmen's restaurant.

It is unclear what the original 1932 layout would have been. In 1942, it was as follows. The main airmen's restaurant took up most of the front elevation. Behind, was the servery and beyond that were the kitchen, yard, staff dormitories, beer store and boiler-room. WAAF recreation, games, reading, and writing rooms and restaurant were all located on the left behind the airmen's restaurant and adjacent to the kitchen. The first floor was used exclusively by corporals and included restaurant and games room. In 1942, the airmen's restaurant was extended with an extension 60 ft long and 28 ft span in temporary brick construction and a pitched roof. It was built in front of the building and joined to it by a flat roof. Access to the new dining-room was through new doorways cut through existing window openings but the top two panes were retained for clerestory lighting. As a consequence of this extra accommodation, the kitchen equipment was also increased with the purchase of an

Cookhouse 184/23 at North Weald. (Photographed 1982)

additional 6 ft cast iron range and a 20-gallon steam kettle.

The institute facilities for airmen from 1942 onwards were in the form of two detached 28 ft span temporary brick huts. One was built on the left side of the main building and functioned as a games room and was 100 ft long. The one on the right, 75 ft long, became the new reading and writing room.

The combined dining-room and institute of 1938 built to accommodate 750–800 corporals and airmen was typical of such buildings in the expansion period. These buildings were planned on two floors with a vertical division between the dining area and institute so that there were two dining-rooms, one on the ground floor, the other directly above on the first floor. The institute was also on two floors with a supper room on the ground floor (requiring a NAAFI service), with games, reading, and writing rooms on the floor above. When required, the ground floor area could be increased by opening a partition that normally separated the two halves, to form a large room for functions. A stage was provided at one end with two dressing-rooms.

The food preparation area, kitchen, and food storage rooms were all located on the ground floor behind the dining area, this portion of the building being single-storey. A small accommodation block for staff was located on the flat roof. The equipment was far superior to that used previously, kitchens were finished with glazed surfaces, and were fitted with the latest types of steam-cooking plant, hot plates. Food preparation areas were of stainless steel, and dish-washing machines were also provided.

The front elevation was symmetrical with a projecting entrance block at each end containing a large hall, cloakroom and staircase. Corporals had their own side entrance leading to their supper and games rooms.

In 1940, another dining block was built at Duxford, for 560 corporals and airmen. This was a permanent brick two-storey building with a hipped roof, featuring a central projecting entrance block with dining rooms each side. An impressive feature of this building was the main entrance, where curved steps led up to three entrance lobbies between double bull nose piers supporting a curved canopy above. Double doors led into a large hallway with

A dining-room for 560 corporals and airmen 6848/39–6851/39 at Duxford. (Photographed 1994)

A combined dining-room and institute 8055/38–8060/38 at Swinderby. (Photographed 1993)

a staircase and coat racks. Through another set of doors and immediately in front was a large servery. Beyond this were the kitchen and ancillary rooms.

Four dining-rooms were provided, each seating 140, two each side of the entrance block. The first floor had the same layout as the ground floor but with a washing-up area behind the servery. Food arrived from below via two lifts. Beyond was the flat roof above the kitchen, ancillary rooms and boiler-room.

The airmen's dining-room on temporary airfields was normally on the main communal site. A double dining-room and kitchen were made up of three temporary brick huts built parallel to each other, each with a 28 ft span with piers spaced at 10 ft centres. There was also a detached ration store. The outer two huts were used as dining-rooms, joined to the kitchen hut at the centre forming a servery for both dining-rooms. Attached to one end wall of the centre hut was a boiler-room. At the opposite end was a yard and cutlery-washing shelter.

Drawing 9028/41 was similar to 9112/41 but, instead of temporary brick, 30 ft span Nissen hutting was used, and the detached ration store was omitted.

The two dining-rooms were designed to accommodate between 800 and 1,000 personnel, depending on the size of the station. The following dimensions were typical.

capacity	length	no. of tables	seating capacity
801	113 ft	51	406
901	125 ft	56	446
1,000	139 ft 5 in	62	496

The kitchen contained the following equipment:

- four 6 ft cast iron ranges arranged in a block, and one other 6 ft range
- two dish-washing machines, one for clean dishes, the other for dirties, both large enough for 6,000 pieces
- two 15-gallon steam kettles for each dining room
- three, 40-gallon portable boilers
- two 60-gallon portable boilers with lifting hoist above
- six 18 inches by 30 inches by 22 inches wet/steam ovens
- one, four-pan fish fryer

The ration store was also of temporary brick construction. With a span of 18 ft and 60 ft long, it was divided into grocery and bread store, meat store, general store, office, and butchers' preparation room.

An even larger complex consisting of three parallel 30 ft span Nissen huts was built to 12957/41 to accommodate between 1,200 and 1,400 personnel. These had two serveries. The two dining-rooms had blackout porches at both ends. The centre hut included a kitchen, a central corridor with rooms each side for food preparation, larders, washing-up, and WAAF changing-rooms. At one end was a detached boiler house in temporary brick with a tall water tank house and an even taller chimney.

Each complex had two dining-rooms of type D, E, F, or G.

Type	length	no. of tables	seating capacity
D	163 ft 3 in	77	616
E	175 ft 9 in	80	640
F	182 ft	84	672
G	188 ft	88	704

Built on the WAAF communal site, a small dining-room complex consisted of two 24 ft span Nissen huts built parallel and joined in the centre by a temporary brick construction to form a servery and crush space. One hut was the dining-room, while the main part of the other formed a kitchen, food preparation area, storage area, and yard, the remaining area housing a small mess for 10–15 sergeants.

The length of the hut containing the kitchen/sergeants' mess was 66 ft 5 in.

drawing no.	dining-room length	no. of tables	seating capacity
13095/41	72 ft 6 in	26	201
	90 ft 7 in	32	250
13095/41			350

drawing no.	184/23	852/32	8055/38–8060/38
examples	Bicester, North Weald, Tangmere	Duxford	Bassingbourn, Bicester, Bramcote

drawing no.	6848/39–6851/39	9028/41	9112/41
examples	Duxford	Gamston, Tibenham, Thorpe Abbotts, Westhampnett	Langham

drawing no.	12957/41	13095/41
examples	Banff	Thorpe Abbotts

Projection Room Extensions

Drawings 932/43 and 6511/43 were for projection room extensions. The extension was built on one end of an existing 24 ft span Nissen hut dining-room to enable it to be converted into a cinema when required. The extensions were added to buildings with the following drawing numbers.

drawing no.	dining-room capacity	cinema capacity
12862/41	201	216
	250	276
	300	326
12863/41	400	216
	500	296
	600	356
12910/41	304	356
	352	356
	399	356

drawing no.	dining-room capacity	cinema capacity
12772/41	601	356
	700	356
	800	356

Drawing 1614/43 was for the construction of a projection room on one end of a temporary brick dining-room with the following drawing numbers.

drawing no.	dining-room capacity	cinema capacity
14390/41	300	340
14387/41	399	420
10106/41 10140/41	600	460
9021/41 10107/41	800	470
9112/41 10108/41	1,000	470
9018/41 10109/41	1,200	470
2070/42 2967/42	1,400	470

Details of the projection room extension to drawings 1614/43, 932/43 and 6511/43 are described in the section dealing with the similar extension (8891/42) to the gymnasium.

drawing no.	9112/41	12772/41
examples	Langham	Attlebridge, Spanhoe, Warboys

Gas Decontamination Buildings

The use of gas in war was outlawed by the Geneva Gas Protocol of 1925 (both Britain and Germany were signatories), but not its production and development. As a result, the British Government, with its previous experience of the ease with which signed agreements were broken during hostilities, decided to develop gas weapons and design methods of protection against their use. This included the construction of specialized buildings, so that in the event of such an attack, personnel who became gas casualties could receive first-aid treatment and be decontaminated. The decontamination building was designed to deal with most types of gases developed during the First World War: lachrymatory agents; respiratory agents; and blister agents.

It was possible to protect oneself from many of the gases by wearing a respirator. Some had distinctive odours which gave sufficient warning of their presence to allow personnel to take cover inside a building or shelter. However, mustard gas has only a faint smell of garlic and its symptoms are not always apparent until some time after the attack, especially the worst effects of the agent. In liquid or vapour form, mustard gas can be absorbed by the skin without being detected. By the time irritation is noticed, the agent has penetrated the surface of the skin and started to cause serious damage. Therefore, special warning posts with metal plates coated with detection paint that changed colour when exposed to mustard gas were placed at intervals along pathways connecting buildings.

Basically, the idea was to get out of all contaminated clothing, dispose of it, wash thoroughly, and change into fresh clothing as soon as possible. If this could be achieved within 20 minutes of the initial contamination, serious injury could be avoided.

On early expansion period stations, the decontamination building resembled an operations block rather than a building to be used for cleansing. Its design was the result of extensive experiments carried out at Orfordness in the mid-1930s on the effects of bomb blast on different types of wall section. It consisted of a windowless single-storey structure with 18-inch thick brick walls protected by angled earth traverses. The annexe to the sick quarters was 107 ft 3 in long, 33 ft wide, 10 ft 6 in high and supported four 2 ft thick reinforced-concrete beams which in turn carried a complicated roof structure.

The roof consisted of a thick-section reinforced-concrete lower subroof and a thin-section reinforced-concrete upper roof, separated by a composite wall made of an inner skin of concrete and faced on the outside with 4.5-inch brick. In the centre of the lower subroof was a hipped-roof water tank house with thick-section reinforced-concrete walls that were cast as part of the lower roof. The protected tank house contained four 500-gallon water tanks for the WCs and showers and was centrally located above the bleaching room. The cavity between the upper and lower roof sections was filled first with sand, then a layer of shingle. So that the tank house had enough protection from the sand and shingle, the centre of the upper roof section was also hipped. It is this centre section that can be seen prominently above a brick parapet wall that hides the remaining flat concrete roof. The whole external surface of the upper roof was covered with asphalt for weather protection.

Entry to the building was through a protected gap in the earth bank via a pathway which sloped down to a foot bath of bleach solution. Along the entrance elevation were seven metal clothes bins, above which were letter-box-like receptacles into which contaminated clothing was discarded from inside the building. This clothing would have to be boiled in large copper boilers to decontaminate them. The concrete floor and internal rendered walls were treated with sodium silicate solution. The floor had a drainage system to allow decontamination to be easily carried out by hosing down.

The first room was a reception area and undressing-room. Because of this it was the only contaminated area in the building. In one corner, was a storeroom where valuables were kept after having been removed from the soiled clothing. An airlock, consisting of two gas-tight doors separated by a gas-proof compartment, led to the bleaching room. The bleaching room contained shower cubicles, sinks, bleach store, towel store, dirty towel store,

Decontamination centre 6224/37 at Bicester. (Photographed 1993)

and WCs. In the bleaching room, uninjured personnel were cleaned up and decontaminated and then used the showers. These were arranged in two groups with a space between so that a person could wet himself under one, move into the space to soap himself and then wash off the soap in the next shower cubicle. It would have been routine procedure to wash out the eyes in warm water – a number of buildings had the slogan 'Don't forget to irrigate your eyes' painted on the wall. After a thorough wash, treatment of the affected areas could begin. As the antidote to mustard gas was bleach, a specially prepared paste would be rubbed into the affected area and then wiped off within 2 minutes.

Next was a dressing area containing a clean clothes store and a waiting area, leading to an exit with an airlock. Where the decontamination block was an annexe to the station sick quarters, the exit led to an 40 ft long enclosed corridor connected to an open-plan waiting-room in the station sick quarters. At the rear of the annexe was the plant room, boiler-room, and fuel store. On the outside wall there was an air-intake shaft for the plant equipment and a tall exhaust chimney for the boilers.

Usually on early expansion period aerodromes there was an SSQ annexe for injured personnel who also required treatment for the effects of gas, and another building that functioned as the decontamination block for unwounded personnel. The latter had a protected entrance and exit, both located on the same side elevation. This building (6224/37) was slightly larger being 28 ft wide and 88 ft long, and was equipped with 18 showers. The protected design was replaced by a less-robust structure in 1939, variations of which were built on late expansion period airfields. Buildings of a similar style were constructed on early temporary airfields between 1940 and 1942. Quite a number survive, many on current RAF stations.

On late expansion period airfields a new annexe (16479/39 and 2425/40) replaced the protected design of SSQ annexe. It was located behind the SSQ so that the entrance elevation faced west. It was a single-storey

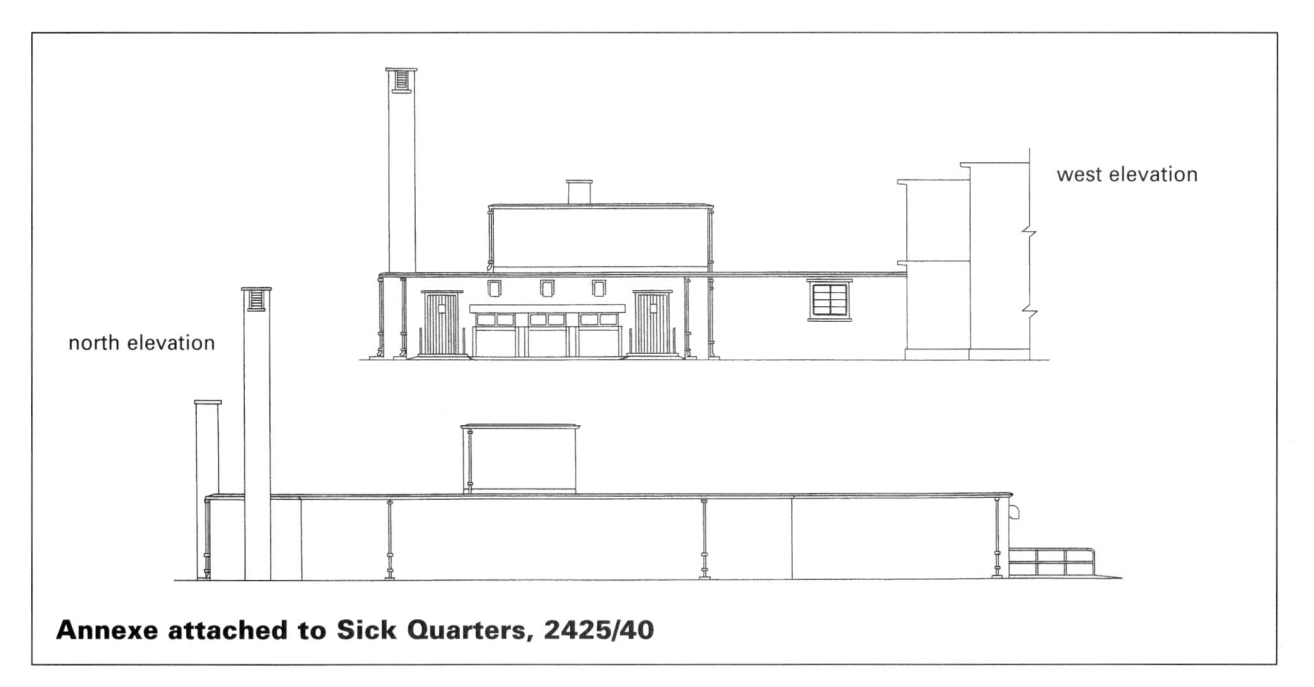

Annexe attached to Sick Quarters, 2425/40

188 British Military Airfield Architecture

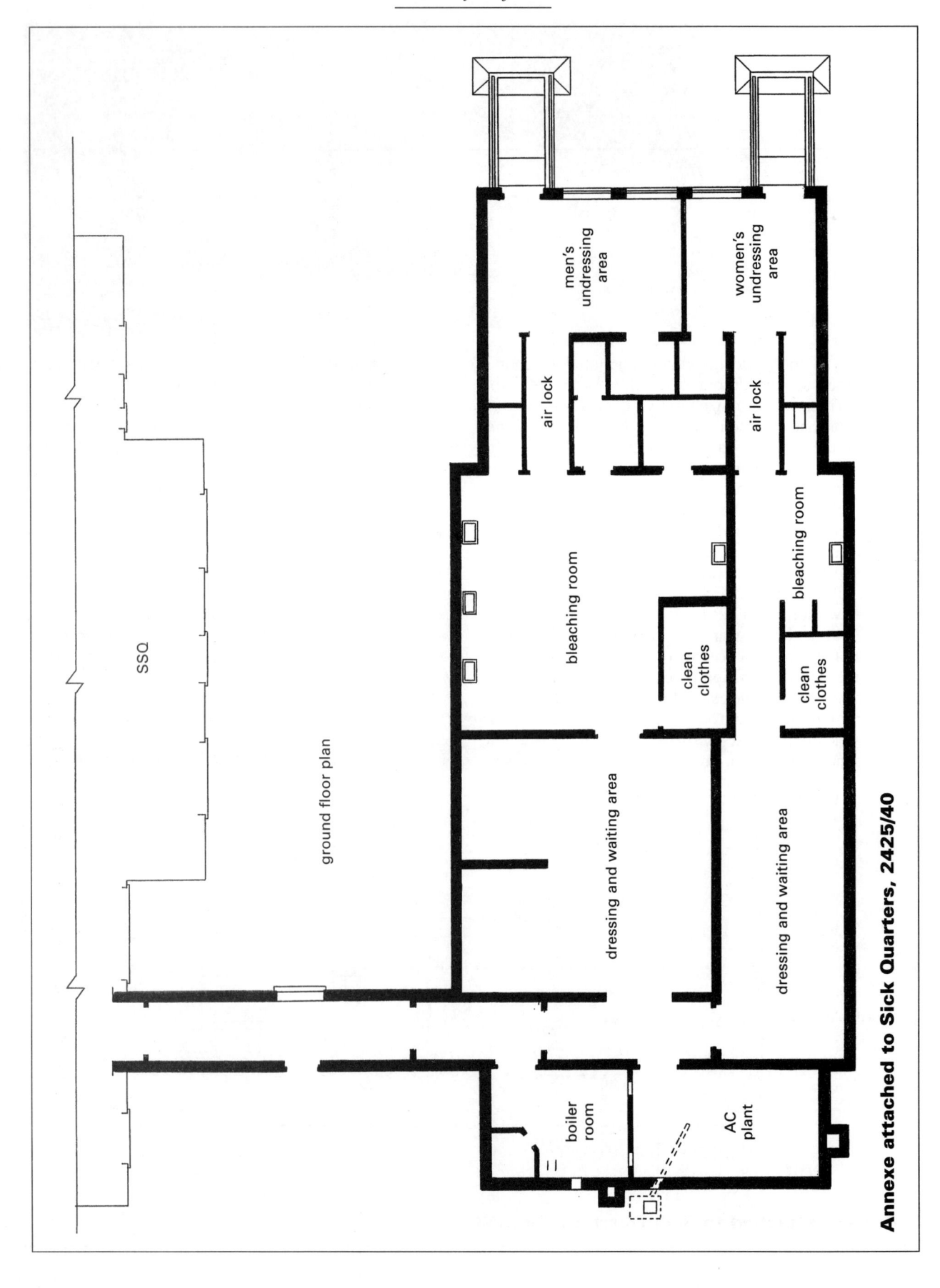

Annexe attached to Sick Quarters, 2425/40

ground floor plan

SSQ

men's undressing area | women's undressing area
air lock | air lock
bleaching room | bleaching room
clean clothes | clean clothes
dressing and waiting area | dressing and waiting area
boiler room | AC plant

Domestic Buildings 189

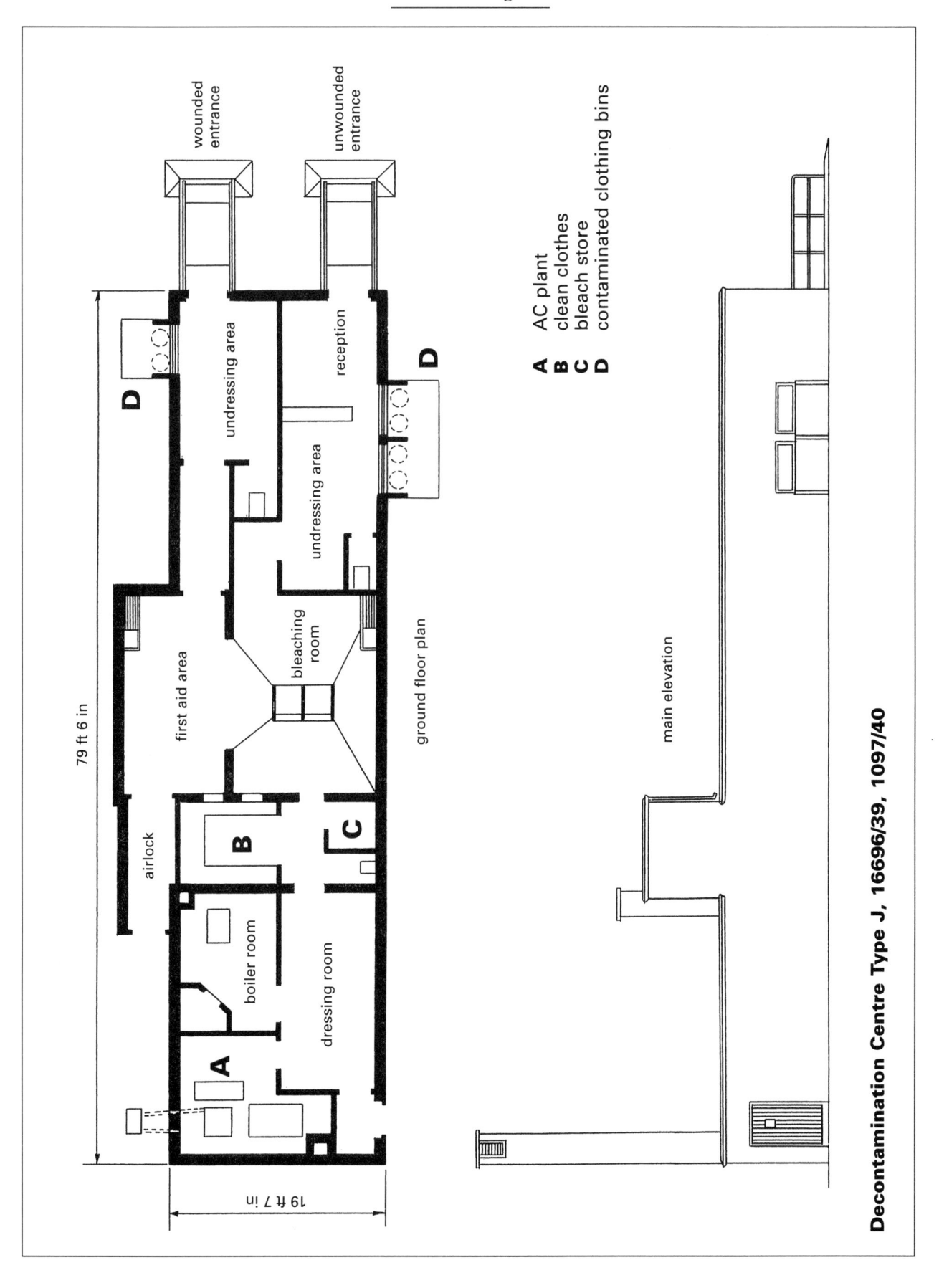

wounded entrance
unwounded entrance

undressing area
reception
undressing area
bleaching room
first aid area
airlock
boiler room
dressing room

A AC plant
B clean clothes
C bleach store
D contaminated clothing bins

ground floor plan

79 ft 6 in
19 ft 7 in

main elevation

Decontamination Centre Type J, 16696/39, 1097/40

windowless building, built of rendered brick with 13.5-inch walls supporting a flat roof of Seigwart precast hollow beam concrete slabs. Approximately in the centre of the roof was a prominent water tank house, which contained two high-level 800-gallon tanks.

On the front elevation were two entrance points, one for women, the other for men (both unwounded) and 'letter-boxes' for discarding contaminated clothing. In a gas contaminated environment, it was possible to raise the internal air pressure to seal the building and prevent gas entering. This enabled the building to be used if gas was still present outside. All doors had rubber seals which formed a perfect seal when shut. The undressing-room had pressure stabilizers on an outside wall to release the pressure when required. An airlock connected the undressing area with the bleaching room where a door led to the dressing-room and waiting area. Here, an enclosed corridor joined both female and male waiting-rooms with the waiting-room of the SSQ. Both female and male halves were similar in layout except that the male side was larger. At the rear of the outside of the main block was the plant equipment complete with tall air-intake shaft supplying clean dry air from above the gas cloud. The boiler-room supplied hot water for the showers and heating, and had a similar but shorter chimney (exhaust).

Later buildings were of a style similar to 16479/39 and were probably a direct development of it after it was decided that this design best-suited temporary airfields. The buildings were located on the main communal site and occasionally on the hospital site where they were used as annexes to the SSQs. There were quite a number of different Types but all were relatively similar. Up to 1940 the main ones were G, J and H; after 1940 came Type KM. Where the drawing number ended in 39 (signifying the year 1939), the buildings were originally designated as temporary brick structures (4.5-inch walls with piers) but after 1940 they were redesigned with thicker 13.5-inch brick walls. For example, the original drawing 16690/39 for a Type G decontamination centre became 1095/40. A deviation drawing (a deviation drawing did not alter the original drawing with which it was associated but was used in conjunction with it), 6347/40 of June 1940, increased the height of the air-intake shaft for the plant equipment from 6 ft above the building to 22 ft 9 in.

The Type J (16696/39 and 1097/40) was for both wounded and unwounded men (or women) and therefore had two entry points on the front elevation. The right-hand entrance for the wounded led into an undressing area and through an airlock to the first-aid room. Here, against a side elevation was an exit airlock. If treatment for the effects of the gas was needed, the injured man was sent to the bleaching room having already been given first-aid. There were normally two buildings, one for men and one for women; their contaminated clothing was removed through openings in a side elevation. The left-hand half, for unwounded personnel, was basically similar to the SSQ annexe 16479/39. The boiler-room and plant room were located at the rear on the side elevation of the part for wounded personnel.

Some buildings had an external lobby at each entry point with a foot bath; for example Type KM (13843/40) as seen at Graveley and Harlaxton. Others, such as Types J and H, had steel railings to guide personnel through the foot bath (this was necessary because one of the symptoms of exposure to mustard gas is blindness). Type H (16711/39, amended to 1096/40) was for use by for both men and women, either wounded or unwounded, and consequently had four entry points on the front elevation. The outer two were for wounded personnel and led to the male and female first-aid sections.

Balloon Depots and aerodromes with timber hutted accommodation such as Jurby and Stormy Down had a timber building to 285/39. It had three pairs of entrance doors on an end elevation, these leading to a reception and undressing area. A WC block annexe was located on one side elevation. On the opposite side wall was an airlock which gave access to the bleaching room. From here, a door led into a first-aid annexe where an exit airlock, or double doors, led to a dressing area, exit airlock and clean clothes store. There was no plant room; instead, the dressing-room had an electric fan connected to an asbestos air-intake duct that was supposed to have a minimum height of 10 ft above the roof ridge.

Fortunately, decontamination buildings were never used for the purpose to which they were designed but some were used for decontamination of another kind; infestation by lice and other parasitic insects. A few were used for the storage of respirators and gas capes, while others were just kept in immaculate condition, ready for use in the event of an actual attack. Postwar, some buildings were used for gas defence training because the nature of their construction made them ideal for this purpose.

In conjunction with the permanent structures, on temporary airfields, the RAF and WAAF mess sites also had buildings of temporary construction with everyday usage as shower blocks and WCs, but which would also function as decontamination centres if required. An example is the 16339/41 series of buildings found on many WAAF communal sites.

This drawing covered several designs of pairs of huts; one was used as a shower block, the other as a drying room. They were usually sited parallel or at an angle to each other but the boiler-room on the shower block had to be within 20 ft of the drying room block. Construction was in temporary brick with walls 7 ft and 8 ft high. The largest was the Type 8a ('a' denoted a communal site; 'b' signified other kinds of site). The ablution and drying room block was split into two halves. One part, with a span of 28 ft and 53 ft long, contained drying and ironing rooms and ablutions for 30 airwomen. Attached to one end was an annexe of 14 ft span and 30 ft long which was a 24-place WC block.

Close by was the decontamination/first-aid block. This building had a span of 18 ft and was 74 ft long. The entrance had a 10 ft span and was 30 ft long. A first-aid annexe was built on to a side elevation. Under a gas attack, personnel entered the building by walking through

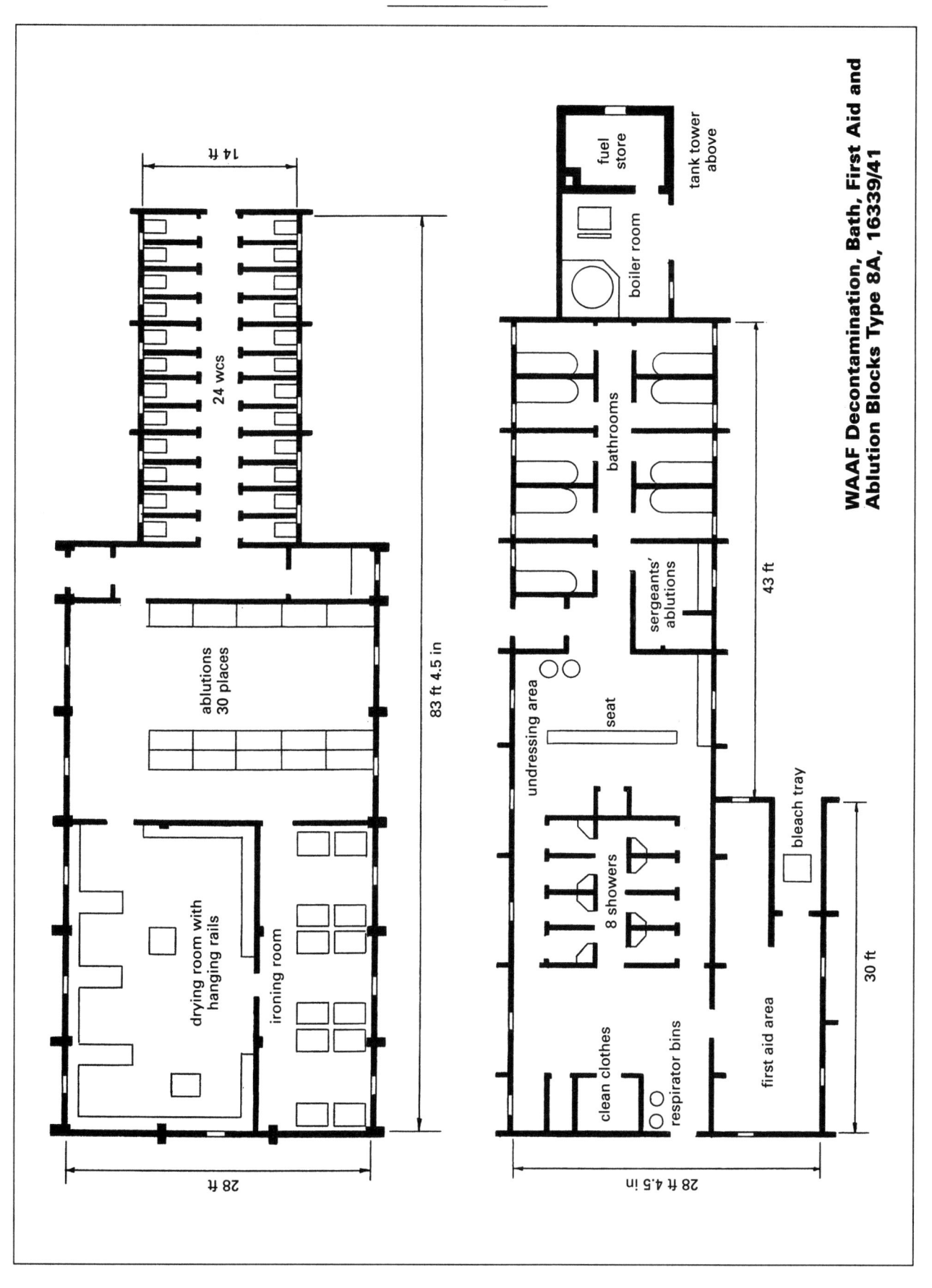

WAAF Decontamination, Bath, First Aid and Ablution Blocks Type 8A, 16339/41

The decontamination centre at Swanton Morley. (Photographed 1993)

a bleach tray. If anyone was contaminated and injured, he could be hosed down while still in the first-aid area, have his wounds treated, then make his way to a dressing area inside the main block. In normal everyday use, a separate entrance was used along a side elevation and on entering a lobby you could choose to have a shower or a bath. At one end of this block was a boiler-room serving both blocks and a fuel store.

A large number of stations had examples of huts built to 16339/41 but it is not always clear exactly which types the were; 6a or 6b, 7a or 7b, or 8a or 8b.

After 1942, the construction of the permanent decontamination centres on new airfields ceased. They were replaced with other types of combination blocks of temporary brick, 16 ft Nissen hutting, or 24 ft Nissen hutting. Generally, the smaller Nissen hut was for officers, while the larger hut was for airmen or airwomen. Drawing 6517/42 is a typical example, built on bomber airfields such as Nuthampstead and Great Dunmow and consisting of 18-bay 24 ft span Nissen huts used as combined shower, ablution and decontamination blocks for airmen. An internal lobby gave access to the undressing area (four bays), then four shower cubicles (five bays) and, further along, to a store for clean clothes (two bays); then came ablutions (five bays), and an exit. The last two bays contained a boiler house complete with high-level water tank mounted 20 ft above floor level. They were normally built adjacent to the combined WC, ablution, laundry and hairdressing block, often sharing the same drawing number.

It is interesting to note that decontamination centres built in the mid-1930s, a time when gas was considered to be a real threat, were very substantial with very thick brick walls and heavy concrete floors and ceilings. Yet by late 1942, new buildings were multi-functional and were of only temporary construction.

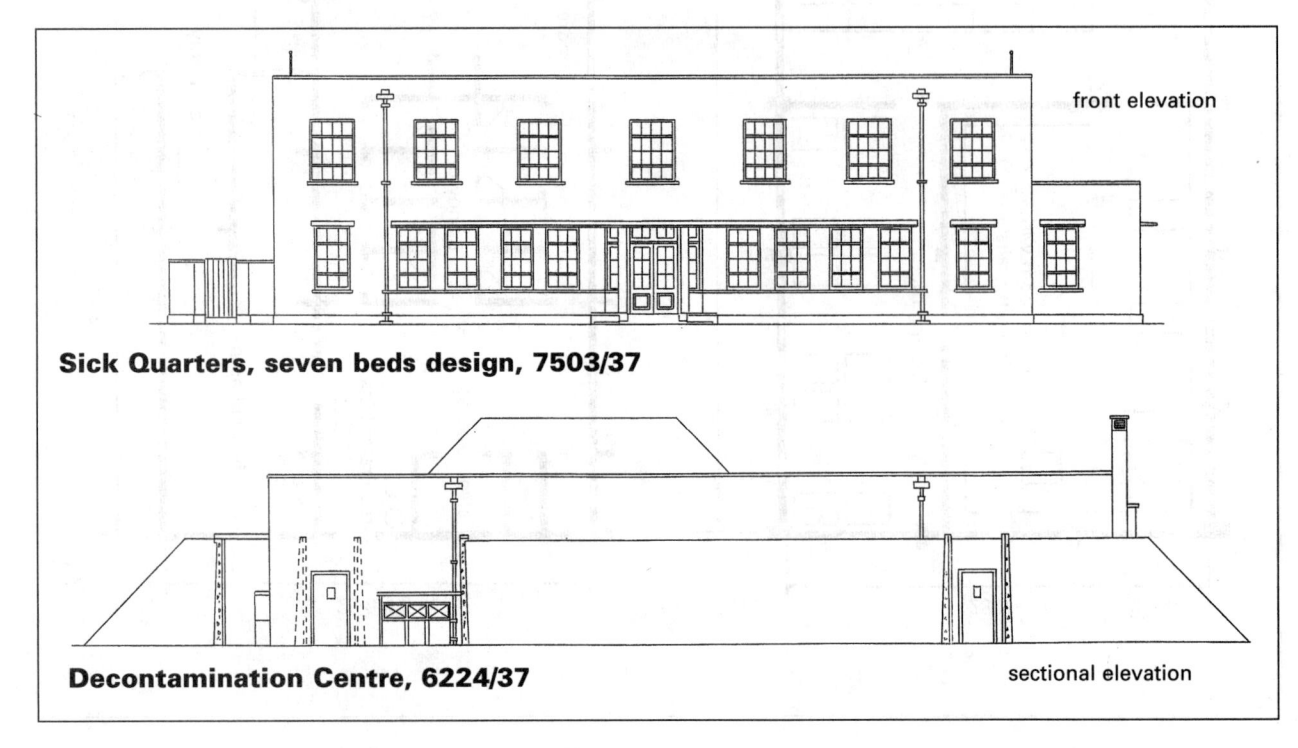

Sick Quarters, seven beds design, 7503/37 — front elevation

Decontamination Centre, 6224/37 — sectional elevation

drawing no.	6224/37	285/39	16479/39, 2425/40
examples	Bassingbourn, Upwood, Watton	Jurby, Rollestone Camp, Yatesbury	Swanton Morley
drawing no.	16690/39, 1095/40, 6347/40	16696/39, 1097/40	16711/39, 1096/40
Type	G	J	H
examples	Honeybourne, North Weald, Riccal	Ouston, Lords Bridge, Wing	Wigtown, Pembray, Dumfries
drawing no.	13843/40	16339/41	6517/42
Type	KM		
examples	Graveley, Harlaxton	Bruntingthorpe, Drem, Eshott	Nuthampstead, Great Dunmow

STATION SICK QUARTERS

Most RAF stations had a well-equipped SSQ with wards to accommodate all ranks. It was run by the station medical officer with support from staff that included the dental officer and his orderly.

A flat roof design of the expansion period was of permanent construction. It was a small two-storey hospital with casualty and out-patients departments. Medical or dental inspections were carried out on the ground floor. Hospital wards for longer-term patients were on the first floor. Construction was in permanent brick cavity walls with reinforced-concrete floor and roof.

Personnel who had been decontaminated following an attack with mustard gas could be treated for other wounds by entering the SSQ via a corridor connecting waiting-rooms in the annexe with the SSQ. Alternatively, patients who were 'conventional' casualties entered the SSQ in the normal way through the main entrance and made their way to the waiting-room – if they were able. Serious casualties requiring immediate attention went into an accident reception area for an examination to ascertain the extent and nature of the injuries which were then treated.

Other rooms on the ground floor were kitchen, medical stores, consulting room, dental surgery, consulting room, office, and dispensary. Upstairs was an airmen's ward with four beds, two individual officers' wards, and an observation ward. Other rooms included an orderly room, baths, and WCs.

Wartime sick quarters were Nissen huts or temporary brick buildings, located on a detached site. Typically, the group of buildings consisted of RAF sick quarters with 22 beds and a WAAF ward with eight beds. Some temporary brick wards were built with an annexe (decontamination centre). Other buildings were sergeants' and orderlies' quarters, an ambulance garage, and mortuary. Examples of temporary construction SSQs could be found on all temporary airfields.

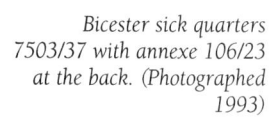

Bicester sick quarters 7503/37 with annexe 106/23 at the back. (Photographed 1993)

A seven-bed SSQ 7503/37 with an annexe at the back.

drawing no. 7503/37
Type flat roof
example Swinderby

WATER SUPPLY

Prior to 1939, water supply to RAF stations was in most cases from the local water authority, but with the rapid increase in the number of aerodromes during the war years, the increased demand severely strained the normal rural water supply. In some cases, the local authority was not capable of supplying the required amount and alternative supplies had to be found.

Water supply from Air Ministry sources came from river, lake, or spring, and had to have water treatment and booster plant equipment installed. Storage tanks of reinforced-concrete or sectional-steel high-level were provided to feed fire hydrants for fire protection and, on wartime dispersed airfield sites, mobile fire pumps and static water tanks were used to supplement the high-level water tank.

Drawing 1178/25 was for a circular reinforced-concrete tank of 30,000-gallon capacity supported on concrete staging. It was built on pre-expansion period aerodromes.

The high-level water-tower 1178/25 at Bicester. (Photographed 1993)

The water-tower with Bath stone cladding at Hullavington. (Photographed 1995)

The height of the tank varied according to the local requirements.

drawing no.	construction	capacity (gal)	height (ft)	examples
1178/25	reinforced concrete, concrete tower	30,000	40	Hornchurch, Upper Heyford, Wittering
			50	Bicester,
			55	Filton
20/40	2 compartments, plate steel	30,000	40	Bodney, Condover, Membury
9526/41	plate steel tank, steel tower	80,000	50	Matching Green, Silverstone, Snitterfield

ELECTRICAL SERVICES

The normal source of electricity was the substation where electrical services to the station were divided into three groups according to importance: general circuits, second circuits, and permanent circuits. General circuits supplied all non-essential services which could first be dispensed with in time of emergency. Second circuits supplied services that were essential to normal station life but could be switched off in emergencies. Permanent circuits supplied services essential to the continued functioning of the aerodrome. All lighting services on this circuit had provision for blue visors, blue lamps, or light-tight windows.

Normally, street lighting and the attack alarm system were controlled by switches on the control panel in the guardroom. However, operational control could be transferred to the operations room control panel, thus making it the master control, in times of imminent attack. This was done by selecting 'remote' on a switch in the substation and by similarly selecting a change-over switch in the guardroom. Street lighting was the first circuit to go off, followed by the general supply, at the first warning of attack. The second circuit was retained for as long as possible before it too was switched off.

The attack alarm system was first introduced in the early part of the expansion period and utilized the existing electrically operated fire alarm system. In order to distinguish between the two, the fire alarm operated at a steady speed whereas the speed of the attack alarm varied in order to produce a 'wailing note'; a siren. Later, the Ministry of Home Security adopted the siren for the public air raid warning system and the Air Ministry soon adopted the same system: the warning 'alert' was a wailing note; the 'raiders past' all clear was a steady note.

On pre-war non-dispersed stations, the normal practice was to put one siren on the roof of an aeroplane shed and another in the barrack area, mounted on the institute or water-tower. On dispersed sites, a siren was mounted on the roof of the picket post at the entrance to each site.

An electrically operated fire alarm system was installed at most pre-war stations. On wartime stations, a hand-rung fire bell was provided at the guard house.

With an electrical system, in the event of a fire, a person could go to the nearest fire alarm point and break the glass, completing the circuit and thereby ringing the fire alarm bell in the guardroom. This also showed the fire party (who had their barracks located in the guard house) which push-button had been used to set off the alarm, its location being indicated on the control panel. The alarm push-buttons were normally mounted at the roadside on red-painted street lighting standards or concrete posts.

Stand-by Supply

In the event of a failure of the outside power supply, the stand-by set could supply electricity to all essential services normally fed by the permanent circuit. It comprised a generator set, powered by a petrol or diesel engine, together with the appropriate switch, control gear, transformer and fuel supply. To effect the switch from one source of supply to another, automatic change-over gear was provided in essential buildings. In the event of a power failure, this would automatically connect to the stand-by circuit. The cables supplying the emergency current from the stand-by set house were run via different routes and separated by at least 50 yd from the permanent circuit cable runs. On expansion period aerodromes, the building was housed on the technical site and electrical distribution was restricted to a small area. By 1940, they were being built on the dispersed main communal site where it was thought to be relatively safe from aerial bombardment.

It would have been uneconomical to provide stand-by current to meet the total requirements of a station and therefore only those buildings which were considered essential to the functioning of the station received a stand-by service. Furthermore, the internal wiring of such buildings was such that only the essential services in those buildings could use it.

The buildings and services which qualified were:

- airfield lighting
- battery-charging room
- beam approach
- contact lighting
- control tower
- crew briefing room
- obstruction lighting
- operations block
- parachute store
- petrol installation
- photographic block
- PBX

The stand-by set house 13243/42 at Rougham. (Photographed 1982)

- sewage works
- speech broadcasting
- stand-by set house/substation
- water service
- works services building
- W/T facility

Where remote dispersed buildings required lighting, a 12-volt 48 amperes per hour battery-operated installation was provided. The function and size of the station dictated the size of the building and the number of sets that were required. Several designs enabled a further set to be added in an extension at a later date.

Stand-by set houses of the expansion period were normally completely surrounded by cavity brick (or concrete) traverse blast walls, the cavity being filled with earth or gravel for protection against bomb blast. In the centre of the area within the traverse walls was the engine room (25 ft by 19 ft) with a single generator set and switch board. Construction was in permanent cavity walls 974/35 or reinforced concrete (607/36); both types had two large steel sashes. The roof was of timber, the close-coupled-type, clad with slate, but the later examples had flat concrete roofs, each with a deep cavity filled with gravel. Six cooling tanks were located in a flat-roofed annexe, and oil storage tanks were positioned in an underground pit between the engine room and traverse wall.

Early wartime buildings were robust structures built of windowless 13.5-inch brick with a flat reinforced-concrete slab roof and reinforced-concrete columns supporting brickwork, roof and platforms. All entrances were protected by reinforced-brickwork traverse blast walls. The design 13244/41 had four main rooms; these were a bulk fuel storage chamber, a transformer chamber, a switchgear chamber, and main engine room with two diesel engine sets. An RSJ carried a crane rail with lifting tackle for the installation of the diesel engines (and their subsequent removal). A concrete platform contained tanks that supplied the engines with fuel and with water to cool the engines. On the floor were cable trenches which led from each engine to the switchgear chamber which obviously contained large-core cables. The diesel engines were fixed to their own concrete beds and were kept in place by large-diameter studs.

Design 16302/41 was similar to 13244/41 but had a larger engine room to accommodate three sets each rated at 187 kW. This larger room also contained the switchgear equipment mounted on a platform on the floor. Building 8760/42 superseded all earlier designs and was clearly a much cheaper alternative. The main difference between it and its predecessors was a steel-framed pitched roof

The stand-by set house 974/35 at North Weald. (Photographed 1982)

The stand-by set house 8760/42 at Melton Mowbray. (Photographed 1980)

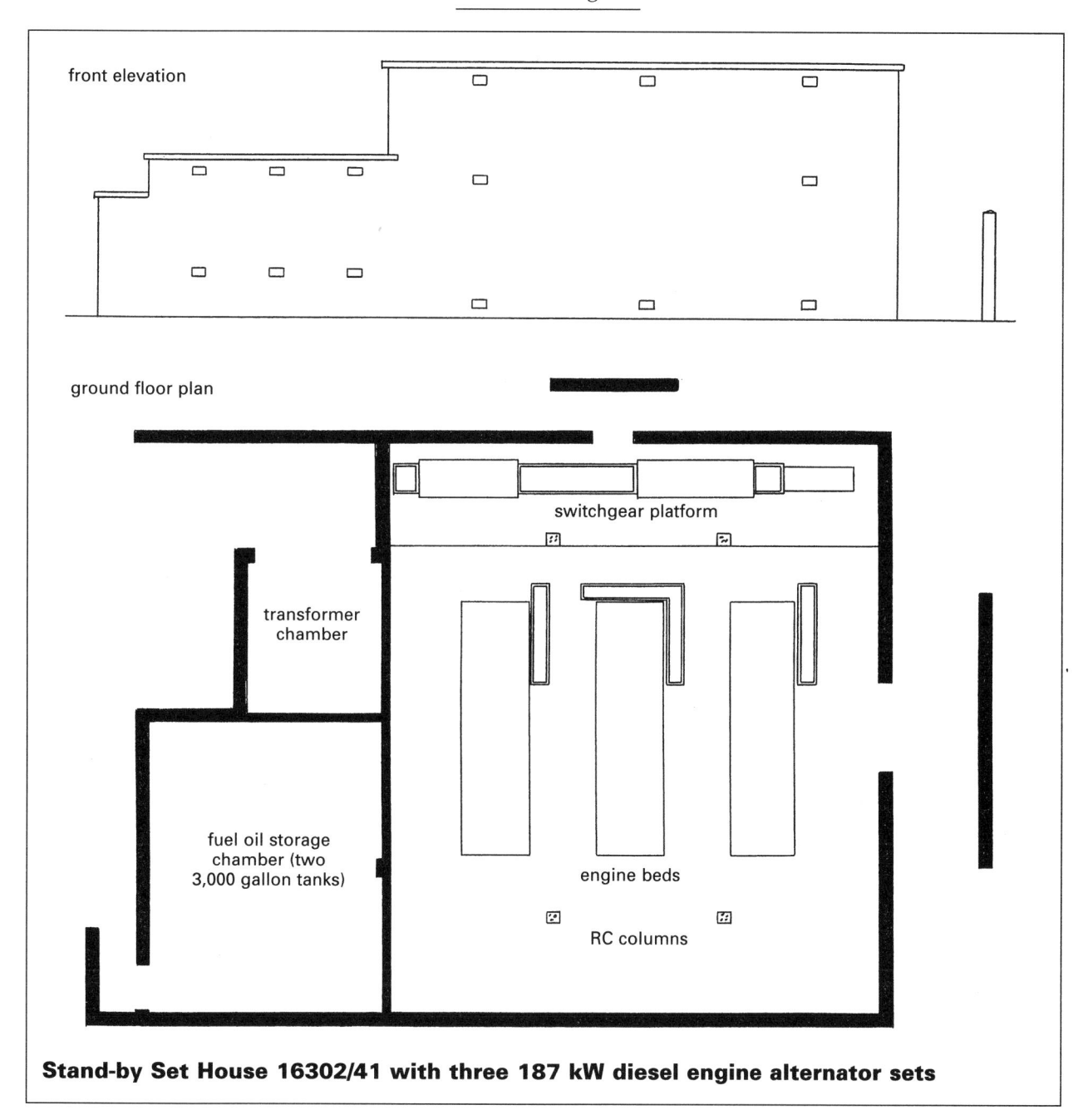

Stand-by Set House 16302/41 with three 187 kW diesel engine alternator sets

instead of flat reinforced concrete. Both the transformer and bulk fuel storage tanks were located outside the main building in their own compounds. The switchgear room, however, retained its flat concrete roof. It was built with bricks laid fair face and so was never meant to be rendered. Size depended on the type of the station and its function, but its unique design meant that it could be easily extended to accommodate a further set by demolishing one gable wall.

drawing no.	974/35	607/36	13244/41
examples	Harwell, Marham	Cottesmore, Driffield, Upwood	Cottam, Spilsby, Thorpe Abbotts

drawing no.	16302/41	8760/42
examples	Halesworth, Leiston, Rackheath	Carnaby, St David's (2 sets), Shepherds Grove (2 sets), Swannington (4 sets)

Power Houses

Power houses needed fuel storage facilities of sufficient capacity to cope with long periods of operation and, unlike the stand-by set, power house plant had to cope with both essential and non-essential loads.

The first power house (207/17) to be built on the North Camp at Biggin Hill was a small building of 20 ft span and 45 ft 5 in long. It consisted of brick piers at 10 ft centres

A First World War power house at Lee-on-Solent. (Photographed 1993)

supporting a composite timber truss clad with corrugated asbestos sheeting. Wall infilling was 3-inch cement breeze slabs. The hut was arranged into four rooms consisting of driver's room, workshop, and store, with battery room and engine room containing two sets (capacity unknown).

The second power house on the Wireless Experimental Establishment on the South Camp at Biggin Hill in 1920 replaced an earlier building which then became the battery-charging room. The new power house also incorporated the South Camp guardroom and this part of the building had a span of 16 ft and was 36 ft long. The power house had a span of 38 ft and was 68 ft long. The main part was devoted to the dynamo house with four sets, two of 50 kW capacity and two of larger capacity. A large fuel tank was located outside in a sunken chamber.

The standard RFC power house for TDSs and AAPs 476/18 had a span of 36 ft and was 59 ft long. It was built of brick piers at 10 ft centres supporting timber king-post trusses with a large ridge-mounted louvred air vent. Wall infilling was cement rendered brick with steel sashes. The main part of the building was the engine room with a small workshop and driver's room.

A power house with fire pumps was originally built of 9-inch walls with brick piers at 10 ft centres to house three generator sets under a pitched roof. The battery room, pump house, and workshop were all located in a separate annexe attached to one end. When it was remodelled in the expansion period to include a larger engine room, it became a protected stand-by set house with a reinforced-concrete roof with blast walls constructed round the building.

drawing no.	207/17, 476/18	1380/24
examples	Biggin Hill, Bracebridge Heath, Filton	Bicester, Upper Heyford

SQUASH RACQUETS COURT

During the First World War, one court or two could be built depending on the size of the station. Where two courts were required, they were built linked-detached, united by a two-storey corridor and WC block. Construction was in external brick piers spaced at 10 ft centres with temporary brick infilling and cement rendering on the inside. Roof trusses were timber king-posts covered with boarding and slates. A large ridge-mounted lantern light with pivot-hung sashes allowed plenty of natural light into the court. There was a single

Two squash racquets courts built to 2078/18 at Thetford. (Photographed 1984)

entrance leading into a corridor connecting a dressing-room for each court, WCs, and stairs to a first-floor viewing gallery. Each court had a span of 21 ft and was 30 ft long; dressing-rooms were 5 ft wide.

During the expansion period a single court was built for officers. It was positioned close to the officers' mess. Sometimes, there was another one, consisting of two courts built back-to-back, for other ranks near the married quarters. Built of permanent brick cavity wall and piers, with walls inside the court cement rendered up to the in-court line, the cement-rendered area being the playing area. The remaining wall surface was left fair face and was painted. Steel roof trusses were clad with corrugated asbestos sheeting. There was a large ridge-mounted lantern light. A single entrance led into a lobby area with stairs to the first-floor gallery on one side and a waiting-room on the other.

Most stations built during the Second World War and existing aerodromes had a temporary brick squash court with walls rendered both inside and out. Roof trusses were initially of the timber king-post type but were later replaced with steel, both types being clad with corrugated asbestos sheeting. On temporary airfields, they were built on the main communal site close to the gymnasium; where two courts were required, they were built back-to-back. The entrance was in the centre of a single-storey annexe containing a waiting-room and dressing-room. The span was 21 ft; the court length was 32 ft. The width of the dressing-room was 5 ft.

The temporary nature of this design is quite apparent from the omission of the ridge-mounted lantern light and viewing gallery.

drawing no.	548/18, 2078/18	1842/35	16589/40
examples	Bircham Newton, Narborough, Thetford	Biggin Hill, Duxford, Mildenhall, Netheravon	Lisset, Rednal, Tuddenham, Skipton-on-Swale

GYMNASIUM

Constructed in a style similar to the squash court, the

Squash racquets court 16589/40 at Lavenham. (Photographed 1982)

gymnasium on First World War aerodromes could be built in any reasonable length to suite the station, normally 60 ft, 80 ft or 100 ft long, and 24 ft wide. Consisting of external brick piers spaced at 10 ft centres with half-brick wall infilling and a single metal window in each bay on each side. Steel or all-timber roof trusses were used; where timber was selected it was of the king-post type covered with diagonal boarding and slates. Ventilation was provided by two ridge-mounted louvered air vents.

The main part of the building was open plan with a single side entrance porch and lobby area, with a storeroom, instructor's office and stairs leading up to a first floor viewing gallery.

One of the most distinctive buildings on many Second World War RAF communal sites was the gymnasium. With the squash court, it was part of the station recreational facilities. The large building (16428/40 and 4911/42) constructed on temporary airfields and existing stations during the Second World War, apart from its obvious use as an indoor sports hall, through clever design, also served a number of other functions for station

The interior of the gymnasium at Bristol Lulsgate Airport. (Photographed 1992)

200 British Military Airfield Architecture

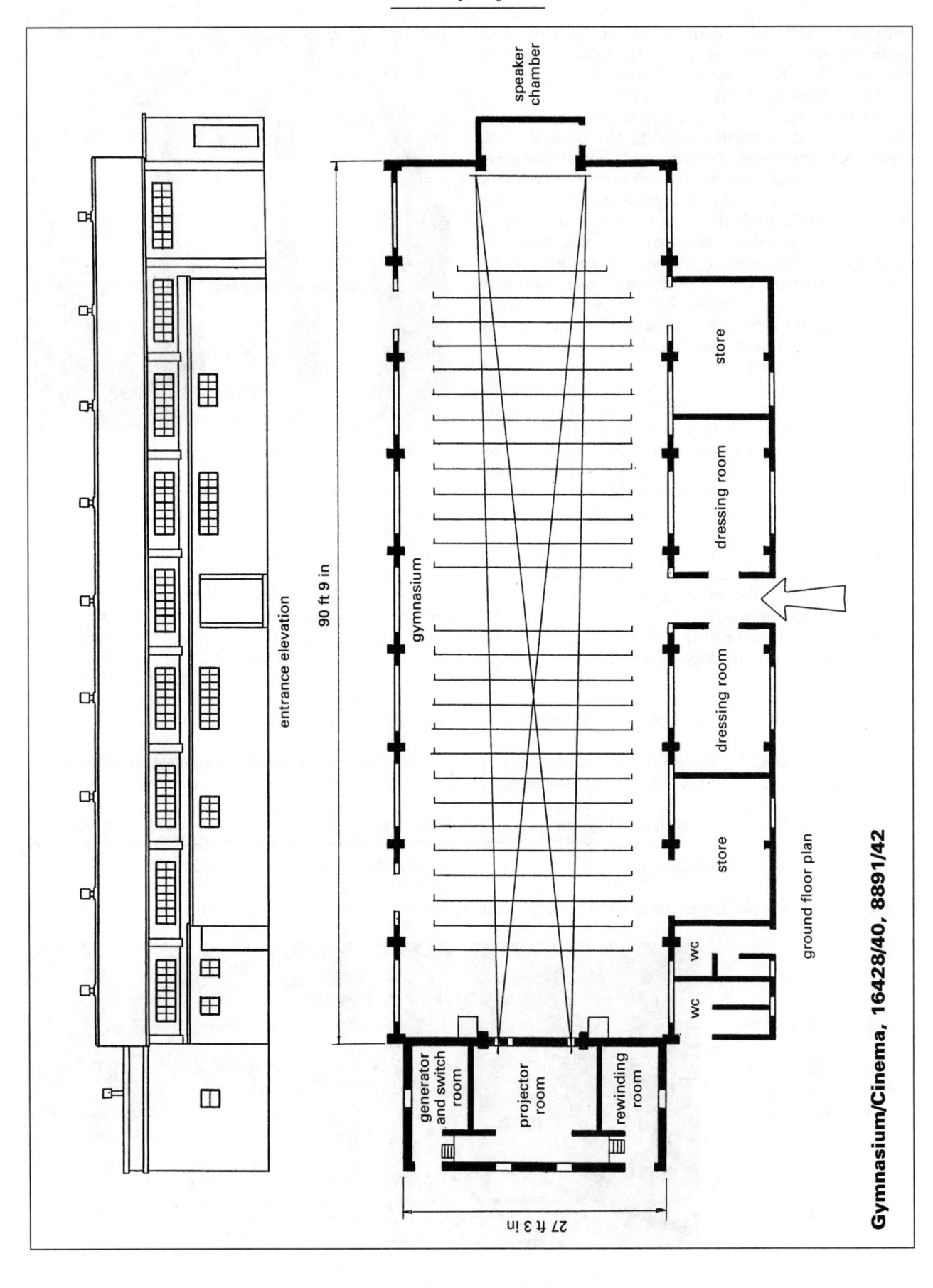

Gymnasium/Cinema, 16428/40, 8891/42

personnel. Separate extensions could be added to each end of the basic gymnasium structure to convert it into a church or cinema. Further variations included a temporary transformation into a large lecture room or even a dance hall.

The basic structure, consisting of just the gymnasium, was built at some airfields such as Lavenham and Swanton Morley. At Market Harborough and Manby the chancel extension was added; all three (including the projection room) were built at Drem and Fiskerton.

Construction was of rendered half-brick walls and piers at 10 ft centres. The original drawing 14604/40 shows the basic gymnasium structure without the chancel extension, the main building being only seven bays long, while later buildings had nine bays. Inside, an RSJ ran the full length of the roof with lugs at regular intervals from which climbing ropes were suspended. Other typical fittings were rope ladders, three-section wall bars, fixing plates for horizontal bars, sockets for boxing-ring standards, and rifle racks.

drawing no.	1840/18	14604/40, 16428/40, 4911/42
examples	Henlow, Kenley	Lavenham, Leicester East, Swanton Morley

Extensions

A church extension (15424/41) of similar temporary brick construction consisted of an annexe, 50 ft by 18 ft, built against one end elevation, subdivided by a partition into a chancel and a Roman Catholic chapel with a vestry. The temporary transformation of the whole building into a sizeable Church of England church was quite simple: a folding wooden partition on sliding rails (normally kept closed when the gymnasium was being used) was drawn back to reveal the altar and chancel, while wooden seats were arranged in the sports hall section to accommodate the congregation. The former gymnasium at RAF Honington became the permanent Church of England church for the station after the Second World War, and still fulfils this role today.

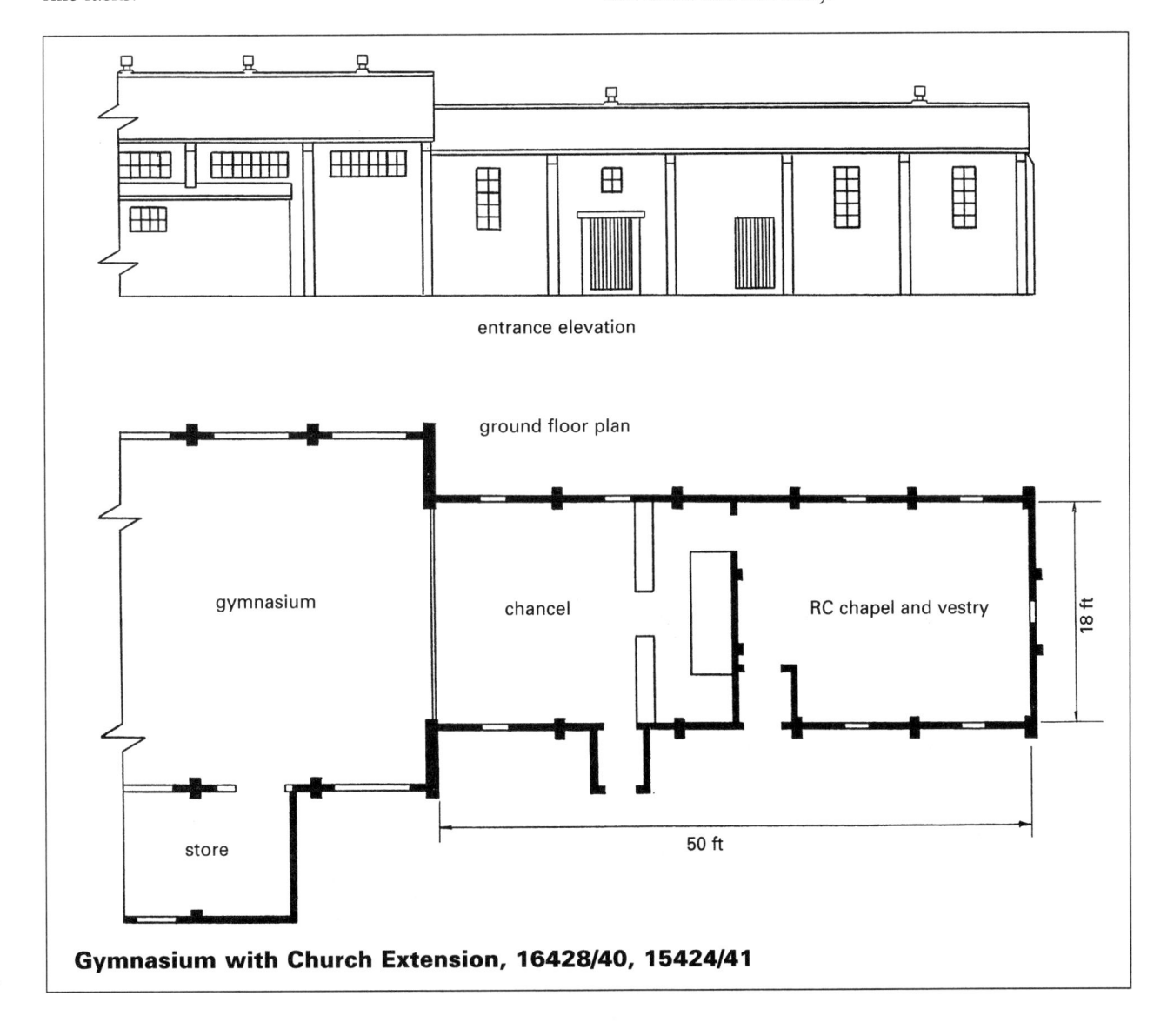

Gymnasium with Church Extension, 16428/40, 15424/41

The final modification to the 'convertible gymnasium' was the addition of a two-storey projection room (8891/42) with 9-inch brick walls (for fireproofing purposes) at one end of the main hall. If the building already possessed a church annexe, the cinema projection box was added to the opposite end. With the fitting of a screen near the far wall or sliding partition, and with all seating *in situ*, the sports hall became a cinema auditorium with a seating capacity of 370 people in 28 rows of 13 seats and one row of nine seats at the front. The maximum picture size on the screen was 11 ft by 7 ft. Buildings without the chancel sometimes had a speaker chamber – an extension 5 ft by 10 ft and 12 ft high, containing the speakers.

The projection box itself (measuring 12 ft 3 in by 15 ft high) was equipped with two 16 mm projectors and was situated at first-floor level between a film rewinding room on one side and a generator and switch room on the other. Films were projected into the auditorium through two 12-inch square protection ports; to help the projectionist to aim correctly and to focus, two 9-inch square sight-holes were positioned near to each projector. Quite often, these holes can be found on many surviving buildings today. Entry to the projection box was gained through two small lobbies at the rear, each of which was connected to the first floor by a steel ladder. The cinema was used extensively during the war for entertainment of service personnel with popular films on general release, news reels, educational films for official training, and propaganda films.

At the end of the Second World War, ENSA operated about 140 RAF cinemas but, with the cessation of hostilities, ENSA had to be wound up as funds from the Treasury and NAAFI were no longer available. The Royal Air Force Cinema Corporation was founded on 5 September 1946 with its head office at Africa House, Kingsway, London. The Corporation took over existing cinema equipment. It became responsible for the provision of cinema entertainment for members of the RAF, their families, and people employed by the Air Ministry on RAF stations at home or abroad. This brought the RAF in line with the Army and Navy which both had similar organizations. In April 1955, the Corporation assumed responsibility for the libraries of all films used for RAF training and instructional purposes.

The 35 mm cinemas usually had a civilian manager and operators, but quite often operating staff was drawn from airmen and airwomen who voluntarily worked in the cinema during their off-duty hours. At small units, where it was uneconomical to establish a permanent cinema, RAF instructional 16 mm projectors were used in temporary premises using film hired from the Corporation's extensive 16 mm entertainment library (subsidized by profits from larger 35 mm cinemas) at very low rates. To avoid competition with nearby commercial exhibitors, films were not shown at stations within 2 miles of a commercial cinema. Furthermore, 35 mm films were not screened in RAF cinemas until civilian exhibitors had screened them, and 16 mm films were not shown until eight months after the London West End release date.

drawing no.	15424/41	8891/42
examples	Hixon, Membury, Silverstone	Methwold, Rednal, Sudbury

GROCERY AND LOCAL PRODUCE STORE

This was sited on the communal site. It was on the same site as the tailor's, shoemaker's and barber's shop. The store was a 24 ft span Nissen hut, the length of which depended on the number of personnel on the station. In some cases, two huts were built. There was also a temporary brick 'empties' yard, built at one end, part of which had a lean-to roof and a fuel store. The hut was divided into a number of storage areas for bacon, groceries, and local produce. There was an issuing area with a counter and an office behind it, and a staff room, a manager's office, and a bathroom.

A gymnasium 16428/40 with projection room extension 889/42 at Methwold. (Photographed 1982)

no. of personnel	length of hut
301–450	54 ft 4 in
451–600	66 ft 5 in
601–800	72 ft 6 in
801–1,250	78 ft 6 in
1,251–1,500	84 ft 7 in
1,501–2,000	90 ft 7 in

drawing no. 12878/41
examples Chipping Ongar, East Wretham, Eshott

Tailor's, Shoemaker's, and Barber's Shop

On the same drawing as the grocery and local produce store was the tailor's, shoemaker's, and barber's shop. This hut was a 24 ft span Nissen hut, but was only 36 ft 3 in long. It was simply divided into three rooms.

drawing no. 12878/41
examples Chipping Ongar, East Wretham, Eshott

PART 8

HUTS

The design branches of the Works Directorate had to produce working drawings for both temporary and permanent buildings that conveyed sufficient information to the site. The adopted scale was 1 inch to 8 feet. The drawings included outline plans of buildings consisting of general arrangements, plans, schedules of fittings, amendments, and superseding drawings; many thousands of designs of this nature were produced. For the main contractor, there was usually a minimum of two drawings for a particular prefabricated hut type: a general arrangement plan showing details of how the building was assembled, and an internal arrangement plan showing three or more alternative layouts. Thus, officers' quarters, sergeants' quarters, or airmen's barracks could all be shown on a single drawing. Quite often, several different hut types shared the same plan. In a lot of cases, it is this drawing number that is listed on the site plan; for example, 13903/41 could be for a Hall, Jane, or Laing hut. Some companies supplied a manufacturer's booklet in conjunction with working drawings, illustrating stage-by-stage assembly, with schedules of parts and details of alternative cladding materials.

Huts were bought in bulk from the manufacturer, supplied in kit form, and stored by the Air Ministry, Ministry of Supply (MoS), or Ministry of Works (MoW) until required at an aerodrome.

At the outbreak of the Second World War, the planning of quarters was based on temporary scales of 120 sq ft per officer, 70 sq ft per sergeant, 45 sq ft per corporal, and 45 sq ft per airman. By 1942, huts were calculated to house larger numbers of personnel, the scale being reduced to 96 sq ft per officer, 58 sq ft per sergeant, 38 sq ft per corporal, and 38 sq ft per airman. After July 1943, the area for corporals and airmen was further reduced to 32 sq ft per man.

During the late expansion period, in the interest of timber economy and speed of production, it became necessary to consider other forms of temporary construction as alternatives to the high-class timber hutting then in general use. As a result, the Gerrard X, Y, and Z timber huts were introduced between 1939 and 1940, which were less robust and inferior in quality to the sectional Type A and Type B huts of 1935–39. By 1940, the timber shortage was so acute that alternative hutting using less timber was developed for the Ministry of Supply. The Magnet timber hut, Thorn hut (plasterboard and timber), Laing hut (plasterboard and timber), and Maycrete and Nashcrete huts (concrete and timber) were all well below the standards normally required by the Air Ministry but this was due to the shortage of raw materials.

Despite a shortage of bricklayers, temporary brick hutting with half-brick walls and piers in spans of 18 ft and 28 ft were used throughout the war. Nissen hutting was re-introduced in 1941 and this system of construction proved to be the most successful of the factory-made huts. Revised Laing, Jane, and Gerrard types were purchased in early 1942 using frames of home-grown timber and corrugated iron sheeting. Later, in 1942, the Interdepartmental Committee on Hutting became the sole arbiter on design and production, and supply of all types changed from the Ministry of Supply to the Ministry of Works. Asbestos hutting made by Uni-Seco (asbestos and plywood), Turners Asbestos (the curved asbestos hut), and Universal (the Handcraft) was introduced. Finally precast concrete huts by British Concrete Federation, Orlit, and Standard Hutting became available between 1941 and 1944. For workshops and stores and similar buildings, the Iris and Romney were designed and built from August 1941. In 1943, the Marston shed was produced but this never replaced the Romney as it was less economical because of its use of steel, and was often used where an overhead gantry or lifting tackle was required.

Camouflage schedules (378/41) were issued to those airfields thought to be liable to attack. They illustrated how huts could be painted to break up the outline, to look like farm buildings (schemes J and M), council cottages (scheme K), old cottages (scheme L), and a cart shed or other farm buildings (scheme M). This could be achieved with imaginative painting, using the colour of the local walls and dark green. Protection against incendiaries for timber hutting on aerodromes liable to bombing consisted of fitting the huts with roof screens of 1-inch mesh Expamat metal lath sheeting laid on battens.

Manufacturers and design companies of the more successful prefabricated huts (British Concrete Federation, Orlit, Turners Asbestos, and Uni-Seco) looked ahead to the postwar housing shortage and produced new designs

Huts 205

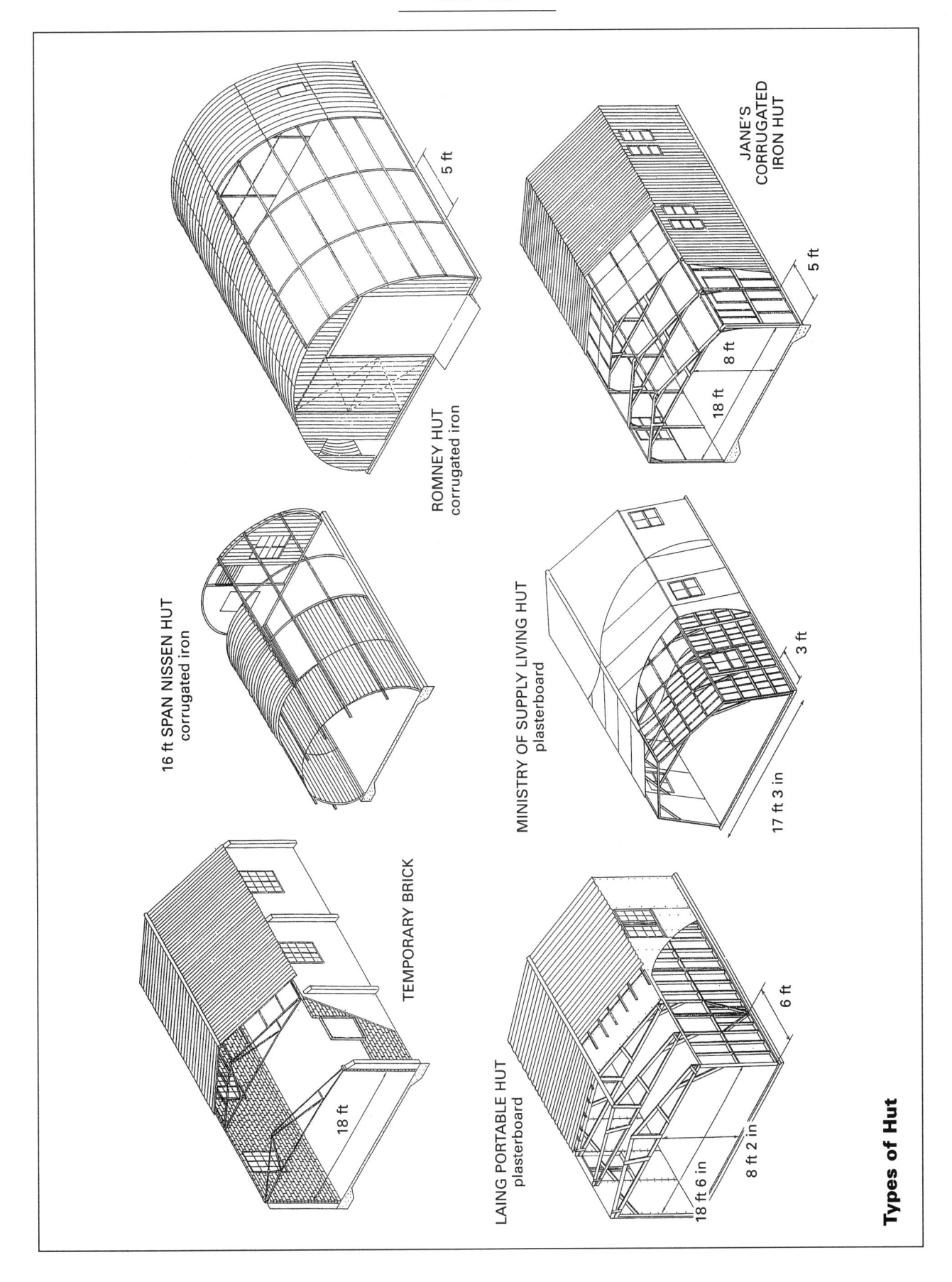

ROMNEY HUT
corrugated iron

JANE'S CORRUGATED IRON HUT
5 ft
8 ft
18 ft

16 ft SPAN NISSEN HUT
corrugated iron

MINISTRY OF SUPPLY LIVING HUT
plasterboard
3 ft
17 ft 3 in

TEMPORARY BRICK
18 ft

LAING PORTABLE HUT
plasterboard
6 ft
8 ft 2 in
18 ft 6 in

Types of Hut

based on wartime hutting. Designs such as the Handcraft and the curved asbestos huts were rejected outright by the MoW, although Universal Asbestos continued to supply their Handcraft hut to the Air Ministry which built them on Bloodhound anti-aircraft missile sites. British Concrete Federation, Orlit and Uni-Seco designs were adopted for postwar housing and many dwellings survive today. The only factory-made buildings still in production in the 1990s are Romney and Nissen huts which are manufactured by both Naylor Buildings Ltd of Wolverhampton and W. W. Leese of Halifax.

Timber Huts

Sectional hutting was designed in 1935 primarily for those RAF stations that were intended to be temporary. It was later used to supplement existing permanent accommodation on new aerodromes. The Air Ministry decided that timber hutting best met the requirements, and designs were therefore prepared for timber-framed units of sectional construction. Each section was designed to be bolted together to form huts of any length, each having peg foundations. The timber-framed panel walls were covered externally with 0.75-inch rebated weatherboarding, internal walls were lined with plasterboard, and standard metal windows were used. Roofs were timber trussed, panelled, and boarded, and floors were of timber in framed and boarded units. A life of about five years was required for Type B hutting and of between 10 and 15 years for Type A. Construction was similar for both of these types but the Type A had weatherboarding of Canadian cedar which contains a natural preservative and is obnoxious to rodents. The roof of Type A huts used corrugated asbestos sheeting while the Type B had a timber and felted roof.

Sectional hutting was used extensively in both domestic and technical accommodation which included decontamination centres 285/39 (Jurby), parachute store 3633/35, and watch office huts at Speke, North Coates, and West Freugh.

Large technical training stations in sectional hutting were first commenced in 1936 at St Athan and Cardington. New Type A hutted Armament Training Schools and Air Observer Schools were also started at Pembrey, Jurby, Penrhos, West Freugh, Evanton, and Acklington. Hutted accommodation was added to existing stations at Henlow, Cranwell and Cosford. In 1937, Type A hutting for instructional and domestic accommodation was also built at Balloon Barrage Depots and Volunteer Reserve Training Centres.

Construction of sectional hutting with 10 ft, 18 ft, and 20 ft spans used a system of four rafters for each bay. Where the bays were joined together, collars were bolted to the two joining rafters, then clad with roof boarding. Hutting with 10 ft span was used for garages and WC blocks, while hutting with spans of 18 ft and 20 ft was used as barracks and other domestic buildings.

Several huts could be bolted together or built side by side to create a large complex. One example was the officers' mess at the Hook Barrage Balloon Depot to

A Type A sectional timber hut. This is a decontamination centre 285/39 at Jurby.

A 28 ft span Type A sectional hut at Jurby.

drawing 5169/37. Three huts of 20 ft span were required, one being 100 ft long and housing the mess facilities. The centre hut contained servery, pantry, WCs, and kitchen; scullery and staff bedrooms were all housed inside the last hut. The entrance to the mess led to a hall and corridor connecting all three huts. In addition, a detached boiler-room and mess servants quarters were also housed inside a 20 ft span Type A sectional hut.

The Hook Balloon Depot used seven 20 ft span huts as a barracks, each in Type A hutting, sleeping 22 airmen in an open-plan barrack room with one bedroom for a single sergeant. Other rooms included WC and a storeroom; total length was 84 ft with 8 ft walls. One other hut of the same dimensions accommodated 17 airmen and three sergeants. The sergeants' mess was effectively three 18 ft span huts bolted together. One 35 ft long hut with a 10 ft wide extension was used as a kitchen. Another, 25 ft long, was used as a billiard room, the last being used as a mess and ante-room, an entrance hall separating the two. The bath house was a 60 ft hut of 18 ft span and contained a drying room, two airmen's and one sergeant's bathroom, eight shower cubicles including one for sergeants, and 11 WCs with one for sergeants.

The timber trusses of the 28 ft span huts consisted of principal rafters joined together by a king-post and angled struts. The truss was fixed to the wall framework with timber knee-braces. Roof sections of purlins and roof boarding spanned the trusses.

A typical example with a hut length of 84 ft was the officers' quarters at Hook, 5169/37. This had a central corridor with five bedrooms and a combined bedroom and sitting-room for senior officers. Two other bedrooms were provided for servants, and other facilities included two bathrooms and WCs for the officers and a box-room containing a small kitchen and bathroom for the servants.

drawing no.	span	bay width	height
1892/35	10 ft	5 ft	8 ft 8 in (to collar)
			9 ft 6 in (garages)
1894/35	28 ft	10 ft	8 ft or 10 ft (to truss)
1897/35	18 ft	5 ft	9 ft (to collar)
1900/35	20 ft	5 ft	9 ft (max internal)
5169/37			
5170/37			

X, Y, Z Huts

From September 1939 until January 1941, Gerrard & Sons of Swinton, Manchester manufactured the X, Y, and Z hutting. These were designed as the Air Ministry replacement of the high-quality peacetime sectional hutting.

Construction was similar to that of Type B 18 ft span sectional hutting, except that there was a reduction in scantlings of the timber framing. It was supplied only in standard lengths and was available in 18 ft spans, unlike sectional hutting which was purchased in several different spans and any length. The hutting was used to supplement existing accommodation at aerodromes already completed where stocks of sectional hutting were exhausted. Eventually, types which used far less timber became necessary and this brought production to end.

A typical airfield using this hutting was RAF Chivenor. For example, building number 35, a Type Y hut, was used as the group captain's and wing commander's quarters. Both officers had an entrance in a side elevation which had a lobby leading off to rooms which included a sitting-room, bedroom, and bathroom; between the quarters was a small servant's room. Along with most of the Gerrard timber hutting at Chivenor, this building has been demolished.

Type	span	internal bay width	length	wall height
X	18 ft	5 ft	50 ft	7 ft
Y	18 ft	5 ft	70 ft	7 ft
Z	18 ft	5 ft	50 ft	8 ft

drawing no. 12673/39   14543/39

Ministry of Supply Timber Hut

Manufactured by Magnet, this consisted of a light timber frame covered with weatherboarding, the walls being internally unlined, and a felt-covered roof. This hut type seems to have been less popular than other MoS huts, probably due to the relatively large amount of timber used in its construction at a time when timber was scarce. Three versions were available: barrack block for one NCO and 16 airmen with a single No. 3 slow-combustion stove; quarters for eight sergeants or eight airmen in five bedrooms with a central corridor, each room having a Queen stove; quarters for four officers with a servants' dormitory and a corridor running along a side wall, each room having a Queen stove. The hut had an internal span of 16 ft and was 54 ft long.

drawing no. 16056/40   16227/40

HALF-BRICK HUTS

The half-brick hut (wall thickness of half a brick), otherwise known as the 4.5-inch brick building, was one of the standard forms of temporary construction. It was used extensively throughout both world wars. Bricks were laid in stretcher bond only (a wall consisting of single bricks laid lengthways along the length of the wall and 4.5 inches wide). The building had brick piers to support roof trusses.

Many First World War 16 ft span barrack huts, offices, and other small living or technical accommodation were built with internal brick piers normally at 10 ft centres. But quite often, where the building was partitioned off into rooms, the dividing wall was used to support the roof truss instead of brick piers. Consequently, the roof trusses were unevenly spaced.

World War Two temporary brick buildings were based on guidelines laid down by drawing numbers 222/40, 223/40 and 3323/40 where huts were built with external brick piers at 10 ft centres. This allowed for simple erection, in spans of 18 ft and 28 ft. These spans were chosen as the most economical for spacing of tables in messes and beds in dormitories. Brickwork was cement rendered externally and left fair face internally, ready for painting. Wall heights varied depending on the function of the building; for example, 7 ft (linked corridors), 8 ft (mess rooms, kitchens), 9 ft (ward block in SSQ), and 10 ft (gymnasium). The maximum height was 13 ft 6 in (floodlight tractor and trailer shed). Floors were concrete with surfaces prepared to receive lino where appropriate. Roofs consisted of standard light steel trusses purchased in bulk and erected at 10 ft centres supporting corrugated asbestos sheeting.

drawing no.	469/17	16428/40	222/40
description	squadron offices	gymnasium	
examples	Biggin Hill		

drawing no.	223/40	3323/40	10041/41
description			Link trainer

drawing no.	633/42	317/43	2077/43
description	officers' mess	combined RAF and WAAF sick quarters	

Plasterboard Huts

Laing Huts

The original Laing hut of 1940 was built in a purpose-built factory established at Elstree, Herts. The hut consisted of standard prefabricated lightweight timber wall sections bolted together. End elevations comprised two corner sections 8 ft 3 in wide by 8 ft 2 in high, and one central door section 2 ft 8 in wide. Side elevations were usually made up of 10 sections, each 6 ft wide and incorporating a steel half-window frame (the window could be used as a half-frame, or combined with a right-hand or left-hand wall section to form a window twice the size) Externally, walls were clad with plasterboard and, to keep the weather out, covered with a layer of felt sheeting. Inside, they were simply lined with plasterboard.

Lightweight composite timber roof trusses were spaced every 4 ft and extra support was provided by timber knee-braces at each end, joined to the wall framework. The roof was clad with Super Six corrugated asbestos sheeting and lined internally with plasterboard, leaving the trusses exposed. The walls were rag-bolted every 3 ft to a thin concrete raft or, in the case of the operations block at Rednal, bolted on top of a brick ground-floor structure 8 ft high.

Laing huts were generally used for minor technical accommodation or, more commonly, as a quarters building for all ranks to drawing number 13903/40. The Type A senior officers' quarters, for example, had a central corridor with six bedrooms each side, plus a single room for three servants. In contrast, the Type B airmen's barrack block had 24 beds in a single room of the same dimensions as the senior officers' block. Airwomen's quarters had a chemical closet inside an external porch, while the airmen's barracks had internal lobbies; the airmen were expected to use detached WC blocks.

Barrack rooms were usually heated by a single Romesse type stove located in the centre of the building; officers had a smaller stove in each room.

drawing no.	11950/40	12292/40	13903/40

MoS Living Hut

The MoS hut was unusual in that the walls had canted sides unlike most other lightweight timber-framed huts which had straight sides. Apparently, the type had several alternative names, including Ripper, Thorn, and Thorbex.

Construction involved a simple system of two knee-braces (small and large) and a collar-beam instead of a roof truss, which ensured that the roof and wall panels were both sturdy and remained at the correct angle. The gable ends were made of five sections of light timber studwork framing which were bolted together, the centre section containing a door. Side elevation walls and roof all shared a common frame section except where windows were required. These were all clad on both sides with plasterboard, the external face being felted. Typically, each 60 ft long hut was constructed from 80 frame sections, each 3 ft wide, making a total of 90 sections when gable end walls were included.

A Laing hut 17917/40, defence accommodation, at East Fortune. (Photographed 1983)

The interior of a MoS living hut H 342/40, clearly showing the canted walls, at Castle Camps.

Although this building type is now rare, the WAAF site No. 6 at Castle Camps still has three MoS living huts still standing. However, they have been modified by being reclad with asbestos sheeting, and the first few feet above the ground have been concreted for conversion into pigsty units. Inside, however, the walls and ceiling are fairly original, the sectional studwork and knee-braces can clearly be seen. The airfield site plan refers to them as Laing huts but, while they may have been assembled by Laing, having been supplied by a subcontractor in kit form, they differ from the true Laing hut in their angled sides and the absence of the Laing composite roof trusses.

Generally, there were three alternative internal arrangements as shown on drawing number 16227/40 (the same drawing as for Maycrete and Magnet hutting):

- large open-plan dormitory for 19 airmen, with a single bedroom for an NCO
- quarters for 10 sergeants or 10 airmen, arranged along a central corridor as four double bedrooms and two single bedrooms, each with a Queen stove, with an exit at each end
- quarters for six officers with a servant's bedroom at the rear

The internal span was 17 ft 3 in, the internal length 60 ft, with a minimum internal height of 7 ft 3 in.

drawing no.   342/40   16057/40   16277/40

MoW Hall Hut

Like others in this group, the Hall hut had walls made of timber-framed panels clad with felted plasterboard on the outside and plain plasterboard inside. Each panel was made of 6 ft 2 in sections bolted together. The roof truss was the standard MoW type similar to that used on Maycrete and Nashcrete huts and clad with timber-framed panels similar to those used on the walls. The joints between the panels were covered with felt, creating the impression of a patched-up building.

Internal span was 18 ft 6 in, internal bay width was 6 ft 2 in and height to truss was 7 ft 10 in. An ex-works hut cost £240; the total cost including foundations, carriage, and erection was £360.

drawing no.   6504/42

CORRUGATED IRON HUTS

Igloo Sheds

Igloos were a range of sheds primarily used for the storage of small-arms ammunition and pyrotechnics. Construction was very basic and consisted of 14-gauge corrugated iron sheeting in 2 ft 4 in sections bolted together to the required length. No frame was required. The building was simply erected above ashes laid on hardcore. The Type A hut had a radius of 2 ft 3 in and had straight sides, looking very much like an Anderson shelter. The Type B had a radius of 5 ft and looked similar to a Nissen hut.

Type	internal width	length	radius	height	drawing no.
A	4 ft 6 in	10 ft 4 in	2 ft 3 in	4 ft 5 in	2677/43, 43110
B	10 ft	14 ft 10 in	5 ft	7 ft	2677/43, 43109

Jane Hut

As an improvement to the earlier plasterboard hutting, the main manufacturers abandoned felted plasterboard and instead used corrugated iron. It's not clear who manufactured Jane huts although it may have been Boulton & Paul.

It was made of lightweight timber-framed panels, covered on the outside with straight sheets of corrugated iron laid vertically, and on the inside with felt reinforced with chicken wire. Each 3 ft wide wall panel contained a timber half-window. The internal partitioning of rooms was usually achieved with 9-inch clayblocks. Roof trusses consisted of unique T-shaped (in section) principal rafters which were lighter than square-section trusses yet retained enough width for attachment of purlins on the top. On the inside, felt was nailed to common rafters, while straight corrugated iron was fixed to the purlins on the outside. The principal rafters were joined by two timber collars, angled timber struts, and a steel knee-brace.

It is not known if the drawings refer to an earlier Jane plasterboard hut or to the later corrugated iron hut. The internal span was 18 ft; bay width was 3 ft; internal height was 8 ft.

drawing no.	2966/42	10844/42
description	(Richmond hut) officer's quarters	officers' quarters
example	Little Staughton	Molesworth

Marston Sheds

Marston shedding was designed as a replacement for the pre-war sectional hutting for technical buildings. Although less economical in its use of steel and slower to erect than 35 ft span Romney hutting, Marston shedding was used where other types of hut would be unsuitable; for example, where vertical sides, overhead travelling cranes, or a larger span was required.

Buildings were supplied in any length or in multiples of 25 ft bays, and erected in single or multi-span units. There were two basic types: high shedding for use when an overhead travelling crane was required; and low shedding for other uses such as gunnery and crew procedure centres. It had an all-steel framework with walls of corrugated asbestos sheeting, the roof being 24-gauge corrugated steel sheeting.

The internal span was 45 ft; bay width was 25 ft; height of high shedding was 25 ft and of low shedding was 16 ft.

Nissen Huts

The Nissen hut was invented in 1915 by a Canadian, Colonel P. N. Nissen, who died in March 1930. His earliest buildings were known as the Nissen bow and the Nissen hospital huts designed to be used on the Western Front of the First World War, and were manufactured from 1916.

Colonel Nissen set up a company called Nissen Buildings Ltd and a factory was built at Rye House, Hoddesdon, Herts in 1922. The last Nissen hut to be manufactured in Hoddesdon was made in late 1960 by Schreiber Wood Industries which had taken over the earlier company in 1958. By 1988, the site had been vacated and remains so in 1995.

In the Second World War, Nissen huts were purchased in bulk from the manufacturers and supplied to

A Jane corrugated iron hut at Panshanger.

A Marston shed at Strubby.

A 24 ft span Nissen hut at Chivenor.

A 16 ft span Nissen hut at Snaith. (Photographed 1981)

A 24 ft span Nissen hut annexe to a hangar at East Fortune. (Photographed 1983)

aerodromes by the Air Ministry. They were used as an alternative to brick construction and soon became one of the standard forms of temporary buildings for all types of accommodation.

Like all Nissen huts, the 16 ft span hut was semicircular in section and could be built to any length in multiples of 6 ft bays (normally six). The frame consisted of steel T-ribs in three sections spaced at 6 ft centres; corrugated steel sheets laid horizontally provided an internal lining and were held in place by the T shape of the rib and by straining wires. The external covering was 26-gauge corrugated iron sheeting; these were attached to timber purlins fixed to the ribs. End walls, each containing two windows and a door frame, were normally supplied with the hut and consisted of timber-framed sections, clad with timber boarding and felt. Alternatively, half-brick walls could be built.

Drawing number 9024/41 quarters and barrack hut is a typical example. Type A senior officers' quarters consisted of four rooms including one for servants. The commanding officer had two rooms while junior officers only had a single room each. In contrast, however, the Type B sergeants' quarters was a single room for eight sergeants, and the airmen's barrack block was a single room for 12 airmen.

The construction of the larger span (24 ft and 30 ft spans) Nissen huts was similar to that described for the 16 ft hut, except that dormer window and door cheeks

212 *British Military Airfield Architecture*

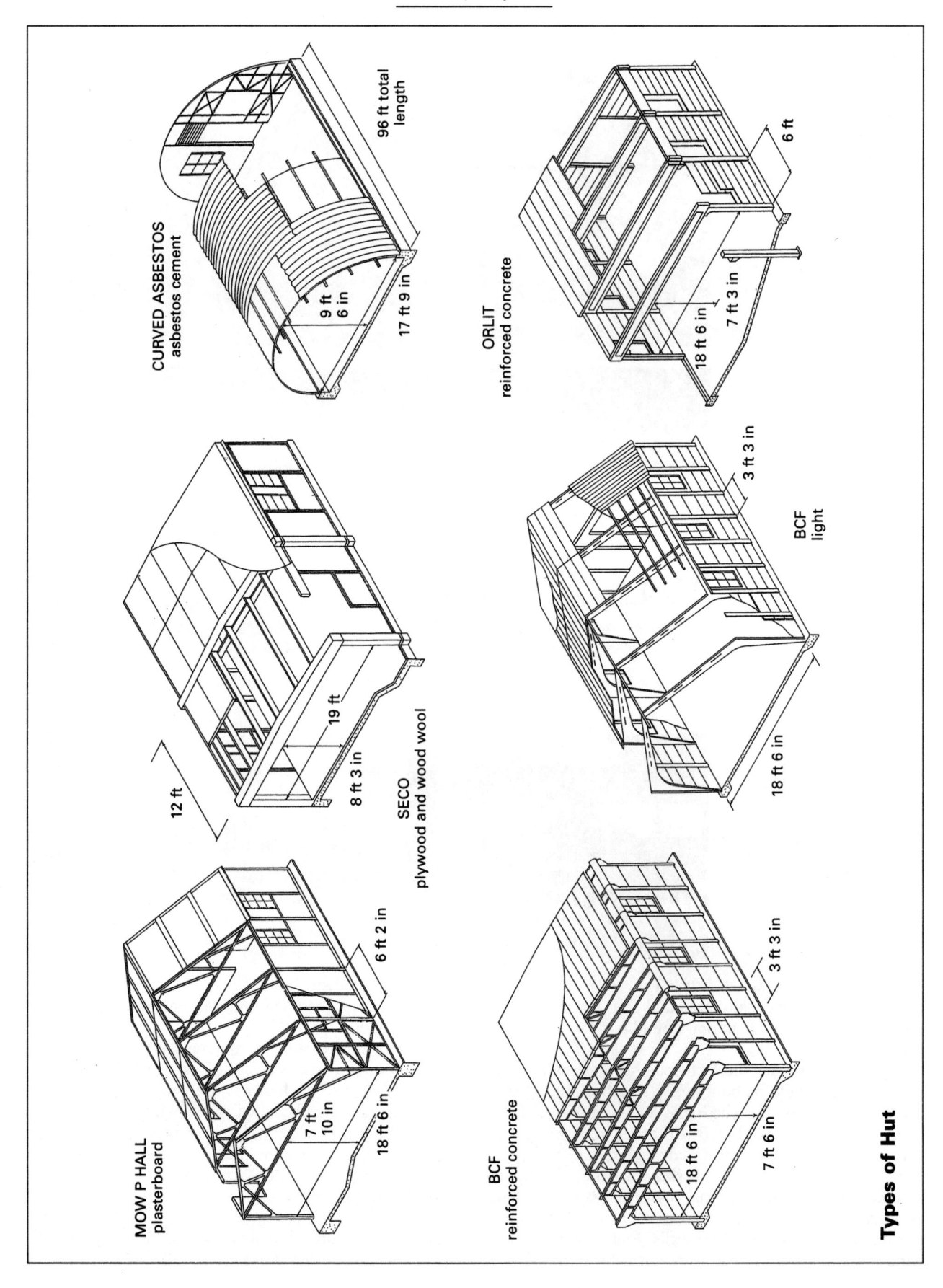

CURVED ASBESTOS
asbestos cement
96 ft total length
9 ft 6 in
17 ft 9 in

ORLIT
reinforced concrete
6 ft
18 ft 6 in
7 ft 3 in

SECO
plywood and wood wool
12 ft
19 ft
8 ft 3 in

BCF light
3 ft 3 in
18 ft 6 in

MOW P HALL
plasterboard
6 ft 2 in
7 ft 10 in
18 ft 6 in

BCF
reinforced concrete
3 ft 3 in
18 ft 6 in
7 ft 6 in

Types of Hut

were often fitted along the side elevations. These were prefabricated from timber and corrugated iron. Internal wall lining could be plasterboard, fibreboard or corrugated iron sheeting. In some cases, timber floor panels were supplied for communal buildings for use as dance halls or cinemas.

The internal spans available were 16 ft, 24 ft, and 30 ft; internal bay width was 6 ft. Examples and drawing numbers can be found in the sections on technical and domestic buildings.

Iris and Romney Huts
Both Iris and Romney hutting were designed at Romney House, London by the Directorate of Fortifications and Works. They were used primarily for storage but could easily be adapted for use as workshops, canteens, and cinemas.

Semicircular in section, the Romney hut was a series of 2.5-inch tubular steel ribs curved to a radius of 17 ft 6 in. A complete rib was made up of four identical sections bolted together through flanged ends. The curved sections were interchangeable. The ribs were secured to their foundations by bolts set into the concrete floor. Each completed rib was connected to the rest by steel angle-section purlins, giving rigidity to the structure.

External covering consisted of curved 24-gauge corrugated iron sheeting bolted to the purlins; store buildings were generally left unlined internally. The end walls were also of steel-framed construction, comprising three channel-section posts and angle rails, clad with straight corrugated iron sheeting. Access was through an 11 ft wide sliding door fitted at each gable end. Natural lighting was achieved by two 'dead lights', one each side per bay. Roof-type air ventilators and gable louveres were not standard but were fitted as required.

A few bomber airfields had two 12-bay Romney sheds to drawing number 2423/43. The internal span was 35 ft; and the length was 96 ft consisting of 12 bays, each 8 ft wide. One building was used as a workshop for power plant assembly and engine stores, and was open plan in layout with a small office for NCOs in one corner. The other shed contained a machine shop for engine repair, a carpenter's shop with a stores area, a fabric worker's shop, and an acetylene welder's and blacksmith's shop. The three main work areas were separated from each other by partitions.

In order that the Romney is not confused with large Nissen huts and curved asbestos hutting, the following points should be remembered. Romney huts were primarily used for workshops and stores, and thus were mainly confined to the technical site (except at few American bases). The framework ribs were tubular whereas the ribs belonging to a Nissen hut are T-shaped in section, and curved asbestos hutting did not have a frame.

Many examples survive today; Knettishall has three excellent examples.

The Iris was similar except that the frame consisted of tubular ribs, 2 inches in diameter, and tubular purlins. The small-diameter tubing made the structure too flimsy and its manufacture was soon discontinued and replaced by the Romney hut.

Romney hut details
drawing no.	2423/43	6191/43	7451/43
description	main workshops		boiler house at American bases

ASBESTOS HUTS

Curved Asbestos Hut
This arched-type of hut was manufactured from May 1942 onwards by the Turners Asbestos Co Ltd of Trafford Park, Manchester. Often mistaken for a Nissen hut, this hut was in fact quite different. No frame was needed. Instead, 'Everite Six' curved asbestos cement corrugated sheets were simply bolted together to form an arch which was fixed to a concrete curb above the floor to a radius of 9 ft. A number of internal purlins supported a lining of flexible asbestos sheets. The end walls were timber framed with plasterboard inside and felted plasterboard outside. Alternatively, cement rendered temporary brick was used.

The internal span was 17 ft 4 in; internal length was 36 ft; internal height was 9 ft 2 in. A typical 36 ft length hut cost £60 and the total cost including carriage, foundations, and erection was only £140.

drawing no. 10837/42
description Link trainer hut

A Romney shed at Enstone.

A curved asbestos hut at Dallachy.

A Handcraft hut at Panshanger.

Handcraft Hut

This building type was manufactured from May 1942 onwards by the Universal Asbestos Co Ltd at their Handcraft Works, Tolpits Lane, Watford, Herts. The hut consisted of trough-shaped asbestos cement sheets bolted together, forming a seven-sided building in cross-section. No framing was needed. Internal lining was of flexible asbestos sheets, and end walls were of cement rendered brick.

The internal arrangement drawing 3472/42 illustrates four layouts. Type A was a senior officers' quarters, divided into three bedrooms for officers and a servants' room with two beds. Type B was an officers' quarters with three rooms, the largest having two beds. Type C was an officers' quarters consisting of a single room with four beds. Type A was a barrack block with a single room of 12 beds for men or women, the airmen having an internal lobby, while the airwomen's quarters had a porch with a night WC.

The internal span was 18 ft; length was 35 ft 9 in; maximum internal height was 9 ft.

drawing no.   2996/42   3472/42   4175/42

PLYWOOD AND ASBESTOS HUTS

Seco Huts

From 1942, Uni-Seco Structures Ltd designed buildings and huts based on a system of standard units for walls and roof. They were manufactured under licence by existing construction companies on a basis of 7.5 per cent profit above costs. The most successful company involved in the construction of the component parts of Seco hutting was En-Tout-Cas which had a purpose-built factory at Thurmaston near Leicester.

Faced with ever increasing Air Ministry demands for this type of hutting, En-Tout-Cas began to employ women for some of the tasks; eventually the company was offered the assistance of Italian prisoners of war. These were brought daily by Army lorries from a camp near Melton Mowbray. The majority worked well and some were made subforemen in charge of the various sections of the work. After some time however, production towards the end of the working day fell off sharply. As they were good workers, it was not at first understood why this happened. The answer was that the men were weak from shortage of food. The provision of food was not the company's responsibility as they were fed by the military authorities in charge of the prison camp. Eventually it was decided that each man should be given one large Spam sandwich and a cup of coffee at midday. This had an astonishing effect; the afternoon session immediately picked up and afternoon production matched morning production.

All went well for three months until one day the managing director received a visit from the officer in charge of the camp who said that he had broken the regulations and that it was illegal to feed prisoners of war. The manager explained why this had been done and told him about the excellent results that had been achieved because of the extra food. He also pointed out that they were trying to obtain the best possible output as the huts were required for the war effort. But this was not accepted and he was told that he would be subject to serious penalties unless it was stopped at once – prisoners of war were given rations strictly in accordance with the Geneva Convention.

The result was immediately apparent. Output by the Italians in the afternoon deteriorated to such an extent that it became worse than before they were given the extra food because their morale was affected as well as their physical state. Eventually, the company had to rely on the stronger men from the camp in order to restore the production levels.

Flat-pack Seco huts were loaded on to railway trucks in the company sidings next to the works. Each morning, a locomotive came with a load of empty trucks and took the loaded ones to the MoW Central Storage Depot at Elstow near Bedford. Here they were distributed to the various contractors for erection on RAF aerodromes.

Seco huts to erection drawings 673, 900–904 and 1128 could be assembled with almost unlimited flexibility into buildings of the clear span type or of the cellular type. The Seco clear span hut consisted of prefabricated, hollow aero plywood beams, columns, and eaves-pieces. Wall and roof cladding consisted of timber-framed units of flat asbestos facing sheets separated by a cavity filled with a mixture of cement and wood wool. All of these component parts were profiled and jointed to fit with other parts. The framework consisted of a series of upright aero columns bolted to a timber keel plate fitted to a concrete base. Columns supported the aero beams and, together with eaves-pieces between two beams, formed the structure of the building. The gap between columns and eaves-pieces was filled with Seco wall units and windows, and door frameworks were attached to the end elevations. The roof was constructed of spars fitted between aero beams and roof ties between eaves-pieces. These supported Seco roof units which were covered with felt.

Seco buildings were designed to be recovered after the war to be used as emergency housing. A typical 19 ft span ex-works hut cost £300; the total cost including foundations, carriage, and erection came to £420.

Seco cellular construction was a much simpler form of construction using the compressive strength of the Seco panel: load-bearing walls and partitions carried the weight of the roof. The internal layout was in the form of a grid system where rooms were arranged each side of a central corridor.

Type	drawing no.	internal span	internal bay width	internal height	examples
clear span	2062/43, 3497/43	19 ft 2 in 24 ft 4 in	12 ft 12 ft	7 ft 6 in 8 ft 2 in	officers', sergeants', airmen's quarters at Thorpe Abbots
cellular		24 ft 4 in 24 ft 4 in	12 ft 12 ft	8 ft 3 in 9 ft 3 in	

Several Seco buildings of both types were built at Binbrook and Bassingbourn.

CONCRETE HUTS

Air Ministry Standard Concrete Hut

This classic late First World War barrack hut, also known as the universal concrete hut, was a large building capable of sleeping up to 86 men. The shape was unique: a tall centre section with a shallow-pitched roof, and two lower outer sections, each with a single-pitched roof. Vertical sides contained clerestory windows. The walls were constructed of 3-inch wide concrete slabwork fitted or cast *in situ* between square-section reinforced-concrete posts. The whole external wall was then coated in a wash of ironite

A Seco hut at Binbrook.

An Air Ministry Standard concrete hut 481/18 at Duxford.

and cement. The roof was timber framed and carried wire mesh and Andrite felt, or slates. Inside, it was divided longitudinally into halves with entrances located in the end walls. Heating was provided by three stoves each side.

An adaptation of the barrack hut was the married solders' quarters 2964/18. The framework, wall slabbing, and windows were manufactured at the National Slab Factory, Yate. The walls were different from the barrack hut and consisted of outer and inner precast concrete blocks separated by a cavity. The roof was of precast concrete slabs. Internal arrangement of a typical semi-detached hut consisted of three bedrooms, parlour, living room, scullery, fuel store, WC, a walk-in larder, and living room. It was 34 ft long and 26 ft 6 in wide.

drawing no.	481/18	2964/18
examples	Andover, Duxford, Orfordness	

British Concrete Federation Huts

From 1942, the British Concrete Federation designed all concrete barrack huts for the MoW, for manufacture by companies within the federation. There were two erection drawings: BCF 32H and BCF 6861. There were also two basic types: those with flat roofs and those with pitched roofs (light).

The flat roof type was one of the few wartime huts to have been tested for resistance to near-miss bomb blast. The tests proved that the hut was resistant to blast and earth shock, much like a typical house of traditional construction. Married quarters had internal partitions which stiffened the structure in both directions, while the resistance of the clear span type to horizontal forces depended entirely on the framework.

A lightweight concrete raft foundation was prepared into which reinforced-concrete posts were fitted at 3 ft 3 in centres. These took the weight of the roof beams and were slotted for insertion of the inner and outer wall panels between which was a cavity. The inner panel was of lightweight 2-inch thick breeze concrete and the outer panel was of dense concrete. Alternative cladding was brick as seen at Rearsby. Each half-bay could have a single metal window if required. The roof beams were in single or half spans bolted together on site. Between each beam were thick breeze concrete slabs.

These huts were also used for nurseries, emergency schools, operating theatres, and clinics.

The ex-works price for a 10-bay hut was £220 and the total cost including carriage, foundations, and erection was £550.

The light hut had a reinforced concrete 3-pin portal frame carrying both roof and walls. Each wall unit consisted of two portal frames spaced at 6 ft 6 in centres with a vertical post between the two frames. Each wall section post had channelling to receive precast concrete walling slabs. These could be anything suitable that was available locally. Internal lining was plasterboard or wallboard. The internal span was 18 ft 6 in; half bay width was 3 ft 3 in; height to beam was 7 ft 6 in.

The roof was precast concrete slabs covered with felt or corrugated asbestos sheeting attached to timber purlins.

A British Concrete Federation hut at Dale, Dyfed.

drawing no.	G1/2191/42	MDH-7
description	airwomen's barracks	airmen's barracks
examples	Riccal	Graveley

Ctesiphon Hut

The idea of this unusual and controversial form of construction came to Major J. H. De W. Waller while stationed in the Middle East. When inspecting an outpost of his unit, he found that a sergeant, unable to find sufficient red earth to camouflage his tent, had applied a coat of cement and water. The cement had hardened and when the tent pole was removed the structure remained in position.

He named his new hut after the 1,600-year-old Palace of Shapur I at Ctesiphon near Baghdad, the hall of which had a great catenary-arched roof which the sergeant's cemented tent resembled. The catenary arch is the ideal theoretical form of concrete construction, the concrete being entirely in compression; Waller's Ctesiphon technique made use of corrugations for stiffening. This allowed the possibility of large spans with a very thin shell of concrete.

This rather unusual hut was developed from 1940 and built from 1943 onwards on some American bases in the UK by the Waller Housing Corporation, a British company which had previously built prefabricated housing based on concrete blocks at places such as Poole and Leeds. The internal span was 19 ft 6 in; minimum length was 36 ft; maximum height was 10 ft. The concrete shell was 2 inches thick.

A temporary arched steel scaffolding was erected, over which hessian was stretched. Concrete was then poured over it and allowed to harden. The weight of concrete between the steel framework caused the fabric to sag between each arch, thus producing a troughed effect. When the steel scaffolding was removed, the result was an all-concrete arched hut with large trough-shaped corrugations rather similar in appearance to a Handcraft hut yet perhaps more accurately described as a jelly mould. Up to four concrete window cheeks could be cast into the side elevations. End walls were of brick with windows and doors, or of Ctesiphon construction with concrete cheek windows and entrance porch.

On the Wethersfield technical site, there were originally 14 buildings of Ctesiphon construction, but by 1987 there was only one example left and this was threatened with demolition. It is not known if this building survives in 1995.

It is interesting to note that a Ctesiphon church was built at Lawrence Weston, near Bristol in 1950. The building consisted of a 40 ft span Ctesiphon hut containing the nave and apse, and a smaller hut of 20 ft span containing kitchen and WCs; unfortunately the building was demolished around 1960.

drawing no.	12403/41	12406/41
description	camera store and office, maintenance unit workshop	lubricant and inflammable stores, and guardroom
example	Wethersfield	Wethersfield

Quetta Hut

This form of construction was developed by Major J. H. De W. Waller in 1936 as a result of the Quetta earthquake in what is now Pakistan. The hut was dodecagonal in plan with a conical roof pitched at about 30°. The structure essentially consisted of a series of applications of a sand-and-cement mix on jute fabric.

First, a small concrete pad was laid down with a timber post at its centre. Precast concrete wall posts were then set into the ground at the correct diameter of the hut and concrete lintels are placed above the posts. A dwarf wall was then built between the posts using concrete poured between shuttering. The remaining earth inside the hut was removed to a depth of 6 inches and was then screeded off with sand. Jute fabric was then placed over the sand and secured. Cement grout was then poured over the

A Ctesiphon hut at Weathersfield.

A Quetta hut at Odiham, now demolished.

fabric. A series of holes at 3 ft centres were made into the subsoil with a crowbar and the holes filled with cement grout. Finally, a layer of concrete was laid over the whole area and screeded off. In time, the earth below the concrete floor shrank, leaving an air space beneath the slab, the floor being supported on concrete piles. On a recent examination of the remains of a Quetta hut at Worthy Down, it was discovered that this technique had indeed worked satisfactorily.

Nails at 6-inch centres protruding from the lintels anchored the jute fabric which was wound round the inside and outside to form a cavity wall. Dummy window frames were inserted both inside and out, and drawn together by thumbscrews. The fabric was then coated with cement grout and the temporary window removed and replaced with a metal one. Sufficient grout was applied until the correct thickness was reached.

Tubular steel scaffolding with tubular rings at the apex and foot of the conical roof was erected first. The top ring provided a fixing for a series of steel rods which fanned out from the apex to the base, acting as a support for the fabric. The fabric was then placed over the whole framework (giving the appearance of an umbrella) so that the whole roof could be coated in cement grout. When this had hardened, reinforcement was added and a further two coats of rendering was applied. Before the scaffolding and rods could be removed, the space between the lintels and the roof was made good. Normally, a central fireplace was built above the concrete pad with its chimney coming out of an opening in the centre of the roof. Alternatively, a small raised conical vent was added.

Quetta huts were quite often built as airfield defence accommodation.

examples Worthy Down, Odiham, Middle Wallop

Maycrete Huts

From 1940, Maycrete Ltd produced concrete and timber

A MoS Maycrete hut, clearly showing the wall panels, at Stoughton, Guildford. This was a barracks.
(Photographed 1993)

barrack huts for both the Ministry of Supply and Ministry of Works.

MoW Maycrete huts had pitched roofs of timber-framed trusses, plywood gussets, and knee-braces, externally clad with corrugated asbestos sheeting or fibrous plaster slabs covered with felt, and supported on timber purlins. The internal roof lining was flat asbestos sheeting. Trusses were supported by reinforced-concrete posts spaced 6 ft apart., The wall filling was moulded panels of Maycrete (sawdust concrete) laid dry. Each 6 ft wall unit consisted of three narrow Maycrete panels laid horizontally up to window level. Each side of a timber window was a single vertical panel, giving it a very distinctive appearance. Internal lining was plasterboard or wallboard.

The main disadvantage of both MoS and MoW Maycrete huts was the great skill required to bolt the wall panels together without breaking them. On a recent inspection of one at Stoughton Barracks at Guildford (now demolished), it was discovered that most of the precast wall panels were cracked as a result of over tightening when the building was assembled in 1940.

The internal arrangements (16058/40 and 16227/40) of MoS Maycrete huts varied according to the function for which they were intended. A barrack block for one NCO and 16 airmen was open plan with a small bedroom for the NCO in one corner. Quarters for eight sergeants or eight airmen had a central corridor with bedrooms each side. Quarters for officers were laid out with a corridor against one side wall and five large bedrooms including one for a servant.

The cost of a typical MoW 10-bay hut, including carriage, foundations, and erection, was £390.

Details of the MoS hut H265 were similar to the MoW Maycrete hut, except for the spacing of wall posts and sizes of wall panels. Walls were two rows of panels bolted together. A simple collar-beam roof truss was used.

Type	drawing no.	internal span	internal length
MoS	16058/40, 16277/40	15 ft 7 in	53 ft 5 in
MoW		18 ft 6 in	60 ft

Ministry of Works Standard Hut

In 1943, the MoW designed concrete hutting as a cheaper alternative to the expensive BCF huts then in production. The main advantage of this system of construction was that any suitable wall cladding material available locally could be used. The first Standard hut to be put into production was of 18 ft 6 in span. This was followed in 1944 by the 24 ft span hut. Hutting on RNAS airfields constructed after 1944 was almost exclusively Standard hutting.

Each building had a reinforced-concrete traverse frame of ribs bolted to bracketed concrete posts. Concrete floor sills and lintels spanned between wall posts. Typical wall infilling was 4.5-inch brick (Anthorn), clayblocks (Dale), mineralized siding board, felted plasterboard, and blocks

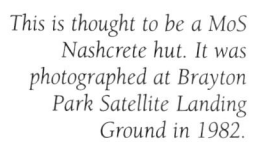

This is thought to be a MoS Nashcrete hut. It was photographed at Brayton Park Satellite Landing Ground in 1982.

A 18 ft 6 in span MoW Standard hut with hollow clayblock walls at Burscough. (Photographed 1982)

An Orlit hut at Wendling.

of wood cement (RAF hospital, Leominster). Internally, walls were covered with plasterboard. The roof consisted of prefabricated gable frames bolted to the ribs and covered with corrugated asbestos sheeting.

The internal span was 24 ft; internal length was 119 ft 8 in (20 bays); height at the eaves was 7 ft 11 in, and 12 ft 11 in at the apex. The average cost was £210. The total cost including carriage, foundations, and erection came to £375.

Nashcrete Huts

Both Nashcrete and Maycrete huts were of similar construction as far as materials were concerned but they differed in the structural arrangement of the walls. Nashcrete was moulded into panels and the huts had slightly different reinforced-concrete posts. The wall units consisted of posts with five moulded Nashcrete panels of similar size, with a window in the middle of the top row. If no window was required, six panels were used. Roof trusses and cladding were exactly the same as for the Maycrete hut.

The only known surviving building on an airfield is that at Brayton Hall (Cumbria), formerly 39 SLG. Nashcrete huts were also used as Army barracks (Aston, Herts), hutted day nurseries for the children of mothers who were engaged in war work (Letchworth, Herts), and emergency housing (Newport, Essex).

Orlit Hut

Manufactured by the Orlit Company of West Drayton, Middlesex, this was similar in appearance to the BCF hut (flat roof type). The huts were purchased by the MoW between August 1942 and July 1943.

Using I-section reinforced-concrete posts spaced at 6 ft centres made it more economical than a BCF hut (posts every 3 ft 3in). This is a convenient way of distinguishing between this and the BCF hut. Walls were of prestressed concrete planks fitted in two layers and separated by a cavity. Each bay had a single metal window on the front and rear elevations. The concrete wall posts supported reinforced-concrete roof beams. Between them, spanned reinforced-concrete slabs covered with felt. The internal span was 18 ft 6 in; length was in multiples of 6 ft. The height to beam was 7 ft 3 in. A typical hut cost £240. Including carriage, foundations, and erection the total cost came to £500.

After the war, Orlit produced reinforced-concrete frame-and-panel houses based on their successful wartime hutting design; many still exist today in city suburbs such as South Oxhey in Middlesex.

examples Great Ashfield, Wendling
(still standing)

INDEX

A & J Main 105
Aberporth 21
Abbots Bromley 108
Abbotsinch 107, 133, 134
Abingdon 16, 92, 111, 124, 178
Acklington 18, 84, 139, 206
Admiralty seaplane sheds 84
Admiralty Type F shed 92
Advanced Landing Ground 23
aeroplane repair section 81
aeroplane shed 12, 16
aeroplane twin shed 82
aircraft equipment store 18, 20
aircraft shed 18
Airfield Construction Service 23
airfield controller 112, 114
Air Observer School 84, 130, 139
Alconbury 133
Aldeburgh 12, 86, 89, 90
Aldergrove 20, 97
Alton Barnes 107
AML bomb teacher 43, 139, 162
Andover 15, 81, 216
Andreas 124
Annan 107, 149, 155
Anthorn 219
anti-aircraft dome trainer 139
Appledram 23
Arbroath 134, 154, 159, 160, 161
Armament Training School 84
armoury 12, 16, 18
Army Track 23
Aston Down 18, 110
Atcham 142, 150
Attlebridge 126
aviation fuel 40
Ayr 107

Babdown Farm 104
Balado Bridge 129
balloon sheds 77
Bar and Rod Track
barrack hut 172, 176
Bardney 127

Barton 21
Bassingbourn 35, 39, 166, 179, 185, 193
battery charging room 20
Bawdsey Manor 112
Beaulieu 12, 118
Beck Row (Mildenhall) 16
Belfast Truss 85, 86, 88, 90
Bellman hangar 101, 102
Bentwaters 132
Bessoneau hangar 82
Bibury 104, 150
Bicester 16, 39, 40, 41, 42, 92, 96, 120, 154, 172, 181, 185, 193, 194, 198
Biggin Hill 12, 16, 25, 39, 81, 82, 88, 166, 175, 178, 198, 199
Binbrook 20, 113, 124, 215
Bircham Newton 16, 39, 120, 179
Blackburn Aeroplane Company Ltd 81
Black Isle 110
blacksmith's shop 12
Blister hangar 106
Blyton 36, 127
Bodney 36, 133, 194
Bomb Stores 18, 40
Booker 34
Boreham 36
Boscombe Down 12, 111
Bottesford 124, 142
Boulton and Paul 110
Bovingdon 39
Bracebridge Heath 12, 39, 81, 198
Brackla 23
Bradwell Bay 130
Bramcote 20, 23, 96, 124, 179, 185
Brayton Hall 220
Bridgenorth 21
briefing room
British Concrete Federation 204
British Steel Corporation 77
Brize Norton 23, 97, 98
Brockworth 12, 86, 88
Bruntingthorpe 143, 193
Brunton 107
Buckminster 12

bulk fuel store 18
Bungay 126
Burnaston 37, 139
Burscough 102, 105, 106, 133
Burtonwood 21, 92, 95, 100, 120, 166
Butler Manufacturing Company 110

Callender Cable and Construction 100, 101
Calshot 9, 84, 88, 89
Calveley 128, 129
Caldale 66
Calveley 155,
Cambletown 105
camera obscura 12, 139
Carew Cheriton 147
Cardington 73, 74, 75, 77, 206
Cark 128
Carnaby 197
Castle Bromwich 19, 166
Castle Camps 209
Castle Coombe 127
Catfoss 19, 90, 92, 108
Catterick 12, 16, 81, 82, 166
CB Projections (Engineering) Ltd 171
changing and locker room 18
Charterhall 143
Chatham 65
Chelveston 21
Chigwell 75
Chipping Norton 23, 25, 127
Chipping Ongar 203
Chipping Warden 21
Chivenor 20, 34, 92, 101, 207, 211
Christchurch 23
Church Fenton 16, 23, 130
Cleave 21
Cleveland Bridge & Engineering Company 65, 74
coal and wood store 12
Coal Aston 81
Colerne 121
Coltishall 20, 124
Condover 104, 194

Coningsby 20, 21
control tower 112, 114
cookhouse 183
Cosford 39, 98, 120, 206
Cottam 127, 197
Cottesmore 53, 166, 179, 197
Coventry Ordnance Works 81
Crail 156, 160, 161, 162
Cranage 23, 166
Cranfield 16, 39, 53, 56, 120, 179
Cranwell 15, 16, 66, 70, 73, 84, 174, 178, 206
Crosby-on-Eden 155
Croydon 111
Ctesiphon hutting 217
Culdrose 106
Culham 133, 134,
Culmhead 129, 133
Curved Asbestos hutting 213

D Anderson and Co. Ltd 88
Dalacombe Merechal & Hervieu Ltd 66
Dale 129, 133, 216, 219
Debach 34
Debden 18, 35, 39, 53
decontamination centre 172, 174, 186, 187, 190, 206
Defence Research Studios 149
Defence Teleprinter Network 112
depot office 12
Detling 12
Dick Kerr Ltd 81
Digby 19
dining room 172, 174
Dishforth 18
Diver Balloon Barrage 77
dope shop 12
Down Ampney 23
Drem 193, 201
Driffield 18, 35, 53, 96, 197
drying tower 35
Dumfries 20, 98, 163, 193
Dundee 9
duty pilot's block 16, 18
Duxford 16, 19, 39, 81, 86, 180, 181, 183, 184, 216

Eastchurch 9, 81, 117
East Fortune 58, 70, 102, 143, 150, 155, 211
Easthaven 105, 133, 134
East Kirkby 46
Eastleigh 86, 87
East Moor 53
East Wretham 203
Edgehill 124
Edmonds direction trainer 139, 155
Edzell 98
elementry deflection trainer 139, 155

Elementry Flying Training School 101, 130, 138, 139
Elmswell 81
Elsham Wolds 21
Elvington 129, 130
Ely 20
engine test house 16, 18, 40
Enstone 127
En-Tout-Cas Ltd 26, 29, 214
Errol 155
Esavian doors 87, 90
Eshott 143, 149, 203
Evanton 18, 84, 166, 206
Eye 104

Farnborough 9, 10, 13, 65, 73, 82, 111, 181, 182
Fearn 133, 134
Felixstowe 9, 120
Feltwell 16, 56, 81, 89, 179
Filton 16, 48, 57, 81, 82, 178, 198
Findlay & Co. Ltd 66
Finmere 104
Finningley 42, 56
Fisher front gun trainer 139
Fiskerton 201
Fitups Ltd 157
flight office 60
flight workshop 59
Ford 13, 88
Fordoun 106
Fort Grange 9
Foulsham 104
Fowlmere 89
Framlingham 56, 104
Francis Morton & Co. Ltd 65, 70
Fromson hangars 107
Funtington 23

Gamston 39, 185
gasholders 73
gas plant house 73
Gatwick 21
Goldhanger 82
Goliath 93
Gosfield 46, 100
Gosport 16, 21, 95, 96, 120, 175, 178
Goxhill 21, 104, 124
Graveley 190, 193, 217
Great Dunmow 192.193
Great West Aerodrome 21
Great Yarmouth 9
Grimsetta 134
Grove 52, 104, 130, 197
guardhouse 12, 16, 18, 30
guardroom 31
Gullane 166
gunnery crew and procedure centre 139
gymnasium 174, 199

Hainault Farm 12
Halesworth 51, 197
Halfpenny Green 101, 130, 142
Halton 15, 16, 119, 174
Handley Page sheds 90
Harlaxton 190, 193
Harwarden 98, 100
Harwarden trainer 139, 148
Harwell 16, 23, 39, 53, 56, 197
Harwell box 143, 147
Hatfield 110
Hawkinge 19, 48, 150
Headcorn 23
Head Wrightson & Co. 100
Hemswell 18, 120, 154
Hendon 21, 35, 57, 88, 89, 120
Henleys (1928) Ltd 97
Henlow 12, 13, 23, 81, 86, 88, 90
Henry Pels Ltd 97
Hensridge 105, 134
Herbertson & Co. Ltd 92
Hereford 92
Hervieu tents 10
Heston 97
High Ercall 39, 53, 100, 155
High Halden 23
Hinaidi aircraft shed 92
Hinton-in-the-Hedges 110
Hixon 56, 143, 202
HMS Excellent 167, 171
HMS Glendower 169
Hollings & Guest Ltd 97
Holme-on-Spalding Moor 21, 122
Home Defence 81
Honeybourne 21
Honington 166, 201
Hook 60, 75, 79, 80, 206, 207
Horsham St. Faith 20
Hornchurch 16, 25, 53, 64, 120, 172, 178, 181, 194
Horne 23
Horsley Bridge & Engineering Company Ltd 97
Howden 66, 70, 72, 74, 75
Hucknall 81
Hullavington 18, 45, 97, 98, 121
Humphreys Ltd 74
Husbands Bosworth 52
hydrogen trailer shed 79

Ibsley 124
Igloo hutting 209
Inskip 106
instruction hut 12
instrument repair shop 20
instrument room 20
Ingham 35, 57
Inchinnan 70
Initial Training Wing 138

institute 173, 184
Isle of Grain 9
Ismailia 74

Jane hutting 209
J hangar 21
Jurby 20, 35, 37, 142, 190, 193, 206

Karachi 74
Kemble 18, 96, 97, 98
Kenley 12, 23, 25, 201
Kidbrook 75
Kidlington 23
Kidsdale 21
Kingscliffe 110
Kingsnorth 9, 23
Kingston Bagpuize 110
Kinloss 20, 21, 98
Kinnal 129
Kirkbride 96
Kirmington 124
Kirton Lindsey 20

Laing hutting 208, 209
Lakenheath 128
Langham 36, 171, 185
Larkhill 9, 75
Larne 66
Lasham 52
Lavenham 142, 199, 201
Leeming 20, 124
Lee-on-Solent 16, 18, 92, 106, 134, 198
Leconfield 18
Leicester East 201
Leiston 197
Leuchars 16, 111
Lichfield 20, 21, 98, 100
Lindholme 20
Link Trainer 139, 140, 159, 161
Linton-on-Ouse 111
Lisset 36, 199
Little Rissington 39, 97, 121, 179
Little Snoring 52, 56
Little Staughton 58, 110, 210
Little Warden 58, 154
Llanbedr 26
Llandwrog 26
London Colney 89
London Air Defence Area 75
Long Newton 104, 155
Longside 66
Lopcombe Corner 12
Lorenze AG 111, 124
Lossiemouth 20, 21, 98
lubricant store 56
Luce Bay 66
Ludford Magna 52
Ludham 150
Lympne 89, 129

Machrihanish 66
Madeley 147
magazine 73
Mainhill Type B 106
main stores 16, 18
maintenance block 20, 58
main worshops 16, 18
Manby 96, 142, 201
Manobier 21, 23
Manston 13
Marham 16, 39, 197
Market Harborough 201
Marske 30, 87
Marston shed 142, 204, 206
Martlesham Heath 93, 119, 175, 178
Matching Green 58, 194
Maycrete Ltd hutting 209, 218, 219, 220
Melbourne 56, 59
Melton Mowbray 52, 154, 163, 196, 214
Membury 35, 194, 202
Mendlesham 58
Merston 25
Metfield 52
Metheringham 52, 56
Methwold 202
Middle Wallop 20, 96
Middleton St. George 20, 21, 32, 35, 39, 56
Mildenhall 92, 111, 120, 171
Milfield 149, 155
Milton 101
Ministry of Works Standard Hutting 219
Miskins & Sons Ltd 106
modified Haskard range 139, 149
modified Hunt range 139, 150
Molesworth 210
Montrose 81, 89, 166
Moreton-in-Marsh 21
Morfa Towyn 21
motor transport yard 12, 16, 18, 36
Mount Batten 84, 154, 176
Moushold Heath 42
Mullion 66

Narborough 199
Nashcrete hutting 209, 220
Netheravon 9, 10, 12, 13, 82, 90, 118, 119, 120, 149, 181
Newton 39, 120, 179
Nissen hutting 32, 39, 42, 52, 53, 56, 57, 58, 59, 60, 130, 143, 150, 185, 192, 193, 206, 210, 211
North Coates 113
North Luffenham 20, 21, 100, 124
Northolt 12, 23, 96, 120, 178
North Pickenham 56
North Weald 16, 25, 36, 48, 53, 56, 64, 82, 92, 129, 175, 179, 181, 182, 183, 185, 193, 196
North Witham 52

Nortons Ltd 92
Norwich 12
Nuneaton 52
Nuthampstead 192

Oakington 20, 21
Oakly 166
Odiham 16, 21, 119, 84, 120, 154
officers' mess and quarters 173, 174
Old Sarum 86, 166
Operational Training Unit 139
operations block 44, 50, 51, 112
operations room 16, 18
Orfordness 31, 36, 37, 39, 48, 216
Orlit hutting 204, 206, 220
Ouston 20, 48
Overton Heath 107

packed balloon store 79
Padgate 21
Painter Brothers 101
panoramic trainer 139
Panshanger 64, 106, 107, 210
parachute store 18, 32, 34
Pembray 20, 84, 171, 193, 206
Pembroke Dock 93
Penrhos 18, 169, 206
Pentad hangar
Peplow 57
Pershore 21
petrol tanker shed 18
Phoenix Dynamo Ltd 81
Pierced Steel Plank 23
Piggott tents 10
plane store 12
Pocklington 21
Polebrook 21, 42
Portsmouth 21
powerhouse 12, 16, 73, 198
Pucklechurch 77, 79
Pulham 66

Quetta hutting 217, 218

radar workshop 20
Radlet 21, 64
ration store 174
Raydon 35
Rednal 50, 124, 201
Regional Control School 111, 124
rest room 18
Riccal 104, 193, 217
Ridgewell 59
Rhu 93
R. Moreland & Sons Ltd 65
Robey & Co. Ltd 81
Rolleston Camp 193
Romney hutting 204, 206, 213
Rougham 53, 154, 195

Royal Aircraft Factory tents 10
Royal Airship Works 73
Royal Engineers 9
Royal Observer Corps 48, 50
Rufforth 126
running shed 90

St. Athan 35, 96, 206
St. Eval 20, 95, 124
St. Hubert Airport 74
St. Marys 66
S Cutler & Sons Ltd 74
sailmakers and carpenters' shop 12
salvage shed 12
Saltby 148
Saughall Masssie 21
Sawbridgeworth 35, 60, 107
Scampton 18
Scatsa 104
Sculthorpe 36, 128
Seething 52
Sealand 16
sergeants' mess 172, 173, 174, 179, 180
Sealand 21
Seighford 126, 166
Service Flying Training School 120
Shawbury 18, 111, 121
Shellingford 130, 131
Shepherds Grove 34
Sherburn-in-Elmet 23
Shipdam 174
Shrewsbury 18
Shobden 35
Shoreham 171
Siddeley Deasy Motor Car Co. Ltd 81
Silloth 92
Silverstone 53, 57, 143, 154, 166, 194
Sir William Arrol Ltd 66, 70
Skegness 9
Sleap 154, 211
Snaith 21, 100, 163
Snitterfield 52, 56, 194
Sommerfeld track 23
Southam 150
South Cerney 23, 121
Southrop 23
Spanhoe 148
speech broadcasting 20
Spencers Ltd 75
Spilsby 197
Spittlegate 92
squadron and flight office 12, 18, 20, 60
squadron armoury 20, 58
Square Mesh Track 23
squash racquets court 173, 174, 198
Standard hutting 204

stand-by-set house 174, 196
Stanhope Engineering 150
Stanmore 18, 75
station armoury 20, 42, 59
station headquarters 16, 18, 43
station sick quarters 173
Staverton 35, 147
Stormy Down 20, 23, 85, 166, 190
Stradishall 16
Strand Electric 150, 157
Stretton 105, 133
Strubby 148, 210
Sutton Bridge 21
Sutton Coldfield 79
Suttons Farm 12, 172
Swannington 197
Swanton Morley 20, 21, 31, 39, 43, 46, 48, 100, 124, 192, 193, 201
Swinderby 20, 21, 46, 181, 184
Syerston 20, 21, 124
synthetic navigation classroom 139
Sywell 18

T2 hangar 20, 21, 58
Tangmere 13, 16, 120, 178, 185
Tarrant Rushton 102
Tealing 143, 155
Teesside Bridge & Engineering Co. Ltd 98, 102, 105
technical store 12
Technicolor Ltd 152, 167, 171
Templehof 111
Tempsford 58, 148
Ternhill 16, 18, 53, 97, 121
Tett Turret 60, 64
Thetford 198, 199
Tholthorpe 133
Thornaby 100, 101, 107
Thorney Island 16, 113
Thorpe Abbotts 58, 185, 197, 215
Tibenham 124, 185
Tilstock 143
Titchfield 79
Topcliffe 21, 104
torpedo attack trainer 139, 155
towed target store 57
transformer enclosure 20
Trussed Concrete Steel Co. Ltd 169
Turners Asbestos Co. hutting 204
Turnhouse 16, 23
turret trainer 139
Turweston 52
Type C hangar 95, 152
Type E aircraft shed 97
Type J aircraft shed 98, 121
Type K aircraft shed 98

Type L aircraft shed 97, 98

Uni-Seco Structures Ltd hutting 204, 206, 214
Universal Asbestos Co. Handcraft hutting 206, 214
Upavon 16, 35, 48, 50, 118, 119, 120, 181, 182
Upper Heyford 16, 39, 53, 90, 92, 172, 178, 181
Upwood 18, 56, 96, 166, 179
Usworth 102
Uxbridge 18, 111, 112, 181

Vickers Bygrave bombing teacher 161
Vulcan Motor and Engineering Company 81

Waddington 16, 21, 111
Warmwell 16
Waterbeach 21, 100
water tower 12, 16, 73
Wattisham 120
Watton 43, 53, 95, 96, 120, 166, 193
Weathersfield 217
Weeton 92
Wellesbourne Mountford 21
Wendling 220
West Freugh 18
West Malling 21
West Raynham 96, 120, 128, 166
Weston-super-Mare 64
Weston Zoyland (Westonzoyland) 104
Wick 21, 41, 42, 95, 122, 124
William Beadmore & Co. Ltd 70
Wimslow 21
Windrush 23, 150
Winfield 130
Winthorpe 35
wireless and instrument shop 18
Wittering 16, 48, 193
Woolfox Lodge 52, 130
Woodbridge 23, 132
Woodley 18, 110
Woodsford 70, 73
workshop (metal) 12
works service yard 18
Wormwood Scrubs 9, 65
Wright Anderson & Co. Ltd 84, 92
Wroughton 96, 97
W/T operational instruction centre 139, 143
Wyton 18, 21, 171

Yatesbury 12, 18, 89, 193
Yeovilton 106